What better way to maximize your Pocket PC productivity than to have a "cheat sheet" that outlines some of the more powerful and interesting Pocket PC features? The *Special Edition Using Pocket PC 2002* how-to topics on this card are designed to help you carry out the most common Pocket PC tasks in just a few steps.

Adjust the Brightness of the Screen

1. Tap the Start menu, and then tap Settings.
2. Tap the Backlight icon, and then tap the Brightness tab.
3. Move the slider bars up or down to adjust the brightness for the device on battery and cradle power, respectively.

Protect Your Device with a Strong Alphanumeric Password

1. Tap Start, and then tap Settings.
2. Tap the Password icon.
3. Select the Strong Alphanumeric Password option.
4. Enter a password at least seven characters long using the soft keyboard, and then enter it again in the Confirm box. Be sure to select a password you won't forget.
5. Tap OK in the upper-right corner, and then tap Yes to save the password settings.

Customize the Start Menu

1. Tap Start, and then tap Settings.
2. Tap the Menus icon.
3. Check and uncheck appropriate items to customize the contents of the Start menu.
4. Tap OK in the upper-right corner to accept the Start menu changes.

Customize the New Menu

1. Tap Start, and then tap Settings.
2. Tap the Menus icon, and then tap the New Menu tab.
3. Check the check box above the document types to turn on the New menu button.
4. Check and uncheck appropriate document types to customize the contents of the New menu.
5. Tap OK in the upper-right corner to accept the New menu changes.

Change the Power-Off Timeout Period

1. Tap Start, and then tap Settings.
2. Tap the System tab, and then tap the Power icon.
3. Tap the combo box next to the On Battery Power check box, and select a new timeout period for the power-off feature. I prefer 5 minutes, but it's up to you.
4. Tap OK in the upper-right corner to accept the Power-Off changes.

Find Out Which Applications Are Currently Running

1. Tap Start, and then tap Settings.
2. Tap the System tab, and then tap the Memory icon.
3. Tap the Running Programs tab to view the Running Program List.

Customize the Word-Completion Feature

1. Tap the up arrow on the Input Panel button, and then tap Options.
2. Tap the Word Completion tab.
3. Tap the combo box next to Suggest Word(s), and select a new number of words for the word-completion feature; I prefer four words. I've found the default settings for the other preferences on this page to work well, but you are free to change them if you like. As an example, you can change the number of letters that are entered before word-completion kicks in (two is the default).

Customize the Word-Completion Feature, *continued*

4. Tap OK in the upper-right corner to accept the word-completion changes.

Copy or Move a File Between Folders

1. Launch File Explorer from the Start menu, and then navigate to the file.
2. Tap and hold on the file to display a menu of file options.
3. Tap Copy to copy the file, or tap Cut to move the file.
4. Navigate to the folder in which you want the file placed.
5. Tap Edit in the lower-left corner of the screen, and then tap Paste. You can also tap and hold in the File Explorer window and then tap Paste on the pop-up menu.

Create an E-mail Message

1. Launch the Inbox application from the Start menu.
2. Tap New near the bottom of the screen to open a blank message.
3. Tap To to select an e-mail recipient from your contact list, or enter an e-mail address in the edit box.
4. Tap the edit box next to Subj to enter the subject of the e-mail message.
5. Tap the body of the e-mail and enter the message.
6. Tap the Send button to queue the e-mail message for sending; this places the message in the Outbox folder.

Store E-mail Attachments on a Memory Card

1. Launch the Inbox application from the Start menu.
2. Tap Tools, and then tap Options.
3. Tap the Storage tab on the Options screen, and then check the Store Attachments on Storage Card check box.
4. Tap OK to accept the new Inbox setting.

Beam Contact Information to Another Device

1. Launch the Contacts application from the Start menu.
2. Navigate to the contact in the contact list.
3. Tap and hold the contact entry.
4. Tap Beam Contact on the pop-up menu that appears.
5. Line up the two devices and wait for the transfer to complete; keep the devices aligned and within a few inches of each other throughout the transfer.

Change the Alarm Sound Used to Signal an Appointment

1. Tap the Start menu, and then tap Settings.
2. Tap the Sounds & Notifications icon, and then tap the Notifications tab.
3. Select Reminders in the drop-down list of notification events.
4. Modify the relevant alarm parameters that are used to notify you of appointment reminders.

Reassign a Hardware Button to a Different Application

1. Tap the Start menu, and then tap Settings.
2. Tap the Buttons icon.
3. Select the button you want to reassign in the list, and then select the application from the Button Assignment drop-down list.
4. Tap OK in the upper-right corner to accept the new button assignment.

Special Edition Using Pocket PC 2002

Michael Morrison

201 W. 103rd Street
Indianapolis, Indiana 46290

Contents at a Glance

SPECIAL EDITION USING POCKET PC 2002

Copyright © 2002 by Que Publishing

International Standard Book Number: 0-7897-2749-8

Library of Congress Catalog Card Number: 2002103975

Printed in the United States of America

First Printing: June 2002

04   03   02   4   3   2   1

Trademarks

Warning and Disclaimer

Associate Publisher
Greg Wiegand

Acquisitions Editor
Stephanie J. McComb

Development Editor
Mark Cierzniak

Managing Editor
Thomas Hayes

Project Editor
Sheila D. Schroeder

Production Editor
Megan Wade

Indexer
Mandie Frank

Proofreader
Andrea Dugan

Technical Editor
Brian Nadel

Team Coordinator
Sharry Gregory

Interior Designer
Lousia Klucznik
Ruth Lewis

Cover Designer
Anne Jones

Page Layout
Cheryl Lynch

CONTENTS

ABOUT THE AUTHOR

Michael Morrison is a writer; developer; toy inventor; and author of a variety of books, including *The Unauthorized Guide to Pocket PC* (Que Publishing, 2000), *Teach Yourself Wireless Java with J2ME in 21 Days* (Sams Publishing, 2001), and *HTML and XML for Beginners* (Microsoft Press, 2001). Michael is the instructor of several Web-based courses for the online learning provider DigitalThink. Michael also serves as a technical director for ReviewNet, a provider of Web-based staffing tools for IT personnel. Finally, Michael is the founder and creative lead of Stalefish Labs, an entertainment company with several Pocket PC games and traditional social games in the works (http://www.stalefishlabs.com/).

When not risking life and limb on his skateboard or mountain bike, trying to avoid the penalty box in hockey, or watching movies with his wife, Masheed, Michael enjoys daydreaming next to his koi pond. You can visit Michael on the Web at http://www.michaelmorrison.com/.

DEDICATION

To my wife, Masheed, who makes every day a pleasure to live.

ACKNOWLEDGMENTS

I'd like to thank Stephanie McComb, Sharry Gregory, Mark Cierzniak, and Sheila Schroeder for their unyielding guidance and support throughout the development of this book. To the other players at Pearson Technology Group whom I didn't interact with directly, I sincerely appreciate your efforts in making this book a reality.

A big thanks goes to my literary agent, Chris Van Buren, for handling the business side of my writing career and making projects like this possible.

I'd also like to thank my parents for always being so supportive. And of course, the biggest thanks of all goes to my wife Masheed for making my writing career possible.

WE WANT TO HEAR FROM YOU!

As the reader of this book, *you* are our most important critic and commentator. We value your opinion and want to know what we're doing right, what we could do better, what areas you'd like to see us publish in, and any other words of wisdom you're willing to pass our way.

As an associate publisher for Que, I welcome your comments. You can e-mail or write me directly to let me know what you did or didn't like about this book—as well as what we can do to make our books better.

Please note that I cannot help you with technical problems related to the *topic* of this book. We do have a User Services group, however, where I will forward specific technical questions related to the book.

When you write, please be sure to include this book's title and author as well as your name, email address, and phone number. I will carefully review your comments and share them with the author and editors who worked on the book.

E-mail: feedback@quepublishing.com

Mail: Greg Weigand
Que
201 West 103rd Street
Indianapolis, IN 46290 USA

For more information about this book or another Que title, visit our Web site at www.quepublishing.com. Type the ISBN (excluding hyphens) or the title of a book in the Search field to find the page you're looking for.

INTRODUCTION

If you own or are considering the purchase of a Pocket PC, you are taking part in nothing short of a technological revolution. Although handheld computers have been around for some time, Pocket PC 2002 devices represent the first devices to truly put the power of a full-blown desktop PC in the palm of your hand. Pocket PCs have endured an extremely tumultuous past to arrive at the point where they are finally set to change the way we use computers. If you think I'm just overly excited because I happened to have written a book on Pocket PCs, I encourage you to take a moment and consider the timing of Pocket PCs. Only recently has widespread wireless Internet access become a reality, and Pocket PCs are entering the mobile device landscape at the precise moment to take maximum advantage of wireless networking. It's the combination of breakthrough hardware, an evolutionary operating system, and wireless Internet access that puts Pocket PCs in a position to dramatically impact the world of computing.

It's important to understand that Pocket PCs aren't just high-end personal digital assistants (PDAs) running a scaled-down version of Windows. Pocket PCs can certainly play the role of PDAs, and some similarities to Windows exist in the Pocket PC operating system, but the Pocket PC platform was designed entirely from scratch with the unique needs of wireless handheld computers in mind. Pocket PC 2002 is literally a new breed of operating system that is based on the notion that it is possible to perform a much wider range of computing tasks on a palm-size computer than anyone had previously believed possible. Prior to the Pocket PC, palm-size computers were thought of as fancy electronic address books, and in many cases that's all they were. Microsoft aimed to take advantage of the fact that hardware now exists to create a device that is powerful enough to do all kinds of interesting things, such as run productivity applications, browse the Web wirelessly, connect to corporate networks, check e-mail, play digital music, and allow you to read digital books, among other things.

The goal of this book is to provide you with the knowledge and skills to maximize the potential of your Pocket PC and get the most out of the Pocket PC 2002 operating system. Whether you are a previous user of a Pocket PC/Windows CE device or a brand-new convert to Pocket PC computing, you will find lots of valuable information in this book that you can put to work in making more productive use of your device. I've made a serious attempt at leaving no stone unturned in exploring the capabilities of Pocket PCs. The hope is that this book will reveal new and interesting things about your Pocket PC that you didn't previously know or understand and ultimately help you get more out of your device and use it more productively.

To give you an idea about what you'll learn throughout the book, following are some of the new features in Pocket PC 2002 devices that you might find interesting, especially if you've used a Pocket PC device prior to Pocket PC 2002:

- A new look and feel that improves the mobile computing experience
- A more customizable Today screen
- Pop-up bubbles that provide notifications and helpful information
- Improved security with support for strong alphanumeric passwords
- A Smart Minimize feature that helps eliminate confusion and improve memory management when you're finished using an application
- An improved Transcriber input method for fast and accurate handwriting recognition
- Support for the Graffiti input method that was made popular on Palm devices
- An integrated spell checker
- Support for the standard OBEX protocol, which is used to share information with other types of devices using an infrared port
- A new Connection Manager for easily creating and managing various types of network connections
- Support for virtual private networking (VPN)
- A Terminal Service Client for accessing enterprise applications
- A greatly improved Pocket Internet Explorer that fully supports HTML 3.2, WAP, JavaScript, and ActiveX, and that also includes a faster rendering engine
- An improved Inbox that can be synchronized with individual folders in Microsoft Outlook
- Support for instant messaging via MSN Messenger
- The capability to upgrade the operating system thanks to required FlashROM memory
- A more refined Reader that supports several levels of eBook security
- Support for MPEG4 video in Windows Media Player

As you can see, Pocket PCs are crammed with features, and the Pocket PC 2002 platform has numerous improvements over previous versions that make it the ideal mobile computing platform as we enter the age of mobile wireless computing.

Who Should Read This Book?

This book is written in such a way to appeal to a broad range of Pocket PC users. Whether you're a seasoned Pocket PC user, a Palm convert, or a new handheld computer user, there is something here for you:

- If you've used devices that ran previous versions of the Pocket PC/Windows CE operating system, you'll find out the many ways in which Microsoft has beefed up the Pocket PC operating system and answered the requests of hardcore users.

- If you've recently converted to a Pocket PC device from a Palm device, you'll appreciate the extensive coverage of Pocket PC features, including many features that simply aren't possible on Palm devices. You also might appreciate the Block Recognizer input method, which enables you to use the popular Graffiti input method on your Pocket PC.

- If you're using a Pocket PC in a business setting, you'll probably be interested in the ways in which Pocket PC 2002 has embraced the corporate computing environment with improved security, seamless network access, and support for accessing enterprise terminal servers.

- If you're completely new to mobile computing and Pocket PCs, you'll hopefully view each unique aspect of Pocket PCs as an opportunity to enrich your business or personal life. At the very least, you should gain an appreciation for the many desktop tasks Pocket PCs enable you to carry out in a mobile environment.

How This Book Is Organized

This book is designed to be read sequentially, but that doesn't mean you can't jump around if you want to learn something specific. Although I've attempted to present the material in a logical order that addresses the needs of most Pocket PC users, you might have a particular topic about which you're interested in learning first. By all means, start wherever you're comfortable and tackle the topics most important to you first. The book uses a lot of cross-references to tie together related topics, so you should be able to refer to an earlier chapter if you read a topic out of order or if you miss something and need to refresh your memory.

Part I, "First Things First"

In this section, you are introduced to the Pocket PC 2002 operating system and its relationship to earlier versions of Windows CE. You learn about the convergence of Pocket PC devices and mobile phones, as well as the ongoing competition between Pocket PCs and Palm devices. You also take a look at the hardware and software that goes into Pocket PCs and learn how to set up and personalize a Pocket PC device. You finish up this part of the book by exploring the various input methods available for entering data into Pocket PCs.

PART II, "NETWORKING YOUR POCKET PC"

In this section, the various networking options for Pocket PCs are explored, along with specifics about how to set up and configure each of them. You find out what is required to use your Pocket PC in a wireless network environment, which is clearly where the Pocket PC movement is headed. You then find out how to use ActiveSync to synchronize Pocket PC data with a desktop PC. You finish up this part of the book by learning the ins and outs of browsing the Web and using instant messaging.

PART III, "POCKET PC INFORMATION MANAGEMENT"

In this section, you examine the Pocket PC in its role as a next-generation personal digital assistant. Although Pocket PC devices are much more than PDAs, this part of the book focuses to some degree on the idea that the applications that comprise Pocket Outlook make for an extremely high-powered PDA. This part of the book also takes a look at how files are stored and managed on Pocket PCs.

PART IV, "GETTING PRODUCTIVE WITH YOUR POCKET PC"

In this section, you examine the role of Pocket PCs as mobile productivity tools. This part of the book delves into the details of using Pocket Word and Pocket Excel to create and manage documents and spreadsheets. You also learn how to manage finances on your Pocket PC with Money for Pocket PC and find your way around strange towns with Pocket Streets.

PART V, "SAFEGUARDING YOUR POCKET PC"

In this section, you find out how to store information safely on your device and then protect it from viruses and the prying eyes of others. This part of the book lays out the various options available for storing and accessing information with a Pocket PC. You then find out how to take advantage of the security features built into the Pocket PC operating system, as well as a few third-party security add-ons. This part of the book finishes by exploring viruses, how they impact Pocket PCs, and how to avoid them.

PART VI, "FUN WITH YOUR POCKET PC"

The last part of the book serves as somewhat of a celebration of what you've learned because it focuses on the entertainment aspects of Pocket PCs. You learn how to read digital eBooks and listen to audible eBooks with Microsoft Reader, not to mention how to play digital music, listen to Internet radio stations, and view Flash animations with the Windows Media Player. This part of the book concludes by touring several popular Pocket PC games, which are surprisingly good considering the relative youth of the Pocket PC gaming industry.

PART VII, "APPENDIXES"

The appendixes include a variety of information about Pocket PCs that you will find useful as you work through the rest of the book. More specifically, you'll find a tour of Pocket PC accessories in Appendix A, "A Pocket PC Hardware Accessory Tour," along with a thorough list of Pocket PC resources in Appendix B, "Where to Go for More About Pocket PCs." And finally, Appendix C, "Resetting Your Pocket PC," shows you how to reset your Pocket PC, with specific details on how the reset process varies across different devices.

FIRST THINGS FIRST

CHAPTER 1

GETTING TO KNOW POCKET PCS

In this chapter

WHAT IS A POCKET PC?

As you no doubt already know, Pocket PC is the name of the operating system that runs on a class of handheld computing devices known collectively as Pocket PCs. The Pocket PC operating system was created by Microsoft and is an evolved version of its Windows CE operating system that has been around since 1996. Pocket PCs are handheld computers that go far beyond the capabilities of traditional personal digital assistants (PDAs), such as Palm devices, which have been extremely popular over the past few years. Although PDAs are certainly useful in their own right, they have their limitations. Pocket PCs have much more to offer the mobile computer user, as you'll learn in this chapter.

This chapter introduces you to the Pocket PC computing platform and helps you to gain some perspective on where it came from and where it's headed. Mobile computing is just now hitting its stride as people are realizing that they can check e-mail, surf the Web, work with desktop documents, read books, and do many other interesting tasks on a device that fits into their pocket. Perhaps even more interesting is the fact that the Pocket PC computing platform enables us to explore new methods of mobile communication. The goal of this chapter is to get you acquainted with the class of devices known as Pocket PCs and the operating system that drives them. This is essential knowledge as you delve deeper into specific facets of Pocket PCs throughout the book.

Even though a wide range of devices could technically be considered pocket PCs, the phrase "Pocket PC" refers to a very specific class of devices that adheres to hardware standards set forth by Microsoft. Microsoft set these standards because it makes the operating system for the devices, which is known as Pocket PC; "Pocket PC" is a trademarked name held by Microsoft. The Pocket PC operating system should be familiar to anyone who has experience with the desktop Windows operating system. In fact, the idea behind Pocket PC is to translate the success of Windows to the handheld computer market. The result of this translation is the Pocket PC 2002 operating system, which is now the standard operating system for Pocket PCs.

Note

The "2002" part of the Pocket PC 2002 name came about with the latest version of the Pocket PC operating system. Prior to the 2002 release, the operating system was referred to simply as "Pocket PC." However, for the sake of brevity, from this point on when I refer to the Pocket PC operating system, please assume that I'm talking about Pocket PC 2002.

So, you know that a handheld computer must run the Pocket PC operating system to be considered a Pocket PC. But remember that Microsoft also has some hardware requirements that must be met. Perhaps the most important of these requirements is that all Pocket PCs must use an ARM microprocessor at a speed of at least 100MHz. ARM microprocessors are 32-bit RISC (reduced instruction set computer) processors that are currently manufactured by Intel, Motorola, and Texas Instruments. The RISC processor requirement is significant because prior to Pocket PC 2002, manufacturers had the capability to pick and choose among several microprocessors. Now, though, manufacturers must stick with a specific type of processor, which might at first seem limiting. However, keep in mind that this alleviates the hassles of software vendors having to offer different versions of their software for each different processor type. And more importantly, it keeps users from having to worry about whether software will work on their devices because of processor differences.

→ To learn more details about the ARM microprocessors used in Pocket PCs, **see** Chapter 2, "Inside Pocket PC Hardware," **p. 23**.

Another important hardware requirement for Pocket PC 2002 is that Pocket PCs must include flash upgradeable ROM. As you might know, ROM stands for read-only memory, and it is actually where the operating system for a Pocket PC is stored. If the memory is read-only, that implies you can't ever change it, which means you are stuck with the same operating system forever. If you've ever needed to upgrade your desktop operating system then you can understand why the inability to upgrade the operating system is a disadvantage with handheld computers. Flash ROM is a special type of ROM that is not entirely read-only; it can be changed through a process known as *flashing*. For Pocket PCs, this means you have the ability to upgrade the operating system by flashing the ROM with a new version, much like you upgrade the operating system on a desktop or notebook PC by installing a new version on a hard drive. This is very important for the future of Pocket PCs because we all know that operating systems are constantly evolving.

In addition to the StrongARM microprocessor and flash upgradeable ROM, other hardware requirements exist for Pocket PCs, such as the screen size and minimum amount of random access memory (RAM). However, I'll save that for Chapter 2, "Inside Pocket PC Hardware," which delves much more deeply into the hardware side of Pocket PCs. Besides, the really exciting things about Pocket PCs are found in the software, which is essentially the Pocket PC operating system. Before we get into the details of the Pocket PC operating system, however, it's important to understand its history.

THE EVOLUTION OF THE POCKET PC OPERATING SYSTEM

Like some celebrities, the Pocket PC operating system never really saw success until it changed its name. The Pocket PC operating system was born under the name Windows CE. Windows CE got its start back in 1994 when Microsoft began developing a PDA known as the WinPad. The WinPad initially was conceived to compete with the Apple Newton, a PDA that eventually crashed and burned due to numerous problems. Many of the Newton's problems had to do with memory, or the lack of it, which led Microsoft to realize that affordable technology wasn't quite there to make the WinPad a success. So, Microsoft cancelled the WinPad project and abandoned the thought of a mobile operating system, at least for the time being.

Note

Although Microsoft never officially divulged the meaning of the "CE" in Windows CE, it is reported to have originally stood for "Consumer Electronics." I've also heard that it stands for "Compact Edition." Because either meaning makes sense, I'll leave it up to you to decide what you want it to mean. Microsoft's official stance is that it means nothing.

SET-TOP INTERNET DEVICES

A few years after the WinPad fizzled, Microsoft turned its attention to set-top Internet devices, which were interesting because they had some of the same hardware and software requirements as the WinPad. The idea behind set-top Internet devices was that they would sit on top of a television set, like a cable box, and provide Internet access. As part of its set-top Internet device development efforts, Microsoft developed an initiative called *SIPC*, which stood for Simply Interactive PCs. Microsoft took a stab at developing an SIPC but eventually aborted the project. Although the SIPC initiative ultimately failed, it rekindled Microsoft's desire to build a compact operating system that would run on handheld devices.

WINDOWS CE

Microsoft's new attempt at a compact operating system was codenamed Project Pegasus and in many ways picked up where the WinPad software left off. However, by now Windows 95 was a big success, and Microsoft wanted the Pegasus graphical user interface (GUI) to have a similar look and feel as Windows 95. Pegasus was publicly unveiled as Windows CE 1.0 at Fall Comdex 1996. It's important to note at this point that Windows CE 1.0 was never perceived as a PDA operating system. Microsoft always had a bigger picture in mind and therefore always looked at Windows CE as a compact version of Windows, not as a fancy contact manager. This perspective is evident in the fact that Windows CE 1.0 had no handwriting-recognition support. Most PDAs on the market used some form of handwriting recognition, but Microsoft was concerned about the quality of handwriting-recognition software and decided to wait on incorporating it into Windows CE. In addition to not including support for handwriting recognition, Microsoft also set Windows CE apart from PDAs by including desktop productivity applications, such as Word and Excel.

Although Windows CE was ultimately just an operating system, Microsoft laid out strict guidelines regarding the hardware configuration of devices that could support Windows CE. A Windows CE 1.0 device was required to have a grayscale screen with 480×480 resolution, 2MB of RAM, 4MB of ROM for Windows CE and standard applications, a serial port, an infrared port, a PCMCIA (PC) slot, and a keyboard. Clearly this was no PDA, but just as clear was the fact that there was no market for such a device at the time; Windows CE 1.0 never caught on. The reality was that at the time it was too expensive to provide notebook computer functionality in a handheld device, which is what Windows CE was trying to accomplish.

Known for getting off to a slow start but eventually getting things right, Microsoft released Windows CE 2.0 in September 1997, and although it had been revamped in several ways, it still didn't make much of an impact on the handheld market. Many critics complained that it felt too much like the desktop Windows, which was clunky on a small screen with no mouse. Windows CE 2.0 was in fact designed to be a lot like the desktop Windows of the time—Windows 95—and Microsoft still hadn't learned that this wasn't really a good thing. Windows CE 2.0 also was noted for being sluggish in terms of performance. Microsoft would later release a much-improved Windows CE 2.1 and still suffer from the same complaints from users who didn't want to use Windows 95/98 on anything but their desktop or notebook computers.

POCKET PC

Then the light bulb went on in Redmond. It was realized that not only did Windows CE need a major GUI facelift, but it also had taken enough of a media beating that it needed a whole new image. This brings us to Pocket PC, which is really Windows CE 3.0. By changing the name from Windows CE to Pocket PC, Microsoft was able to get a clean start and establish a recognizable brand with no negative history to drag it down. This strategy has clearly paid off. Even though Pocket PC is still trailing in second place to the dominant Palm handheld computing platform, it is well on its way to getting there. Like I said, Microsoft has a history of getting it wrong a few times and then hitting a home run on the third or fourth revision. So, the success of the Pocket PC platform really shouldn't be too much of a surprise.

Note

Pocket PC, or Windows CE 3.0, was codenamed Rapier prior to its release. Interestingly enough, Microsoft originally tried to use the name "Palm PC" for an earlier version of Windows CE, but Palm Computing and its parent 3Com, promptly took Microsoft to court to defend the Palm name. The lawsuit was eventually settled, and Microsoft was able to take home the name "Palm-size PC." The name "Pocket PC" didn't come about until later, when Microsoft was able to obtain the name from a company called Pocket PC, Inc. I think it's safe to say the name "Pocket PC" has finally stuck.

Microsoft has released two versions of Pocket PC: the original Pocket PC operating system and the latter version, Pocket PC 2002. Pocket PC 2002 represents an incremental improvement in the Pocket PC operating system and refines many of the GUI features to fit in better with mobile devices. Keep in mind that, even though handheld computers aren't really new, the idea of a high-powered operating system for handheld computers is certainly new. In my opinion, the bumpy road from Windows CE 1.0 to Pocket PC 2002 has been necessary in the evolution of handheld computers. As users, we all benefit from the knowledge Microsoft has gained through several failures and now a couple of successes. Figure 1.1 shows a timeline that reveals the history of the Pocket PC operating system.

Figure 1.1
The Pocket PC 2002 operating system began as Windows CE 1.0 in late 1996 and evolved from there.

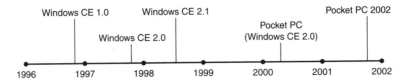

If you own a device that uses the original Pocket PC operating system and you want to upgrade it to Pocket PC 2002, see "Upgrading a Device to Pocket PC 2002" in the "Troubleshooting" section at the end of the chapter to find out whether your device is upgradeable and how to carry out the upgrade.

WHAT POCKET PCS CAN AND CAN'T DO

With all the excitement surrounding Pocket PCs and the future of handheld computing, it's easy to get carried away and think that the future of the computing world lies in the palms of our hands. Although handheld computers are poised to change the way we live and work in the very near future, they don't necessarily change the role of desktop and notebook computers. For this reason, I want to address the role of Pocket PCs, including what they can and can't do, before going any further.

To understand the capabilities of Pocket PCs and their role with respect to desktop and notebook PCs, you first must consider the individual needs of computer users. If you don't travel much and don't have the need for information access while away from your home or office, you might not need a handheld computer at all. On the other hand, some business travelers, corporate computer users, and information junkies such as myself enjoy being able to check e-mail, synchronize data, and perform various other computing tasks while away from the ball-and-chain desktop or notebook PC. Granted, it might be a little harsh to refer to a non-handheld computer as a "ball and chain," but you tend to get spoiled when you get accustomed to a computer small enough to slip into your pocket. Getting back to the point, the usefulness of Pocket PCs is largely dictated by your personal mobile computing needs.

It turns out that a lot of people appreciate the power and flexibility of Pocket PCs. Does that mean Pocket PCs will eventually replace the notebook computer, or possibly even the desktop computer? I think I can safely answer this question with a "no." Although Pocket PCs pack a lot of punch in a small footprint, they still serve as complementary devices to a traditional PC. Granted, you can buy a keyboard for your Pocket PC, plug in one of IBM's 1GB micro hard drives, and use Pocket applications to the max, but at some point you will undoubtedly want to have a desktop or notebook PC on which to do serious work. Pocket PCs are designed for mobility, and for those times when you're mobile, they are incredibly useful. But then again, so are notebook computers. So when would you choose a Pocket PC over a notebook?

→ For more information on micro hard drives, **see** Chapter 19, "Finding a Home for Your Storage," **p. 357**.

It's important to understand the constraints of Pocket PCs with respect to notebook computers in order to understand why you would use one over the other. First, and perhaps most importantly, Pocket PCs don't have keyboards so entering text is much harder on Pocket PCs than on notebook PCs. Even the most skilled stylus handwriting experts will fall far short of a decent typist using a notebook keyboard. Of course, you can buy a portable keyboard for your Pocket PC and alleviate this problem, but I doubt this is high on the wish list of most Pocket PC users. So, first and foremost, Pocket PCs aren't particularly adept at text entry, which makes it difficult for someone such as me, a computer book author, to do a lot of my primary work on a Pocket PC.

→ For more information on portable keyboards, **see** Appendix A, "A Pocket PC Hardware Tour," **p. 479**.

Strike number two against Pocket PCs, at least with respect to notebook PCs, is their small displays. Don't get me wrong, the displays on Pocket PCs have improved dramatically from early handheld devices and now have brilliant color that doesn't fade in sunlight, but the fact remains that you're dealing with 240×320 resolution. Most notebook and desktop computers these days are at 1024×768 and higher resolutions, which gives you a great deal more screen real estate with which to work. Figure 1.2 shows a comparison between the display sizes of Pocket PCs, Palm devices, and notebook PCs. Of course, the importance of screen real estate is highly dependent on the type of application you're using. The usefulness of Pocket Excel is diminished to some extent if you're working on a spreadsheet with 60 columns of data and you have to scroll for days on your Pocket PC to get anything done. On the other hand, you probably didn't buy your Pocket PC to hack away on unwieldy spreadsheets, which is the point I'm trying to make.

Figure 1.2
The size of the display dramatically impacts the usefulness of any mobile device.

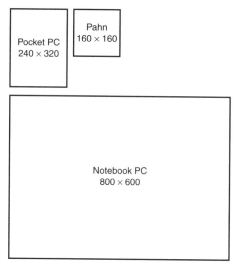

Just in case I haven't made the point, computers are tools, and it's important to always fit the right tool with a particular task. Pocket PCs can be unbelievably useful if leveraged properly as tools for mobile people who need to carry out certain tasks when a notebook or desktop computer is inconvenient or unavailable. That can mean checking e-mail wirelessly in an airport, editing a Word document memorandum, tracking expenses in a financial application, interacting remotely with a legacy database, reading eBooks, keeping up with each shot during a round of golf, or any number of other activities that suit your needs when you can't or don't want to lug around a notebook PC. Assess your needs, and you'll figure out the best way to fit your Pocket PC into your lifestyle and work style.

THE CONVERGENCE OF POCKET PCs AND MOBILE PHONES

Now that I've made a sufficient comparison/contrast between Pocket PCs and notebook computers, I'd like to turn your attention toward another type of device that is closely related to Pocket PCs: mobile phones. Although few have realized it, mobile phones and handheld computers have been on a collision course for some time. Mobile phones have steadily acquired new capabilities as their processing power has increased, while Pocket PCs have steadily enjoyed increasing wireless connectivity options. What this means is that mobile phones are now capable of performing some of the same tasks as handheld computers, and handheld computers are now capable of acting as mobile phones. The question remains as to whether anyone is interested in having such an all-in-one device.

Keep in mind that no matter how rugged a Pocket PC is manufactured, it's unlikely to be capable of withstanding the abuse unleashed on a typical mobile phone. Along the same lines, the small size of mobile phones is in part what allows them to be so rugged. With their relatively large displays, it's going to be difficult to build a Pocket PC that is as compact and durable as even the bulkiest mobile phone. So does that mean we'll never see Pocket PCs and mobile phones converge in a single device? Of course not. In fact, it's already happening.

In late 2000, Microsoft formally announced an initiative that involved injecting the Pocket PC operating system into mobile phones. This project was codenamed Stinger, and a lot of excitement was generated over the prospect of Pocket PC-powered mobile phones. Apparently, the early excitement was justified because several phone manufacturers signed on to produce Stinger phones. Of course, these phones aren't called Stinger phones anymore because the Stinger project was later formally named Smartphone 2002. Smartphone 2002 is essentially the Pocket PC operating system modified to work within the constraints of mobile phones. If you think Pocket PCs are constrained with their small displays and lack of a keyboard, think about the constraints of mobile phones.

If you're concerned about the Pocket PC user interface not working too well in the confines of a mobile phone, think again. Microsoft did its homework on the Smartphone user interface and has designed it specifically for one-handed use without a stylus. That means you can run through the airport carrying a bag and still check messages on your Smartphone mobile phone. The really cool thing about the Smartphone platform is that it finally bridges the information gap between handheld computers and mobile phones; you can now maintain a single contact list between both devices.

On the other side of the fence are global system for mobile communications (GSM) expansion cards available for Pocket PCs that enable you to use your Pocket PC as a mobile phone. GSM is a leading communication technology used by mobile phones. GSM support in a Pocket PC could work out especially well if you add a headset to your Pocket PC that enables you to talk hands-free. I'm not sure how I feel personally about using my Pocket PC as a mobile phone because I tend to be hard on mobile phones, but it's a pretty neat option to have. You also can use mobile phone networks to establish Pocket PC data connections. Mobile phone networks such as General Packet Radio Service (GPRS) enable you to establish an always-on wireless Internet connection with your Pocket PC.

→ For more information on using mobile phone technology for wireless networking with your Pocket PC, **see** "Using a Mobile Phone for Wireless Internet Access," **p. 120**.

Whereas Smartphone 2002 addresses devices that don't use a stylus, Microsoft recently announced Pocket PC 2002 Phone Edition, which is a version of the Pocket PC 2002 operating system designed for wireless devices with a screen and stylus. In fact, Pocket PC 2002 Phone Edition is really just the Pocket PC 2002 operating system with telephony features added so you can make calls and communicate via Short Message Service (SMS) messaging. Pocket PC 2002 Phone Edition in some ways represents the middle ground between handheld computers and mobile phones in that it legitimately blends aspects of both devices. One of the first devices to use the Pocket PC 2002 Phone Edition operating system was Hewlett Packard's Jornada 928 Wireless Digital Assistant. Devices such as the HP Jornada 928 are similar to traditional Pocket PCs, but they are physically designed to function more as phones.

Note

The term *wireless digital assistant (WDA)* is a new term you'll likely hear more and more to describe the next generation of wireless PDAs.

The question still remains as to whether Pocket PCs will kill mobile phones or mobile phones will kill Pocket PCs. In truth, I don't expect either of these scenarios to play out anytime soon. Compelling reasons (size, price, durability, and so on) still exist to have both a handheld computer and a mobile phone, at least for the foreseeable future, so I expect most people to have one of each device if they have the need to both compute and make phone calls on the go. On the other hand, Microsoft is clearly trying to push the idea of an all-encompassing device with Pocket PC 2002 Phone Edition. This is one issue that will likely be decided by the marketplace because no one yet has a feel for how users will take to a single device that serves as a handheld computer, PDA, and mobile phone.

POCKET PC VERSUS PALM

It is currently impossible to speak of handheld computers without addressing the incredibly popular Palm line of handheld devices. Although Palm devices and compatible clones have suffered somewhat in the marketplace as of late, they still have a huge user base and occupy a considerable share of the handheld computer market. This is for a number of reasons, not limited to a sleek design, great marketing, and a very affordable price tag. A few years ago Palm devices set the standard for modern PDAs. As PDAs, Palm devices provide a rich set of features that are intuitive and easy to use. Unfortunately, the Palm operating system was designed purely around the PDA concept and doesn't necessarily scale well to the demands of a full-blown handheld computer.

In today's hectic workplace, PDAs are a necessity for some, which explains the popularity of the Palm devices. However, in many ways the PDA approach to handheld computing is no different from the original spreadsheet approach to personal computing. In case you weren't wired for the early days of PC history, most of the original PCs were sold purely because of spreadsheet software that enabled people to crunch numbers much more effectively than using calculators. The spreadsheet was the killer application that initially put computers on so many desks. However, spreadsheet software eventually settled in as one of many important computer applications. Do you still perceive the spreadsheet as the killer PC application? I doubt it. Are PC sales still driven primarily by the need for everyone to run Lotus 1-2-3? Absolutely not.

The same usage shift is currently taking place in the handheld world as Palm devices cling to their killer application (PDA software) and Pocket PCs introduce a complete mobile computing experience. Granted, some Palm devices are expanding their capabilities by supporting MP3 music and even acting as mobile phones, but at their cores they are still designed to be PDAs. In addition to functioning as traditional PDAs, Pocket PCs also serve as word processors, spreadsheets, navigational maps, financial managers, e-mail clients, Web clients, digital Walkmans, digital voice recorders, digital book readers, and portable video games, to name a few applications. These features are due to both the hardware and software of the Pocket PC platform, which are much more in line with a full-featured computer than with a PDA such as a Palm device. It's worth noting that some of the functionality built into Pocket PC devices can be added to Palm devices via third-party hardware and software, but these add-ons still run contrary to the original PDA design of Palm devices.

 If you recently purchased a Pocket PC to replace a Palm device, you might be interested in moving your address book over to the Pocket PC from the Palm device. See "Migrating from Palm to Pocket PC" in the "Troubleshooting" section at the end of the chapter to find out how this is done.

Although the feature list of the Pocket PC operating system is certainly a clear indicator of its technical superiority over the Palm operating system, let's dig a little deeper and really see why Pocket PCs are more powerful devices. Following is a list of the major aspects of Pocket PC devices that make them clear-cut winners over Palm devices:

- **Faster processor**—Pocket PCs all have 32-bit processors with speeds in the range of 100MHz to 206MHz, whereas the fastest Palm devices have 33MHz processors. To the credit of Palm devices, most of their applications require less processing power than their Pocket PC counterparts, which makes the processor speed difference not quite as dramatic as it appears.

- **More memory**—Pocket PCs all have between 32MB and 64MB of RAM and 32MB of ROM, whereas the most powerful Palm devices have 16MB of RAM and 2MB of ROM. Palm applications tend to require less memory than Pocket PC applications, which offsets the memory difference somewhat. However, media files such as images and MP3 music are memory hogs regardless of which type of device they are used with, which gives Pocket PCs a distinct edge.

- **Better screens**—Pocket PCs all have screens that are 240×320 in resolution, whereas most Palms have 160×160 resolution. Also, most Pocket PCs have color screens; however, only a couple of the newer, more expensive Palm devices have color screens. The end result is that a lot of the Palm software was developed without color in mind. On the other hand, color Pocket PC screens are a bigger drain on batteries, which means that Pocket PCs tend to have a shorter battery life than Palm devices.

- **Standard expansion slot**—Pocket PCs include one or more standard expansion slots, either CompactFlash (CF) or Secure Digital (SD), whereas many Palm devices do not. Newer Palm devices and HandEra Palm-compatible devices include Secure Digital slots, and the various Handspring Visor devices include a proprietary Springboard expansion slot.

- **Natural handwriting recognition**—Pocket PCs include natural handwriting-recognition software, which enables you to write very closely to how you're accustomed to writing and have it automatically translated into text. Palm devices use a special Graffiti language for handwriting recognition; although many Palm users are fond of the Graffiti language, it has a fairly steep learning curve. If you're migrating from Palm to Pocket PC and can't stand the thought of giving up Graffiti, you can use Graffiti on your Pocket PC with the Block Recognizer input method.

- **Full Web browsing**—Pocket PCs include Pocket Internet Explorer, which enables you to view any Web page, provided you don't mind scrolling around a little; there is a Fit to Screen option that does a fairly decent job of scaling pages down to fit on the Pocket PC screen. Many Palm devices don't support any direct Web browsing—you must view Web content as text snippets that are available only from specific Web sites.

This list isn't intended to be all-inclusive; there are obviously other areas in which Pocket PC devices shine over Palm devices. However, it does reveal the most significant areas in which Pocket PC excels over Palm. Keep in mind that both Pocket PCs and Palm devices continue to evolve rapidly and acquire more features, so this list is likely to change as new models of each respective device are released. Even so, the Pocket PC platform is considerably more demanding of its hardware, so I don't expect the technological gap to close any time soon.

Perhaps the only significant advantage Palm devices still have at the moment is price, which isn't surprising given the extensive feature set of Pocket PCs, both in terms of hardware and software. Everything has its price, and in this case the rich features of Pocket PCs result in Pocket PCs being more expensive than Palm devices. However, Palm device manufacturers are quickly beefing up their devices in an attempt to catch up with Pocket PCs, which is driving up their price. At the same time, Pocket PC sales are escalating, which is helping lower the price of Pocket PCs. The price gap will likely still exist for some time between Pocket PCs and the low-end Palm devices that are pure PDAs, which makes sense. However, these are very different types of devices that really aren't in direct competition. Pocket PCs are targeted at those users who are looking for more than a PDA; this is a market segment Palm is unlikely to retain given the strength of the Pocket PC platform.

WIRELESS POCKET PC CONNECTIVITY

In the discussion earlier about the convergence of Pocket PCs and mobile phones, I mentioned that you can use a Pocket PC as a mobile phone. In actuality, this is but one facet of the wireless communication capabilities of Pocket PCs. Many of us in the computing world have been anxiously awaiting the widespread and affordable availability of wireless communications, and the time has finally come. The good news is that Pocket PCs are poised to take full advantage of wireless communications. The wireless connection itself is quite likely the killer app that puts Pocket PCs in the hands of most serious computer users. That's why I feel the need to discuss wireless communications with Pocket PCs in this opening chapter, even though you don't get into the specifics of Pocket PC networking until later in the book.

→ For details on Pocket PC networking, **see** Chapter 6, "Evaluating Networking Options," **p. 111**.

To understand why wireless connectivity is so important to Pocket PCs, consider the fact that they are the most mobile of computers, and therefore the computers that are most encumbered when a wire is required for communications. Few people care that a wire connects their desktop computers to a LAN, cable modem, or phone line, and not all that many people are upset about plugging their notebook computers into a docking station for the same net effect. However, try finding a wire long enough to follow you around everywhere you go, and you'll quickly see why wireless connectivity is so important to Pocket PCs. The situation is really no different from mobile phones. Most of us initially saw mobile phones as a simple convenience, and now most of us don't know how we got by without them in the past. In the very near future, we will feel the same way about wireless e-mail and instant messaging, and Pocket PCs will be the devices that make it possible.

Note

If you're like me, maybe the idea of wireless instant messaging is a bit worrisome because you have limits as to how "connected" you need to be. Fortunately, you can make your own rules regarding how much you allow wireless communications to invade your privacy or disrupt your lifestyle. Pocket PCs are very flexible devices and can be customized to your own personal needs. The main thing is that the capabilities exist for you to be as wirelessly "available" as you want to be.

When it comes to the technical details of wireless Pocket PC connectivity, several distinct networking options are available to Pocket PC users. These options correspond to the various kinds of networks currently available for wireless networking:

- Wide Area Network (WAN)
- Wireless Local Area Network (WLAN)
- Personal Area Network (PAN)

WIDE AREA NETWORK

Although you can establish wireless network connections in any of these networks, the topology of each network dictates exactly how you go about doing so. So, for example, connecting your Pocket PC to a wide area network (WAN) requires different hardware than it does to connect to a PAN. To better understand why this is so, let's quickly go over what constitutes the various kinds of networks and how a Pocket PC might interact with each.

Although there are certainly wide area networks connecting computers, when you think in terms of wireless Pocket PCs, WANs usually involve a mobile phone network. More specifically, you take advantage of the existing wireless network used by mobile phones to establish a wireless WAN connection for your Pocket PC. This network can be one of several types, such as Cellular Digital Packet Data (CDPD), GSM, or Code Division Multiple Access (CDMA). It isn't really important for you to understand the differences between these networks—just understand that they are all designed for mobile phones. For a Pocket PC to communicate over a network designed for mobile phones, it must have special hardware (via an expansion card or directly integrated into the device) that can recognize and handle data on the specific network being used.

WIRELESS LOCAL AREA NETWORK

A LAN used for wireless networking is actually referred to as a *wireless LAN (WLAN)*. WLANs differ from WANs both in terms of their range of communication and their bandwidth. WLANs have significantly less range than WANs, but they are much faster; for example, WLANs offer speeds up to 11Mbps, whereas WANs offer speeds of only 9.6bps. On the other hand, the range of WANs is limited only by the area of a mobile phone network, which is typically quite large, whereas WLANs have a range in the neighborhood of 100 yards. The idea behind WLANs is to provide seamless wireless network access for Pocket PCs that are reasonably close to an existing LAN. For example, you might connect to a WLAN with your Pocket PC when you arrive at your place of work to synchronize e-mail and contacts.

Similar to WANs, WLANs also require special hardware on the part of Pocket PCs; several expansion cards are available that adhere to the popular Wi-Fi (802.11b) wireless networking standard, and a few Pocket PC devices have integrated support. You might already be familiar with Wi-Fi wireless networking due to it having become popular for home and small business use simply because it eliminates a lot of the wiring hassles associated with small computer networks.

PERSONAL AREA NETWORK

Chances are you might not yet have heard of personal area networks (PANs), which are the smallest and most personal of the three types of networks to which you can wirelessly connect your Pocket PC. PANs are purely wireless networks consisting of devices that are within about 30 feet of each other. The technology behind PANs is the much-hyped Bluetooth wireless networking standard, which is designed to remove many of those unsightly wires meandering between devices in a typical office. With the proper Bluetooth hardware in place, you can walk into a room and establish an instant wireless connection between your Pocket PC and another device, such as a printer or desktop PC. Unlike WLANs, Bluetooth isn't intended to be an all-purpose wireless networking standard; it is primarily designed to facilitate one-to-one wireless device connections. Several Bluetooth expansion cards are available for Pocket PCs, not to mention a few devices with built-in support.

Figure 1.3 shows the relationship between WANs, WLANs, and PANs as they relate to Pocket PC wireless connectivity. To help you remember the distinction between each, just understand that PAN involves Bluetooth, WLAN involves Wi-Fi (802.11b), and WAN involves a mobile phone network such as GSM.

Figure 1.3
The types of networks available for wireless Pocket PC connectivity vary widely.

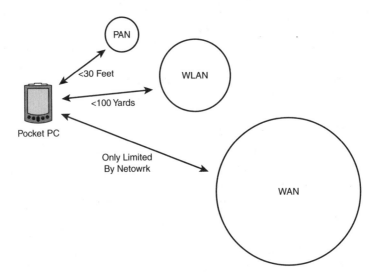

Regardless of whether you are leaning toward a WAN, WLAN, or PAN for connecting your Pocket PC to a wireless network, you should definitely consider wireless connectivity for your device in one form or another. Pocket PCs simply offer too many benefits when coupled with wireless communications to not take advantage of them. You might even end up using some combination of the three wireless networking options. For example, you could use a Bluetooth PAN connection to synchronize data with a desktop PC and then take advantage of a WAN connection to check e-mail and browse the Web while traveling—the possibilities are virtually limitless when it comes to wireless communications and Pocket PCs.

TROUBLESHOOTING

UPGRADING A DEVICE TO POCKET PC 2002

I own a Pocket PC device that uses the original Pocket PC operating system. How do I upgrade the device to the Pocket PC 2002 operating system?

Depending on your specific device, you might not have the option of upgrading to the Pocket PC 2002 operating system. More specifically, the Compaq iPAQ H3600 and H3100 series of devices are the only legacy Pocket PC devices with upgradeable flash ROM, which means they are the only devices that can be upgraded to Pocket PC 2002. The upgrade is available for free on a CD-ROM that you can order directly from Compaq at `http://www.compaqordercenter.com/ipaq2002upgrade/`.

MIGRATING FROM PALM TO POCKET PC

I recently bought a Pocket PC 2002 device after having used a Palm device for years. How can I import my Palm address book into my Pocket PC?

Fortunately, Pocket PCs are designed with Palm users in mind so transferring your Palm address book to your Pocket PC isn't difficult. The most straightforward approach is to beam the contact information across using the infrared port on each device; Pocket PC 2002 supports the UBEX standard, which allows information to be shared via infrared across a wide range of devices. You learn how to beam contacts through your Pocket PC's infrared port in Chapter 13, "Using the Pocket Outlook Contacts and Calendar."

If you want additional control over the migration of data from Palm to Pocket PC, you might consider using a commercial application such as Peacemaker by Conduits Technologies, which includes advanced information sharing features. You can learn more about Peacemaker by visiting its Web site at `http://www.conduits.com/products/peacemaker/`.

REAL-WORLD EXAMPLE—PLANNING FOR THE FUTURE OF POCKET PCS

The convergence of Pocket PCs and mobile phones will likely continue to be a significant issue as the wireless device market continues to evolve and mature. To determine how this convergence might affect you, you need to assess your own unique wireless communication needs. Do you use a mobile phone regularly for business or personal use? If so, would you realistically consider getting rid of it and using your Pocket PC as a mobile phone? I suspect an upgrade for Pocket PC 2002 Phone Edition will be available at some point so that existing Pocket PC 2002 devices could be upgraded and used as mobile phones, assuming you've added appropriate wireless hardware. Because this option is on the horizon, I encourage you to consider the prospect of an all-in-one handheld device and try to determine whether it would benefit you.

CHAPTER 2

INSIDE POCKET PC HARDWARE

In this chapter

POCKET PC HARDWARE FUNDAMENTALS

Although the Pocket PC operating system is a pretty impressive piece of software technology, the hardware behind Pocket PC devices is quite amazing considering their small size. To fully understand the capabilities of a Pocket PC, it's important to have a solid grasp on the underlying hardware that makes them tick. And rather than ask you to pry open your device with a screwdriver to see for yourself, I'd prefer telling you about the hardware inside. Trust me, it will save you some time, and you won't have to buy another Pocket PC when you realize that yours won't go back together.

This chapter explores the inner workings of Pocket PCs and gives you some insight into the physical characteristics of these intricate little machines. Pocket PCs include an unprecedented array of features packed into a small footprint, which makes them quite interesting gadgets. Although this chapter admittedly doesn't delve much into Pocket PC software, it will hopefully leave you with a newfound appreciation of Pocket PCs and enable you to better understand their overall design.

MAJOR HARDWARE COMPONENTS

As with all modern computers, Pocket PCs are electronic devices that rely on a variety of subsystems, or *components*, to carry out different operations. Some of these components are hidden from the user (the microprocessor), whereas others are right there in plain view (the display). Following are the major hardware components that drive a typical Pocket PC:

- Microprocessor
- Memory
- Power
- Display
- Stylus
- I/O ports
- Multimedia hardware

The microprocessor, or processor for short, is at the heart of a Pocket PC and is responsible for executing software instructions and coordinating other hardware subsystems. Memory can come in several forms and is used both as a place for software applications to run and as a place to store installed applications and data. Because Pocket PCs are electronic devices, they wouldn't be of much use without power, which comes in the form of batteries. The display of Pocket PCs is extremely important because it enables you to view information and interact with applications by tapping the stylus. I/O ports give you the ability to connect Pocket PCs to networks and other devices. And finally, multimedia hardware consists of the speaker, headphone jack, and microphone that are prevalent in all Pocket PCs.

POCKET PC MODELS

The remainder of this chapter explores the various Pocket PC hardware components and examines their roles in making Pocket PCs such powerful handheld devices. I'll also point out the minimum hardware requirements for each component as set forth by Microsoft for Pocket PC 2002. These requirements are extremely important because they establish the minimum hardware characteristics of Pocket PC devices. Before getting into the characteristics of each hardware component, however, it's worth taking a quick look at some of the Pocket PC devices that are currently available. Although new Pocket PC devices are being released on a regular basis, following are some of the popular models available as of this writing:

- Casio Cassiopeia E-200
- Compaq iPAQ H3800 Series
- HP Jornada 560 Series
- Toshiba e570
- NEC MobilePro P300
- Audiovox Maestro

I'll be referring to these devices throughout the chapter to illuminate similarities and differences between them. My goal is to simultaneously reveal the hardware that drives Pocket PCs in general as well as point out the unique hardware approaches taken by various Pocket PC manufacturers. Even with minimum hardware requirements firmly in place, there is still a wide range of hardware features available in Pocket PCs. Toward the end of the chapter, I'll break down these devices according to their specific hardware features.

PROCESSORS: THE BRAINS OF THE OUTFIT

The *processor* is the brain of Pocket PC devices and therefore is critical in determining how much power is packed into them. Even though desktop and notebook PC processor speeds are now over 2GHz (2,000MHz), it was only a few short years ago when a 200MHz PC was considered speedy for most applications. Knowing this, it's pretty impressive that most Pocket PCs now use processors running at 206MHz. In fact, the Pocket PC 2002 platform dictates that all Pocket PCs must use a 32-bit processor running at a speed of at least 100MHz. Additionally, Pocket PCs must now use a specific type of processor based on the ARM processor technology.

Simplifying the Processor in Pocket PC 2002

Prior to Pocket PC 2002, Pocket PCs were capable of using a variety of processors with widely varying architectures. In fact, five different processors were used in devices prior to Pocket PC 2002 with speeds ranging from 70MHz to 206MHz. Although this processor diversity might have seemed like a good idea, it presented a problem for software distribution. Because Pocket PC processors were each distinctively different, applications had to be compiled to each specific processor. More importantly, software vendors had to release different versions of their software for different processors. From the user's perspective, this was extremely confusing, which is probably why Microsoft decided to do away with processor diversity in Pocket PC 2002.

ARM is actually a processor architecture created by Advanced RISC Machines (ARM) Ltd., which means that various chip manufacturers license the architecture and develop their own ARM processors. All ARM processors are 32-bit RISC processors, which means they shuttle around data in 32-bit chunks and rely on a reduced instruction set. The *reduced instruction set* used by RISC processors enables them to perform many of the most common operations faster than CISC processors that rely on a complex instruction set. RISC processors also tend to be much cheaper to manufacture, which is extremely important for Pocket PC manufacturers given the need to keep Pocket PC prices down.

Note

In addition to Pocket PCs, ARM processors are used in a variety of other devices, such as Nintendo's Game Boy Advance. It probably seems strange that your Pocket PC that is used for executive e-mails is powered by the same processor technology that grade school kids are using to play Super Mario World. Keep in mind, however, that a Game Boy Advance is a handheld computer with many of the same processor requirements as a Pocket PC.

Most of the current Pocket PC devices use Intel's StrongARM SA-1110 processor running at 206MHz. What few people realize is that this StrongARM processor is actually capable of running at speeds of anywhere between 162MHz and 236MHz. Higher speeds result in increased power consumption, which is presumably why device manufacturers settled on 206MHz as a reasonable tradeoff of processor speed and battery life. The interesting thing, however, is that you can change the speed of the processor on some devices with the appropriate software. For example, the JS Overclock utility by Jimmy Software (`http://www.jimmysoftware.com/`) enables you to set the processor speed for Compaq iPAQ Pocket PCs in the range of 162MHz–236MHz. Setting a processor to a speed higher than its default (206MHz in this case) is known as *overclocking* the processor. Overclocking is not recommended or endorsed by device manufacturers, but it is an option to some Pocket PC users who are willing to trade off battery life for a speedier processor.

Caution

Another problem with overclocking is that it puts more stress on a processor because higher speeds result in more heat; heat is the enemy of any electronic circuit. So, overclocking your processor can decrease its life. Because no manufacturer endorses overclocking, gauging the risks associated with overclocking is difficult, which means the safe route is to avoid it.

The good news about Pocket PC processor speeds is that overclocking shouldn't be necessary, except for the greediest of Pocket PC users. Keep in mind that a considerable amount of thought and design work has gone into matching up hardware and software in Pocket

PCs. In other words, the majority of applications available for Pocket PCs should run perfectly well on a device with its processor running at the default speed.

UNDERSTANDING MEMORY

Next to processor speed, the most significant factor in the performance of any computer is memory. Because Pocket PCs are inherently compact devices with every design decision carefully weighed against size, cost, weight, and ruggedness, it stands to reason that memory is the only real Pocket PC bottleneck. All Pocket PCs are required to have at least 16MB of flash upgradeable ROM and 16MB of RAM, although Microsoft recommends 32MB of RAM. Although the ROM is sufficient for storing the Pocket PC operating system and standard applications, the RAM is where things quickly get tight. ROM (read-only memory) is used in Pocket PCs to store the Pocket PC operating system and built-in applications. *Flash ROM* is a type of ROM that can be rewritten through a process known as *flashing*, which enables you to upgrade the Pocket PC operating system.

Note

New in Pocket PC 2002 is the concept of Execute In Place (XIP) installation, which enables built-in applications to reside in separate segments of flash ROM. This allows you to selectively upgrade individual built-in applications without touching the operating system. Built-in applications are those that are installed in the ROM of your device straight from the factory, as opposed to applications you purchase and install yourself. XIP technology would come into play if you wanted to upgrade Pocket Word, for example, which is an application that is built into the ROM of every Pocket PC device.

RAM (random access memory) basically serves as the main memory in Pocket PCs. Whereas the contents of ROM are fixed and change only if you perform a rare operating system upgrade, RAM changes constantly. This is due to the fact that RAM houses both applications and data. Any time you install a new application or edit a document in an application you are changing RAM. The downside to RAM is that it is volatile, which means you lose its contents if power goes away. That's why it's so important to never let a Pocket PC's battery completely drain down to nothing. Likewise, you don't want to leave the batteries out of your device for more than a few minutes; most Pocket PCs are designed to be capable of surviving without their main batteries for a little while.

Now that you understand how ROM and RAM fit into the Pocket PC hardware equation, it's time to break some bad news to you about the limitations of Pocket PC memory. When you consider that desktop and notebook computers have exploded in recent years in terms of their memory and hard disk capacities, it's not too surprising that people haven't argued much as applications and data files have ballooned in size. When you literally have tens of gigabytes of hard disk space to spare, who cares if a file is 120KB or 120MB? Obviously, there are reasons to care, but in the big picture it isn't that big of a deal when you almost always have room to spare. Such is the situation in the world of desktop and notebook computing.

Unfortunately, handheld devices live by a very different set of rules than desktop and note-book computers, and memory is the one area where this is painfully evident. The primary issue is the cost of compact memory, which is higher than the cost of desktop or even note-book memory and incredibly higher than the cost of hard drives. The comparison to hard drives is important because Pocket PCs typically don't have hard drives, in which case they must rely on some form of memory as residual storage. When you look at trying to replace the storage space of a hard drive with memory, cost suddenly becomes a big problem.

Because compact RAM for handheld devices is relatively expensive, Pocket PC manufactur-ers decided to design them with enough RAM to handle average usage but not enough to handle extreme applications such as storing a lot of photographs, MP3 music, or videos. For those users with large memory requirements, the extensibility of Pocket PCs saves the day. More specifically, all Pocket PCs are required to support some form of memory expansion through one or more expansion slots. Several types of expansion slots are supported across Pocket PC devices, which we'll get to in just a moment. When it comes to extra memory, it's really a matter of economics; if you can afford it, get a bunch and you won't have to worry so much about running out. So let's explore the various options made possible by Pocket PC expansion slots.

Three options are available for adding extra memory to Pocket PCs, which correspond to the three types of expansion cards currently supported by Pocket PCs:

- PC
- CompactFlash (CF)
- Secure digital (SD)/multimedia card (MMC)

Note

I didn't entirely tell the truth when I said that expansion cards are the only way to increase the memory capacity of Pocket PCs. If you don't mind the thought of sending off your device and having someone open it up and tinker with its internals, you can increase your device's memory without using an expansion slot. A company called Portable Computer Enhancements specializes in this type of memory upgrade, which can increase your device's internal RAM up to 256MB. To find out more, visit the Portable Computer Enhancements Web site at http://www.pce2000.com/.

PC

PC is a type of expansion card formerly known as PCMCIA that originated more than a decade ago as a means of adding accessories such as modems and network interfaces to notebook computers. PC cards have found their way into Pocket PCs as a means of adding memory as well as accessories such as wireless modems and network interface cards. In fact, you can use some PC card accessories designed for notebook computers with Pocket PCs. PC cards are roughly the size of credit cards and somewhat thicker. There are three types of PC cards (I, II, and III), so it's important to ensure that your device supports the correct type of card if you purchase expansion memory or an accessory as a PC card. In terms of memory, PC cards are currently capable of storing up to 5GB and are relatively inexpensive as an expansion storage option. However, few Pocket PCs support PC cards because they are somewhat power hungry.

COMPACTFLASH

By far, the most popular memory expansion option for Pocket PCs is CompactFlash (CF) cards, or CF cards. CF cards originated in 1994 and are specifically designed for use in small consumer devices, such as digital cameras, MP3 music players, and handheld computers. CF cards are available in two types: Type I and Type II. CF Type I cards are roughly the size of a matchbook and weigh about half an ounce, whereas Type II cards are slightly thicker and weigh a little more. Devices with Type II slots will also accept Type I cards, but devices that support only Type I cards will not accept Type II cards. Memory is typically packaged in CF Type I cards, which makes it usable in the widest range of devices. CF cards are extremely rugged, which makes them perhaps the best all-around expansion card for Pocket PCs. The slight downside to CF cards is the fact that they currently can store up to only 1GB. Don't get me wrong—that's a lot of memory. But when you start to enter the realm of digital music and video with Pocket PCs, memory can get sparse in a hurry. Even so, CF cards are an extremely viable memory expansion solution because of their durability and relatively inexpensive prices.

Note

Although CF cards are considerably different in size (smaller than) from PC cards, you can use a PC card adapter to use a CF card in a PC card slot. This adapter could be particularly useful with Compaq's dual-slot PC card expansion sleeve, which includes two PC card slots but no CF slots.

SECURE DIGITAL/MULTIMEDIA CARD

The newcomer to the Pocket PC memory expansion scene is the secure digital card, or SD card. The primary benefit of SD cards is that they are extremely small and lightweight—a little larger than a postage stamp and not much thicker! Their incredibly small size and lack of weight also make SD cards quite durable. The other big benefit of SD cards is that they have built-in security features for distributing licensed content, such as digital music and eBooks. Similar cards without encryption capabilities are also marketed as multimedia cards, or MMCs. Because SD cards are considerably newer than PC and CF cards, they still cost more and aren't as widely supported across Pocket PC devices. Even so, don't be surprised if SD cards eventually catch on; they are just too small and compact not to make sense. In addition to price, the other downside to SD cards at the moment is that you can't get them any larger than 128MB. However, I've heard that 1GB SD cards are on the near horizon, so this isn't likely to be a problem for very long.

Note

You might have also heard of SmartMedia cards, which are small, thin expansion cards used as memory cards in many consumer devices. For example, the popular Creative Labs Nomad MP3 player uses SmartMedia cards as a means of storing digital MP3 music. However, no Pocket PCs have adopted SmartMedia cards as of yet, and they might not now that SD cards provide a similar option in terms of size. Yet another type of memory card is Sony's Memory Stick, which is popular in Sony's CLIE Palm device.

MEMORY SELECTION CONSIDERATIONS

Even though it would be great to pretend that you could pick and choose exactly what type of memory expansion card to buy based on price, durability, and so on, the reality is that your Pocket PC will likely dictate your options for you. In other words, you're pretty much limited by the expansion slots built into your device. The exception to this rule is the Compaq iPAQ line of Pocket PCs, which supports expansion sleeves that can be slid over the device to add different kinds of expansion slots. PC and CF expansion sleeves are available for iPAQs, and the newer iPAQs have a built-in SD slot in addition to the expansion sleeves. That means you have the option of using any of the expansion card types with the newer iPAQ devices. I expect other Pocket PC manufacturers to eventually follow Compaq's lead in this area simply due to the flexibility it gives users. Table 2.1 provides a recap of the differences between the types of Pocket PC memory expansion cards.

TABLE 2.1   COMPARING POCKET PC MEMORY EXPANSION CARDS

Card Type	Maximum Memory	Physical Size	Cost*
PC	5GB	Medium	$
CompactFlash (CF)	512MB	Small	$$
Secure digital (SD/MMC)	128MB	Very small	$$$

* The dollar signs ($) under the Cost column indicate the relative cost of each type of memory expansion card, with more dollar signs indicating a higher cost.

Memory expansion cards are interesting in that they actually function as removable disk drives because data is stored on them persistently. In other words, if all the power to your Pocket PC is lost or if you perform a full reset on the device, the data on a memory card will still be intact. Because memory cards function more as disk drives—as opposed to traditional RAM—you will likely want to store both applications and data files on them. One obvious use for memory cards is storing MP3 music files, which are notorious for taking up a lot of space. You also might decide to store maps for Pocket Streets, e-mail attachments, or eBooks on memory cards. Basically, any data can be stored on a memory card, and most applications can be safely installed and executed from a memory card as well.

It wouldn't be fair to make the comparison between memory cards and hard drives without pointing out an impressive piece of technology that in some ways makes the most sense of all in terms of memory expansion. I'm referring to miniature hard drives by IBM and

Toshiba that are capable of storing enormous amounts of Pocket PC data. The IBM drives are known as Microdrives and are packaged as CF expansion cards. IBM Microdrives are currently available in 340MB, 512MB, and 1GB sizes. Toshiba's micro hard drives are packaged as either PC or CF cards and are available in sizes of 2GB, 5GB, 10GB, and even 20GB.

THE IMPORTANCE OF POWER

A Pocket PC with no power wouldn't be of much use, so power is certainly an important part of the Pocket PC hardware picture. All Pocket PCs include a main battery that is used to power the device during normal use. In addition to the main battery, some devices also include a backup battery that is used when the main battery is dead or otherwise not functioning. The Pocket PC operating system is designed to keep close tabs on battery power and inform you of impending low power. It's important to heed low power warnings, recharge/replace the main battery, and possibly replace the backup battery, if one exists.

PART

I

CH

2

As of Pocket PC 2002, Microsoft has placed an increased emphasis on devices providing longer battery life. For example, devices with color displays are required to supply a minimum of 8 hours of battery life, whereas grayscale devices must supply 15 hours of battery life. In addition to these requirements on how long the main battery must last with a full charge, there are also some interesting power requirements related to system RAM. Keep in mind that regardless of how careful you are about keeping the main battery charged, the possibility always exists that the main battery could go bad and need replacing. Obviously, you need a way to replace the main battery without losing everything in system RAM. Fortunately, all Pocket PC 2002 devices are required to keep system RAM intact for a minimum of 30 minutes with the main battery removed. Additionally, devices must retain RAM for 72 hours after a low battery system shutdown. This occurs when the battery level is determined to be too low to enable you to use the device, in which case you have 3 days to recharge or replace the main battery.

 If you need to recharge the batteries in your Pocket PC when you're away from a traditional power source, see "Recharging Batteries Without a Traditional Power Source" in the "Troubleshooting" section at the end of the chapter.

Caution

If your Pocket PC allows access to its batteries, it is important to never remove the main battery and the backup battery at the same time unless you are intentionally trying to clear the memory of your Pocket PC. Without either battery, you are sure to lose all data and any customized settings you made to the device. If both batteries require replacement at the same time, be sure to replace the main battery first.

Most Pocket PCs use a rechargeable lithium-ion or lithium-polymer battery for primary power. Lithium-ion batteries are a little more popular, whereas the newer lithium-polymer batteries offer improved battery life. Keep in mind, however, that Microsoft's power requirements guarantee you decent battery life regardless of the underlying battery technology. Most devices support charging the main battery through a cradle, as well as enabling you to use AC and automobile adapter cords for recharging.

Note
Unfortunately, most Pocket PC 2002 devices don't include user replaceable batteries, which means you must ship your device back to the manufacturer whenever your battery dies. I suppose the logic is that the lifetime of a battery is sufficient to outlast the usefulness of the device, but that's debatable. Hewlett Packard and Casio are two manufacturers in particular who allow you to replace the batteries in their devices.

THE ALL-IMPORTANT DISPLAY

When you think about the displays used in most mobile devices, such as mobile phones, it's hard to look at a Pocket PC without appreciating the display. All Pocket PCs are required to support a screen resolution of 240×320 pixels with a 0.216mm or 0.24mm dot pitch. Although the dot pitch might be hard to visualize, hopefully you can appreciate the fact that 240×320 resolution is pretty amazing for a device that fits in the palm of your hand. Although not a strict requirement, most Pocket PCs also include color screens, which adds significantly to their usability. Devices with color screens are required to have a color depth of at least 8-bit color (256 colors), whereas most devices are now up to 16-bit color (64,000 colors). Grayscale devices must have either 2-bit (4 shades of gray) or 4-bit color (16 shades of gray).

Caution
Be careful when cleaning the screen of your Pocket PC. Some commercial glass cleaners, such as Formula 409, contain solvents that can damage the top layer of the liquid crystal display (LCD) screen, which is made of plastic. More specifically, avoid using a cleaner that contains acetone, ethanol, isopropyl alcohol, or toluene. Kensington Computer Screen Cleaner is a safe option and is available at most computer stores.

As you might have noticed, the display quality on Pocket PCs rivals that of the best notebook computers. This has a lot to do with the reflective TFT LCD display technology used by newer Pocket PCs. TFT stands for thin film transistor, which is a technology that results in displays that are brighter than other types of LCD displays although they have a tendency to wash out more in direct light such as outdoor sunlight. TFT displays are considered *active displays*, which means they use individual transistors to control each pixel on the screen; *passive displays* use a grid of horizontal and vertical wires to accomplish the same task. The upside to active displays is that they provide a sharper image and a broader viewing angle than passive displays. Not surprisingly, active displays are more expensive to produce than passive displays, but the improvement in display quality appears to be well worth the added cost.

I mentioned a moment ago that active displays have a tendency to wash out if viewed in direct light. Pocket PCs handle this problem by using a reflective TFT display; the reflective part of the display addresses the wash out problem. A *reflective* display is a display that relies on ambient light to light up the display, as opposed to a backlight that shines behind the screen. The reflective TFT display used in Pocket PCs not only solves the wash out problem by adjusting the display according to the intensity of surrounding light, but it also uses much less power than backlit displays. You might notice that reflective displays aren't quite as bright as backlit displays in normal indoor light, but they perform much better all-around.

PART

I

CH

2

Tip from
Michael

> Because the top layer of a Pocket PC display is plastic, it is relatively easy to scratch it, which can be very frustrating. Believe it or not, an inexpensive way to fix minor scratches on your Pocket PC's display is to spray a little STP Son of a Gun tire cleaner on the screen and lightly buff it off. It contains a polymer that bonds with the top layer of the LCD display and fills minor scratches.

ASSESSING I/O CAPABILITIES

The Pocket PC platform dictates that all Pocket PCs have several input/output (I/O) ports to provide the utmost in flexibility when it comes to communicating with the outside world. I/O ports such as USB and infrared are important in enabling Pocket PCs to connect and communicate with desktop PCs and other mobile devices. Although some Pocket PC devices also include a serial port for desktop synchronization, Pocket PC 2002 requires all devices to have a USB port. This is due to the fact that USB ports provide considerably much faster transfer speeds than serial ports. More specifically, a Pocket PC serial port is limited to a data transfer rate of 115Kbps (kilobits per second), whereas a USB port can move data at speeds of 1,500Kbps. That's more than 10 times as fast, which can make a big difference when transferring large files such as digital MP3 or WMA music files.

In addition to a USB port, all Pocket PCs must include an infrared port that can be used to communicate with other devices via an invisible beam of light. The infrared port is convenient because it doesn't require a physical connection for two devices to communicate with each other. The speed of the infrared port clocks in at 115Kbps, which is the same as serial ports. This type of infrared port is known as an SIR port, which stands for serial infrared. SIR differs from FIR (fast infrared) in that it supports speeds up to only 115Kbps, as opposed to the 4Mbps supported by FIR. Speed isn't quite as big of an issue with the Pocket PC infrared port, however, because it is designed more for mobile communication between devices—as opposed to hardcore networking. For example, you can use the infrared port with some mobile phones to establish a wireless Internet connection. Because most mobile phones have limited bandwidth for data connections, the speed limitation on Pocket PC infrared ports doesn't really present a problem.

> **Note**
>
> The infrared port found in Pocket PCs conforms to the Infrared Data Association (IrDA) infrared communications protocol, which is important because this is an industry standard used by many devices.

GETTING TO KNOW THE STYLUS, BUTTONS, AND DIALS

Although they tend to get overlooked when considering the impressive technology behind Pocket PC processors and memory, the physical controls used to interact with Pocket PCs are an integral part of Pocket PC hardware. I'm referring to the stylus, buttons, and dials used to enter data, control applications, and otherwise interact with Pocket PCs. The majority of interaction carried out with a device is done through the stylus, which serves as an intuitive means of navigating through the Pocket PC GUI. The stylus can also serve as an interesting control for games and other interactive applications. Figure 2.1 shows a Compaq iPAQ H3800 Series Pocket PC, whose stylus is accessed from the top of the device.

Figure 2.1
Most Pocket PCs, such as the Compaq iPAQ H3800 Series, conveniently store the stylus in a slot that is accessible from the top of the device.

Microphone   Infrared Port
Stylus
Speaker
Launch Buttons
Navigation Button

Whereas styli are fairly consistent across Pocket PC devices, buttons are where you see significant differences when comparing various models of Pocket PCs. Each manufacturer has its own opinion about what types of buttons are useful and the ergonomics of where they are located. I don't have too strong of an opinion regarding button styles or placement other than to say I really like Pocket PCs that include a navigation button or gamepad. Fortunately, most late-model Pocket PCs have adopted such a button. Although few of us will purchase a Pocket PC solely for games, it's nice to have the option to play games, and a navigation button is practically a necessity for many games. Figure 2.2 shows a Casio Cassiopeia E-200 Pocket PC, which includes an innovative navigation button with an integrated speaker.

Note

Older versions of the Compaq iPAQ Pocket PCs had only a four-direction navigation button, and they didn't recognize more than one button being pressed at a time, which is critical for most games. Both of these problems were solved in the iPAQ H3800 Series, which now boasts an eight-direction navigation button and recognizes multiple button presses. Additionally, the navigation button can be pressed to activate a selection.

PART

I

CH

2

Figure 2.2
Most Pocket PCs, such as the Casio Cassiopeia E-200, include a navigation button for use in playing games and performing other types of multidirectional navigation.

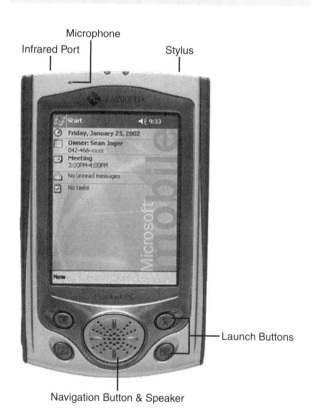

Microphone

Infrared Port

Stylus

Launch Buttons

Navigation Button & Speaker

You might notice in the figure that a few other buttons surround the gamepad on the iPAQ H3800 Series device. These *launch buttons* are used to launch the following applications: Calendar, Contacts, E-Mail, and iTask StarTap (the standard Compaq task launcher). This button configuration varies slightly from device to device, but the idea is generally the same. Figure 2.3 shows an HP Jornada 560 Series Pocket PC, which also includes a navigation button and launch buttons, as well as an action button just below the navigation button.

Infrared Port   Stylus

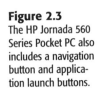

Figure 2.3
The HP Jornada 560
Series Pocket PC also
includes a navigation
button and applica-
tion launch buttons.

Jog Dial

Launch Buttons

Speaker

Microphone

Action Button

Navigation Button

Another button common to all Pocket PCs is the Record button, which is used to record audio via the built-in microphone. Every Pocket PC also has an Action button that is used primarily to scroll the display up and down or to select an item in a list above or below the currently selected item. Pressing the Action button is akin to pressing the Enter key on the keyboard; it activates a selected item. The combination of being able to use this button to both navigate and select items enables you to use a Pocket PC with one hand. It is up to Pocket PC manufacturers how they want to implement the Action button. For example, the iPAQ H3800 Series devices incorporate the Action button into the navigation button (you press the middle of the button to invoke an action), whereas the HP Jornada 560 Series devices include an Action button just below the navigation button (refer to Figure 2.3).

Although it isn't required of all devices, some Pocket PCs include a jog dial that enables you to move up and down within a list of items. If you look closely at Figure 2.3, you'll notice that the HP Jornada 560 Series jog dial appears on the side of the device just to the left of the Record button. The jog dial can be quite handy when combined with the Action button—you use the jog dial to scroll through a list of items and then press the Action button to select an item.

If you own a Pocket PC that doesn't have a jog dial, see "Navigating Without a Jog Dial" in the "Troubleshooting" section at the end of the chapter to find out how to perform jog dial navigations without a jog dial.

YOUR DEVICE IS A GOOD LISTENER

The last hardware facet of Pocket PCs of interest in this chapter is audio hardware, which enables you to both play and record digital audio. Pocket PCs are required to support 16-bit stereo audio, which should be high enough quality to accommodate your portable audio needs. Following are the major audio hardware components of a Pocket PC device:

- Speaker
- Headphone jack
- Microphone

The speaker is an obvious piece of hardware that is a necessity for hearing sounds and music emitted by a Pocket PC. Similarly, the headphone jack provides a convenient way to hear a Pocket PC through headphones without disturbing anyone else. The microphone can be used for verbal note taking, dictation, recording meetings, or maybe even recording your child's first word. The locations of these audio components vary widely according to each specific Pocket PC device. As an example, the Compaq iPAQ H3800 Series devices have the speaker located near the top of the device, whereas the HP Jornada 560 Series devices have the speaker located near the bottom-right corner, as shown in Figure 2.3. Similarly, the microphone of the iPAQ devices is located on top of the device, whereas the Jornada microphone is located on the bottom. I'm sure each manufacturer has its own reasons for the positioning of audio components, but from a usability perspective, you can probably get comfortable with any of the locations.

Note

In the past, some Pocket PCs have been criticized for not having powerful enough audio to listen to digital music, especially when there is background noise such as riding in a car or plane. If you feel you aren't getting enough volume out of your Pocket PC, you might want to check out the Boostaroo audio amplifier. It is a small device that increases the gain of a Pocket PC's headphone jack, thereby giving you more volume. The Boostaroo also includes three headphone jacks, which enable several people to listen in together. For more information, visit the Boostaroo Web site at
http://www.boostaroo.com.

COMPARING POCKET PC DEVICES

Now that you have a pretty good understanding of the hardware that goes into Pocket PCs, it's worth taking a step back and looking at how the current crop of Pocket PC devices differ with respect to major hardware features. One area where devices don't vary much at the moment is in the processor—all Pocket PCs released as of this writing rely on the Intel StrongARM SA-1110 processor, which runs at 206MHz. Additionally, all color Pocket PCs currently use reflective TFT displays with support for 16-bit color (65,536 colors). This is a dramatic improvement over the displays used in some older Pocket PCs and helps to add some uniformity to the quality of displays in all Pocket PCs. Although the processors and displays might be similar across Pocket PCs, their other hardware components do vary to some degree. Table 2.2 provides a breakdown of some of the more popular Pocket PC devices, along with the major hardware features found in each.

TABLE 2.2 COMPARING POCKET PC DEVICE FEATURES

Device	ROM	RAM	Built-In Slots	Add-On Slots	Battery Life (Hours)
Cassiopeia E-200	32MB	64MB	CF II/SD	PC	10
Compaq iPAQ H3800 Series	32MB	64MB	SD	PC/CF	12
HP Jornada 560 Series	32MB	32/64MB	CF I	PC	14
Toshiba e570	32MB	64MB	CF II/SD	—	8
NEC MobilePro P300	32MB	32MB	CF II/SD	—	10
Audiovox Maestro	32MB	32MB	CF II/SD	—	8

As you can see in Table 2.2, all the devices conform to the minimum 32MB ROM standard, and all have at least 32MB RAM. Additionally, all devices except the Compaq iPAQ have a built-in CF slot; the iPAQ is unique in that you can add CF support to it via an expansion sleeve that slides over the device. The battery life for every device is a little different and reflects the unique hardware characteristics of the devices. You might be thinking that the hardware differences between these devices aren't really very dramatic, and in fact this is true. Keep in mind, however, that each device manufacturer has its own approach to style, ergonomics, ruggedness, and built-in software, among other things.

TROUBLESHOOTING

RECHARGING BATTERIES WITHOUT A TRADITIONAL POWER SOURCE

I often find myself away from a traditional power source, but I'd still like to recharge the batteries of my Pocket PC. Is this possible?

Yes, you can recharge your Pocket PC without access to a traditional power source such as a cradle, an A/C power outlet, or a cigarette lighter jack in an automobile. The solution is an innovative product called the iPowerPak by Data-Nation, which uses four standard AA batteries as a means of recharging Pocket PC batteries. To use the iPowerPak, you simply insert four AA batteries, connect your Pocket PC, and wait up to an hour and a half. To find out more about the iPowerPak, visit its Web site at `http://www.data-nation.com/`.

NAVIGATING WITHOUT A JOG DIAL

I own a Pocket PC that doesn't include a jog dial. How do I perform up/down navigations similar to those provided by a jog dial?

The multidirectional navigation button on iPAQ Pocket PCs is used in lieu of a jog dial. To use the navigation button in a similar manner as a jog dial, just press up or down on the navigation button to navigate up or down in the Pocket PC 2002 user interface.

REAL-WORLD EXAMPLE—ASSESSING YOUR DEVICE'S CAPABILITIES

Although this chapter painted a general picture regarding the type of hardware used in Pocket PC devices, it's important to have a clear understanding of the hardware capabilities of your specific device. This is important because it not only impacts the speed and usability of a device, but it also dictates the expansion options you have when adding memory or hardware accessories such as modems or portable keyboards. The documentation for your device should provide details regarding the specific hardware features, including the processor speed, built-in memory, and expansion slots, among other things.

CHAPTER **3**

NAVIGATING THE POCKET PC GUI

In this chapter

THE INITIAL STARTUP PROCEDURE

Because the Pocket PC operating system is based on the success and popularity of Microsoft Windows, it includes a similar look and feel as its desktop counterpart. However, mobile devices with constrained resources have their own special usability needs, which require the Pocket PC operating system to include features unique to mobile devices. This chapter gets you started using your Pocket PC and introduces you to the main components of the Pocket PC graphical user interface (GUI). After setting up your device and connecting it to a desktop computer, you explore some of the main facets of the Pocket PC GUI.

Your Pocket PC is a very sophisticated piece of computer hardware that must be fine-tuned to suit your needs. For this reason, you must set up a few things before you can begin using the device. If you've already gone through the setup process with your device, you can probably speed through this section. I still recommend that you read it just to ensure you properly set up everything on your device.

> **Note**
>
> If you ever let the batteries in your device drain down completely, you'll have to repeat the setup process.

The first step in setting up a Pocket PC is to personalize it by telling it who you are and what time zone you live in. But before you do that, you need to align the screen. This takes place when your Pocket PC first powers up out of the box. If the screen isn't aligned properly, the stylus will misinterpret taps and drags and you'll have a difficult time navigating the Pocket PC user interface. Align the screen by tapping the stylus on a series of crosshairs as they appear on the screen.

SETTING THE SYSTEM CLOCK AND TIME ZONE

After aligning the screen, you are prompted to enter your time zone. This information is important to keep the system clock running properly. Keep in mind that the system clock is used to schedule appointments and meetings, which is why accuracy is a must. Speaking of the system clock, you'll probably have to set it unless your device magically has the correct date and time already set when you get it. Following are the steps required to set the date and time on your device:

1. Go to the Today screen, which is the main screen you see when you turn on your device (if you aren't sure whether you're there, tap Start in the upper-left corner of the screen, and then tap Today).

2. Tap the date just below Start, near the top of the screen, which brings up the Clock Settings page (see Figure 3.1).

3. Use the arrows to set the correct date and time for the Home setting; you can also tap the analog clock and drag the arms around to set the time. The Visiting setting enables you to set another time for when you're traveling and are in another time zone.

4. Tap OK in the upper-right corner, and then tap Yes to save the changes to the clock settings.

Figure 3.1
The Clock Settings page is where you set the date and time for your device.

Tip from
Michael

Make sure the time zone is set properly on your desktop computer; otherwise, you will find that your Pocket PC's clock will get reset each time you synchronize.

ENTERING OWNER INFORMATION

With the date and time set, you are ready to enter owner information, which is very important in case you ever misplace your device. The following steps guide you through entering owner information:

1. Go to the Today screen (you will automatically return to the Today screen after setting the date and time).

2. Tap the Owner band just below the date and time, which brings up the Owner Information page (see Figure 3.2).

Figure 3.2
The Owner Information page enables you to enter information about yourself, which can be important if you ever lose your Pocket PC.

3. Fill in the text fields with your name, company, street address, telephone number, and e-mail address. The Input Panel (soft keyboard) automatically appears when you tap one of the text fields. To enter the @ symbol in your e-mail address, tap the Shift key on the Input Panel followed by the @ key, which appears where the number 2 key was.

4. Check the check box below the text fields if you want the device to display owner information on a Power-On screen when it is first turned on. The idea is that someone would immediately know to whom a lost device belongs when it's first turned on. This option is a necessity if you plan to set a password on the device (covered in Chapter 4, "Personalizing Your Pocket PC").

5. Tap the Notes tab at the bottom of the screen if you want to add any notes about yourself. The check box on the Notes page enables you to designate that the notes are displayed when the device is first turned on.

6. Tap OK in the upper-right corner to accept the owner information.

Caution

If you plan to set a password for your Pocket PC, be sure to check the box on the Owner Information screen that displays owner information when the device is turned on. If you don't, and if the device is lost, the person who finds it won't be able to get past the password screen to find out who owns the device.

NAMING YOUR DEVICE

Now that your Pocket PC knows your name, it's time for you to give it a name of its own. Naming your device is important because this name is used to identify the device when you *synchronize* it with a desktop computer. Altering the name is more difficult after you've set up the ActiveSync synchronization software and connected to your desktop computer, so I encourage you to do it now. The device name also comes into play if you perform a hard reset after having set up the device for synchronization; you'll need to restore the original device name to synchronize and restore the device from a backup. Following are the steps required to enter a name for your device:

1. Tap Start, and then tap Settings.

2. Tap the System tab, and then tap the About icon.

3. Tap the Device ID tab.

4. Enter a name for the device (no spaces), along with a device description. The Pocket PC device name must start with a letter and consist of the letters A–Z and the numbers 0–9. Underscores are also allowed and can be used instead of spaces if you want to separate words.

5. Tap OK in the upper-right corner to accept the device name and description.

Note

> A hard reset involves completely restoring your device to its factory settings, which means all the memory is cleared. Even though this sounds harsh, it can be valuable on occasion, especially if your device is crashing or otherwise acting strangely. The key is to back up your device on a regular basis so you can restore important information if you need to perform a hard reset. Keep in mind that you must perform all these initial setup steps again if you perform a hard reset.

→ **See** Appendix C, "Resetting Your Pocket PC," **p. 497**, to find out how to perform a hard reset on your device.

Your Pocket PC is now set up in terms of knowing who you are and having a name for itself. Now, you need to get connected to your desktop PC so you can install additional software and synchronize with desktop applications.

CONNECTING TO YOUR DESKTOP PC

The Pocket PC operating system comes standard with a wide range of applications and utilities. Because these applications and utilities are stored in ROM, you don't ever have to worry about reinstalling them. Even with this rich set of functionality built into your Pocket PC, you will undoubtedly want to expand its horizons by installing new software. Perhaps even more important is the capability to share and synchronize data with your desktop PC. To accomplish any of this, you must establish a connection between your Pocket PC and desktop PC.

MAKING A PHYSICAL CONNECTION

The physical connection between a Pocket PC and desktop PC is pretty straightforward and involves one of the following types of connections:

- Universal Serial Bus (USB)
- Serial
- Infrared
- Ethernet

Note

> Because most desktop PCs don't have an infrared port, an infrared connection with a Pocket PC is usually established with an infrared USB adapter. An infrared USB adapter plugs into the USB port of the desktop computer and provides an infrared port. Practically all notebook PCs include an infrared port these days, so you can probably forego the infrared USB adapter if you have a notebook PC. To communicate with a desktop or notebook PC via infrared, just align the Pocket PC's infrared port with the port on the desktop or notebook PC, and you're good to go.

USB is the preferred connection type for most users because it's the fastest among non-Ethernet connections. However, if you are still using Windows NT on your desktop computer, USB is not an option because NT doesn't support USB ports—you must use a serial port. If you have the capability of connecting to your desktop computer via an Ethernet connection, you might want to consider purchasing an Ethernet CF card for your Pocket PC. Ethernet connections are extremely fast (up to 10MBps) and result in very quick synchronization. Short of Ethernet, a USB connection is your best bet for reasonably speedy synchronization. Besides, most Pocket PCs come with a cradle designed to accommodate a USB or serial connection and to also serve as a battery charger.

INSTALLING MICROSOFT ACTIVESYNC

Your device's cradle is handy because it provides a convenient way to establish a physical connection between the device and a desktop PC. The first step in connecting your Pocket PC to a desktop PC is to install Microsoft's ActiveSync software on your desktop computer.

ActiveSync ships on a CD-ROM with all Pocket PCs and is responsible for detecting a Pocket PC connection and allowing you to synchronize and share data between a Pocket PC device and desktop computer. Synchronization is quite powerful and is handled at the application level. In other words, you set the applications whose data you want to have synchronized, and ActiveSync handles the rest. ActiveSync also provides a means of accessing the Pocket PC file system from your desktop PC, which can be very useful. The good news is that ActiveSync is a very straightforward application to use.

Caution

In case you're itching to hook up the cradle, let me warn you that the ActiveSync installation is specifically designed to work smoothly if you install the software first and then connect the hardware. So, be sure to install ActiveSync first; you'll get an opportunity to connect the cradle during the ActiveSync installation in just a moment.

Note

You might be wondering whether the ActiveSync software is available for Macintosh computers. Unfortunately, as of this writing it is not. However, you can use the Windows version of ActiveSync on a Macintosh with the help of a Windows emulation software package called Virtual PC. Virtual PC emulates a Windows environment within the Macintosh operating system and enables you to install ActiveSync and use it as if it were actually running on a Windows system.

To begin installing the ActiveSync software, insert the ActiveSync CD-ROM into the CD-ROM drive of the desktop PC with which you are synchronizing your Pocket PC. After a few moments, you will see the window shown in Figure 3.3, which is the beginning of the ActiveSync Installation Wizard.

Tip from
Michael

If, for some reason, you have the CD-ROM Autorun feature of Windows disabled, you'll need to manually run the ActiveSync setup program by selecting Run from the Start menu and then selecting Setup.exe from the CD-ROM.

Figure 3.3
The beginning of the ActiveSync Installation Wizard is the first window you see when installing the ActiveSync software.

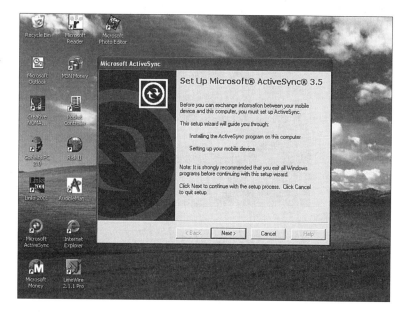

Clicking the Next button starts the installation process. The next window displayed enables you to select the installation folder for ActiveSync. I recommend keeping the default setting, but clicking the Change button allows you to put ActiveSync anywhere you want.

Clicking Next moves you along to a screen that confirms you have physically connected your Pocket PC to the desktop PC. Of course, this involves connecting the cradle to the desktop PC (via USB or serial) and plugging the cradle into a power source. After the cradle is properly connected, set your Pocket PC in the cradle, power it up, and click Next in the ActiveSync Installation Wizard. Upon clicking Next, the Installation Wizard searches for a connected Pocket PC device on the available USB and serial ports. If the device isn't found, double-check that the cradle is properly connected to the desktop PC, the Pocket PC is firmly seated in the cradle, and the Pocket PC has a charge on its batteries.

When the device is found, the window in Figure 3.4 is displayed, which asks whether you want to set up a *partnership*. To synchronize application data, such as the e-mail in your Inbox or tasks in the Tasks application, you must create a partnership between the two machines. Although a partnership is not required to establish a connection and share files between the Pocket PC and desktop PC, without a partnership you are limited to copying or moving files back and forth between the machines and installing applications. In other words, you won't be able to synchronize data with applications.

Figure 3.4
The next window of the ActiveSync Installation Wizard enables you to set up a partnership, which is necessary for synchronizing application data.

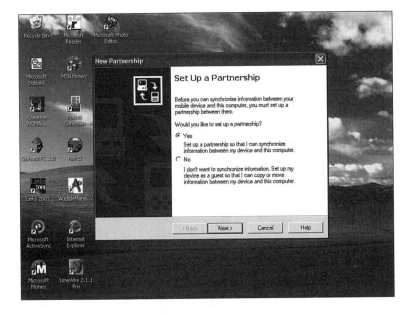

If you own two Pocket PCs and are having trouble synchronizing them both with one desktop PC, see "Identifying Multiple Pocket PCs" in the "Troubleshooting" section at the end of the chapter to find out how to solve the problem.

Assuming you selected the Yes radio button to set up a partnership, the Select Synchronization Settings window is displayed next (see Figure 3.5). This window enables you to select the specific applications with which you want to synchronize. Resist the temptation to select all of them because you will likely be interested in synchronizing only certain types of information. As an example, I typically synchronize only the Calendar, Contacts, Inbox, and Tasks applications. This is ultimately a personal decision, however, and it has everything to do with how you intend to use your device and what Pocket PC applications you plan to use on a regular basis. Following are the applications whose data can be synchronized:

- AvantGo
- Calendar
- Contacts
- Favorite
- Files
- Inbox
- Notes
- Pocket Access
- Tasks

Note

AvantGo is a Web-based information service that specializes in offering Web content in a form that is easily viewed on handheld devices such as Pocket PCs. AvantGo content is designed for offline browsing and is therefore synchronized with your Pocket PC through ActiveSync.

Figure 3.5
The Select Synchronization Settings window enables you to select applications with which you want to synchronize.

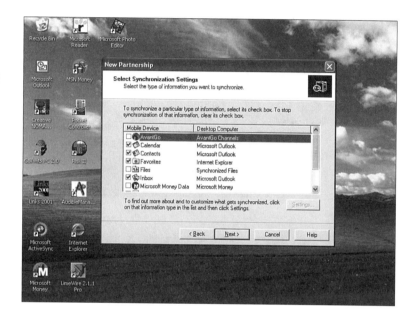

You can fine-tune the settings of the synchronized applications by selecting an application in the list and then clicking the Settings button. Figure 3.6 shows the settings available for the Inbox application.

If you compare the options selected in this figure to the default settings of your Pocket PC, you can see that I made a few changes to the default settings. The Include File Attachments option enables you to receive attachments along with e-mail messages. Although this is a very useful feature, you need to be careful about limiting the size of the attachments so that you don't receive enormous files along with e-mail. You'll notice that the standard Outlook e-mail folders are listed in the Mail Synchronization Settings window. If you have created subfolders beneath the Inbox folder, you can open the Inbox folder and check specific sub-folders to be synchronized; by default, only the Inbox folder itself is synchronized. E-mail synchronization is useful because it enables you to create e-mail messages at any time and then send them when you synchronize with your desktop PC.

Figure 3.6
The Mail Synchronization Settings window allows you to customize the manner in which e-mail messages are synchronized via the Inbox application.

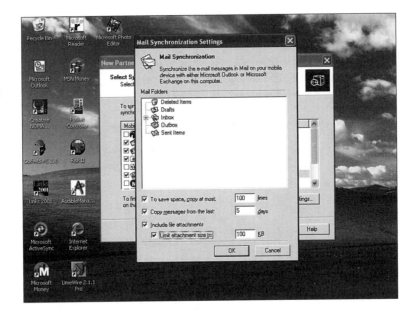

Tip from
Michael

I've found that turning on the Include File Attachments option and limiting the attachment size to 100KB is useful. That way, when a friend sends you a whopping 2MB MPEG wedding video, you won't be wasting precious RAM or synchronization time.

Click OK to accept the Mail Synchronization settings, and then click Next to accept the Synchronization settings. You will then see the screen shown in Figure 3.7, which is the end of the ActiveSync Installation Wizard.

At this point, you can click the Finish button to finish the installation and begin using ActiveSync. ActiveSync automatically begins synchronizing the applications you selected during installation, which might take a few minutes depending on how much information you have stored in each application (see Figure 3.8). The really neat thing about ActiveSync is that it's automatic in its approach to synchronization. To test it, try modifying a piece of synchronized information on the desktop PC, such as an e-mail message, and watch for Active Sync to spring into action and synchronize it on the Pocket PC. The same thing applies to modifying synchronized data on the Pocket PC—it automatically updates on the desktop PC.

You can tell that synchronization is complete because the circular green icon in the upper-right corner of the ActiveSync window stops its animation; the small, green ActiveSync icon in the system tray also stops its animation. More importantly, the status of each of the types of synchronized information turns to Synchronized in the ActiveSync window.

Figure 3.7
The final step of the ActiveSync Installation Wizard clarifies the completion of the ActiveSync installation.

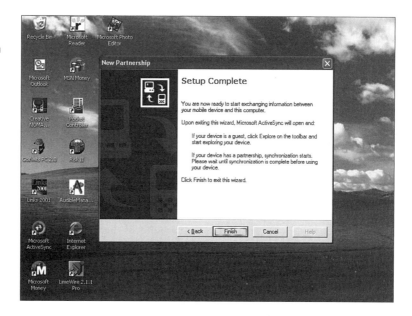

Figure 3.8
Synchronization can take a few minutes if you have a lot of information to be synchronized.

TAKING A LOOK AROUND THE POCKET PC GUI

If you're new to the Pocket PC platform, you're in for a pleasant surprise when it comes to the Pocket PC GUI. Pocket PC 2002 represents the fourth major revision of the GUI, and Microsoft has done a good job of answering the requests of users over the past few years as the technology has evolved. A few things might take some getting used to, especially if you're coming purely from a desktop environment such as Windows XP, but rest assured that the Pocket PC GUI is organized the way it is for a reason. Screen real estate is extremely limited on mobile devices, which dictates a very tight GUI where everything has a practical reason for its location. Additionally, the uniqueness of entering most information via a stylus results in subtle differences between the Pocket PC GUI and a desktop GUI. All things considered, however, you should be able to adjust to the differences very quickly.

The Pocket PC GUI can be broken down into four major components:

- Navigation bar
- Today screen
- Command bar
- Text input

Figure 3.9 shows how the first three components of the Pocket PC GUI fit into the overall scheme of things; the fourth is accessible only within the context of an application. The next few sections explore these pieces of the Pocket PC GUI puzzle, along with another little GUI feature you'll find interesting.

Figure 3.9
The major components of the Pocket PC GUI are the Navigation bar, Today screen, and Command bar.

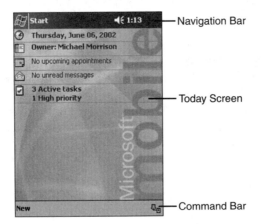

THE NAVIGATION BAR

The Navigation bar is located at the top of the screen (refer to Figure 3.9) and is visible in most applications. In addition to displaying the speaker volume and current time on the right side of the screen, the Navigation bar is responsible for housing the Start menu on the left side. The Start menu is a convenient place to launch applications, much like you would find in Windows XP. When you run an application, the word "Start" in the Start menu changes to reflect the name of the application. However, you can still access the Start menu by clicking the Start menu icon (the little colored window) to the left of the application name. Figure 3.10 shows the opened Start menu.

Figure 3.10
The Start menu provides a convenient starting point for launching Pocket PC applications.

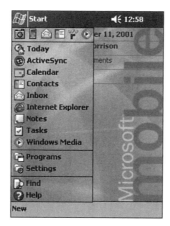

The contents of the Start menu consist of applications that you can launch. One neat feature of the Start menu is the line of icons at the top of the menu just above the Today menu item. These icons indicate the last six applications that were run and provide a quick way to launch any of the applications again. This icon list changes to reflect the last six applications you've used, which is one example of how the Pocket PC GUI accommodates usability needs.

THE TODAY SCREEN

The Today screen is located just below the Navigation bar (refer to Figure 3.9) and serves as the default screen that is displayed when you aren't working in an application. The Today screen displays the current day and date; the owner of the Pocket PC; and any upcoming appointments, messages, and tasks for the day. In conjunction with the Navigation and Command bars, the Today screen serves as a great starting point for performing most Pocket PC operations. You can customize the Today screen considerably by using themes and altering the graphics that appear within it.

→ To find out how to customize the Today screen, **see** Chapter 4, "Personalizing Your Pocket PC," **p. 61**.

THE COMMAND BAR

Below the Today screen you'll find the Command bar (refer to Figure 3.9), which is used to display system information, perform application-specific operations, and enter text information via the Input Panel button. On the left side of the Command bar is a menu that changes with respect to the currently active application. For example, on the Today screen the menu consists solely of a New submenu, which displays a list of menu items that enable you to create a new appointment, contact, e-mail message, Excel workbook, note, task, or Word document. On the right side of the Command bar there can appear various icons that display system information; these icons function as a minimal system tray to give you clues regarding the status of the device. For example, if you establish a network connection, a small icon will appear to indicate that the connection is active.

The Command bar icons are displayed only when the Today screen is active; if an application is executing, the Input Panel button is displayed instead. Figure 3.11 shows the Pocket Word application, which uses a more interesting menu in the Command bar, and the Input Panel button. The Input Panel provides several alternatives to entering text, which you learn about next.

Figure 3.11
Pocket Word is an example of an application that takes advantage of the Command bar for its menu and uses the Input Panel button.

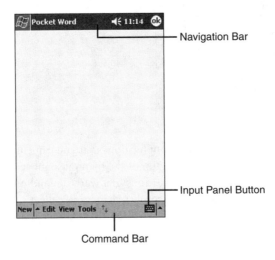

Navigation Bar

Input Panel Button

Command Bar

TEXT INPUT

The Input Panel button is located on the right side of the Command bar in applications that support text entry. This button enables you to select the method of input used to enter text and provides access to four types of text input:

- **Soft keyboard**—The soft keyboard is a scaled-down keyboard that is displayed on the screen. You can type on the soft keyboard by tapping its keys with the stylus, which is similar to how you might peck at keys on a real keyboard if you have no typing background.

- **Letter Recognizer**—The Letter Recognizer is a handwriting interface that enables you to write individual characters and have them recognized and converted into text. Although the handwriting recognition is quite effective, it can be time-consuming writing individual characters one at a time.

- **Transcriber**—The Transcriber provides a more powerful means of entering handwritten text by allowing you to write anywhere on the screen. This gives you plenty of room to write a few words or an entire sentence. Transcriber uses natural handwriting recognition, which means you can write on your Pocket PC screen as if you were writing on a piece of paper and Transcriber will convert it into text. To carry out this ambitious task, Transcriber relies on fuzzy logic and neural network algorithms, which is a techie way of saying that Transcriber uses some very sophisticated artificial intelligence to interpret handwriting.

■ **Block Recognizer**—If you've migrated to the Pocket PC from a Palm device, you might be interested in the Block Recognizer input method, which is new to Pocket PC 2002 and offers a text-entry solution to people who have grown accustomed to using the Graffiti input system on Palm devices. The idea behind the Block Recognizer is to provide a smooth path for Palm users to migrate to the Pocket PC platform without having to relearn their approaches to text entry.

You will likely select a single input method and stick with it as you get comfortable entering information into your Pocket PC. Keep in mind, though, that you also can purchase a portable keyboard for your device in the event that you want to do some heavy-duty text entry.

➔ For more information about portable keyboards, **see** Appendix A, "A Pocket PC Hardware Accessory Tour," **p. 479**.

➔ To learn more about the four text input methods, **see** Chapter 5, "Making the Most of Input Methods," **p. 83**.

BUBBLE NOTIFICATIONS

Although it might not qualify as a major component of the Pocket PC GUI, the bubble notification is a feature new to Pocket PC 2002 that nonetheless proves to be quite useful. Whenever a relatively small piece of information needs to be presented to you, a small pop-up window known as a bubble notification appears. It is similar to a comic strip bubble. Bubble notifications are used throughout the Pocket PC GUI in various scenarios. One of the quickest ways to get acquainted with bubble notifications is by tapping the time on the Navigation bar, which results in a bubble notification appearing that resembles the one shown in Figure 3.12.

Figure 3.12
Bubble notifications are used to present relatively small pieces of information to the user without being too disruptive.

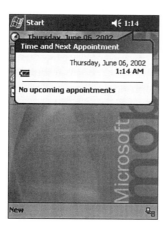

Unlike dialog boxes in the desktop Windows GUI, bubble notifications are designed so that they don't disrupt what you're doing to any significant extent. For example, many bubble notifications automatically disappear after a few seconds if they don't require any information from you; you can also tap outside a bubble notification to make it go away. The idea is to quickly notify you of something, such as an appointment, and then get out of the way. Bubble notifications are a very efficient and highly intuitive improvement to the Pocket PC GUI that you'll no doubt come to appreciate.

MEMORY MANAGEMENT AND CLOSING APPLICATIONS

If you have any experience with the first release of the Pocket PC operating system, you no doubt recall the confusion surrounding the closing of applications. Unlike desktop operating systems, in which you must manually shut down applications to unload them from memory, the Pocket PC operating system enabled you to leave applications running. The idea was that the operating system itself is vigilant enough at managing memory that it will automatically unload lesser-used applications as it sees fit. In fact, there was no X (Close button) in the upper-right corner of applications in the original Pocket PC operating system, which meant there was no intuitive way to shut down applications manually. Although this concept seemed like a good idea, it gave users fits because they felt powerless to close applications. Additionally, the memory management wasn't as good as Microsoft had hoped, and the operating system ended up not doing such a great job of keeping things running smoothly.

Pocket PC 2002 solved the closing application problem in two ways: with a revamped memory manager and a Close button. The new memory manager in Pocket PC 2002 does a much better job of targeting "stale" applications and removing them from memory, which is the most important fix to the problem of applications hogging memory. The new Close button isn't quite as significant of a fix because it doesn't really function as a Close button. The X in the upper-right corner of applications is there in Pocket PC 2002, and even though I'm referring to it as a Close button, it actually functions as a Minimize button. When you click the X to close an application, you're really minimizing the application and sending it to the bottom of the application pile. The application is still in memory, but you've relegated it to being the first to go if the memory manager decides to clean house.

The functionality of the Close button is definitely misleading because an X button in any desktop version of Windows has always meant "close," not "minimize." On the other hand, Pocket PCs don't really have a notion of minimized applications, at least in terms of seeing their icons along the bottom of the screen. So, the distinction between an application being closed or minimized really comes down to an issue of memory and performance. For efficiency reasons, Microsoft opted to minimize applications in response to users clicking the X, as opposed to actually closing them. If you return to a recently "closed" application, it will still be in memory, and therefore you won't experience a delay for it to reload. Of course, this relies on the Pocket PC memory manager to do a good job of unloading applications whenever necessary, which fortunately it does.

 If your device is acting a little strange and you feel it could benefit from a clean start, see "Restarting Your Device" in the "Troubleshooting" section at the end of the chapter to learn how to restart your device.

The good news about this entire discussion is that the whole close/minimize application issue is pretty much transparent to you as a user. As far as you're concerned, when you click the Close button, the application disappears from the screen and therefore appears to be closed. If you're the obsessive type who simply must have complete control over a situation, you can always look to the Memory section of the system Settings screen to see exactly which applications are loaded in memory. The following steps show you how to find out which applications are currently running:

1. Tap Start, and then tap Settings.

2. Tap the System tab, and then tap the Memory icon.

3. Tap the Running Programs tab to view the Running Program List.

Figure 3.13 shows the Running Program List, which in this case consists of five applications.

Figure 3.13
The Running Program List displays the applications that are currently loaded and running in memory.

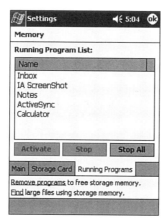

The buttons just below the Running Program List enable you to activate an application, stop (close) an application, or stop all applications. This is a good way to manually exercise some control over the memory management of applications, although you might not need to use it very often.

Tip from
Michael

If you want to close an application without having to rely on the Running Program list, tap the Ctl key (Control) on the soft keyboard, followed by the q key. This is the equivalent of issuing a Ctrl+Q command on a normal keyboard, which closes an application.

Caution

On the main Settings screen is a Remove Programs icon. Although your first impression might be that this removes a program from memory, it actually removes (uninstalls) the selected application from your device. Use this option only if you want to completely remove an application from your device, not just close it.

TROUBLESHOOTING

IDENTIFYING MULTIPLE POCKET PCS

I have two Pocket PCs and want to synchronize them both with the same computer, but my desktop PC is recognizing only one device.

When using more than one Pocket PC, it is very important to give each device a unique name so that the desktop PC can distinguish between the devices. You then can create a partnership for each device in ActiveSync. To set or change the name of a device, follow these steps:

1. Tap Start, and then tap Settings.
2. Tap the System tab, and then tap the About icon.
3. Tap the Device ID tab.
4. Enter a name for the device (no spaces), along with a device description. The Pocket PC device name must start with a letter and consist of the letters A–Z and the numbers 0–9. Underscores are also allowed and can be used instead of spaces if you want to separate words.
5. Tap OK in the upper-right corner to accept the device name and description.

RESTARTING YOUR DEVICE

My device is acting a little strange, and I want to perform a restart like I do with my desktop PC. Is this possible?

Yes, a restart on a Pocket PC is referred to as a *soft reset* and is easily accomplished. All Pocket PCs have a small recessed reset button that is usually accessible only using the stylus. To perform a soft reset, grab your stylus and follow these steps:

1. Turn on the power.
2. Press the reset button with the stylus and hold it for a couple of seconds.

Similar to performing a restart on a desktop PC, a soft reset on your Pocket PC results in data loss if you haven't saved opened documents and closed running applications. So, be sure to save or close anything you're working on before performing a soft reset.

REAL-WORLD EXAMPLE—SYNCHRONIZING WITH TWO PCS

If you use more than one PC regularly, such as a desktop PC and a notebook PC, you might benefit from synchronizing your Pocket PC with both machines. To do this, you must set up a partnership with your Pocket PC on both computers and be sure to synchronize the exact same types of data in both partnerships. For example, if you want only e-mail and contacts synchronized, select only Inbox and Contacts in the ActiveSync options for each partnership. Also, when you first set up the partnership with the second computer, you are given an option to declare that you're synchronizing the device with two computers—be sure you select this option.

CHAPTER 4

PERSONALIZING YOUR POCKET PC

In this chapter

PASSWORD-PROTECTING YOUR POCKET PC

The whole idea behind Pocket PCs is that you can stick them in your pocket and carry them wherever you go. This use makes Pocket PCs somewhat similar to a wallet or purse in terms of how personal they can become. Knowing this, it makes sense to be able to personalize Pocket PCs to suit your individual needs and tastes. Just as you might place a photo of your spouse or significant other in your wallet, you might also want to use a similar photo as "wallpaper" on your Pocket PC display. On the more serious side of things, it can be a good idea to protect the contents of your Pocket PC from others by password-protecting the device. This chapter explores the various ways you can personalize your Pocket PC, from themes that enable you to tweak the "window dressing" of your device to password protection and extending the battery life.

Note

As you well know, *PC* is a popular acronym for personal computer. Even though PC applies to a variety of types of computers, such as desktop PCs, notebook PCs, and Pocket PCs, it's safe to say that Pocket PCs are the most personal of all these computers. Pocket PCs can be carried in your pocket and often contain personal information. Because Pocket PCs are very personal devices, it's important to protect them in case someone else gets their hands on your device.

The Pocket PC operating system enables you to set a system password that is required each time the device is turned on. If the password is entered incorrectly, the device won't let you get past the password-entry screen. Setting a password is a personal preference and has a lot to do with how you plan to use your Pocket PC. If you store sensitive information such as credit card numbers or business information that could be detrimental in the wrong hands, a password is a necessity. You also might want to set a password if you plan to use Money for Pocket PC because your personal financial information is something I'm sure you'd like to protect.

→ To learn how to use Money for Pocket PC to manage your finances on the go, **see** Chapter 17, "Managing Money with Your Pocket PC," **p. 319**.

Note

If you want to take things a step further, third-party applications are available that enable you to encrypt sensitive information such as credit card numbers, passwords, and business information. You learn about some of these applications in Chapter 20, "Beefing Up Your Pocket PC's Security."

Tip from
Michael

If you decide to password-protect your Pocket PC, be sure to set the device so it displays owner information when turned on. That way, if your device is lost, the person who finds it can track you down.

The Pocket PC 2002 operating system offers two approaches to password protection, which differ by how much security protection they provide:

- Four-digit numeric password (PIN code)
- Strong alphanumeric password

A four-digit *numeric password* is similar to a PIN code that you use at an ATM (Automated teller machine) to withdraw cash from your bank using a debit card. Four-digit numeric passwords are easy to remember and can be entered quickly. However, four-digit numeric passwords can be hacked easier than strong alphanumeric passwords. Fortunately, the Pocket PC operating system includes a nifty little feature that makes hacking passwords more difficult—more on that in a moment.

Strong *alphanumeric passwords* consist of letters (both uppercase and lowercase) and numbers and can be virtually as long as you want them to be. This makes them much more secure than four-digit numeric passwords at the expense of taking a little more effort to enter. The idea behind offering both types of passwords is to meet the needs of users—those who simply want to protect their data against others poking around and those who need robust security features for protecting highly sensitive data. If you simply want to keep co-workers from taking a peek at your net worth on Pocket Money, a four-digit numeric password will probably suit your needs. On the other hand, if you're toting around sensitive information that could seriously damage you or your employer if placed in the wrong hands, then a more secure strong alphanumeric password is probably what you need.

→ To find out about additional security options for your Pocket PC, **see** Chapter 20, "Beefing Up Your Pocket PC's Security," **p. 375**.

If you're on the fence regarding the security level of Pocket PC passwords, you might consider using the four-digit numeric password because it is still tough to hack. Microsoft added a slick new feature to Pocket PC 2002 where the duration of time between entering incorrect passwords increases with each attempt. For example, if someone steals your device, he might attempt to hack your password using a brute-force approach in which he repeatedly goes through all the possible four-digit combinations. This approach would work quite well if it wasn't for the fact that the delay between being able to try another password grows with each incorrect attempt. As an example, by the time 20 incorrect password attempts are made, the delay grows to around 10 seconds, and it continues to climb higher from there. Because more than a million combinations of four-digit password possibilities exist, a brute-force hack is virtually impossible on a Pocket PC.

To set a four-digit numeric password and password-protect your device, follow these steps:

1. Tap Start, and then tap Settings.
2. Tap the Password icon.
3. Select the Simple 4 Digit Password option.
4. Enter a four-digit password by tapping the numeric keys on the screen (see Figure 4.1).
5. Tap OK in the upper-right corner, and then tap Yes to save the password settings.

PART

I

CH

4

Figure 4.1
Setting a four-digit numeric password provides an adequate level of security for most users.

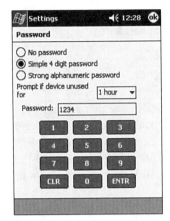

Caution

Be sure to select a password you won't forget. If you forget your password, the only way to get back into your Pocket PC is to perform a hard reset, which blitzes the device memory. If you're like me and still run the risk of forgetting the password, just be sure to back up your device regularly. Then, if you ever have to perform a hard reset, you can still restore everything.

→ For more information on how to perform a hard reset for your particular device, **see** Appendix C, "Resetting Your Pocket PC," **p. 497**, or check the manuals that came with your device.

The steps for setting a strong alphanumeric password are similar to the steps for setting a four-digit numeric password. Even so, let's go over them just to make sure you've got it:

1. Tap Start, and then tap Settings.

2. Tap the Password icon.

3. Select the Strong Alphanumeric Password option.

4. Enter a password at least seven characters long using the soft keyboard, and then enter it again in the Confirm box (see Figure 4.2).

5. Tap OK in the upper-right corner, and then tap Yes to save the password settings.

In addition to setting a password, you might have noticed that the Password Settings page has an option for determining how long your device goes unused before prompting for a password. The idea behind this option is to protect your device in the event that you leave it unattended for a while without explicitly turning it off. You can set the amount of time that must pass before the password prompt is displayed. Keep in mind that this time starts ticking only when the device is unused; if you're using your device, you won't be hassled with a password prompt. The default setting for this option is 1 hour, and it's ultimately a personal preference as to how fast you want password protection to kick in when your Pocket PC is left unattended.

Figure 4.2
If you need the
utmost in security for
your device, you
should set a strong
alphanumeric pass-
word.

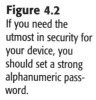

DRESSING UP YOUR DEVICE WITH THEMES

Even though password protection is certainly important, there is a fun side to personalizing your Pocket PC. I'm referring to *themes*, which are used to alter the appearance of the Today screen, Start menu, and colors used throughout the Pocket PC GUI. More specifi-cally, a Pocket PC theme includes an image that is displayed in the background of the Today screen, an image that is displayed in the background of the Start menu, and a set of color schemes that are applied to the following portions of the Pocket PC GUI:

- Today text
- Navigation bar
- Command bar
- Navigation tray
- Message notification
- Important message notification

Themes provide a great way to personalize the appearance of your Pocket PC to reflect per-sonal tastes. You can dress up your device with a family portrait, your favorite sports team, a company logo, or maybe just an interesting photograph that catches your eye. Although you don't have to modify the default colors used in the Pocket PC GUI, it's generally a neat effect to match the color scheme to the images used on the Today screen and Start menu, if possible. Of course, this all assumes you're going to be creating your own themes, which you learn how to do a little later in the chapter. But what if you aren't that ambitious? Fortunately, there are quite a few themes out there just waiting for you to download and use. Following are a few Web sites you can visit to download free themes:

- **Microsoft's Pocket PC Themes**—http://www.microsoft.com/mobile/pocketpc/downloads/themes.asp
- **Pocket PC Themes**—http://www.pocketpcthemes.com/
- **Pocket Themes**—http://www.pocketthemes.com/

PART

I

CH

4

I'm sure you'll find plenty of interesting themes on these Web sites, but one extra theme is already included on your Pocket PC that you can try in the meantime. This theme is called Fire, and its filename is `Fire.tsk`; all Pocket PC themes have the file extension .tsk, which stands for theme skin. The next section steps you through setting the built-in Fire theme on your device.

Note

In case you were wondering, Windows XP desktop themes are in a different format than Pocket PC themes are, and therefore they can't be directly used with Pocket PCs. I say "directly" because you can create your own Pocket PC theme by "borrowing" images and colors from a Windows XP theme. You learn how to create your own Pocket PC themes a little later in the chapter.

It's worth pointing out that themes take up valuable storage space on your device and therefore shouldn't be overused. If you can't settle on a single theme, consider having two themes installed on your device at any given time; beyond that, you're probably wasting space that could be used for more important information. You can always store themes on your desktop PC and then change them out on your Pocket PC as necessary.

SETTING THEMES

To set a new theme for your device, you first must copy the theme to a location on the device where it is accessible. Following are the two acceptable locations for storing Pocket PC themes:

- The Windows folder in system RAM
- The My Documents folder in system RAM or in a memory storage card

You can use the Explore button in ActiveSync on your desktop PC to navigate to one of these directories on your Pocket PC, and then copy the theme file over from your desktop PC. Or, for the purposes of learning how to set a theme, just use the built-in Fire theme. To set a theme on your device, follow these steps:

1. Tap Start, and then tap Settings.
2. Tap the Today icon.
3. Select the desired theme from the list of themes (see Figure 4.3).
4. Tap OK in the upper-right corner to set the theme.

→ For more information about exploring your Pocket PC from a desktop PC, **see** Chapter 8, "Using ActiveSync to Synchronize Data," **p. 145**.

Although the new theme is now set, you probably won't notice much of a change until you return to the Today screen. Upon returning to the Today screen, notice its new appearance, as well as the new appearance of the Start menu (see Figure 4.4).

Figure 4.3
All the themes installed on your device are available for selection on the Today Settings page.

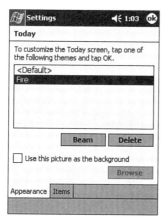

Figure 4.4
Setting the theme for your Pocket PC alters the appearance of the Today screen, Start menu, and system colors.

PART

I

CH

4

Most themes impact the Today screen dramatically, and often the Start menu as well. The Navigation bar is also altered by most themes, but this can be harder to see at first if the color changes are subtle.

CREATING YOUR OWN THEMES

Although many interesting themes are available and ready for you to download, there is nothing like the satisfaction of creating your own personal theme. The good news is that cooking up your very own Pocket PC theme is surprisingly easy thanks to an application called Theme Generator. Theme Generator is a freely available desktop PC application from Microsoft that you can download from the following Web site: http://www.microsoft.com/mobile/pocketpc/downloads/themegenerator.asp. Theme Generator is extremely easy to use, as you'll find out in a moment. Before getting into that, however, it's important to understand a few things about the makeup of themes.

Pocket PC themes are comprised of three components:

- A Today screen background image
- A Start menu background image
- A color scheme

To create a theme, you must create the Today and Start images and then select colors that are applied to specific parts of the Pocket PC GUI. It's important to create the Today and Start images so that they are the appropriate size. Following are the sizes for each of these images, in pixels:

- Today screen image: 240×268
- Start menu image: 158×290

Note

The Theme Generator application enables you to use a single image for both the Today screen and Start menu and then crop or stretch it appropriately for each, but you'll probably want to provide two different images.

It's up to you how you want to create these images. If, for some reason, you have trouble sizing them perfectly, don't worry because Theme Generator gives you the option to crop or stretch the images to perfectly fit the Today screen and Start menu. You usually get much better results by cropping larger images to fit the Pocket PC screen, as opposed to stretching smaller images. Figure 4.5 shows the Theme Generator application upon first being executed.

If you're having trouble running Theme Generator on your desktop or notebook PC, see "Problems Running Theme Generator" in the "Troubleshooting" section at the end of the chapter.

Figure 4.5
The Theme Generator application begins by showing you a virtual Pocket PC screen as it appears with the default system theme.

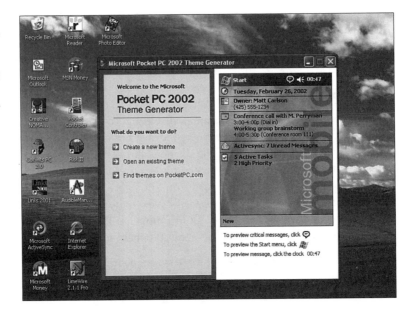

DISSECTING EXISTING THEMES

Before you get started creating a theme, a good way to get a feel for Theme Generator is to take a look at an existing theme. Figure 4.6 shows the America theme, which is available for download from Microsoft's Pocket PC Themes Web page at `http://www.microsoft.com/mobile/pocketpc/downloads/themes.asp`. The neat thing about Theme Generator is that it enables you to click the virtual Pocket PC screen to see how the theme is applied to different parts of the GUI. For example, clicking the Start button results in the Start menu being displayed, just as if you had clicked the button on your device.

Figure 4.6
The America theme is a good example of a theme that is worth dissecting in Theme Generator.

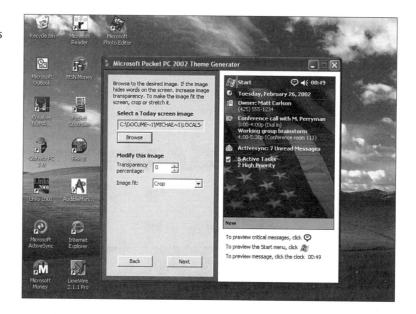

You can click the Next button to step through the various facets of the America theme and see how it is put together, or you can click the Back button and get started creating your own theme from scratch. Figure 4.7 shows the first step in the creation of a theme, which involves setting the image for the background of the Today screen.

Click the Browse button to browse and find the image on your computer, and then set the transparency and fit of the image if necessary. In this example I'm creating a theme for my board game, Inc. The Game of Business, which has bull and bear characters. Because the bull illustration used for the background is bold and vivid, I need to make it somewhat transparent so that there is contrast between it and the text that appears on the Today screen. I decided to use a value of 50 for the image transparency, which means the image is 50% transparent. Also, I sized the image exactly to fit the Today screen (240×268), which means that I don't have to crop or stretch it to fit; leaving the default fit setting of Crop is sufficient because no cropping will actually be performed. Click the Next button to move to the next step in Theme Generator (see Figure 4.8).

PART

I

CH

4

Today Image

Figure 4.7
The first step in creating a theme involves setting the image for the Today screen background.

Transparency Percentage

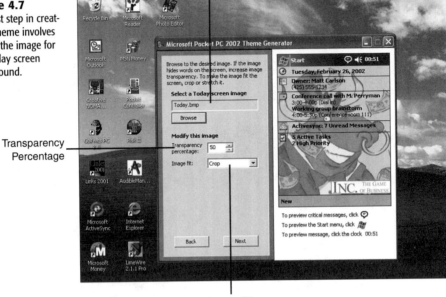

Image Fit

Start Menu Image

Figure 4.8
The second step in creating a theme involves setting the image for the Start menu background.

Transparency Percentage

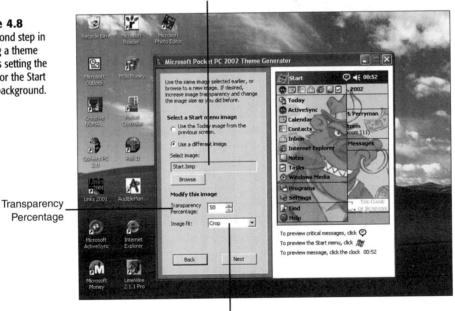

Image Fit

SELECTING THE BACKGROUND IMAGE

Selecting the background image for the Start menu is similar to setting the Today image. Keep in mind that the Start image is smaller, so you might have to crop or stretch it if you didn't size it exactly to fit the Start menu (158×290). Instead of providing an image of your own, you have the option of reusing the Today image and cropping it down to fit the Start menu. After selecting an image and determining how to fit it properly, you'll need to set the transparency. In this example I'm using another vivid illustration, so I set the transparency to 50 again. Be sure to click the Start menu on the virtual Pocket PC screen to take a look at what the Start image will look like in context. Click the Next button to move on to selecting the colors of the theme (see Figure 4.9).

Figure 4.9
The final component of the Pocket PC theme is the color scheme, which applies colors to various parts of the Pocket PC GUI.

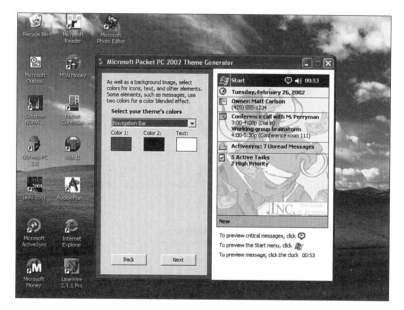

PART

I

CH

4

The colors for a theme apply to specific parts of the Pocket PC GUI, such as the Navigation bar and Command bar. You must select each GUI component in the drop-down menu of Theme Generator and then alter its colors. It's important to take note of the virtual Pocket PC screen as you make each color change because it will reflect the changes. After you finish setting all the colors, click the Next button to complete the theme by giving it a name (see Figure 4.10).

The theme name is actually the filename of the theme, so you must name it according to the same rules of naming files under Windows; the resulting theme file will have the name *ThemeName*.tsk. This theme name is also the name you'll see in the Today Settings page when you set the theme on your device, so it should be somewhat descriptive. If your device is connected to your desktop PC, you can click the Send Theme to Device When Finished check box to have the theme automatically transferred to your device upon creation. Otherwise, you must manually copy it over after creating it. Click the Finish button to complete the theme and generate the .tsk theme file.

Theme Name

Figure 4.10
The theme name is the name of the theme as it will appear in the Pocket PC Today Settings page, as well as the theme's filename (ThemeName.tsk).

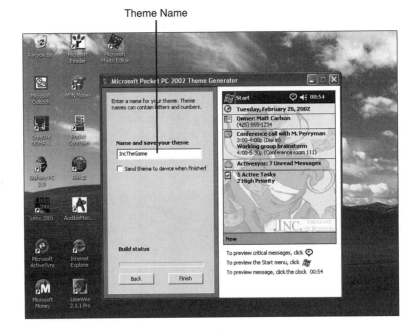

After creating the theme and copying it to your device, you'll find it ready to be selected in the Today Settings page. Figure 4.11 shows the IncTheGame theme as it appears on the Today Settings page, ready to be applied.

Figure 4.11
The IncTheGame theme is installed and ready to be used.

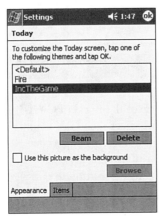

APPLYING A THEME

If you recall from earlier in the chapter, applying a theme is as simple as selecting it in the list on the Today Settings page and then clicking OK in the upper-right corner of the screen. Figure 4.12 shows the IncTheGame theme as it appears on the Today screen of my device.

Figure 4.12
The IncTheGame theme definitely adds some spice to the Today screen.

As Figure 4.12 reveals, custom themes enable you to customize the appearance of your device with personal imagery or a company logo.

DRESSING UP YOUR DEVICE WITHOUT THEMES

I've talked a lot about themes, but it's worth pointing out that there are ways to dress up your Pocket PC without relying solely on themes. You might have noticed an option on the Today Settings page that enables you to specify an image to be used as a background for the Today screen. This provides a quick and easy way to set a background image for the Today screen without having to create a custom theme. Of course, it won't affect the colors on the Today screen, but that might not matter to you.

SELECTING A BACKGROUND IMAGE WITHOUT A THEME

Although this might seem strange, the background image size for the Today screen differs in this case from when you created one for a custom theme; the image size for a background image used directly on the Today screen is 240×299. So, you need to create an image of this size to have it properly fit the Today screen.

Note

Although the Today screen image must be 240×299, the visible portion of the Today screen is still only 240×268. This means that the lower 31 pixels of the background image are covered up by the Command bar and therefore aren't visible onscreen.

To select an image for use as the Today background, you must first copy it to a folder on your Pocket PC. The most convenient place to store this image is in the My Documents folder of your device because the Today Settings page will look there first when you browse to find the image. To set a background image for the Today screen, follow these steps:

1. Tap Start, and then tap Settings.
2. Tap the Today icon.

3. Check the Use This Picture As the Background check box, and then tap the Browse button to select the image (see Figure 4.13).

4. After selecting the image file, tap OK in the upper-right corner to set the image as the background.

Tip from
Michael

There is a shortcut to setting the Today background image that might save you some time if you're prone to changing the image frequently. Using File Explorer on your Pocket PC, you can tap and hold any GIF or JPEG image and then select Set As Today Wallpaper from the pop-up menu to set the image as the Today background.

Figure 4.13
Setting a background image for the Today screen without using a theme is as simple as browsing to select the image on your device.

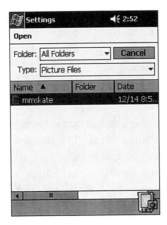

After you've selected a background image, you can return to the Today screen to see it in action; just tap Today on the Start menu to return to the Today screen. Figure 4.14 shows a picture of me skateboarding (mmskate.jpg) that I set as the background image on my device.

Figure 4.14
A skateboarding image is set as the background for the Today screen.

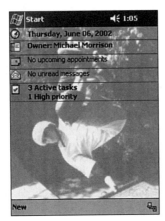

CUSTOMIZING THE MY INFO PAGE

You now know how to bypass using a theme to set the background image of the Today screen, but if you're the curious type you're probably wondering about another potential customization. I'm referring to the My Info page that pops up when your device starts; this page appears only if you have the Owner Information setting selected that shows the owner information when the device is turned on. By default, this page includes a small, horizontal image across the top of the screen, along with your owner information text below it. This image is named `myinfo.gif` and is stored in the Windows folder of your device. You can copy your own image in place of this image to change the appearance of the My Info page. For this to work, your image must be sized 240×60, and you must replace the image in the Windows folder with yours.

 If you're having trouble finding the file `myinfo.gif` on your device, see "Missing the My Info Page Image" in the "Troubleshooting" section at the end of the chapter to find out where this mysterious file is hiding.

Figure 4.15 shows the My Info page with a custom image of the bull character you saw earlier in the chapter.

Figure 4.15
The bull character from the Inc. The Game of Business board game appears on the My Info page thanks to the custom `myinfo.gif` image.

Customizing the My Info page with an image is useful because the My Info page is displayed even if your device is protected by a password. So, if you were to lose your device, the person who found it would not only see the owner information on the My Info page, but also the image you selected.

MAKING THE TODAY SCREEN MORE ACCESSIBLE

In addition to customizing the background images on the Today screen, you might also want to consider making an additional, more practical change to the way the Today screen is accessed. Because the Today screen serves as a starting point in the Pocket PC user interface, it makes sense that it should be readily available. Granted, you can always get to it from the top of the Start menu, but I like the idea of my Pocket PC automatically taking me back to the Today screen if I haven't used the device for a while. Fortunately, this feature is built in to the Pocket PC operating system, and you can alter it to have the Today screen displayed more often.

By default, your Pocket PC is set up so the Today screen is displayed if the device is idle for 4 hours. I prefer the minimum setting for this feature, which is 1 hour. To change the idle period for the Today screen, follow these steps:

1. Tap Start, and then tap Settings.
2. Tap the Today icon.
3. Tap the Items tab.
4. Select the idle period in the combo box near the bottom of the screen (see Figure 4.16).
5. Tap OK to accept the Today Settings changes.

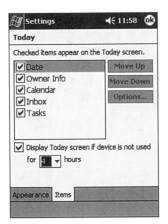

Figure 4.16
The Items tab of the Today Settings page enables you to set the idle period that must elapse before your device automatically returns to the Today screen.

You might have noticed in the Today Settings screen that you can customize the information that is displayed on the Today screen. To do so, you check and uncheck the information that you want to have displayed. By default, all the items are checked, which results in the most information being displayed on the Today screen. This is my personal preference because there is plenty of room on the Today screen, and you might as well use it. However, if you want the Today screen to be a little tidier, you can selectively turn these items on and off, as well as alter the order in which they are displayed on the Today screen using the Move Up and Move Down buttons. Additionally, the Calendar and Tasks items enable you to further customize their appearance on the Today screen by tapping the Options button.

TWEAKING THE START AND NEW MENUS

The Start menu is the anchor of the Pocket PC user interface and is typically used frequently to launch applications. In fact, the Start menu enables you to be only two taps away from any application. Therefore, it is important that it contain exactly the applications you plan to use regularly, and nothing more. The first item displayed in the Start menu is a series of icons that indicate the last six applications you've used. This icon list is automatically maintained by the Pocket PC GUI and is intended to provide a quick means of accessing recently used applications; tap an icon to launch the given application.

ALTERING THE APPLICATIONS IN THE START MENU

The applications listed in the main part of the Start menu can be customized. The following steps show you how to control exactly which applications appear on the Start menu:

1. Tap Start, and then tap Settings.
2. Tap the Menus icon.
3. Check and uncheck appropriate items to customize the contents of the Start menu (see Figure 4.17).
4. Tap OK in the upper-right corner to accept the Start menu changes.

Caution

The Start menu is capable of holding only nine items as selected on the Menu Settings page.

Figure 4.17
Customizing the Start menu is as simple as checking and unchecking the items you want to appear in the menu.

CONTROLLING THE CREATION OF DOCUMENTS WITH THE NEW MENU

Another important part of the Pocket PC GUI is the New menu, which is located in the lower-left corner of the screen. The New menu provides a convenient place to create new documents. Following are the types of documents that can be created with the New menu, along with the applications used to modify them:

- **Appointments**—Calendar
- **Contacts**—Contacts
- **E-mail messages**—Inbox
- **Excel workbooks**—Pocket Excel

- **Notes**—Notes
- **Tasks**—Tasks
- **Word documents**—Pocket Word

The New menu helps add a document-centric feel to Pocket PCs, which means you can think in terms of documents rather than applications. As an example, the New menu enables you to focus on creating a spreadsheet or e-mail message, as opposed to focusing on running Pocket Excel or Inbox. The shift from applications to documents is subtle, but it has been taking place in the desktop Windows environment for quite some time.

The New menu can be customized, in which case you specify which types of documents you want to be able to create via the menu. The other customization available with the New menu is enabling the New menu button, which is a small up arrow that appears next to the New menu. On the Today screen, the button doesn't add any functionality, but within an application, the button enables you to create new documents of any of the previous types listed. Without having the button enabled—which is the default setting—you can use the New button to create only new documents of the same type as the application you are using. Of course, you always have full access to creating different document types via the New menu when you are on the Today screen.

To customize the New menu, follow these steps:

1. Tap Start, and then tap Settings.
2. Tap the Menus icon, and then tap the New Menu tab.
3. Check the check box above the document types to turn on the New menu button.
4. Check and uncheck appropriate document types to customize the contents of the New menu (see Figure 4.18).
5. Tap OK in the upper-right corner to accept the New menu changes.

Figure 4.18
Customizing the New menu primarily involves determining which types of documents you want to be able to create via the New menu.

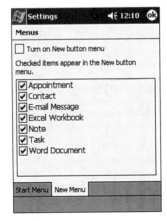

Your New button is now customized and ready to help you create new documents with ease. Let's now turn our attention to the backlight that many find annoying because it seems to be constantly dimming itself.

EXTENDING THE BACKLIGHT AND POWER

With battery life a consistent concern for any PDA owner, your Pocket PC, by default, is most likely set up to preserve power to its fullest. One of the features that preserves battery life is the automatic dimming of the backlight on the screen when the device sits inactive for a given period of time. Although this "auto-dim" feature is handy, it can be set too short. I don't mind a little extra battery drain if it means not having to worry about tapping the screen every 15 seconds. Besides, even the most battery-hungry Pocket PCs still have reasonable battery life—the battery life of newer Pocket PCs ranges from 8 to 14 hours.

AUTOMATICALLY TURNING OFF THE BACKLIGHT

To alter the timeout period for the backlight, follow these steps:

1. Tap Start, and then tap Settings.

2. Tap the System tab, and then tap the Backlight icon.

3. Tap the combo box next to the Turn Off Backlight if Device Is Not Used for check box, and select a new timeout period for the auto-dim feature; I prefer 2 minutes (see Figure 4.19).

4. Make sure the Turn On Backlight When a Button Is Pressed or the Screen Is Tapped check box is checked if you want the backlight to automatically come on when you tap the screen or press a button.

5. Tap OK in the upper-right corner to accept the backlight changes.

PART

I

CH

4

Figure 4.19
The Backlight Settings page enables you to control the timeout period that must elapse before the backlight is automatically turned off.

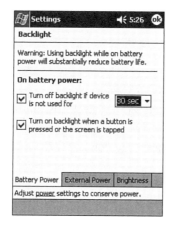

AUTOMATICALLY DIMMING THE SCREEN

You might have noticed on the Backlight Settings page a tab named External Power. This tab enables you to set auto-dim for an external power source, such as when your device is sitting in its cradle connected to a desktop PC. Because there isn't much of a reason to conserve external power, this option is turned off by default. You are certainly free to change it if you'd like, but I like the default setting myself.

ALTERING THE BRIGHTNESS LEVEL

Another setting related to the backlight is the brightness level of the display, which can be set from the Brightness tab of the Backlight Settings page. This tab displays the brightness level for the display under two circumstances: battery power and external power. Some devices don't even allow you to alter the battery-powered brightness because they include an automated means of adjusting the brightness based on ambient light shining on the device. However, you can change the external-powered brightness if you want, or you can check the Automatic check box to enable the device to automatically adjust it. Because my device always gets its external power from the connection to my desktop PC, I choose to leave the external-powered brightness at its maximum level.

AUTOMATICALLY TURNING OFF THE DEVICE

Another setting related to preserving battery life is the power-off setting, which is available on the Power Settings page. The power-off feature is responsible for automatically turning off the device when it sits idle for a certain period of time. By default, this timeout period is set to 3 minutes, which is a little short for my taste. Although I can appreciate the logic behind wanting to save precious battery life, 3 minutes goes by pretty fast, and it can be a hassle having to turn on your device after every 3-minute lapse; I would rather lose a little battery life than have to constantly keep turning the device back on. This is ultimately a personal preference, however, so by all means feel free to be as miserly as you want with battery life.

To change the power-off timeout period, follow these steps:

1. Tap Start, and then tap Settings.
2. Tap the System tab, and then tap the Power icon.
3. Tap the combo box next to the On Battery Power check box, and select a new timeout period for the power-off feature. I prefer 5 minutes, but it's up to you (see Figure 4.20).
4. Tap OK in the upper-right corner to accept the Power Off changes.

Similar to auto-dim, you can also set power-off to work with an external power source. Not surprisingly, this option is unchecked by default because power savings isn't a big deal when running a Pocket PC off an external power source.

Figure 4.20
The Power Settings page enables you to adjust the timeout period for the power-off feature.

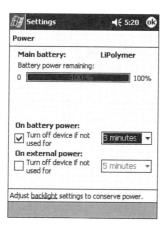

TROUBLESHOOTING

PROBLEMS RUNNING THEME GENERATOR

I can't get the Theme Generator application to run on my desktop/notebook PC.

The Theme Generator application is specifically designed to run on Windows XP or Windows 2000 and will not run on Windows Me or Windows 98. If you are using Windows Me/98, you won't be able to run Theme Generator, and therefore you won't be able to create your own themes. However, if you don't have access to a computer running Windows XP or Windows 2000, all hope for a custom Pocket PC appearance is not lost. See the section "Dressing Up Your Device Without Themes," earlier in this chapter, to learn how to bypass themes and directly set the wallpaper for the Today screen.

MISSING THE MY INFO PAGE IMAGE

I can't find the file myinfo.gif *on my device, even though it is supposed to be image displayed on the My Info page.*

The myinfo.gif image is hidden from view in File Explorer, so you can't see it if you try to browse to it on your device. However, the Explore feature of ActiveSync enables you to see the file on your desktop PC. To change the image, all you must do is copy your version of myinfo.gif into the Windows folder of your device, and it will appear on the My Info page when you turn on the device.

REAL-WORLD EXAMPLE—GIVING DEVICES A BUSINESS LOOK

In case you haven't noticed, Pocket PCs have a tendency to be interesting to people who aren't familiar with them. This primarily has to do with the fact that Pocket PCs are incredibly powerful for their size, and some people still aren't aware of the fact that such a technically advanced handheld computer is available. Knowing that people are likely to take a look at your Pocket PC, investing some time in creating a theme that reflects your personal interests or business affiliation is worthwhile. For example, let's say you work for a company that has several employees who use Pocket PCs. It would be worth the effort to create a theme with your company logo that is used by all the Pocket PC users so that anyone who comes into contact with them can immediately see the business affiliation. In fact, you could go a step further by including a company logo on the My Info page, which effectively makes the My Info page somewhat of a business card.

CHAPTER 5

MAKING THE MOST OF INPUT METHODS

In this chapter

THE CHALLENGE OF HANDHELD INPUT

The compactness of Pocket PCs is what makes them so handy for anyone who needs mobile computing power. Unfortunately, their small size also makes Pocket PCs somewhat of a challenge when it comes time to enter text information. Although the mouse has taken much of the credit in an era of graphical user interfaces, the trusty keyboard still plays an incredibly important role in desktop computing. The stylus plays the role of the mouse in Pocket PCs, but nothing in the way of hardware fills in the gap left by not having a keyboard. Granted, portable keyboards are available for the Pocket PC, but those aren't ideal in every situation; portable keyboards include thumb keyboards that function like the keypads on high-end alphanumeric pagers and foldout keyboards that require a flat surface. Fortunately, the Pocket PC operating system includes several options for inputting text information using the stylus. This chapter focuses on those options and helps you get the most out of each.

→ To learn more about portable keyboards for Pocket PCs, **see** "Keyboards," **p. 485**.

It's not until you first use a handheld computer without a keyboard that you start to fully appreciate the significance of a keyboard in everyday computing. Being somewhat of a power user myself, I depend on a keyboard even more because I like to learn shortcut keys and avoid the mouse for repetitious tasks. When I first started using handheld computers, I was convinced there was no way to realistically do anything serious in the way of text entry because of the limitation of not having a keyboard. Although I'm still faster on a traditional keyboard, I've found that the Pocket PC does an amazing job of providing alternative *input methods* for entering text in the absence of a traditional keyboard.

The input methods available for use in the Pocket PC operating system are made available by the Input Panel button, which automatically appears in the lower-right corner of the screen whenever you need to enter text. Figure 5.1 shows the relationship between the Input Panel button and the Input Panel.

Figure 5.1
The Input Panel button provides access to the various input methods and also shows and hides the Input Panel.

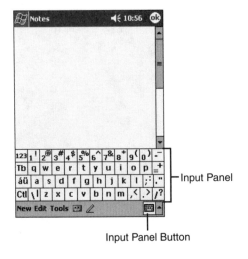

Input Panel

Input Panel Button

The input method shown in Figure 5.1 is the Keyboard input method, which simulates a keyboard and enables you to enter keys by pecking at them with the stylus. The Input Panel actually supports a total of four input methods, which follow:

- Keyboard
- Letter Recognizer
- Block Recognizer
- Transcriber

These input methods vary widely in terms of how they enable you to enter text. I encourage you to experiment with all of them to see which one suits your needs the best. The Keyboard input method is perhaps the quickest to learn, but it can be a slow go pecking out letters one at a time. The same thing applies to the Letter Recognizer, which enables you to draw one letter at a time on the screen with the stylus. If you've ever used a Palm handheld device, you might find the Block Recognizer interesting because it simulates the Graffiti input method that has become so popular on Palm devices. However, the most powerful Pocket PC input method by far is Transcriber, which uses *natural handwriting recognition* to enable you to write complete words and sentences on the screen in your own handwriting.

Note

A few portable foldout keyboards on the market can be used with Pocket PCs. If you've never seen one of these keyboards, I encourage you to check them out because they are technical marvels in terms of how they fold open from a little compact case. Although you probably won't find it convenient to unfold a portable keyboard every time you want to enter information into your Pocket PC, it can be extremely useful if you end up using your Pocket PC as an alternative to a notebook computer. In addition, portable keyboards are available with small keys you press with your thumbs, which can be handy in situations in which a foldout keyboard isn't a viable option. Both types of portable keyboards are covered in Appendix A, "A Pocket PC Hardware Accesssory Tour."

PART
I

CH
5

The remainder of this chapter focuses on the four Pocket PC input methods and explores how you can tweak their settings to get the most out of each. You might fall in love with a particular input method, or you might decide to use several of them in various situations.

Note

The Notes application is used throughout this chapter to demonstrate the use of input methods. Notes is a standard Pocket PC application used to enter small pieces of information, including text, handwriting, and graphics. Keep in mind that the input methods apply to any Pocket PC application that requires text input, not just the Notes application.

➜ To find out more about the Notes application, **see** "Jotting Down Ideas with Notes," **p. 264**.

INSIDE THE SOFT KEYBOARD

The Keyboard input method is also known as the *soft keyboard,* or *virtual keyboard* because it simulates a physical keyboard on the display screen. The idea behind the soft keyboard is to provide a means of accessing the familiar keys on a keyboard using the stylus. Although the soft keyboard is probably not the most efficient input method available on Pocket PCs, it could be the most intuitive and least error-prone simply because we're all familiar with using keyboards. I find myself using the soft keyboard for entering small amounts of text where accuracy is important.

The soft keyboard is activated by selecting Keyboard from the pop-up menu associated with the Input Panel button (see Figure 5.2). You can also customize the soft keyboard by selecting Options from the Input Panel pop-up menu.

Figure 5.2
The soft keyboard is activated for input by selecting Keyboard on the Input Panel pop-up menu.

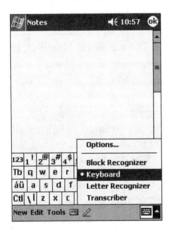

Even though the default settings for the soft keyboard are suitable, you might consider altering them to fit your input style. For example, you can change the size of the virtual keyboard keys and establish gestures with the stylus that correspond to commonly used keys, such as Shift and Enter. *Gestures* are special strokes you make with the stylus that perform a special function, such as capitalizing a letter, deleting a character, or imitating a control key such as Shift or Enter. Gestures are performed over the soft keyboard in the Input Panel and are interpreted as control entries rather than character entries.

→ If you're interested in learning about stylus options beyond what came with your device, **see** "Pointing Tools," **p. 488**.

Gestures are available only with large keys, but I encourage you to try them. I got used to them in a matter of minutes and found them to be efficient in avoiding having to peck the Space, Shift, Backspace, and Enter keys; you can also perform gestures anywhere on the keyboard. The main benefit is the Shift gesture, which applies to the key over which you perform the gesture. For example, to enter a capital M, you tap the M key and drag upward with the stylus.

To customize the Keyboard input method, follow these steps:

1. Launch any application that involves text entry, such as Notes.
2. Tap the up arrow on the Input Panel button, and then tap Options.
3. To use large keys, tap the Large Keys radio button (Small Keys is the default setting).
4. To enable gestures, tap the Gestures check box (see Figure 5.3).
5. Tap OK in the upper-right corner to accept the Keyboard input method changes.

Figure 5.3
The soft keyboard settings can easily be changed to accommodate a larger keyboard and gestures.

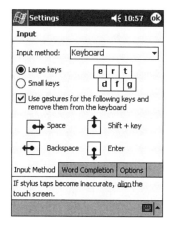

Tip from
Michael

When you turn on Gestures for the soft keyboard, the Space and Shift keys are removed from the keyboard to make room for additional keys. The Space and Shift gestures appear on the screen in the Input Settings page (refer to Figure 5.3) and are easy to remember.

 If you can't seem to find the arrow keys on the soft keyboard, see "Missing Arrow Keys on the Soft Keyboard" in the "Troubleshooting" section at the end of the chapter to find out where they're located.

PART

I

CH

5

USING THE LETTER RECOGNIZER

The Letter Recognizer input method is used to enter letters and numbers one at a time by drawing them on a special region of the screen. You can think of the Letter Recognizer as somewhat of a handwriting version of the soft keyboard in that you must enter text one letter, number, or symbol at a time, as opposed to entering entire words or sentences. Nonetheless, if you like the idea of quickly jotting down letters to enter information into your Pocket PC, you might find the Letter Recognizer input method to be a suitable means of entering text.

ENTERING TEXT WITH THE LETTER RECOGNIZER

After selecting Letter Recognizer from the Input Panel pop-up menu, you'll see the Letter Recognizer as it appears in Figure 5.4. Similar to the Keyboard input method, there are a few ways to customize the Letter Recognizer to suit your own style of input.

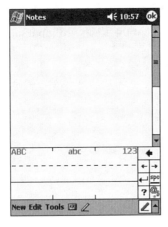

Figure 5.4
The Letter Recognizer enables you to enter text one character at a time by drawing each character in the Input Panel.

If you examine Figure 5.4 closely, you'll notice that the Input Panel is divided into three regions when the Letter Recognizer input method is in action. These three regions determine the type of text being entered and are listed from left to right as follows:

- **Uppercase area**—Used to draw uppercase letters
- **Lowercase area**—Used to draw lowercase letters
- **Number area**—Used to draw numbers

If you want to enter an uppercase letter, you must draw it in the leftmost region, whereas lowercase letters must be drawn in the middle region. Regardless of whether you're drawing in the uppercase or lowercase area, the standard approach to drawing letters in the Letter Recognizer is to use lowercase. So, for example, if you want to enter an uppercase *E*, you would draw a lowercase *e* in the left region (the uppercase area) of the Letter Recognizer. Remember this, the region in which you draw a letter determines its case, not the manner in which you draw it.

Note

If you have an unconventional handwriting style, like me, and prefer to draw letters in uppercase, you should consider using the Block Recognizer input method instead of the Letter Recognizer. You learn about the Block Recognizer in the next section, "Using the Block Recognizer."

You can enter symbols in the Letter Recognizer by tapping the Symbol button on the toolbar to the right of the Input Panel. This results in the display of the symbols keyboard, which is shown in Figure 5.5.

Figure 5.5
The Letter Recognizer's symbols keyboard enables you to enter symbols.

Many symbols can also be drawn in the number area of the Input Panel. For example, Figure 5.6 shows how to draw an ampersand (&) using the number area.

Figure 5.6
The number area of the Letter Recognizer can be used to draw many symbols.

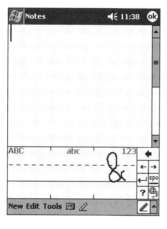

PART
I
CH
5

Tip from
Michael

If you are having trouble drawing a particular symbol, it's probably not supported via drawing in the number area. In this case you must rely on the symbols keyboard, which is accessible by tapping the Symbol button on the toolbar to the right of the Input Panel.

CUSTOMIZING THE LETTER RECOGNIZER

A few settings are available for customizing the Letter Recognizer input method. These settings enable you to tweak the manner in which certain characters are drawn, and they are accessible by following these steps:

1. After selecting the Letter Recognizer input method, tap the up arrow on the Input Panel button, and then tap Options.

2. Tap the Options button to view the options for the Letter Recognizer input method.

3. Check the options you want to set (see Figure 5.7).

4. Tap OK in the upper-right corner to accept the Letter Recognizer input method changes.

Figure 5.7
The Letter Recognizer options enable you to customize the manner in which characters are interpreted as you draw them.

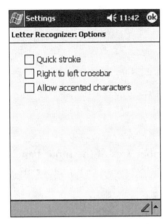

The Quick Stroke option requires you to write all letters using a single stroke, which can be convenient if you're into highly efficient data entry. The downside to this approach is that you'll need to learn a few tricks to drawing some characters that typically require two strokes, such as the letter *t* or *x*. Keep in mind that you can normally draw any letters using a single stroke; the Quick Stroke option simply forces you to use the single-stroke approach, which presumably helps minimize error because it doesn't allow you to attempt to draw with two strokes.

The second option for the Letter Recognizer input method involves the direction you use to cross the letters *t* and *f*, as well as the plus sign (+). Most people cross these characters from left to right, but there are no doubt folks who go against the grain and cross the other way. If you're one of those people, check the Right to Left Crossbar option to reverse the manner in which these characters are crossed. This option obviously applies only to two-stroke character entry, which means that it doesn't apply if you have the Quick Stroke option set. In fact, the Right to Left Crossbar option will gray out if you check the Quick Stroke option.

The final option in the Letter Recognizer determines whether you're allowed to draw accented characters. If you want to be able to draw accented characters, just check the Allow Accented Characters option. To actually draw an accented character, you must draw the accent mark just above the character immediately after drawing the character. You usually have to be pretty quick drawing the accent for the Letter Recognizer to catch it and know that it is part of the character. If you aren't quick enough with the accent, it will likely be misinterpreted as a single quotation mark (').

You might be a little concerned about the fact that I've provided a text description of how to draw letters, numbers, and symbols using the Letter Recognizer input method. Unfortunately, current technology doesn't allow me to include interactive animations in the pages of this book. However, your Pocket PC includes a very useful feature that aids in learning how to draw characters using the Letter Recognizer input method. I'm referring to the demo that is built in to the Letter Recognizer. To access this demo, tap the Help button on the Letter Recognizer toolbar, and then tap the Demo button. Once inside the demo, you can tap any key on the soft keyboard to view an animation of how it should be drawn in the Letter Recognizer (see Figure 5.8).

Figure 5.8
The Letter Recognizer demo uses animated graphics to demonstrate how to draw letters, numbers, and symbols.

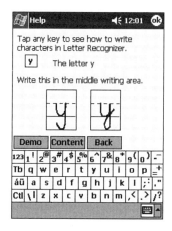

Now that you have a pretty good feel for the Letter Recognizer input method, it's time to push onward and learn about another input method available for use on your Pocket PC.

PART

I

CH

5

USING THE BLOCK RECOGNIZER

When Microsoft first created the Pocket PC platform, it found itself in an unfamiliar position as a minority player in the handheld marketplace. Things have changed dramatically since then, but Microsoft still finds itself in the position of trying to lure users of Palm devices to Pocket PCs. Because Palm users don't want to have to relearn a completely new approach to handheld computing, Microsoft has tried to ease the transition as much as possible. One of the significant ways in which the Pocket PC operating system smoothes the Palm to Pocket PC transition is with the Block Recognizer input method, which simulates the popular Graffiti input method employed by Palm devices.

→ For a detailed comparison of Pocket PCs and Palm devices, **see** "Pocket PC Versus Palm,"
p. 15.

The Graffiti input method is actually quite similar to the Letter Recognizer input method except that the specific strokes used to draw characters differ between the two methods. The Letter Recognizer represents Microsoft's own unique approach to character entry via drawing, whereas the Block Recognizer represents a concession for migrating Palm users.

Knowing this, if you don't have a background using Palm devices or the Graffiti input method, you might not find the Block Recognizer to offer any significant advantages over the Letter Recognizer.

To begin using the Block Recognizer, select Block Recognizer from the Input Panel pop-up menu. You'll see the Block Recognizer as it appears in Figure 5.9, which looks surprisingly similar to the Letter Recognizer.

Figure 5.9
The Block Recognizer enables you to enter text one character at a time with strokes popularized by the Graffiti input method used on Palm devices.

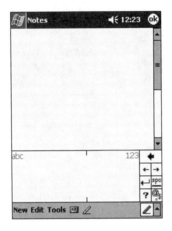

Similar to the Letter Recognizer, the Block Recognizer consists of areas that are used to draw different kinds of characters. However, in this case the Input Panel is divided into two regions for the Block Recognizer, as opposed to three for the Letter Recognizer. These two regions determine the type of text being entered and are listed from left to right as follows:

- **Letter area**—Used to draw letters
- **Number area**—Used to draw numbers

All letters drawn in the letter area appear as lowercase letters unless you activate Shift mode, which is accomplished by drawing a short vertical line up the letter area of the Input Panel. The specific approach used to draw letters and numbers in the Block Recognizer strictly follows the Graffiti input method, which is beyond the scope of this chapter. Keep in mind that a demo is available for learning how to draw characters in the Block Recognizer—just tap the Help button on the Block Recognizer toolbar, and then tap the Demo button. You can use the demo to view an animation of how characters should be drawn in the Block Recognizer (see Figure 5.10).

The Block Recognizer demo is a great way to learn how to use the Block Recognizer input method to enter characters. If you plan to use the Block Recognizer input method, I encourage you to spend some time with the demo and get acquainted with the entry of most characters.

Figure 5.10
The Block Recognizer demo uses animated graphics to demonstrate how to draw letters, numbers, and symbols based on the Graffiti input method.

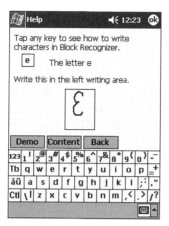

WORKING WITH TRANSCRIBER

The final input method available for use on your Pocket PC is without a doubt the most interesting and powerful input method of all. I'm referring to Transcriber, which is an input method that uses natural handwriting recognition to enable you to write complete words and sentences anywhere on the screen. Unlike all the other input methods, Transcriber enables you to write complete words anywhere on the screen and automatically convert them to text. It also supports cursive handwriting and can be customized to fit your writing style.

Note

If you're a lefty and you've used a previous version of Transcriber, you'll be glad to know that the Pocket PC 2002 version of Transcriber includes extensive support for left-handed writing.

PART

I

CH

5

WHAT IS TRANSCRIBER?

As you might already know, Microsoft has a strong track record for either acquiring or licensing powerful technologies and incorporating them into its products. One such technology that made its way into Pocket PC via a licensing deal is Transcriber, which is based on the Calligrapher handwriting-recognition software by ParaGraph (http://www.paragraph.com/). Calligrapher made its mark as the only handwriting-recognition software for handheld devices that could recognize both cursive and printed text. Transcriber uses similar technology found in Calligrapher to bring advanced handwriting recognition to Pocket PCs.

Transcriber is surprisingly accurate at recognizing handwriting and will likely change the way you use your Pocket PC. The interesting thing about Transcriber is how you can customize it to suit your personal writing style. I use a lot of capital letters and tend to print everything I write, as opposed to using cursive writing. I can customize Transcriber so that it expects me to write in printed uppercase and doesn't look for cursive writing.

Customizing Transcriber in this way can improve the accuracy and speed of the handwriting recognition.

In addition to recognizing handwritten text, numbers, and symbols, Transcriber also supports several gestures, which simulate control keys such as Space and Enter and perform common tasks such as cut, copy, and paste. Transcriber gestures are similar to the gestures that are part of the Keyboard input method. Like the Keyboard gestures, Transcriber gestures are easy to learn and significantly speed up the entry of text information.

→ If you like the idea of using handwriting on your Pocket PC, you might want to consider using handwriting recognition as a security measure for protecting your device from unauthorized access. To find out more, **see** "Going Sci-Fi with Biometric Authentication," **p. 388**.

USING TRANSCRIBER

To get started with Transcriber, select Transcriber from the Input Panel pop-up menu. You'll be presented with an Intro window that provides a quick overview of how to use Transcriber, including a description of some of the more commonly used gestures (see Figure 5.11). If you don't want to see this window the next time you change the input method to Transcriber, check the Don't Show This check box near the bottom of the window. Tap OK in the upper-right corner of the Intro window to close it and begin using Transcriber.

Figure 5.11
The Transcriber Intro window presents you with a quick overview of how to use Transcriber.

The best way to learn how to use Transcriber is by doing. So, go ahead and try hand-writing a sentence on the screen using the stylus. Figure 5.12 shows a sentence I wrote by hand.

When you finish writing, Transcriber kicks in and attempts to recognize the handwriting and convert it to text. The converted text is inserted into the current application at the insertion point, which in this case is the start of a note. Figure 5.13 shows the resulting text that Transcriber successfully recognized. It's important to understand that Transcriber begins recognizing your handwriting when you pause long enough to indicate that you are finished writing a particular word or phrase; as long as you keep writing, Transcriber will wait. This period of time in which Transcriber waits before recognizing the handwriting is known as the *recognition delay* and can be adjusted. You learn how to adjust the recognition delay in a moment.

Figure 5.12
Transcriber enables you to write any-where on the screen and have it recog-nized as text.

Figure 5.13
I got a little lucky because Transcriber perfectly recognized my handwritten sen-tence on the first try.

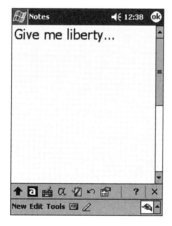

PART
I

CH
5

SELECTING TEXT

As good at handwriting recognition as Transcriber is, it's still common for it to make mis-takes. More accurately, unavoidable inconsistencies in our handwriting are what actually result in the mistakes. If you see a mistake or decide to change a portion of the text recog-nized by Transcriber, you can easily block off the text and try again. For example, if I decided I wanted to change the sentence so that it says "death" instead of "liberty," I could tap and hold briefly just in front of the word "liberty." After about a second you will hear a beep and can then drag the stylus to select the whole word. With text selected, you can write on the screen again, and the writing will be recognized and replace the selected text.

Caution

> If you wait too long while tapping to select text, the Notes application will interpret the tap as a tap and hold, and it will display a pop-up menu. Hold the tap just long enough to hear the beep, and then quickly drag to select the text you want.

Another good way to select text while using Transcriber is to double-tap the text with the stylus. You can even triple-tap a word to select an entire paragraph of text. One other Transcriber feature that you'll find useful is the selection stroke. The *selection stroke* enables you to select text by drawing a line through the text. For example, Figure 5.14 shows how I'm selecting the word "liberty" by drawing a line through it.

Figure 5.14
The selection stroke is applied by drawing a line through a word or group of words.

COMMUNICATING WITH GESTURES

Although Transcriber's handwriting-recognition capabilities are impressive, you have to start using gestures to really appreciate its power. Gestures are special strokes you make with the stylus that are interpreted as commands rather than characters or words. Transcriber supports the following commands via gestures:

- **Enter**—Inserts a carriage return
- **Space**—Inserts a space
- **Backspace**—Deletes the selected text or the character to the left of the insertion point
- **Quick Correct**—Suggests a correction for a word or opens the Transcriber keyboard
- **Case Change**—Changes a letter's case
- **Undo**—Undoes the previous action
- **Copy**—Copies the selected text to the Clipboard (equivalent to Ctrl+C)
- **Cut**—Cuts the selected text to the Clipboard (equivalent to Ctrl+X)
- **Paste**—Pastes the text on the Clipboard over the selected text or at the current insertion point (equivalent to Ctrl+V)

- **Tab**—Inserts a tab
- **Correction**—Opens the Transcriber Correction window

Each of these gestures has a unique stroke that is used to enter the gesture. Figure 5.15 shows what the various strokes look like; you can also view them in Transcriber Help in the section titled "Microsoft Transcriber Gestures." The arrows in the gesture strokes indicate the direction in which the stroke must be performed. As an example, the Enter stroke requires you to tap, drag the stylus down, drag it to the left, and then release.

Tip from
Michael

I've found that the gestures are recognized better if you make large strokes. It takes a little practice, but the gestures provide an incredibly powerful and efficient way to perform common editing tasks.

Figure 5.15
Transcriber gestures involve the use of special strokes that are made with the stylus.

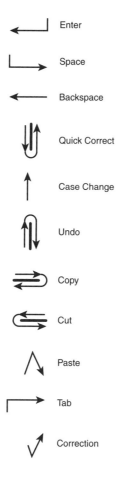

Enter

Space

Backspace

Quick Correct

Case Change

Undo

Copy

Cut

Paste

Tab

Correction

PART
I
CH
5

The only gestures whose functions aren't immediately obvious are the Quick Correct and Correction gestures, which are used to correct mistakes in the currently selected text. As an example of how these gestures work, check out Figure 5.16, which shows the Quick Correct gesture in action. In this figure, Transcriber has incorrectly recognized the word "deeth," so I used the Quick Correct gesture to display a list of possible corrections. The corrections are displayed in the Alternates pop-up menu, as shown in the figure; tapping the word "death" on this menu quickly corrects the mistake.

Tip from
Michael

Transcriber uses a dictionary to suggest words when using the Quick Correct gesture. You can add a word to the dictionary by selecting the word, making the Quick Correct gesture, and tapping Add to Dictionary in the Alternates pop-up menu that appears.

Figure 5.16
The Quick Correct gesture provides a convenient technique for correcting words that are incorrectly recognized.

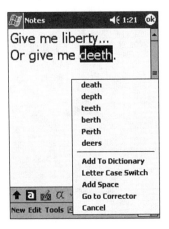

The Quick Correct gesture actually has another use in addition to correcting words: If you make the Quick Correct gesture with a punctuation character selected, the Transcriber keyboard is displayed. This keyboard contains punctuation characters that are difficult to make using strokes. Figure 5.17 shows how I used the Transcriber keyboard to change a period to a comma.

Note

The Transcriber keyboard is also displayed if you make the Quick Correct gesture with nothing selected.

CORRECTING MISTAKES WITH THE CORRECTION GESTURE

The other gesture used to make corrections is the Correction gesture, which you saw in Figure 5.15. The Correction gesture differs from the Quick Correct gesture in that it opens the Correction window, which provides a more comprehensive approach to correcting mistakes. Figure 5.18 shows the Correction window, which includes a toolbar you use to carry out the correction.

Figure 5.17
The Transcriber keyboard provides a user interface for entering punctuation characters that are difficult to make using strokes.

Figure 5.18
The Correction gesture provides a more comprehensive approach to correcting Transcriber mistakes by opening the Correction window.

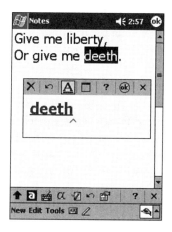

PART

I

CH

5

Tip from
Michael

You can also open the Correction window by selecting Go to Corrector from the Alternates pop-up menu or by tapping the Correction button on the Transcriber icon-bar, which appears near the bottom of the screen when Transcriber is in use.

Within the Correction window you can use one of two approaches to correct mistakes in a word or sentence:

- Write directly over a letter or word to change it.
- Double-tap a letter or word to open the Alternates pop-up menu, where you can select a replacement.

If you choose to double-tap a letter or word to change it, the Alternates pop-up menu that appears enables you to change the case of the letter or word or turn it into a space.

You might have noticed a row of buttons along the top of the Correction window. These buttons are used to carry out commands while making corrections. Following are the commands, from left to right, that correspond to the buttons in the Correction window:

- **Delete**—Delete the highlighted text
- **Undo**—Undo the previous action
- **Text/Draw**—Use the stylus to underline misspelled words
- **Full screen**—Enlarge the Correction window to fill the screen
- **Help**—Open Transcriber Help
- **OK**—Close the Correction window and save changes
- **Exit**—Close the Correction window without saving changes

Of course, if you run into trouble with the Correction window, you can always refer to Transcriber's online help by tapping the Help button. Fortunately, correcting mistakes in Transcriber becomes second nature after you've done it a few times. Hopefully, you'll get the hang of writing in Transcriber so that there aren't too many corrections to be made.

CUSTOMIZING TRANSCRIBER

The Transcriber input method is capable of being customized to a considerable degree. Some of the customizations involve the user interface, whereas others are more significant and impact the manner in which handwriting is recognized. To customize Transcriber, tap the up arrow on the Input Panel button and then tap Options followed by the Options button. You will see the Transcriber Options page, which is shown in Figure 5.19.

Figure 5.19
The Transcriber Options page enables you to customize Transcriber settings.

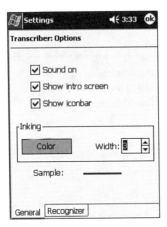

Following are the most important settings on the Transcriber Options page, as shown in Figure 5.19:

- **Sound On**—Determines whether Transcriber makes sounds as you write and make gesture strokes. You can obviously use Transcriber effectively without sound, but the subtle cues it provides, such as the sound played when you've performed an undo action, help ensure you don't make errors.

- **Show Intro Screen**—Determines whether the introduction screen is displayed when you select Transcriber as the input method.

- **Show Iconbar**—Determines whether the Transcriber iconbar is displayed; this bar is displayed near the bottom of the screen and provides access to some interesting Transcriber features, as well as Transcriber Help. You learn more about the iconbar in a moment.

The other settings in the Transcriber Options page enable you to customize the look of the ink displayed when you draw strokes. More specifically, you can change the color and width of the ink to suit your personal preferences. Since the ink should stand out, it's a good idea not to set it to black or make it any narrower than the default width. Keep in mind that this setting affects only the ink that is displayed while you're drawing in Transcriber, not the resulting text that is recognized.

TWEAKING THE RECOGNITION OF HANDWRITING

You might have noticed a tab named Recognizer at the bottom of the Transcriber Options page. The Recognizer tab enables you to customize the manner in which handwriting is recognized. Figure 5.20 shows the options that are available under this tab.

Figure 5.20
The Recognizer tab in the Transcriber Options provides a means of customizing how handwriting is recognized.

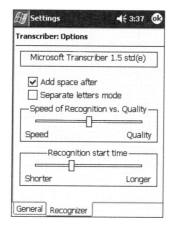

PART
I

CH
5

Following are the settings available in the Recognizer tab of the Transcriber Options page:

- **Add Space After**—Determines whether a space is inserted after each word or fragment recognized by Transcriber. I find that keeping this setting activated is very helpful because it keeps me from having to manually add spaces when writing one word at a time.

- **Separate Letters Mode**—Instructs Transcriber to recognize words that are written with letters that aren't connected. In other words, it instructs Transcriber to accept only printed words, as opposed to words written in cursive.

- **Speed of Recognition vs Quality**—Enables you to set the accuracy of Transcriber; of course, accuracy comes at the expense of decreased speed. If you find that Transcriber is making a lot of mistakes, you might want to consider inching the slider toward Quality. On the other hand, you might lean toward Speed if you think Transcriber is taking too long to recognize your writing.

- **Recognition Start Time**—Determines how long it takes Transcriber to begin recognizing text after you finish writing. Keep in mind that you sometimes pause while writing multiple words, which impacts the delay in which you want Transcriber to jump into action. If you move the slider all the way to the left, you will probably not have enough time to accurately write multiple words. On the other hand, the right end of the delay spectrum is probably too slow for most users.

> **Note**
>
> You might wonder why you would want to enable such a seemingly limiting option as Separate Letters Mode. The reason is because it significantly improves the performance of Transcriber. So, if you're like me and your natural writing style is printing, you definitely should set this option to speed up Transcriber. Of course, many people use all cursive or a mixture of print and cursive writing, in which case the performance improvement won't be worth the limitations in Transcriber's handwriting recognition.

> **Tip from**
> *Michael*
>
> The speed of Transcriber's recognition is dependent on several factors, the most important being the processor speed of your device. A good way to find the best setting is to start out with the slider pegged on the Quality end. As you gain experience with Transcriber and get comfortable entering text with it, you can inch the slider back toward Speed.

> **Tip from**
> *Michael*
>
> I've found that, to start, it's best that you keep the default value for the Recognition Start Time setting. However, if you are a particularly slow or speedy writer then by all means change the delay to suit your style.

HONING YOUR WRITING STYLE WITH THE TRANSCRIBER ICONBAR

A little earlier I mentioned the Transcriber iconbar as an option you could turn on or off in the General tab of the Transcriber Options page. The Transcriber iconbar is located across the bottom of the screen in Transcriber and includes several icons for fine-tuning the entry and recognition of text. The recognition settings available for customization via the Transcriber iconbar are incredibly detailed and enable you to really dial Transcriber into your writing style. You can see the Transcriber iconbar near the bottom of Figure 5.18, earlier in this chapter. Following are the meanings of the icons displayed in the Transcriber iconbar, from left to right:

- **Control of Writing Orientation**—Changes the screen orientation to allow you to write at various angles
- **Recognition Mode**—Changes the recognition mode used to recognize handwriting (uppercase, lowercase, or numerical)
- **Transcriber Keyboard**—Shows/hides the Transcriber keyboard
- **Letter Shape Selector**—Changes the stroke shapes expected for letters and symbols
- **Correction**—Opens the Correction window
- **Undo**—Undoes the previous action
- **Options**—Opens Transcriber Options
- **Help**—Opens Transcriber Help
- **Close**—Closes Transcriber

The Control of Writing Orientation icon enables you to change the screen orientation so you can write at different angles. Maybe you like to rotate your Pocket PC to the left at a 45° angle for optimal writing comfort. If so, tap the Control of Writing Orientation icon once, and Transcriber factors the angle of the device into the recognition.

The Recognition Mode icon enables you to change the recognition mode used to recognize handwriting, which can be one of the following modes: lowercase, uppercase, and numerical. Lowercase mode actually recognizes both lowercase and uppercase text, whereas uppercase mode is exclusively for writing uppercase text. When writing in uppercase mode, everything you write is automatically capitalized regardless of the case in which it is entered. Numerical mode is used to enter numbers and is handy if you need to enter mathematical information, such as equations or fractions.

PART

I

CH

5

Tip from
Michael

Transcriber includes a built-in calculator that enables you to enter mathematical equations and have them solved automatically. For example, if you draw the partial equation "3 + 1 =", Transcriber will calculate the result and display the complete equation "3 + 1 = 4".

The Transcriber Keyboard icon shows and hides the Transcriber keyboard, which you learned about earlier in the chapter. If you recall, the keyboard provides access to punctuation characters and symbols that are difficult to enter using strokes.

The Letter Shape Selector icon is probably the most interesting of all the icons on the iconbar and is where you can really customize Transcriber to fit your personal writing style. Tapping this icon opens the Letter Shape Selector, which enables you to customize the strokes used to write individual letters and symbols. Figure 5.21 shows the Letter Shape Selector with the letter A selected for customization.

Figure 5.21
The Letter Shape Selector enables you to customize the strokes used to write individual letters and symbols.

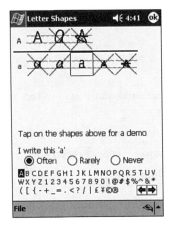

As Figure 5.21 shows, the Letter Shape Selector shows various ways in which a letter can be written and enables you to set whether you use a certain stroke Often, Rarely, or Never. In Figure 5.21 I've already customized the A letter to suit my writing style. By default, all the strokes are set to Often, which means that Transcriber attempts to recognize a wide range of writing styles. By fine-tuning each letter and symbol to your own personal style and eliminating as many unused strokes as possible, you improve both the accuracy and speed of Transcriber.

Some of the strokes shown in the Letter Shape Selector might look similar to you. That's because the application is showing you the finished stroke, which can sometimes be the same for different strokes. To really be able to distinguish between strokes, you must see an animation of how they are made. To do this, tap the stroke in the Letter Shape Selector to select it, and then tap it again to see its animation.

Tip from
Michael

The File menu in the Letter Shape Selector enables you to set the letter shape settings as either Master or Guest. You should set your letter shape settings to Master and leave the Guest settings as an option if you will allow someone else to use your device.

Although setting letter shapes can be a tedious and time-consuming process, if you use Transcriber often enough, you will appreciate the effort in the long term.

 If you're having trouble with Transcriber recognizing your handwriting, see "Recognition Errors in Transcriber" in the "Troubleshooting" section at the end of the chapter to learn how to resolve the problem.

FINE-TUNING USER INPUT

Throughout the chapter you probably noticed a couple of other tabs in the familiar Input Settings page that you've been using to customize input methods. One of these tabs is the Word Completion tab (see Figure 5.22), which enables you to turn on and customize the word-completion feature. The word-completion feature applies to all the input methods and suggests words in a pop-up window while you're entering text. Ideally, this feature suggests the word you're entering, and you can quickly tap it to avoid the extra text entry. The default setting for word-completion is to suggest one word after you enter two letters. Although the two-letter setting seems to work well, I prefer having more words from which to choose.

Figure 5.22
Fine-tuning the word-completion feature can help make you more productive as you enter information into your Pocket PC.

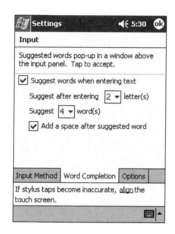

To raise the number of words suggested by the word-completion feature, follow these steps:

1. Tap the up arrow on the Input Panel button, and then tap Options.

2. Tap the Word Completion tab.

3. Tap the combo box next to Suggest Word(s), and select a new number of words for the word-completion feature; I prefer four words. I've found the default settings for the other preferences on this page to work well, but you are free to change them if you like. As an example, you can change the number of letters that are entered before word-completion kicks in (two is the default).

4. Tap OK in the upper-right corner to accept the word-completion changes.

The other tab present in the Input Settings is the Options tab, which enables you to customize input settings such as the audio format used for voice recording, the zoom level used for writing and typing text, and a couple of other neat text-entry features. I find it beneficial to make a slight modification to these settings. First, I think the option 8,000 Hz, 16 Bit, Mono (16 KB/s) for audio provides a better trade-off of quality and storage space for voice recordings than the default setting. If you aren't so concerned about minimizing storage space and prefer higher-quality audio, you might consider changing this setting to a higher quality, such as the option 11,025 Hz, 16 Bit, Stereo (43 KB/s). Just keep in mind that these settings apply to voice recordings, which rarely have to be of superior sound quality.

→ Technically, you might consider the Record button an input method because it enables you to create audio voice recordings. To learn all about the Record button, **see** Chapter 14, "Working with the Pocket Outlook Tasks and Notes," **p. 257**.

PART

I

CH

5

To alter the input settings within the Options tab on the Input Settings page, follow these steps:

1. Tap the up arrow on the Input Panel button, and then tap Options.

2. Tap the Options tab.

3. Tap the first combo box and select 8,000 Hz, 16 Bit, Mono (16 KB/s) for the voice recording format. Feel free to adjust this setting for your own purposes if you are familiar with audio formats.

4. Tap the second and third combo boxes, and select 150% for each (see Figure 5.23).

5. Tap OK in the upper-right corner to accept the input options changes.

Figure 5.23
The Options tab on the Input Settings page enables you to set the voice recording format, as well as some input parameters for text entry.

The zoom level settings you modified in step 4 determine the zoom level used for writing and typing text; you might want to experiment with these values to determine your own preferences.

TROUBLESHOOTING

MISSING ARROW KEYS ON THE SOFT KEYBOARD

I can't find the arrow keys on the soft keyboard.

The arrow keys on the soft keyboard in the Keyboard input method are immediately visible only when you're using the keyboard with small keys. If you have the keyboard set to use large keys, you must tap the 123 key in the upper-left corner of the keyboard to access the arrow keys, as well as other control keys and symbols. To change the soft keyboard setting between large keys and small keys, follow these steps:

1. Tap the up arrow on the Input Panel button, and then tap Options.

2. To use small keys, tap the Small Keys radio button.

RECOGNITION ERRORS IN TRANSCRIBER

Transcriber isn't doing a very good job recognizing my handwriting.

There are several possible problems associated with Transcriber not recognizing your handwriting. The first place to start is your handwriting—make sure you are writing letters and punctuation as clearly and consistently as possible. If you feel you're doing a pretty good job with the handwriting, the next thing to check is the Speed of Recognition vs. Quality setting in the Recognizer tab of the Transcriber Options page. Make sure the slider for this setting is set all the way over to Quality, which helps ensure that Transcriber does the best possible job of recognizing handwriting. The last thing to do to help Transcriber along is to use the Letter Shape Selector by tapping the Letter Shape Selector icon on the Transcriber iconbar. If you recall from earlier in the chapter, the Letter Shape Selector allows you to specify exactly how you write individual letters and symbols, which can dramatically improve Transcriber's capability to recognize your handwriting.

REAL-WORLD EXAMPLE—DEVELOPING A HANDHELD WRITING STYLE

Not all of us are graced with exemplary penmanship, but that doesn't necessarily mean you can't use natural handwriting recognition to enter information on your Pocket PC just because you don't have great handwriting. The key to successfully using Transcriber for handwriting recognition is consistency. If you commit to using the Letter Shape Selector to isolate the manner in which you write letters and symbols, and then work on writing them consistently, you can get pretty efficient at writing text on your Pocket PC. Granted, it's not as free-form as jotting down information on paper, but you'll find that a consistent writing style can go a long way toward improving your handheld computing experience. I encourage you to take some time and experiment with Transcriber as the primary input method for your Pocket PC. See whether you can't develop a writing style that is both efficient and accurate.

NETWORKING YOUR POCKET PC

EVALUATING NETWORKING OPTIONS

In this chapter

THE BASICS OF POCKET PC NETWORKING

It was only a few short years ago that most people thought of personal computers as self-contained machines with no communication capabilities. Even though personal computers have always had some degree of networking capability, it has been only in the last five or so years that we've come to view personal computers as portals to a larger virtual world. Broad, affordable, reliable Internet access has given even the most casual computer user the ability to connect to the rest of the world electronically and share in the online experience. This connection of a computer (and its users) to the Internet has generally become known as being *wired*. We are all part of the wired generation.

Of course, the technology industry changes fast, and the term *wired* has already fallen out of favor to some degree. This is due to the fact that we are now in the midst of a wireless revolution that will eventually connect us all together without wires. Many of the pieces of the wireless Internet puzzle are already in place, with others rapidly being developed. We are only a few short years away from looking back at the term *wired* and wondering how we could have been dependent on such a primitive means of shooting bits at each other.

As you can no doubt guess, the computer connectivity evolution from nothing to wired to wireless impacts Pocket PCs considerably. Any mobile machine is limited by the degree to which it is dependent on fixed objects. Consider the earliest remote-control toys that graced toy store shelves a couple of decades ago. These toys included a wire that connected the remote control with the toy, which meant your control extended only as far as the wire. Eventually, radio-control toys would enter the picture and give kids the freedom to remotely control toys and vehicles without concern for wires.

Similar to remote-control toys, Pocket PCs are devices that are infinitely more useful if given the freedom to move around without any strings (wires) attached. Although some wired approaches to networking Pocket PCs are quite acceptable in some situations, such as synchronizing with a desktop PC, Pocket PCs simply beg to be networked wirelessly. Wireless networking options for Pocket PCs range from infrared connections between devices and other computers to dial-up connections involving mobile phones to wireless expansion packs into which you plug your device. It's important to have a clear understanding of all the options surrounding Pocket PC networking, both with wires and without.

Following are the four general networking options available to you when it comes to establishing a network connection for your Pocket PC:

- The cradle
- Local area networks (LANs)
- Wired modems
- Mobile phones and wireless modems

These networking options vary widely, with each having unique benefits and drawbacks. The next few sections dig more deeply into each networking option and illuminate some of the important considerations regarding the usefulness of each. Keep in mind that you will in all likelihood end up relying on a combination of networking approaches that use two or more of these options.

THE TRUSTY CRADLE CONNECTION

The simplest and most reliable of all network connections for your Pocket PC involves the cradle that came with your device. This cradle is a hardware device that serves to connect your device to your desktop PC using a USB or serial connection. In addition to providing a means of synchronizing data between your desktop PC and Pocket PC, the cradle also serves to provide a pass-through Internet connection, assuming that your desktop PC has Internet access. This is a significant feature because it means you can explore the Internet from your Pocket PC without any special hardware; just sit your device in the cradle and go!

Tip from *Michael*	The cradle is handy for synchronizing Web content with your device, even if you opt to not browse the Web directly via the pass-through Internet connection made possible by the cradle.

The type of connection used by the cradle determines the speed of the connection. A USB connection is considerably faster than a serial connection, with USB offering data transfer rates of 12Mbps, as opposed to the significantly slower 115Kbps of serial. When you consider that you'll be potentially transferring and synchronizing megabytes of files across this connection, along with using it as a pass-through Internet connection, the speed of your cradle connection is incredibly important. So, if your cradle gives you the option of USB or serial, be sure to use USB.

In the event that your device didn't come with a cradle, or maybe you need to synchronize with a notebook computer without a cradle, another connection option is available that simply involves using a USB or serial cable. Keep in mind that a cradle is really just a convenient way to establish a USB or serial connection between your Pocket PC and desktop PC, as well as a good way to charge your device's batteries. Knowing this, you can accomplish the same connectivity goal by connecting your Pocket PC with your desktop PC via a USB or serial cable.

One more interesting option for getting around the cradle is to use infrared to connect your Pocket PC to your desktop PC. Most notebook PCs these days include an infrared port that can be used to communicate with your Pocket PC. Additionally, you can purchase an infrared port adapter for your desktop PC that effectively turns a USB or serial port into an infrared port. With a suitable infrared port on your desktop or notebook PC, you can synchronize your Pocket PC without having to plug it into a cradle or use any cables. The net effect is a USB or serial connection, but you get to do so without a physical connection.

PART

II

CH

6

Note

> The XTNDAccess infrared adapter by Extended Systems enables you to turn a USB or serial port on a desktop computer into an infrared port that can communicate with your Pocket PC's infrared port. To find out more, visit the Extended Systems Web site at http://www.extendedsystems.com/.

LOCAL AREA NETWORKS

If you regularly use a local area network (LAN) of some sort, you might want to consider using it as the basis for providing network connectivity to your Pocket PC. Most LANs these days include Internet access, which means you can connect to a LAN and use it to get on the Internet. In regard to Pocket PCs, there are two fundamental approaches to accessing LANs: wired and wireless. *Wired* LAN access involves using a network card in your Pocket PC that connects the device to the LAN with a network cable. *Wireless* LAN access involves a network card or expansion sleeve that includes a wireless radio for communicating using a wireless networking standard, such as Wi-Fi (802.11b) or Bluetooth.

→ For more information on wired LAN cards available for use with Pocket PCs, **see** "Wired LAN Cards," **p. 484**.

 If your device is limited in terms of available expansion slots and you're worried about trading memory for a wireless network card, see "Wireless Networking Without a Free Expansion Slot" in the "Troubleshooting" section at the end of the chapter.

Although a wired network card certainly provides all the benefits of a LAN connection, and does so through high speeds, it is less than ideal because it doesn't give you much flexibility in terms of roaming around with your device. With wireless LANs becoming so prevalent, it makes much more sense to use a Wi-Fi or Bluetooth network card to establish a wireless connection to a LAN. Using this approach in a corporate environment, your device automatically connects to the LAN when you arrive at work, as long as you're within the range of the wireless network hub. For Wi-Fi, this distance is about 100 yards, whereas Bluetooth is more limited with a range of about only 30 feet.

Note

> If you'd like to add wireless capabilities to an existing LAN, you can do so with a wireless access point, which is also known as a *wireless base station*. The main role of this hardware is to provide a bridge between Ethernet and wireless. This hardware is relatively inexpensive and doesn't take up much space. If you want to wirelessly connect directly to a PC, as opposed to a LAN, then a wireless base station isn't necessary.

The main benefit of a wireless LAN connection is that it enables you to be more flexible with how you use your device. For example, you can carry your device from your desk into a board room and still send and receive e-mails. Or, if you're like me and work from a home office, you have the flexibility of surfing the Web while lounging on the patio with a martini. Okay, maybe that's just me, but you get the idea that wireless LANs are a good thing.

→ For more information on wireless LAN cards available for use with Pocket PCs, **see** "Wireless LAN Cards," **p. 484**.

The specific Pocket PC hardware used to connect to a wireless LAN currently comes in one of two types: an expansion card or an expansion sleeve. Actually, there is a third type because some Pocket PCs, such as Compaq's iPAQ H3870, come with built-in support for wireless network connectivity. In the case of the H3870, Bluetooth is used to provide wireless network access, but a few other manufacturers are readying Wi-Fi devices for release as well. Getting back to the expansion types, a wireless *expansion card* requires a CF or PC card slot. A wireless *expansion sleeve*, on the other hand, doesn't take up an expansion slot but must be used with a specific model of Pocket PC. The upside to the expansion sleeve approach is that it often provides you with an extra expansion slot, as with the Compaq Bluetooth expansion sleeve.

It's worth pointing out that Wi-Fi and Bluetooth aren't really competing technologies. Wi-Fi is designed as a true wireless networking standard, whereas Bluetooth is designed to accommodate wireless connections between individual devices. What this means is that I've been using the phrase *wireless LAN* kind of loosely in this section. If you want to establish a legitimate wireless LAN connection with your Pocket PC, you should use a Wi-Fi expansion card or sleeve. On the other hand, if you just want to establish a wireless connection with an individual desktop PC for synchronization or pass-through Internet access, Bluetooth will work fine.

→ For more information on Bluetooth network hardware available for use with Pocket PCs, **see** "Bluetooth Networking," **p. 484**.

 If your Pocket PC has built-in Bluetooth support and you can't figure out how to make it communicate wirelessly with your desktop PC, see "Using Bluetooth with a Desktop PC" in the "Troubleshooting" section at the end of the chapter.

WIRED MODEMS

Wired modems represent one of the oldest forms of networking known to computers. Even though technologies now exist that in some ways make wired modems look obsolete, the fact of the matter is that we have an extremely reliable telephone network that is well-suited for modem communication. Even if you use a more advanced form of wireless communication with your Pocket PC as your primary form of networking, a wired modem is not a bad backup to have for situations in which you need a simple no-frills, dial-up Internet connection. A wired modem connection is inexpensive and is also faster than some wireless options that you learn about a little later in the chapter; modems these days can communicate at speeds up to 56Kbps.

To establish a wired modem connection with your Pocket PC, you need a modem, phone line, and dial-up Internet service. The modem can be packaged as a wireless expansion card or as an external device with an infrared port. Either way, the modem is physically wired to the phone line using a phone cable. Your Pocket PC is then connected to the modem either by plugging the expansion card into the device or by establishing an infrared line-of-sight with the modem if it is an external modem. Keep in mind that regardless of what type of wired modem you use, you must have a dial-up Internet service.

PART

II

CH

6

→ For more information on wired modem cards available for Pocket PCs, **see** "Wired Modem Cards," **p. 482**.

MOBILE PHONES AND WIRELESS MODEMS

Whereas wired modems provide a means of connecting to a wired dial-up Internet service, mobile phones and wireless modems enable you to connect to a wireless dial-up Internet service. The difference between these two types of services is that one relies on a physical phone line, whereas the other relies on a wireless wide area network (WAN). This network can be one of several types, such as Cellular Digital Packet Data (CDPD), Global System for Mobile Communications (GSM), Code Division Multiple Access (CDMA), or Time Division Multiple Access (TDMA). It isn't important for you to understand the differences between these networks—just understand that they are all designed for wireless communication between mobile phones. For a Pocket PC to communicate over a wireless network designed for mobile phones, it must use a special wireless modem or directly take advantage of a modem built into a mobile phone.

Many newer digital mobile phones include built-in modems, which enables you to connect your Pocket PC to a mobile phone and then establish a wireless dial-up Internet connection. The connection between the Pocket PC and phone can involve a wire, or it can be wireless thanks to either infrared or Bluetooth. Regardless of how you connect your Pocket PC to a mobile phone, the important thing to remember about this approach to wireless networking is that your Pocket PC is relying on the mobile phone to provide access to a wireless network.

An even better option in terms of convenience is a wireless modem, which can come in the form of an expansion card or sleeve. A wireless modem basically consists of enough mobile phone hardware to enable you to establish a wireless dial-up Internet connection. In other words, wireless modems use the same networks as mobile phones, but they alleviate the need to have two discrete devices (Pocket PC and mobile phone). I really like the expansion sleeve option for wireless modems because you don't have to give up an expansion slot, which means you could feasibly still use a wireless LAN card in the slot. This provides the utmost in wireless flexibility because you can dial up the wireless Internet when you're away from a LAN and then automatically jump on a wireless LAN when you're in range.

→ For more information on wireless modem cards available for use with Pocket PCs, **see** "Wireless Modem Cards," **p. 482**.

The current drawback to mobile phone and wireless modem networking is that they aren't very fast. The network speed is determined by the type of network used, which is determined by the service provider you use. Following are two of the major types of wireless WANs in use today:

- General Packet Radio Service (GPRS)
- Cellular Digital Packet Data (CDPD)

The next couple of sections take a closer look at these wireless WANs to understand the speed limitations of each, along with the basics of how they work.

GENERAL PACKET RADIO SERVICE

General Packet Radio Service is a wireless mobile phone network that is currently in use in North America, Europe, Asia, and Australia. GPRS is based on GSM and uses TCP/IP to send and receive data as packets of information over a continuous network connection. GSM is widely used throughout Europe, Asia, and Australia and is gaining in popularity in North America. Because of the relationship between GPRS and GSM, you sometimes see GPRS referred to as GSM/GPRS. GPRS currently offers speeds up to 28Kbps, but there are plans to increase its capabilities up to 171Kbps in the very near future. AT&T is the primary provider of GPRS service in North America.

Note

Even though GPRS is currently theoretically capable of speeds up to 28Kbps, realistic throughput is closer to 20Kbps.

CELLULAR DIGITAL PACKET DATA

Cellular Digital Packet Data is a wireless network standard used only in North America. Similar to GPRS, CDPD uses TCP/IP as the basis for its network. The speed of a CDPD connection is dependent on the number of users on the system and the signal strength of the connection. The maximum speed that is possible with CDPD is 19Kbps, which is one-fourth the speed of a wired modem. Popular providers of the CDPD service include GoAmerica and OmniSky; you can also get CDPD access through some mobile phone companies.

Note

Even though 19Kbps is technically the maximum speed for CDPD networks, realistic throughput is unfortunately much lower, in the range of 3Kbps.

FINDING A WIRELESS INTERNET SERVICE PROVIDER

Now that you have an understanding of the various options available when it comes to networking your Pocket PC, I'd like to take a moment to focus on wireless networking. More specifically, you might be in the process of trying to decide how to proceed in terms of establishing a wireless Internet service. A critical part of this process is the selection of a wireless Internet service provider (ISP). Although my goal isn't to endorse specific providers, I want to give you some ground rules to use when trying to determine the best wireless ISP for your particular needs.

Keep in mind that many options are available in terms of wireless ISPs. It might at first appear to be difficult deciding how to distinguish between them, but you might already have needs that help you narrow down the field. If not, then I'll help you with some criteria you can use to make the selection a little easier. Following are the four main considerations you should make when comparing wireless ISPs:

PART

II

CH

6

- Accessibility
- Cost
- Performance
- Compatibility

The next few sections explore each of these considerations in more detail. As long as you carefully weigh the importance of each consideration and factor in your own needs and resources, you should be able to make an informed choice of a wireless ISP. This up-front work will not only help save you money in network charges, but it might also avoid you signing on with a service that isn't compatible with your hardware.

ACCESSIBILITY

Accessibility is probably the most significant consideration to make when comparing wireless ISPs. Similar to a mobile phone, your ability to connect to the Internet with your Pocket PC is entirely dependent on the coverage area of the ISP's wireless network. If you live on the outskirts of town, or if you regularly travel off the beaten path, accessibility becomes even more important. You might opt to choose an ISP that is a little more expensive if it means having better accessibility to its network. On the other hand, if you're a casual user who doesn't necessarily need wireless Internet access everywhere you go, you might opt to put other considerations—such as cost—ahead of accessibility.

Although this might not be an option for everyone, I encourage you to try testing a wireless ISP's coverage area if possible. If you have a friend who is using a certain provider, borrow her mobile phone or Pocket PC and see whether you get good coverage near your home and office. As an example of how this can be a problem, my mom's mobile phone worked great everywhere except inside her house. This meant that her connection would get dropped if she started a conversation away from home and then continued it into her house. She eventually tested a different provider whose service worked fine both around and inside her house, and she made the switch. The point is that you should try to test the range of a wireless ISP if at all possible.

Tip from	A good place to start when assessing the coverage of a wireless ISP is the ISP's Web
Michael	site, which typically has a map showing areas of coverage. Although coverage maps are useful for determining general coverage, it's still a good idea to perform a realistic coverage test if possible.

COST

Depending on how you use your device and whether you can claim a wireless Internet service as a business expense, the cost of wireless service might or might not be a critical factor in determining a suitable wireless ISP. However, it's worth making the point that wireless Internet services can be expensive, so you should definitely shop around. Each provider will likely have different pricing plans based on usage, so you should carefully consider how much time you plan on staying connected. Do you plan on using the service primarily to send and receive e-mail, or do you plan on doing a lot of online Web browsing? If the latter is the case, you probably should spring for an unlimited plan or a plan without too many limitations.

Whereas mobile phone services typically charge you by the minute for talk time, or *airtime*, wireless data providers typically charge by the amount of data exchanged. So, you must think in terms of how many kilobytes (KB) of data you plan on transferring, which is admittedly a difficult thing to pinpoint. Some wireless ISPs also charge differently based on the connection speed, with faster speeds costing more money. Again, it's entirely up to your specific needs as to what you're willing to pay for. One other thing to consider is whether the ISP charges extra for roaming; this can get very expensive if you travel out of its network coverage area frequently.

Caution

Believe it or not, some wireless ISPs charge for both airtime and data exchanged, which can be quite costly. Certainly, other factors should be considered when deciding on a wireless ISP, but I would generally try to avoid providers who charge for both airtime and data exchanged.

PERFORMANCE

Performance is a key factor in any computer networking situation because it directly determines how quickly you can access information. In the case of wireless network service for Pocket PCs, most wireless services are considerably slower than their wired counterparts, so even the fastest service is still slow by most network standards. However, the difference between 19Kbps and 28Kbps is significant, so be sure to get the fastest connection you can afford. The connection speed is determined by the type of network being used, which will likely be GPRS or CDPD; you learned about these two networks earlier in the chapter. Other types of networks are available, but these two are the most common when it comes to Pocket PC wireless services.

COMPATIBILITY

The last consideration to make with respect to selecting a wireless ISP for your Pocket PC is compatibility. This basically boils down to ensuring an ISP is compatible with your hardware setup. If your device came bundled with a GPRS expansion sleeve, you'll need to find an ISP that uses the GPRS network. Similarly, if your device has integrated CDPD support, you'll need to use a CDPD network. If you win a wireless expansion sleeve in a giveaway and it is compatible only with some obscure network then you should find an obscure ISP to provide you with service. The main point I'm trying to make here is that you need to coordinate your hardware purchase with the ISP you choose. This means you should ideally do some ISP investigation before purchasing any wireless hardware.

PART

II

CH

6

Assuming that you have the option of purchasing hardware after selecting an ISP, it's important to ensure that you purchase hardware that works with your device. For example, a wireless PC card won't help you much if your Pocket PC has only a CF slot. Conversely, neither a CF nor a PC card will help if you have only an SD memory slot. Of course, most devices that have only an SD slot also offer expansion sleeves that include CF or PC slots. Just be sure to factor the cost of such an expansion sleeve into your wireless budget.

Caution

Don't forget that the type of slot used by an expansion card can also impact how much of a drain the card puts on your device's battery. More specifically, PC cards tend to require considerably more power than CF cards.

USING A MOBILE PHONE FOR WIRELESS INTERNET ACCESS

Earlier in the chapter, I explained how mobile phones provide a means of establishing a wireless connection between your Pocket PC and the Internet. Because this is such a viable wireless connectivity option for so many people, I thought it would be helpful to explore it further. More specifically, I want to shed more light on the specifics of how you use a mobile phone to provide wireless Internet access to your Pocket PC. You might already have a mobile phone that is suitable for this type of connectivity, in which case you might not need any additional hardware to get connected to the wireless Internet.

The first determination to make in regard to how you can use your mobile phone for wireless Internet connectivity is whether your phone has a built-in modem. You can probably find this out from the documentation that came with your phone, from the manufacturer's Web site, or by calling your mobile phone service provider and asking them. If your phone has a built-in modem then you have more options, but if it doesn't then you're still okay.

For phones that don't have built-in modems, the only way to establish a wireless Internet connection is with the help of a modem expansion card—also known as a *digital phone card*—that plugs into your Pocket PC. This modem card fills the role of the missing modem in your phone. More specifically, it handles the details of converting data transmission from your Pocket PC into a form that can be sent and received over a wireless phone network. Several digital phone cards are available for use with Pocket PCs.

→ For more information on specific digital phone cards available for use with Pocket PCs, **see** "Digital Phone Cards," **p. 483**.

If your mobile phone already has a modem built into it, you might have more options at your disposal. More specifically, the phone probably also has an infrared port, in which case you can use a wireless infrared connection to get on the Internet. If you have a really fancy phone, it might have built-in Bluetooth support, which means you can use Bluetooth to communicate with the phone wirelessly and establish an Internet connection.

To recap, following are the options for connecting a Pocket PC to the wireless Internet via a mobile phone:

- Modem card
- Infrared port
- Bluetooth

The next few sections examine each of these mobile phone networking approaches in more detail.

Connecting with a Modem Card

Connecting your Pocket PC to the wireless Internet via a modem card (digital phone card) involves inserting the modem card into your device and then connecting your device to a mobile phone via a special cable. This cable is usually a serial cable of some type, and it plugs into a jack on the modem card, as well as a port on the mobile phone. These cables are typically designed for specific model phones, so be sure to get the appropriate cable for your phone. Figure 6.1 shows how a Pocket PC is connected to a mobile phone in this scenario.

Figure 6.1
Connecting a Pocket PC to the wireless Internet via a modem card and mobile phone requires a cable to connect the Pocket PC to the mobile phone.

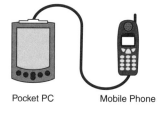

Pocket PC   Mobile Phone

Note

If your mobile phone has a built-in modem but you don't want to use infrared to connect it with your Pocket PC, you can use a modem card as a basis for establishing a connection between the devices. In this case, the modem card serves only as a means for connecting the two devices with a cable—the modem built into the phone overrides the modem on the card.

Modem cards are usually CF cards, which makes them available to the widest range of Pocket PCs. Keep in mind that you must select a modem card that is compatible with the mobile phone network used by your phone. More specifically, this means purchasing a modem card that is compatible with GPRS, CDPD, or whatever wireless network your phone uses.

Taking Advantage of the Infrared Port

All Pocket PCs are required to have infrared ports, which enable them to communicate with other devices via an invisible beam of light. Although infrared communication with Pocket

PCs is typically thought of in terms of beaming contact information between Pocket PCs, it also comes into play with mobile communications. More specifically, if your mobile phone has a built-in modem and an infrared port, you can line up the ports on the phone and your Pocket PC and establish a wireless Internet connection. Figure 6.2 shows how a Pocket PC and mobile phone are physically connected in this networking scenario.

→ To find out how to beam contact information using the infrared port on your Pocket PC, **see** "Beaming Contacts via Infrared," **p. 245**.

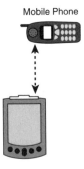

Mobile Phone

Figure 6.2
Connecting a Pocket PC to the wireless Internet via the infrared port on a mobile phone requires a line-of-sight between the infrared ports on the two devices.

Pocket PC

Note

Infrared communications on a Pocket PC is sometimes referred to as *IrDA*, which stands for Infrared Data Association. IrDA is a standard to which infrared hardware must adhere to be compatible. Virtually all computer infrared ports adhere to the IrDA standard.

The primary benefit of the infrared approach to connecting your Pocket PC to the wireless Internet is that it doesn't require any additional hardware, assuming your mobile phone has a built-in modem and an infrared port. On the other hand, the obvious drawback is that infrared communication requires a line-of-sight between the ports with a distance of no more than about a foot. This might not pose a problem if you're working with your device on a flat surface, but in a cramped space keeping the ports aligned can be difficult.

EXPLORING THE BLUETOOTH SOLUTION

The newest and most interesting approach to bridging the communication between a Pocket PC and mobile phone is Bluetooth, which is the long-awaited wireless technology that will hopefully replace the rat's nest of wires in my office. Although Bluetooth has larger aspirations than simply providing a good way to connect Pocket PCs with mobile phones, this particular application is useful as a means of establishing Bluetooth as a wireless standard. To take advantage of Bluetooth, both your Pocket PC and your mobile phone need Bluetooth capabilities. Assuming this is the case, you can maintain a Bluetooth connection between a Pocket PC and mobile phone with a range in the neighborhood of 30 feet. Figure 6.3 shows how a Pocket PC communicates with a mobile phone using Bluetooth.

Figure 6.3
Connecting a Pocket PC to the wireless Internet via Bluetooth and a mobile phone requires only that the Pocket PC and mobile phone be within about 30 feet of each other.

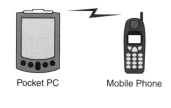

Pocket PC   Mobile Phone

One thing to keep in mind about Bluetooth is that it is a wireless radio technology, which means it doesn't require any kind of visual line-of-sight. This makes Bluetooth considerably more appealing than the infrared approach you learned about in the previous section. Of course, you must have Bluetooth support in both your Pocket PC and your mobile phone for it to be an option. Pocket PCs are already available that include built-in support, and you can add Bluetooth capabilities through expansion cards and sleeves. In addition, several mobile phones are available with Bluetooth support, and even some Bluetooth modules are available that you can add to existing phones. It is expected that Bluetooth will eventually replace infrared in mobile phones, but only time will tell.

Note

The Bluetooth technology is named after the Viking king Harald Bluetooth, who lived in Denmark between 910 and 940 AD. King Bluetooth is known for having united Denmark and Norway during his reign. I'm not exactly sure how this relates to wireless communications, but at least you now know from where the name originates.

TROUBLESHOOTING

WIRELESS NETWORKING WITHOUT A FREE EXPANSION SLOT

I'd love to connect my device to the Internet through a wireless network connection, but I'm already using a memory storage card in my device's only free expansion slot.

If you own a Pocket PC that is compatible with a wireless expansion sleeve, you can purchase an expansion sleeve to acquire wireless networking capabilities. The wireless network hardware is built into the expansion sleeve, which leaves your expansion port free for other accessories, such as memory. Additionally, some expansion sleeves include extra expansion ports, which make the sleeve an even sweeter option.

If, however, your device isn't compatible with any wireless expansion sleeve options then you have some hard decision making to do. You basically must decide what's more important to you: memory or wireless connectivity. And if you simply can't choose between the two, you might consider alternating between them. This involves using the memory storage card for storing information that you don't need while you're online. Then, you can remove the memory card and replace it with the wireless network card to get online. If you need access to the information on the storage card, just swap the cards again.

USING BLUETOOTH WITH A DESKTOP PC

I have a Pocket PC with built-in Bluetooth support, and I can't figure out how to make it communicate with my desktop PC.

To communicate with a desktop PC using Bluetooth, the PC must have Bluetooth capabilities. More specifically, you need to purchase a Bluetooth adapter for your desktop PC. The simplest solution is to purchase a USB Bluetooth adapter that plugs into a USB port on your desktop PC. Several companies manufacture such adapters, and they aren't very expensive. With a Bluetooth adapter connected to your desktop PC, you can communicate with your Pocket PC wirelessly via Bluetooth.

Although I'm not aware of any desktop PCs with Bluetooth integration, several manufacturers are offering notebook PCs with integrated Bluetooth support. So, you might opt to purchase a notebook PC that already has Bluetooth capabilities, in which case you can connect it to your Pocket PC without any special adapters.

REAL-WORLD EXAMPLE—COMING UP WITH A WIRELESS GAME PLAN

To get the most out of wireless networking with your Pocket PC, I encourage you to come up with a wireless game plan. Don't worry, I'm not suggesting you write down a long, tedious description of your wireless networking needs; I'm just suggesting that you take a moment to consider exactly how you plan on using your device in a wireless environment. What do you already find the most beneficial about using your Pocket PC? Now consider how wireless connectivity might add to that usefulness. More importantly, think about what types of wireless solutions would benefit you the most.

The goal of this wireless game plan is to determine the wireless products and services that best suit your needs. As an example, I don't travel a whole lot, so a wireless LAN connection suits my needs 90% of the time. For this reason, my best solution is a Wi-Fi or Bluetooth card or expansion sleeve. If I decide to worry about the other 10% of my time, I might consider a wireless modem card. It's important to realize that each of these individual decisions impacts the other. If I go with Bluetooth for the wireless LAN connection, it probably makes more sense to get a Bluetooth-compatible mobile phone for network access when I'm away from the LAN. On the other hand, I already have a Wi-Fi network in place, so it might make more sense to stick with Wi-Fi for the LAN connection and then rely on a modem card for network access away from the LAN.

Hopefully, my sample scenario can help you to do some thinking about your own wireless network needs. All I ask is that you spend some time thinking about it before committing to any products or services.

CHAPTER 7

WORKING WITH NETWORK CONNECTIONS

In this chapter

GETTING TO KNOW CONNECTION MANAGER

You learned in the previous chapter that a variety of options are available to you when it comes to networking your Pocket PC. These options range from traditional wired network solutions, such as dial-up modems and Ethernet expansion cards, to completely wireless solutions, such as mobile phone connectivity and wireless modem expansion packs. Although it might seem complicated figuring out which type of network connection is appropriate for a given situation, the Pocket PC operating system takes most of the decision making out of your hands, which is a good thing. This is made possible by Connection Manager, which is a fundamental part of the Pocket PC 2002 operating system.

Connection Manager is a part of the Pocket PC control that serves as a central location for managing network connections. Connection Manager enables you to set up a variety of network connections, which are then automatically invoked when needed based on the context of a particular application. More specifically, Connection Manager is smart enough to decide which type of connection is most appropriate for a given task. This decision-making process has a lot to do with where you are located—home or work. The reason for this is because networks in a work environment typically require different login procedures from your home environment. Your home "network" might consist of no more than a cradle connection for your device, whereas your work connection might have more complex security requirements.

Although the benefits of tying network connection details to a location are relatively obvious, the secondary benefits of Connection Manager have to do with its integration into Pocket PC applications. More specifically, you don't have to specify connection details to any of the networked Pocket PC applications, such as Inbox or Pocket Internet Explorer. Every standard Pocket PC application with network support derives its connection from Connection Manager, which makes Pocket PC networks extremely straightforward.

Connection Manager divides your networking needs into two distinct groupings: Internet and Work. The idea here is to make a distinction between a direct Internet connection, such as a dial-up modem connection, and a corporate network connection that might require a proxy server. Technically speaking, the distinguishing factor between these two network options is that the Internet option presumes you're accessing a public network, whereas the Work option presumes a private corporate network. The accessibility of a network is therefore the fundamental consideration that determines whether your device uses the Internet or Work connection type. After you establish how a network connection is to be made through these two approaches (Internet and Work), the rest is handled automatically by Connection Manager.

To help put this Connection Manager stuff into perspective, let's consider a practical scenario. You set up the Internet networking option to use a dial-up modem connection that dials up your Internet service provider (ISP) and logs you in with a user ID and password.

You then set up the Work networking option to use a Wi-Fi wireless LAN card and to connect with a LAN at your workplace by logging you in to the network with a username and password, using the appropriate proxy. If you attempt to access a corporate intranet from a dial-up connection while traveling, Connection Manager knows to automatically establish a virtual private network (VPN) connection because you must access the intranet securely through a remote connection. On the other hand, if you connect with your wireless LAN card in the office, you get a direct connection to the network. The point is that Connection Manager factors in the type of network connection when determining the specifics of how to access a network.

The capability of Connection Manager to intelligently determine your networking needs is very important. The sheer number of networking options available to Pocket PCs makes them more complex than desktop PCs in terms of connectivity. The Pocket PC operating system could have easily included a complicated network control panel that forces you to manually switch between different types of networks. Connection Manager provides an elegant solution to a tricky problem.

CREATING CONNECTIONS WITH CONNECTION MANAGER

You're no doubt itching to get started with Connection Manager, so let's jump right in. To use Connection Manager, tap Settings on the Start menu, select the Connections tab, and finally tap the Connections icon. This opens the Connections screen, which is shown in Figure 7.1.

Figure 7.1
The Connections screen is home to the Pocket PC Connection Manager, which allows you to control and manage different kinds of network connections.

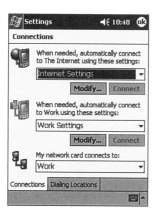

The Connections screen is your starting point for configuring network connections of all types. Before getting into specific connections, however, it's important to set a few general parameters related to your phone line. Tap the Dialing Locations tab to access settings related to the dialing properties of your phone lines (see Figure 7.2).

PART

II

CH

7

Figure 7.2
The Dialing Locations tab of the Connections screen provides access to the dialing properties of your phone lines.

The Dialing Locations tab is important because it enables you to specify important properties about any phone lines you might use to access a network through a dial-up connection. Even if you don't currently plan on using a dial-up connection, it's not a bad idea to go ahead and provide this information. Near the top of the screen, the location defaults to Work, which means you are setting dialing properties for your work phone line. You need to enter your work area code and country code, along with whether the phone line uses tone dialing (most do). You should also specify how to disable call waiting, if it exists. Finally, if your work phone line requires any special prefixes to access an outside line or make a long-distance call, tap the Dialing Patterns button and enter them (see Figure 7.3).

Figure 7.3
The Dialing Patterns screen prompts you to enter any special dialing prefixes for a phone line, such as the prefix used to access an outside line in an office environment.

When you're finished setting up your work phone line, tap the Location drop-down list and select Home. Next, repeat the same process to set up your home phone. Again, this might not seem necessary if you don't plan to dial up a network from home, but it takes only a second and will help to make things smoother if you ever decide to use a dial-up connection. When you're finished with the Dialing Locations settings, tap the Connections tab to return to the main Connection Manager screen.

With the dialing properties set up, you're now ready to set up some real network connections. Four fundamental types of network connections can be used with a Pocket PC, at least in terms of how they are configured in Connection Manager:

- Pass-through connections
- Dial-up modem connections
- LAN connections
- Mobile phone and wireless modem connections

These types of connections are important because you must configure each of them a little differently. Fortunately, Connection Manager enables you to have multiple connections configured simultaneously, which is convenient if you tend to access several different networks using different approaches. The next few sections explore each of these connection approaches and describe exactly how to establish connections with each one.

USING ACTIVESYNC FOR PASS-THROUGH CONNECTIONS

The simplest network connection you can make is a *pass-through* connection that relies on ActiveSync and your device's cradle to get you on the Internet. When connecting to the Internet in this manner, your device is effectively using your desktop PC as a proxy, even though you don't really have to set it up as one. The key to establishing a successful pass-through connection is making sure your device knows to use the proper location for the connection. More specifically, this means you must properly identify the location of the network card setting in the Connections screen, which is the last setting on the screen. Follow these steps to make the appropriate change in Connection Manager:

1. Tap Settings on the Start menu, and then tap the Connections tab.
2. Tap the Connections icon, and then tap the Connections tab.
3. Select the appropriate setting in the last setting, My Network Card Connects to (see Figure 7.4).
4. Tap OK to finish configuring the connection.

Figure 7.4
Setting up a pass-through connection on your Pocket PC simply involves selecting the appropriate setting (The Internet) for the device's network card.

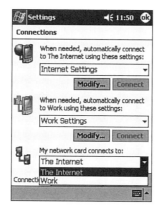

> **Note**
>
> Your Pocket PC might work fine with a pass-through connection out of the box with no changes, but it's still a good idea to ensure it is set the way you plan on using it. For example, my device worked fine initially with the default Work settings, but it would have run into problems when I changed the Work settings because I actually use the cradle on my home computer.

When changing this setting, keep in mind that Work corresponds to a cradle on a work computer, whereas The Internet corresponds to a cradle on a home computer. This takes care of the Pocket PC side of the pass-through configuration, but you need to make another change in ActiveSync on your desktop PC. Follow these steps to get ActiveSync ready for the pass-through connection:

1. Launch ActiveSync on your desktop PC, and then click the Options button.

2. Click the Rules tab to display Rules options for ActiveSync.

3. Change the Pass-Through Connection setting near the bottom of the screen to reflect your connection location; select Work for a work computer or The Internet for a home computer (see Figure 7.5).

4. Click OK to accept the settings.

Figure 7.5
The desktop PC side of the pass-through connection must be tweaked in ActiveSync to match your Pocket PC settings.

Caution

> You can't access a secure corporate network using a pass-through connection. This is because pass-through connections currently don't support VPN, file sharing, or terminal services. If you need access to a corporate network using any of these features, you must establish a legitimate LAN connection with your Pocket PC.

ACCESSING A DIAL-UP ISP

Dial-up modem connections are a good option if you want to be able to get on the Internet from virtually anywhere. This has to do with the fact that land lines are available just about anywhere, although wireless coverage for network access isn't as far-reaching. The hardware specifics of a dial-up connection can vary widely depending on whether you use a modem card or a mobile phone to establish the connection. Fortunately, Connection Manager doesn't really care about the hardware specifics—all it knows is that the hardware must somehow use a phone line to dial out and establish a connection with an ISP.

Even though Connection Manager doesn't get into the specifics of dial-up networking hardware, it does care about the type of network you're accessing. More specifically, it makes a difference whether you're connecting to the Internet via an ISP or to a corporate network via Remote Access Server (RAS). An ISP connection is less stringent and doesn't involve the extra layers of security required of a RAS connection. For this reason, you must set up a dial-up connection differently depending on which type of network you're using.

Note

> Be sure to plug your modem into your Pocket PC before setting up a modem connection. If your modem came with an installation CD-ROM, be sure to use it to install any necessary drivers.

To set up a dial-up ISP connection using Connection Manager, connect the modem to your device and then follow these steps:

1. Tap Settings on the Start menu, and then tap the Connections tab.
2. Tap the Connections icon, and then tap the Connections tab.
3. Select Internet Settings in the first drop-down list, which determines how you connect to the Internet.
4. Tap the Modify button, and then tap New in the connection list to create a new connection (see Figure 7.6).
5. Enter a name for the ISP connection, and then select a modem from the list (see Figure 7.7).

PART

II

CH

7

Figure 7.6
The Internet Settings screen enables you to manage and create connections for use in connecting to the Internet.

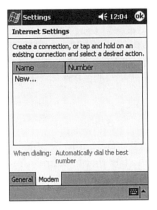

Figure 7.7
The Make New Connection screen enables you to enter information about a new ISP connection, including its name and the modem used to access it.

6. Select the baud rate for the connection, which is typically the maximum speed of your modem.

7. If your ISP requires advanced settings such as special port preferences, a specific IP address, or specific name server addresses, tap the Advanced button and enter them; leave these settings alone if you're unsure.

8. Tap the Next button.

9. Enter the country code, area code, and access phone number of the ISP (see Figure 7.8). Then, tap the Next button.

10. The default settings on the last screen of the connection setup are okay, so tap Finish to finish setting up the connection (see Figure 7.9).

Figure 7.8
The access phone number is required so that the connection knows what number to dial.

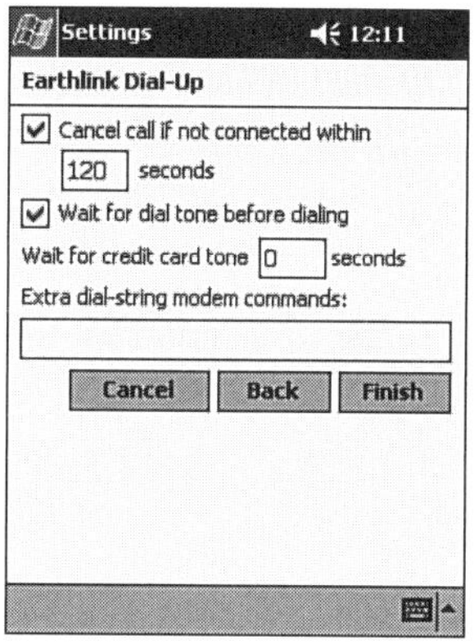

Figure 7.9
The default settings in the last step in the ISP connection setup are sufficient for the vast majority of connections.

11. Tap OK in the Internet Settings screen to return to the Connections screen.

12. Select The Internet in the last setting, My Network Card Connects to.

13. Tap OK to finish configuring the connection.

Tip from
Michael

> Even if your ISP's access number is a local number, enter the area code when setting up the connection so that the Pocket PC dialer will know whether the call is a local or long-distance call. This is important because you can set up multiple locations from which you establish a modem connection, and these locations can have different area codes.

The dial-up connection is now properly configured and ready to roll. To establish a connection, make sure your modem is connected to a phone line and then launch Pocket Internet Explorer. The first time you make a connection, you must enter the usual account information (password and username) for your dial-up ISP account. To avoid having to enter your password every time you connect to the service, check the Save Password check box.

Although security is certainly an issue, your dial-up password is probably not as sensitive as other information that you'd like to protect. Besides, you can always password-protect the device itself, in which case no one will be able to get into your Pocket PC to use your dial-up account.

 If you have trouble establishing a dial-up connection with your ISP, see "Dial-Up Connection Problems" in the "Troubleshooting" section at the end of the chapter.

→ To find out how to password-protect your Pocket PC, **see** "Password-Protecting Your Pocket PC," **p. 62**.

REMOTE NETWORKING WITH REMOTE ACCESS SERVER

Connecting to a network via a dial-up Remote Access Server connection is similar in many ways to a normal dial-up ISP connection, except that RAS connections are a little more stringent in terms of access. From the perspective of your Pocket PC, the differences are very subtle. To set up a dial-up RAS connection, follow these steps:

1. Tap Settings on the Start menu, and then tap the Connections tab.

2. Tap the Connections icon, and then tap the Connections tab.

3. Select Work Settings in the second drop-down list, which determines how you connect to work.

4. Tap the Modify button, and then tap New in the connection list to create a new connection (see Figure 7.10).

Figure 7.10
The Work Settings screen enables you to manage and create connections for use in connecting to work.

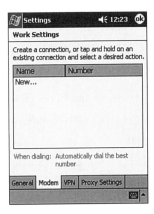

5. Enter a name for the RAS connection, and then select a modem from the list (see Figure 7.11).

6. Select the baud rate for the connection, which is typically the maximum speed of your modem.

7. If your RAS server requires advanced settings, tap the Advanced button and enter them.

8. Tap the Next button.

Figure 7.11
The Make New
Connection screen
enables you to enter
information about a
new RAS connection.

9. Enter the country code, area code, and access phone number of the RAS server, and then tap the Next button.

10. The default settings on the last screen of the connection setup are okay, so tap Finish to finish setting up the connection.

11. Tap OK in the Work Settings screen to return to the Connections screen.

12. Select Work in the last setting, My Network Card Connects to.

13. Tap OK to finish configuring the connection.

You now have a RAS dial-up connection that is set up and ready to be connected.

CONNECTING TO PUBLIC LANs

Unlike a dial-up modem connection, which is temporary because of its dependence on a phone call, a LAN connection is more instantaneous because no dialing is required. If you're using a wired LAN card, your device basically has a dedicated network connection for the duration of time that it's plugged into the network. For wireless LAN connections, the connection is maintained as long as your Pocket PC is in range of a wireless signal. Regardless of whether it is wired or wireless, a LAN connection is typically much faster than a traditional dial-up network connection.

Whether a LAN connection uses a wired or wireless approach, the underlying technology is a familiar Ethernet connection. *Ethernet* networking offers significant benefits because it is so much faster than most other Pocket PC networking options. Ethernet blows away all dial-up networking options and is considerably faster than USB or serial connections through the cradle. If you want the fastest connection possible for your Pocket PC, Ethernet is the way to go.

In terms of setup and configuration, Ethernet LAN connections can be divided into two types: public LAN connections and corporate LAN connections. *Public* LAN connections correspond to a whole new breed of network that is now popping up in unlikely places. For example, Starbucks is now offering wireless Internet access through public LANs in many of its stores. Also, many college campuses offer public LAN access for similar purposes.

PART

II

CH

7

Corporate LANs consist primarily of private networks associated with businesses that allow remote network access to employees. Some hotels offer a combination of the two types of LANs through the LodgeNet service, which provides access to corporate LANs over the Internet.

Note

Be sure to properly install your Ethernet hardware on your Pocket PC before setting up a LAN connection. If the hardware came with an installation CD-ROM, be sure to use it to install any necessary drivers.

Connecting to a public LAN with your Pocket PC is incredibly simple. Just make sure you've properly installed the appropriate Ethernet hardware for your Pocket PC, and then follow these steps:

1. Tap Settings on the Start menu, and then tap the Connections tab.
2. Tap the Connections icon, and then tap the Connections tab.
3. Select Internet Settings in the first drop-down list, which determines how you connect to the Internet.
4. Select The Internet in the last setting, My Network Card Connects to.
5. Tap OK to finish configuring the connection.

These settings reveal how automatic Pocket PC networking truly is. You basically just let your device know that you're connecting to the Internet, and it's smart enough to determine that it can use Ethernet hardware to establish the connection.

CONNECTING TO CORPORATE LANS

Connecting to a corporate LAN is similar to connecting to a public LAN, except that you have to take into account the fact that corporate LANs often use proxy servers to provide Internet access. Following are the steps required to configure a corporate LAN connection:

1. Tap Settings on the Start menu, and then tap the Connections tab.
2. Tap the Connections icon, and then tap the Connections tab.
3. Select Work Settings in the second drop-down list, which determines how you connect to work.
4. Tap the Modify button.
5. Tap the Proxy Settings tab, and enter appropriate proxy information for the network (see Figure 7.12). Tap the Advanced button if you need to enter advanced information about the proxy server.
6. Tap OK to return to the Connections screen.
7. Select Work in the last setting, My Network Card Connects to.
8. Tap OK to finish configuring the connection.

Caution

If your corporate LAN requires a virtual private network connection, skip ahead to the section titled "Pocket PCs and Virtual Private Networks," later in the chapter.

Figure 7.12
The Proxy Settings tab in the Work Settings enables you to specify details about a proxy server, if necessary.

The corporate LAN connection is now set up and ready for action.

 If you have trouble connecting your device to a LAN, see "LAN Connection Problems" in the "Troubleshooting" section at the end of the chapter.

MOBILE PHONE AND WIRELESS MODEM CONNECTIONS

Although not nearly as speedy as Ethernet LAN connections, mobile phone and wireless modem connections can't be beat when it comes to flexibility. It's hard to argue the benefits of a network connection that can be made while lounging on the beach away from civilization. Granted, you must be within the coverage area of a mobile phone network, but beyond that, no limitations exist on how you access a mobile phone network with your Pocket PC. Of course, the limited bandwidth of wireless modem connections is certainly a limitation, but the benefit is flexibility in accessing a network.

Before you configure a connection for a mobile phone or wireless modem, be sure to install any hardware required for the connection, along with any drivers that accompanied the hardware. Of course, if you're using an infrared connection with a mobile phone, no additional hardware is involved. On the other hand, a wireless expansion card or sleeve might require special drivers, which you should install before attempting to set up a connection. After you've gotten the hardware squared away, follow these simple steps to configure a connection on your Pocket PC:

1. Tap Settings on the Start menu, and then tap the Connections tab.
2. Tap the Connections icon, and then tap the Connections tab.
3. Select Internet Settings in the first drop-down list, which determines how you connect to the Internet.
4. Select The Internet in the last setting, My Network Card Connects to.
5. Tap OK to finish configuring the connection.

If you've been really paying attention, you might recognize these settings as the exact same settings used to configure a public LAN connection earlier in the chapter. How can it possibly be that the same settings apply to such radically different types of connections? Keep in mind that earlier I mentioned how Connection Manager handles the details of determining how to establish a connection given the basic connection settings you put in place. In this case, you're letting the hardware speak for itself; Connection Manager automatically uses the hardware that makes the most sense for a particular type of connection, which in this case is a mobile phone or wireless modem.

STAYING MOBILE WITH CONNECTION MANAGER

The whole idea behind Connection Manager is to make network access seamless across the entire spectrum of connection possibilities made available to Pocket PCs. Even though you've now learned how to configure network connections for work and home, you haven't fully explored the flexibility made possible by Connection Manager. For example, if you travel considerably, you might find yourself having to constantly tweak certain settings in Connection Manager to account for dialing out of different locations, or maybe even accessing different corporate networks.

To make your connected life even easier, Connection Manager enables you to create new dialing locations for dial-up connections. Taking things a step further, you can even create entirely new connections to go along with the standard Work Settings and Internet Settings connections.

ADDING NEW DIALING LOCATIONS

A dialing location specifies phone line properties that are associated with a particular location such as home; work; or maybe even a particular chain of hotels, such as Hilton. Hopefully, you aren't so much of a road warrior that you need a dialing location for a hotel chain, but if you are, Connection Manager is here to help. Follow these steps to create a new dialing location, which can then be used with a dial-up connection:

1. Tap Settings on the Start menu, and then tap the Connections tab.
2. Tap the Connections icon, and then tap the Dialing Locations tab.
3. Tap the New button to create a new location (see Figure 7.13).
4. Enter the phone line information for the new dialing location.
5. Tap OK to finish.

Keep in mind that the dialing location is selected in the Dialing Locations tab of Connection Manager. So, after creating a new dialing location, make sure it is the one selected in the Location drop-down list in the Dialing Locations tab; this should take place automatically when you create a new dialing location. To switch between dialing locations, just return to the Dialing Locations tab and select a different location.

Figure 7.13
Creating a new dialing location first requires you to enter a name for it.

ADDING NEW CONNECTIONS

If you find yourself connecting to different networks that require different configurations, you should consider creating an entirely new connection. This is advantageous only if you constantly have to change the settings for the standard Work and Internet connections. If you think this is necessary, you can easily create a new connection in Connection Manager by following these steps:

1. Tap Settings on the Start menu, and then tap the Connections tab.
2. Tap the Connections icon, and then tap the Connections tab.
3. Tap the Modify button for the appropriate type of connection you'd like to create (Internet or Work).
4. Tap New to create the new connection.
5. Enter the appropriate settings for the new connection.
6. Tap OK to finish creating the new connection.

With the new connection created, you can start using it by selecting it in the Connections tab of Connection Manager. For example, if you create a new work connection, you can put it into use by simply selecting it from the second drop-down list in Connection Manager, which indicates the connection your Pocket PC should use to connect to Work.

POCKET PCs AND VIRTUAL PRIVATE NETWORKS

Earlier in the chapter you learned how to connect to corporate networks using a dial-up connection. For security purposes, many corporate networks now require remote users to use a relatively new technology known as virtual private networking (VPN) to establish remote network connections. VPN adds a layer of security not possible with other forms of remote network access and is a good method of accessing private corporate networks remotely.

PART

II

CH

7

WHAT IS A VPN?

Virtual private networking is a technology designed to provide remote access to private networks in a secure manner. VPN is interesting because it involves both public and private networking. More specifically, VPN allows a remote user to use the public Internet to establish a secure connection to a private corporate network. The process of going through a public network to access a private network is known as *tunneling*, which means that you are essentially using one network (the Internet) as a tunnel to connect to another network (the private corporate network).

VPN offers significant advantages to businesses because it enables them to forego costly dial-up access points. Not only that, but accessibility is greatly increased because you can tunnel into a VPN from any Internet connection. Beyond cost reduction and accessibility, VPNs also offer security advantages because they use authentication and encryption throughout the connection. For all these reasons, VPNs are a good option for most businesses that require remote network access for their employees. Therefore, VPNs are likely to continue to grow in popularity, which means you need to be able to connect to them with your Pocket PC.

CONNECTING TO A VPN

Connecting to a VPN isn't really very different from connecting to a LAN using RAS, except that you must specify details regarding the VPN server. Following are the steps required to configure a VPN connection for your Pocket PC:

1. Tap Settings on the Start menu, and then tap the Connections tab.
2. Tap the Connections icon, and then tap the Connections tab.
3. Select Work Settings in the second drop-down list, which determines how you connect to work.
4. Tap the Modify button, and then tap the VPN tab.
5. Tap New in the connection list to create a new VPN connection (see Figure 7.14).

Figure 7.14
The Work Settings screen enables you to manage and create VPN connections for use in connecting to Work.

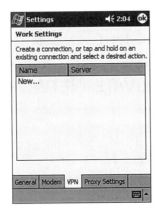

6. Enter a name for the VPN connection, along with the hostname or IP address of the VPN server (see Figure 7.15).

Figure 7.15
Creating a VPN connection primarily consists of naming the connection and identifying the VPN server.

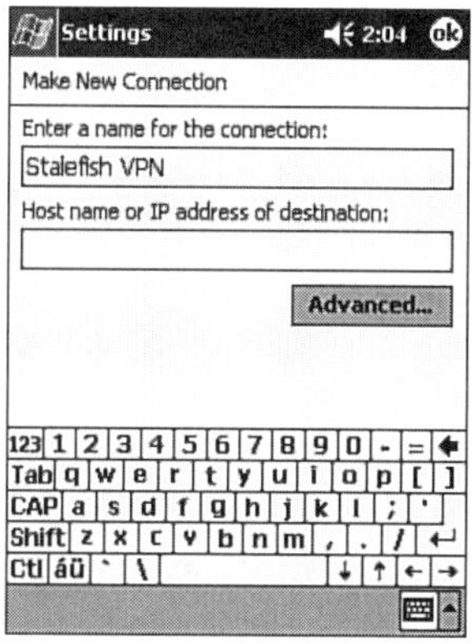

7. If your VPN server requires advanced settings, tap the Advanced button and enter them.

8. Tap OK to finish setting up the connection, and then tap OK to return to the Connections screen.

9. Select Work in the last setting, My Network Card Connects to.

10. Tap OK to finish configuring the connection.

The VPN connection is now created and ready to be used for tunneling into a VPN. Connection Manager is smart enough to automatically use the VPN connection whenever it is needed to access a resource on a corporate network.

THE POCKET PC AS A TERMINAL SERVICES CLIENT

One of the most powerful network features in the Pocket PC 2002 operating system is support for using Pocket PCs as Terminal Services clients. Terminal Services are used to provide remote access to server applications, thereby enabling a remote computer to run the applications remotely. Terminal Services are useful in enterprise environments where applications are often distributed across several servers.

UNDERSTANDING TERMINAL SERVICES

Terminal Services are used to give remote users the capability of running applications directly from a server. Unlike a remote network connection, which simply connects you to a network, Terminal Services actually puts you in the driver's seat of applications on a network.

PART

II

CH

7

In other words, you are able to run an application across a network entirely through a remote connection. The way this works is that Terminal Services delivers the user interface of a server application to the remote client and then keeps track of client key presses and mouse clicks to provide interaction with the application. You can think of it as having a monitor, keyboard, and mouse connected to a computer that is physically located somewhere else.

Note

To run the Terminal Services server software, the server must be using the Windows 2000 or Windows XP operating system.

The interesting thing about Terminal servers is that they are capable of serving many users simultaneously. Each client user that accesses a Terminal server has a discrete session that is completely independent of other users. It's not hard to see the benefits of such an environment because it provides a means of allowing multiple remote users to access a single application on a Terminal server. The other benefit of Terminal servers is that they don't require much of clients in terms of power. In fact, Terminal Services clients are often referred to as *thin clients* because they play such a small role in the processing part of a Terminal application.

Terminal Services enters the picture with Pocket PCs because it enables Pocket PCs to act as thin clients and run applications remotely. The only drawback to using Pocket PCs with Terminal Services is that Terminal applications are typically designed for desktop monitors, in which case the application screen won't fit on the smaller Pocket PC screen. However, Terminal Services provides some navigational features for moving around a larger application screen on your Pocket PC.

BECOMING A MOBILE TERMINAL SERVICES CLIENT

Using Terminal Services to connect to a Terminal server with your Pocket PC is very straightforward. The Pocket PC 2002 operating system includes an application called Terminal Services Client that handles the details of establishing a Terminal Services connection and providing client capabilities to a Terminal application. Following are the steps required to run the Terminal Services Client application and access a Terminal server:

1. Tap Programs on the Start menu, and then tap the Terminal Services Client icon.

2. Enter the server name of the Terminal server, or select a recently used server from the list (see Figure 7.16).

3. Tap the Connect button to connect to the Terminal server.

Tip from
Michael

Recent Terminal servers are listed in the Terminal Services Client application and act as good shortcuts whenever you need to visit one of the same servers again.

Figure 7.16
The opening screen of the Terminal Services Client application prompts you to enter a Terminal server and then connect to it.

After connecting to a remote Terminal server, you can run applications just as if you were sitting in front of the remote computer. Figure 7.17 shows how Terminal Services Client provides access to the desktop of a remote computer.

Figure 7.17
The Terminal Services Client application provides access to server applications, including a remote desktop.

Notice in Figure 7.17 that Terminal Services Client includes a toolbar along the bottom of the screen with little boxes in the buttons. These buttons are used as a navigational aid to help you move around a larger remote computer screen on your Pocket PC. Because your Pocket PC screen can be as much as five times smaller than a desktop monitor, these buttons can prove useful in quickly moving around within a Terminal application.

TROUBLESHOOTING

DIAL-UP CONNECTION PROBLEMS

I can't seem to get my dial-up modem to connect to my ISP.

First, check that your modem is properly configured and that it's properly connected to your device. If that checks out okay, make sure the cable for the phone line is connected to the modem and to the phone line itself. The next step is to ensure you have a dial tone, which can quickly be determined by picking up a phone connected to the same line. That takes care of the hardware side of things.

In terms of software settings, make sure you have the correct dialing location selected and that its properties are set up properly for the phone line you're using. Then, double-check the access number for your ISP and ensure that it matches what you're using in the connection settings. You also should make absolutely sure that you're entering your user ID and password correctly. If none of this helps, perform a soft reset on your device and try establishing a connection again. If you still don't have any luck, try establishing the same dial-up connection with a desktop computer to ensure that there isn't a problem with your ISP.

LAN CONNECTION PROBLEMS

My device won't connect to a LAN even though I've set up the connection in Connection Manager.

The first thing to do when having trouble with a LAN connection is to perform a soft reset on your device. Network hardware tends to be sensitive, and often a soft reset resolves problems associated with this sensitivity. The next step is to make sure your network hardware is properly configured, with all appropriate drivers installed. If you're using a physical network connection, ensure that the network cable is attached well at both ends. If you're using a wireless connection, make sure you're within range of the network's base station.

If you're still having trouble, you might need to make some advanced network settings in Connection Manager. If you're connecting to a corporate LAN, double-check that you're entering the correct login ID and password, and then ask your network administrator to clarify the settings that need to be made if you still can't get connected. If you're connecting to a public LAN, ask for information regarding how the LAN should be accessed.

REAL-WORLD EXAMPLE—MAKING THE MOST OF PUBLIC LANS

Earlier in the chapter you learned that public LANs are popping up in some surprising places, such as coffee shops. Public LANs likely represent the future of mobile wireless networking because they provide a means of obtaining temporary Internet access without having to pay anything. When you think about it, you might not really need wireless Internet access all the time. If you knew that you could hop on the Internet at certain places you frequent, it might be sufficient for checking e-mail and browsing a Web site here and there.
I encourage you to do some investigating and see what public LANs are available where you live. Good places to start include college campuses, libraries, coffee shops, book stores, and airports.

CHAPTER

USING ACTIVESYNC TO SYNCHRONIZE DATA

In this chapter

EXAMINING ALTERNATIVE SYNCHRONIZATION OPTIONS

At this point, you're probably fairly comfortable using ActiveSync to synchronize data between your Pocket PC and desktop PC. You connected your device to your desktop PC back in Chapter 3, "Navigating the Pocket PC GUI," when you first installed ActiveSync. Now it's time to look a little more deeply into ActiveSync and find out what else it is capable of doing. More specifically, you might not have realized that you can use ActiveSync outside a typical cradle connection. For example, if your notebook PC has an infrared port, you can use it with ActiveSync to synchronize with your Pocket PC.

ActiveSync is actually quite flexible in terms of how you establish a connection between a Pocket PC and a desktop or notebook PC. The steps explained in Chapter 3 to synchronize your device with ActiveSync assumed you were using the cradle that came with your device. Following are some other types of ActiveSync connections you might find useful in situations in which a cradle isn't a viable option:

- Ethernet connection
- Infrared connection
- USB connection

The really powerful thing about this connection flexibility is that it takes place automatically; you establish the appropriate physical connection, and ActiveSync automatically recognizes your device and connects for synchronization. In this way, using an Ethernet, an infrared, or a USB connection with ActiveSync is really no different from using a cradle. This also means you can use the *pass-through* networking feature of the Pocket PC 2002 operating system regardless of the physical connection used with ActiveSync. For example, you can synchronize wirelessly with your Pocket PC and a notebook PC and browse the Web using Pocket Internet Explorer through the same connection.

Although the ability to use pass-through networking with various types of ActiveSync connections is certainly powerful, it might not be as powerful as the ability to synchronize your device over a remote connection. This synchronization technique enables you to dial into a network server with a modem to establish a synchronization connection. This can be very handy when traveling because it gives you the ability to synchronize e-mail, appointments, and other important information from virtually anywhere. Remote synchronization serves to explain why the ActiveSync application on your Pocket PC includes the same status information shown in the desktop ActiveSync application (see Figure 8.1). This is significant when synchronizing remotely because you can't see what's happening on the other end of the connection.

 If your device isn't connecting to ActiveSync even though it has done so in the past with no problems, you probably need to perform a simple fix. To learn more, see "What to Do When ActiveSync Won't Connect" in the "Troubleshooting" section at the end of the chapter.

Figure 8.1
The Pocket PC side of ActiveSync shows exactly what is going on with the ActiveSync connection, which is important when synchronizing remotely.

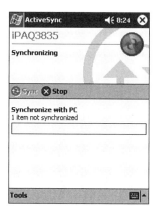

USING DRAG AND DROP TO SHARE FILES WITH YOUR DESKTOP PC

Synchronizing via ActiveSync is the automated way to keep your Pocket PC and desktop PC on the same track in terms of application data. ActiveSync also supports exploring the Pocket PC, which basically lets you use your desktop PC to explore the file system of the Pocket PC. In doing so, you can move, copy, or delete files between the Pocket PC and desktop PC. To explore your Pocket PC from the desktop, connect the device to your desktop PC and click the Explore button on the main ActiveSync toolbar. This results in an Explorer window appearing that shows the My Documents folder in the Pocket PC file system (see Figure 8.2).

Note

As long as ActiveSync is running, you can also explore your Pocket PC by clicking the Mobile Device icon that appears just beneath My Computer on your desktop. You can open the Mobile Device icon to reveal the entire file system of the Pocket PC.

Double-clicking the My Pocket PC icon takes you to the root level of the file system, where you can directly access the familiar My Documents and Program Files folders, among others. You are free to copy and move files by dragging and dropping them between Explorer instances. So, to copy or move files between the Pocket PC and desktop PC, you just open another Explorer window and explore your hard drive. From there, you can drag and drop between the two Explorer instances with ease. Behind the scenes, ActiveSync is handling the actual file transfers, but it is seamless from your perspective.

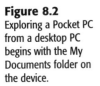

Figure 8.2
Exploring a Pocket PC
from a desktop PC
begins with the My
Documents folder on
the device.

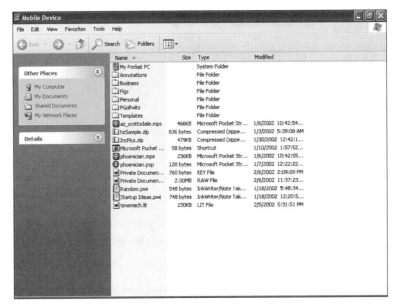

FINE-TUNING ACTIVESYNC

Most of the time, synchronization between a Pocket PC and desktop PC takes place very smoothly. However, occasionally the same information has changed on both machines between synchronizations, in which case a *synchronization conflict* occurs. This is a problem because ActiveSync doesn't know which version of the data to use as the basis for synchronization. When this type of conflict occurs, ActiveSync flags the data item as unresolved during synchronization. It is then up to you to resolve the conflict by selecting one of the versions of the item as the correct one.

RESOLVING SYNCHRONIZATION CONFLICTS

One option for handling synchronization conflicts is to always let your desktop computer win. In other words, you're saying that in the event of a synchronization conflict, always replace the version on the Pocket PC with the desktop version. This makes sense for many users because your desktop PC is likely to have the latest versions of all application data. You set this option in ActiveSync on your desktop PC by following these steps:

1. Click the Options button on the main toolbar.

2. Click the Rules tab.

3. Click the Conflict Resolution drop-down list and select Always Replace the Item on My Device, which indicates that the item on the device should always be replaced (see Figure 8.3). The other radio buttons correspond to options that enable you to leave a conflict unresolved or replace the version on the computer with the Pocket PC version.

4. Click OK to accept the Conflict Resolution options.

Figure 8.3
ActiveSync enables you to determine exactly how it should respond when a synchronization conflict occurs.

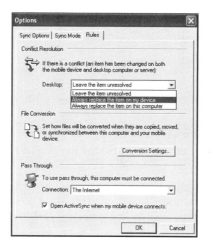

Keep in mind that this approach to synchronization results in your desktop PC always "winning" when it comes to a synchronization conflict. Practically speaking, this means if you've modified information on both devices, the modifications on the Pocket PC side will be lost. If you want to avoid the risk of losing important information on your Pocket PC, a good solution is to back up your device to a storage card prior to synchronization.

SETTING THE SYNCHRONIZATION MODE

Another synchronization option is the synchronization mode, which is available under the Sync Mode tab in the ActiveSync Options dialog box (see Figure 8.4).

Figure 8.4
ActiveSync provides three synchronization modes that determine when and how often synchronization occurs.

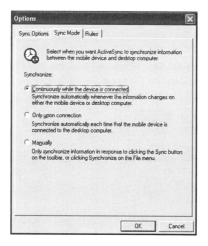

Three settings are available for the synchronization mode, which determine when synchronization takes place:

- Continuously While the Device Is Connected
- Only upon Connection
- Manually

The default setting is the first one, which is guaranteed to provide the most accurate level of synchronization because the device is constantly synchronizing as data changes. Continuous synchronization is especially handy if you synchronize Web content that changes regularly. If you aren't so concerned about up-to-the-minute synchronization, the second option is reasonable, too. In this case, the device is synchronized upon being connected to the desktop PC. This approach works well if you want to synchronize only when you first connect your device to your desktop PC, and it is primarily useful for synchronizing relatively constant information, such as contact information and tasks. Keep in mind that you can still manually synchronize whenever you want by clicking the Sync button on the main ActiveSync toolbar.

BACKING UP WITH ACTIVESYNC

ActiveSync includes a powerful backup feature that I encourage you to use on a regular basis. By regularly backing up your Pocket PC, you minimize the chances of losing valuable data due to a battery problem or some other, more serious accident, such as dropping your device in water. A backup also provides an image of your system that you can restore in a new device if your device gets lost or stolen.

→ To find out how to reduce the risks of theft and improve the chances of recovering a lost device, **see** "Antitheft Devices," **p. 377**.

The backup feature is available in the desktop version of ActiveSync and is accessed via the Tools menu; just select Backup/Restore on the Tools menu. This results in the display of the Backup/Restore dialog box, which is shown in Figure 8.5.

Figure 8.5
The Backup/Restore dialog box in the desktop ActiveSync application enables you to perform a backup on your device or restore a previous backup to your device.

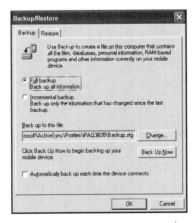

The two radio buttons in the Backup tab of the Backup/Restore dialog box enable you to choose between a full or an incremental backup. A *full backup* always backs up everything on your device regardless of whether you've backed it up before, whereas an *incremental backup* backs up only information that has changed since the previous backup. Incremental backups are faster, take up less space on your desktop computer's hard drive, and are probably the best backup approach to use unless you don't plan to back up your device very often.

Near the bottom of the Backup/Restore dialog box is a check box that enables you to automatically back up your device each time it connects via ActiveSync. Although this might seem like a lot of overhead in terms of information transfer, if you choose the incremental backup approach, automatic backups are pretty quick. This is a great way to guarantee that your device's contents are always safely stored on your desktop computer in case of a problem. The Change button in the Backup/Restore dialog box enables you to change the name and location of the backup file on the desktop computer.

Tip from
Michael

It's generally a good idea to back up your Pocket PC at least once a month at a bare minimum.

When you are ready to perform a backup, click the Back Up Now button in the Backup/Restore dialog box. Figure 8.6 shows the backup process taking place.

Figure 8.6
The backup process can take a while if your device is full of data.

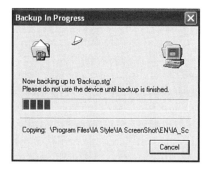

After performing a backup, you can easily restore information to your device. To restore a previous backup, click the Restore tab in the Backup/Restore dialog box. Figure 8.7 shows this tab, which is pretty straightforward.

Before restoring backed-up data to your device, be sure to close all applications running on the device. After closing all applications, click the Restore Now button in the Restore tab of the Backup/Restore dialog box. Unlike the backup process, you can't abort the restore process after it begins. It is important that you don't attempt to use your device until the restore process finishes.

→ To recap how to manually close all applications that are running, **see** "Memory Management and Closing Applications," **p. 56**.

Figure 8.7
The Restore tab in the Backup/Restore dialog box enables you to restore backed-up data.

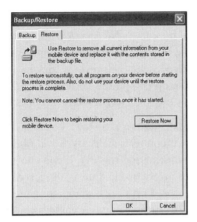

TAKING A LOOK BEYOND ACTIVESYNC

Thus far in this chapter, you've focused on some of the more interesting features and options in ActiveSync that make synchronization possible between a Pocket PC and desktop or notebook PC. One significant limitation of ActiveSync is that it enables you to synchronize data only with Microsoft Outlook. Although Outlook is certainly a popular information management application, others are in use as well. For example, many companies rely solely on Lotus Notes for information management. In fact, Lotus Notes represents Outlook's most significant competitor. It's unfortunate that ActiveSync isn't designed to accommodate Lotus Notes.

Another limitation of ActiveSync has to do with the amount of control you have over a device when it is connected to a desktop PC. Although you can explore the file system of a device using ActiveSync, you don't have the ability to actually take control of the device by running applications and interacting with data. Granted, not everyone has the need for this type of feature, but it could be useful in situations in which you want to access data on your Pocket PC without having to remove the device from its cradle. Besides, you might have data on your device that can't be synchronized with a desktop PC, in which case you must interact with it directly on the device. In this situation, being able to interact with the device from a desktop PC would be convenient. In other words, the desktop PC would display an image of the Pocket PC display and then enable you to use the mouse pointer to tap the screen and simulate the stylus.

The following is an introduction to a couple of interesting third-party applications that provide solutions to the problems I just described. The next two sections examine these applications and show you how to use them to do some things that are beyond the scope of ActiveSync.

SYNCHRONIZING WITHOUT ACTIVESYNC

If you use an information management application other than Microsoft Outlook, you've probably been frustrated by the fact that ActiveSync doesn't do much in the way of enabling you to synchronize information with your Pocket PC. For example, if your company uses Lotus Notes as an information manager for handling e-mail, contacts, scheduling, and so on, you're basically out of luck in terms of synchronizing information with Pocket Outlook. Even though ActiveSync doesn't offer any solution to this problem, a few third-party applications provide synchronization options for Lotus Notes, Novell GroupWise, and other workgroup-based information managers:

- Intellisync
- PDAsync
- Cadenza

The next few sections introduce you to these synchronization applications and provide you with enough information to decide whether any of them can meet your synchronization needs.

INTELLISYNC

Intellisync is a synchronization application by Pumatech that enables you to synchronize a Pocket PC with a variety of information management applications, such as Lotus Notes, Novell, GroupWise, and ACT!, as well as the familiar Microsoft Outlook. Intellisync is particularly useful if you need to synchronize data with an application other than Outlook, or if you use both Outlook and another application such as Lotus Notes. This might be the case if you use Lotus Notes at work and Outlook at home. Intellisync enables you to synchronize with both applications. To learn more about Intellisync, visit the Intellisync Web site at `http://www.pumatech.com/intellisync.html`.

PDAsync

PDAsync is another synchronization application for your Pocket PC that enables you to synchronize data with information applications other than Microsoft Outlook. PDAsync was created by LapLink, a company that has a lot of experience with data synchronization; the original LapLink synchronization software for desktop PCs has been extremely popular for years. PDAsync addresses the same synchronization issues as ActiveSync and even goes a few steps further by enabling you to synchronize contact information with mobile phones that have an infrared port or Bluetooth wireless networking capability.

→ To learn more about Bluetooth wireless networking, **see** Chapter 6, "Evaluating Networking Options," **p. 111**.

PDAsync is compatible with Lotus Notes, ACT!, and Microsoft Outlook, to name a few of the major information management applications. To find out more about PDAsync, visit the PDAsync Web site at `http://www.laplink.com/products/pdasync/overview.asp`.

CADENZA

Cadenza is different from Intellisync and PDAsync in that it is specifically geared toward integrating Pocket PCs with the Lotus Domino messaging and database system employed by Lotus Notes. More specifically, Cadenza turns your Pocket PC into a Lotus Notes client that is capable of directly accessing information from a Lotus Domino server. With Cadenza, you can connect to a Domino server from your Pocket PC and replicate e-mail, contacts, appointments, and tasks just as if you were using a desktop Lotus Notes client. Cadenza is a product of CommonTime and can be found on the Web at http://www.commontime.com/ProductsCadenza.htm.

CONTROLLING YOUR POCKET PC WITH POCKET CONTROLLER

If you've ever used pcAnywhere to control a desktop PC remotely, you have an understanding of how useful directly taking control of a computer from another computer can be. Even if you haven't used pcAnywhere or a similar product, it isn't difficult to see how being able to control one computer from another computer can be advantageous in some situations. For example, remote control software enables you to troubleshoot problems remotely without having to physically sit in front of a computer. Beyond troubleshooting, it can also be handy when you need to remotely access an application that is installed only on a particular computer.

The remote control functionality of pcAnywhere is now available on Pocket PCs thanks to Pocket Controller by Soft Object Technologies. Pocket Controller enables you to control your Pocket PC from a desktop PC. Granted, this isn't exactly a form of synchronization, but it is nonetheless an interesting way to interact with a Pocket PC from a desktop PC. Pocket Controller displays a view of the Pocket PC screen directly on a desktop PC monitor and interprets mouse clicks on the virtual screen as stylus taps on the Pocket PC screen. As you click the virtual Pocket PC screen on the desktop computer, you can see the Pocket PC respond as if you were actually tapping it.

Pocket Controller can be set up to use either an ActiveSync or a TCP/IP connection, which opens up lots of interesting opportunities for remotely controlling a device. For example, you can establish a wireless network connection between the Pocket PC and desktop PC and then remotely control the Pocket PC from the desktop PC. This could come in extremely handy for traveling professionals who are having technical difficulty with their devices. A tech support person could use Pocket Controller to take control of the device through a remote wireless network connection and help solve the problem by directly changing device settings and installing software upgrades.

Pocket Controller can also be used for training and presentations because it enables you to view the screen of a Pocket PC on a desktop computer monitor or an LCD projector. For example, Pocket Controller could be employed in a training session for a mobile sales force to demonstrate step-by-step instructions for using productivity applications. Similarly, presentations created in PowerPoint or Macromedia Flash could be displayed on a desktop computer monitor or projector via Pocket Controller. You can even specify a landscape view in Pocket Controller, which rotates the Pocket PC display by 90° to provide a view that is wider than it is tall.

→ To learn more about viewing PowerPoint and Macromedia Flash presentations, **see** Chapter 23, "Multimedia and Video in Your Pocket," **p. 433**.

Pocket Controller is available from the Soft Object Technologies (SOTI) Web site at http://www.soti.net/. You can download a free trial of the software or purchase the full version online. The first time you run Pocket Controller, it prompts you to select the type of Pocket PC you're using. Figure 8.8 shows the initial Configuration dialog box that appears when you first run Pocket Controller.

Figure 8.8
The opening Configuration dialog box in Pocket Controller prompts you to select the type of Pocket PC you're using.

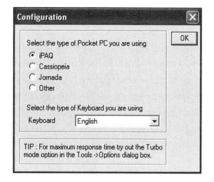

After selecting the appropriate Pocket PC, the Pocket Controller application launches. Before connecting and establishing a connection to take control of your device, it's worth taking a look at the options for Pocket Controller. Just click Options on the Tools menu to access the Options dialog box, as shown in Figure 8.9.

Figure 8.9
The Options dialog box in Pocket Controller enables you to fine-tune the manner in which you control your Pocket PC.

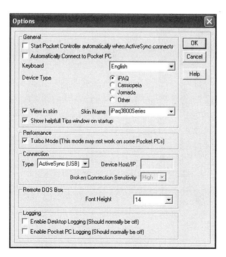

One of the most interesting settings in the Options dialog box involves the use of *skins*, which simulate the physical appearance of a Pocket PC device on the desktop screen. Without using skins, all you see on the desktop is your Pocket PCs screen. With skins, however, you see the entire device, and you can even click hardware buttons on the front face of the device. Pocket Controller includes skins for most Pocket PCs, but if for some reason yours isn't available, you can probably download it from the SOTI Web site at http://www.soti.net/.

Note

Device skins used in Pocket Controller are completely different from the skins used to customize the appearance of Windows Media Player.

Another setting in the Options dialog box worth trying is Turbo Mode, which speeds up the connection between the Pocket PC and desktop PC, resulting in better performance. Turbo Mode doesn't work with all Pocket PCs, but it's worth a try because performance is an issue when using any type of remote-control software. One other important setting you should take a look at is the connection type for the remote device access. The connection type can be either ActiveSync or TCP/IP; if you're controlling your device from a cradle then you should select ActiveSync as the connection type.

After you've decided on the Pocket Controller settings, you can take control of your device by selecting Connect from the File menu or clicking the Connect button on the toolbar. Figure 8.10 shows the virtual device screen for my Pocket PC as it appears on my desktop monitor.

Figure 8.10
Pocket Controller provides a virtual screen for your Pocket PC that is viewed on your desktop monitor.

Notice in Figure 8.10 that I'm using the skin for a Compaq iPAQ H3800 series device, which is why the entire device is visible onscreen. Controlling the Pocket PC is as simple as clicking the virtual screen just as if you were using a stylus on the real Pocket PC screen. For example, Figure 8.11 shows how I've launched the Calendar application to take a look at appointments for the month.

Figure 8.11
Launching applications via Pocket Controller is as simple as clicking the virtual Pocket PC screen with the mouse.

You can access any application on your Pocket PC using Pocket Controller. In fact, Pocket Controller gives you the ability to do anything on your device with mouse clicks that you could do directly on the device with a stylus. When you're finished using Pocket Controller, you should terminate the device connection by selecting Disconnect from the File menu in the Pocket Controller application.

 When you're finished using a skin in Pocket Controller to control your device, you might be a little confused by the fact that there is no obvious way to exit the skin or Pocket Controller. See "Closing Pocket Controller When Using a Skin" in the "Troubleshooting" section at the end of the chapter to find out how to close Pocket Controller when using a skin.

TROUBLESHOOTING

WHAT TO DO WHEN ACTIVESYNC WON'T CONNECT

Although ActiveSync appears to recognize it when I place my Pocket PC in its cradle, I can't get ActiveSync to establish a connection with my device.

This is a tricky little problem that can be very annoying until you figure out how to fix it. The problem is that your device can at times get itself into a state where it won't connect with ActiveSync on your desktop PC. There are no warnings other than ActiveSync never being able to connect. The simple solution is to perform a soft reset on your device and then synchronize again—this has fixed the problem for me every time.

CLOSING POCKET CONTROLLER WHEN USING A SKIN

I can't close Pocket Controller when controlling my device via a skin; clicking the power button on the skin doesn't do anything.

You can't close Pocket Controller using the skin for a device you're controlling. The skin is provided as an interface for interacting with the device, but it doesn't allow you to interact with the Pocket Controller application itself. This is evident by the fact that the Pocket Controller application window is still open along with the skin. To close the skin (and Pocket Controller), just click the Pocket Controller application window and then close it just as you would any other desktop Windows applications.

REAL-WORLD EXAMPLE—CLONING A DEVICE

If you are upgrading to a new Pocket PC or think you might run the risk of losing or having your Pocket PC stolen, you should perform a full backup on a regular basis with ActiveSync. As long as you perform regular backups, you have the capability of effectively cloning a Pocket PC even if you restore the backup to a different physical device. You can even clone a device without using a desktop PC by backing up to a memory storage card and then restoring the backup image from the card on another device. Most Pocket PCs include a built-in backup application that supports backing up to a storage card.

Although cloning a device is a security measure for an individual with a single device, it can be a good way to initialize multiple devices in a corporate environment. For example, if you want users in a workgroup to have the exact same applications and settings on their Pocket PCs, you might consider setting up one device, backing it up, and then restoring the backup to several other devices. Again, you could use a single memory storage card to "install" the setup image of the master device to the other devices.

CHAPTER

9

STAYING IN TOUCH WITH INSTANT MESSAGING

In this chapter

INSTANT MESSAGING BASICS

I have a prediction: Now that wireless connectivity is rapidly becoming a regular part of the Pocket PC experience, instant messaging will emerge as the killer application of Pocket PCs. I know, you're thinking that wireless Web browsing is where the real excitement's at, or maybe even wireless e-mail, but I'm here to tell you that wireless instant messaging will be the king of mobile wireless communication. There is no doubt that wireless Web browsing is important, and I feel even more strongly about the flexibility of being able to communicate via e-mail from anywhere. However, the immediacy of instant messaging is hard to top. Granted, wireless instant messaging won't be for everyone, especially when it comes to communication that is more efficient by voice with a mobile phone, but I think we will see a considerable increase in instant messaging as people begin to realize its usefulness.

The only limiting factor in regard to wireless instant messaging is the relative inefficiency of entering text on a Pocket PC. I suppose what I'm saying here is that although I'm standing by my prediction of wireless instant messaging being the next big thing, it might take longer to catch on because some people will be frustrated over the manner in which they have to enter messages. Pecking the soft keyboard with a stylus isn't very efficient, and even though Transcriber is an impressive technology, I'm not sure whether it offers a speedy enough solution for entering chat messages. The ideal solution is a miniature keyboard such as the ones used on Blackberry messaging devices, which are already available for Pocket PCs. Although they don't compare with typing on a real keyboard, you can get quite adept at pecking out messages on these little keyboards.

→ To find out more about keyboards available for use with Pocket PCs, **see** "Keyboards," **p. 485**.

Instant messaging is a type of communication involving two or more people exchanging small text messages with each other. Instant messages are similar to the *short message service (SMS)* messages that can be sent between pagers and mobile phones. However, instant messages are designed for use on full-blown computers through an Internet or a LAN connection. Instant messaging is also distinguishable from SMS-type messaging systems because it allows conversations between multiple parties, sort of like a message-based conference call.

Wireless instant messaging has many benefits. Mobile phones have their place, but they tend to be too imposing. How many times have you seen people roll their eyes when someone accepts a mobile phone call in a setting that is deemed "inappropriate," such as a movie theater, restaurant, or business meeting? Wireless e-mail is the logical alternative to mobile phones, but in many ways it isn't immediate enough. I, for one, don't have the expectation of getting a response to an e-mail any sooner than a few hours. If I need an immediate response from someone, I either call him or instant message him.

So, why is instant messaging better than making a phone call? Well, in many cases it isn't. Plenty of conversations simply must be carried out verbally because of the complexity of expressing certain thoughts and ideas. However, a great deal of communication is going on in e-mail and on mobile phones that could easily be carried out via wireless instant messaging. The obvious benefit instant messaging offers over making a phone call is that it isn't as distracting; you can quickly look and respond to an instant message with much less distraction than answering a phone and carrying on a conversation. Not only that, but instant messaging is much more discrete than taking a phone call. For example, SMS-based pagers are already being used to communicate discretely across the conference table in business meetings; think of it as high-tech note passing.

I could be wrong, and wireless instant messaging could end up being nothing more than a gimmick that comes and goes. But, if you spend some time with an instant messaging application on your Pocket PC and attempt to use it as a serious communication medium, I think you'll agree that wireless instant messaging could very well have a bright future.

COMMUNICATING WITH MSN MESSENGER

Although several instant messaging services are available for carrying out "conversations" through instant messages, one particular service has built-in support in Pocket PCs. I'm referring to Microsoft's MSN Messenger, which includes a client application in the ROM of the Pocket PC 2002 operating system. A version of Messenger is available for desktop PCs called Windows Messenger, which integrates well with the Windows XP user interface. You can download the desktop version of the Windows Messenger application for free from the MSN Messenger Web site at `http://messenger.msn.com/`. Just to clarify, MSN Messenger is the Pocket PC instant messaging application, whereas Windows Messenger is its desktop counterpart; both applications rely on the Microsoft Network (MSN) for communications.

Note

Microsoft is clearly trying to extend the reach of Messenger across multiple platforms. For example, a version of Messenger is available for Apple Macintosh computers, as is a version for the Microsoft TV set-top Internet appliance. You can find out more about these versions of Messenger on the MSN Messenger Web site.

To communicate with any version of Messenger, you must have a special instant messaging account that identifies you to the instant messaging service. MSN Messenger supports two kinds of accounts:

- .NET Passport accounts
- Exchange accounts

.NET Passport accounts are the likely choice if you don't already use instant messaging in a corporate environment with Microsoft Exchange Server. Exchange accounts are associated with Exchange Server and are used by businesses to provide instant messaging services in a secure environment. If you already have an Exchange account, by all means use it with MSN Messenger. If not, you might need to set up a Passport account, assuming you don't already have one through Hotmail or MSN.

SIGNING UP FOR A .NET PASSPORT

Before getting started with MSN Messenger on your Pocket PC, you must have a .NET Passport account set up with Microsoft. Microsoft's *.NET Passport service* is a free service designed to serve as a unified storage location for information about yourself that can be used anywhere on the Web. The goal is to eliminate the redundancy associated with keeping track of multiple user IDs and passwords for different Web sites and services. In the case of MSN Messenger, a Passport account is used to identify who you are, which is necessary to log you in to MSN Messenger and identify you to other Messenger users.

If you've never used the desktop Windows Messenger application and you have no .NET Passport account, you can sign up for a free account at http://www.passport.com/. It's important to clarify that a Passport account is actually a security measure designed to keep your personal information all in one place. As support for Passport spreads around the Web, you'll be able to exert more control over your personal information because it will be held in one place—your Passport account. You also can use your Passport account as a financial tool that enables you to make electronic payments at supported Web sites. It's ultimately up to you how you decide to use your Passport account, but you do need it at least for use with MSN Messenger.

The end result of setting up a .NET Passport account is a sign-in name and password, which are then used in MSN Messenger to sign in to the instant messaging service. Store your Passport password in a safe place so you don't forget it.

STARTING MSN MESSENGER

The MSN Messenger application is located in the Programs folder of your Pocket PC, which is accessible by tapping Programs on the Start menu. From there, just tap MSN Messenger to launch MSN Messenger. The first thing you see when you start MSN Messenger is a title screen that prompts you to tap and sign in (see Figure 9.1).

Figure 9.1
The MSN Messenger title screen presents a prompt that requires you to sign in before you can start communicating with instant messages.

If you tap the phrase Tap Here to Sign In, you are taken to the Sign In screen, which is shown in Figure 9.2.

Figure 9.2
Signing into MSN Messenger simply involves entering a sign-in name and password.

PART

II

CH

9

Tip from
Michael

If you later want to switch MSN Messenger to a different type of account, you can easily do so. For example, your company might add instant messaging support through Exchange Server, in which case you might decide to switch from a Passport account to an Exchange account. To make the switch, tap Options on the Tools menu, and then select the Accounts tab. Check the appropriate account type and enter your sign-in name and password. You actually can use both types of accounts simultaneously if you want to distinguish between personal and business chatting; just indicate which account should be used first at sign-in.

Signing in to MSN Messenger simply involves entering your sign-in name and password for your .NET Passport or Exchange account. If you're using a Passport, the sign-in name is actually the e-mail address you entered when creating your Passport account, and it typically ends in `passport.com`. If you've had a Passport account for a while, you might have a sign-in name that ends in `hotmail.com` or `msn.com`. After successfully entering your sign-in name and password, MSN Messenger displays a list of your messenger contacts, along with the status of each (see Figure 9.3).

Caution

If you use Windows Messenger on your desktop PC, you'll quickly learn that you can't use it at the same time as MSN Messenger. This limitation has to do with the fact that you can't be signed in with a Passport account on two different devices simultaneously. So, you can use only one Messenger application at a time.

Figure 9.3
The contact list in MSN Messenger displays messenger contacts, along with their current statuses; the contacts are divided according to those who are online and those who aren't online.

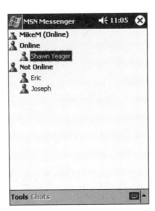

Notice in Figure 9.3 that I have three contacts set up in MSN Messenger. The status of each contact is very important because it determines with whom I can communicate via instant messages. In this case, two of my contacts (Eric and Joseph) are offline, whereas Shawn Yeager is online; this means I can chat only with Shawn. To initiate a chat with a contact, just tap them in the contact list. Figure 9.4 shows part of an MSN Messenger chat with my good friend and Internet guru, Shawn Yeager.

 If you've tried unsuccessfully to start a chat with a particular contact in MSN Messenger, see "Problem Establishing a Chat" in the "Troubleshooting" section at the end of the chapter to find out how to resolve the situation.

Figure 9.4
Chatting with MSN Messenger is as simple as choosing a contact and entering text messages in the chat window.

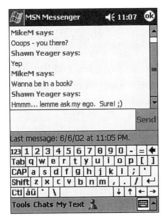

Figure 9.4 reveals a few interesting things about MSN Messenger. First, notice that the soft keyboard is visible, which is my preferred method for entering instant messages. When you enter a message, all you must do to send it is tap the Send button or tap the Enter key on the soft keyboard. Similar to Windows Messenger on desktop PCs, MSN Messenger clearly distinguishes messages by showing the name of each person just above her message in the chat window.

Tip from
Michael

You can have multiple chats going on in MSN Messenger at the same time, in which case you can use the Chat menu item to quickly switch between chats. Of course, this requires a unique ability to juggle multiple conversations at the same time.

ADDING CONTACTS

Just as with verbal conversations, instant message conversations don't work too well without two willing participants. You therefore must add any desired business associates, friends, and family members to MSN Messenger as contacts so that you can communicate with them via instant messages. To add a new contact to MSN Messenger, tap Add a Contact on the Tools menu. This displays the Add a Contact screen, which is shown in Figure 9.5.

PART
II

CH
9

Figure 9.5
The Add a Contact screen prompts you to enter the sign-in name of the new contact, which is her Passport account name.

After entering the sign-in name of the new contact, tap Next to finish setting up the new contact. If the contact addition is successful, you'll see a confirmation screen similar to the one in Figure 9.6.

Figure 9.6
MSN Messenger displays a confirmation whenever you add a new contact.

In this example, I've added myself as a contact just to demonstrate how the process works. The other important thing to note about this process is that you are notified by MSN Messenger when someone else adds you to his contact list. Figure 9.7 shows the notification displayed by MSN Messenger when you're added to someone else's contact list.

Figure 9.7
MSN Messenger gives you control over who is allowed to chat with you by displaying a notification whenever someone adds you to his contact list.

Note how MSN Messenger gives you the option of blocking your addition to someone's contact list. This gives you control over who is able to initiate chats with you, and it ultimately provides privacy.

Tip from
Michael

If you want to temporarily block people from contacting you with instant messaging, you can do so by tapping Options in the Tools menu and then selecting the Privacy tab. Just move contacts to the Block List to block them from chatting with you. You can always unblock them later by moving them back to the Allow List.

USING MY TEXT MESSAGES

You might have noticed the My Text menu command on the MSN Messenger menu near the bottom of the screen. This command enables you to quickly enter commonly used phrases without actually having to type them out. For example, if you want to say "Where are you?" you can just tap My Text and then select the phrase from the pop-up menu of choices (see Figure 9.8).

The real power of the My Text feature is that you can customize the messages to suit your own personal tastes. To edit the My Text messages, tap Edit My Text Messages in the Tools menu. This displays the My Text Messages screen, which enables you to modify the standard My Text messages (see Figure 9.9).

Figure 9.8
The My Text pop-up menu enables you to enter commonly used phrases with a single tap.

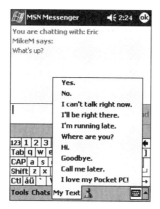

Figure 9.9
The My Text Messages screen enables you to customize the My Text messages to include phrases that are personal to you.

CHANGING YOUR STATUS

For instant messaging to be useful, you must update your status as frequently as possible. Your status indicates your availability for chatting and can be easily changed to reflect the fact that you aren't available. Following are the various status settings you can use to indicate your availability:

- Online
- Busy
- Be Right Back
- Away
- On The Phone
- Out To Lunch
- Appear Offline

The Online status setting is the only setting that enables other people to initiate a chat with you. In other words, all the other settings make you unavailable and therefore shield you from an unwanted chat. It's a good idea to use these status settings any time you're away from your device or are otherwise unavailable or uninterested in chatting.

To change your status setting in MSN Messenger, just tap your name in the contact list and then select a status setting. You can also change your status by tapping My Status on the Tools menu, followed by the desired status setting. Your icon and status change in the MSN Messenger contact list to reflect the changed status, as shown in Figure 9.10.

Figure 9.10
When you change your status, the icon next to your name in the contact list changes, along with your status that appears in parentheses.

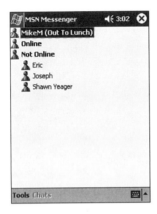

Your status is not the only status reflected in MSN Messenger on your Pocket PC. Any time one of the people in your contact list goes from being offline to online, a notification appears in MSN Messenger to alert you of his availability. A little MSN Messenger icon along the top of the Pocket PC screen is used to relay these notifications. Figure 9.11 shows one of these notifications, which states that one of my contacts (me!) has just signed in.

Figure 9.11
This notification indicates that a contact has just signed in and is therefore available for chatting.

 If you run into a situation where you start a chat on your Pocket PC and then want to continue it on your desktop PC because of the faster input capabilities of a full-size keyboard, see "Chatting from Your Pocket to the Desktop" in the "Troubleshooting" section at the end of the chapter.

GETTING TO KNOW OTHER MESSAGING SERVICES

Earlier in the chapter, I mentioned that several instant messaging services are available. I've focused on Microsoft's Messenger service because MSN Messenger is already installed on all Pocket PCs and is therefore readily available without installing any additional software. Although MSN Messenger will likely meet the needs of most mobile chatters, you might already be using a different instant messaging service on your desktop PC. If you already have a group of people you communicate with using that service, it might be a huge hassle to switch over to Microsoft's Messenger service. For this reason, it's worth taking a moment to explore other instant messaging options for your Pocket PC.

When it comes to Pocket PCs, two other significant instant messaging services beyond Microsoft's offering are available:

- AOL Instant Messenger
- Yahoo! Messenger

Both of these services are extremely popular, and both include clients for Pocket PCs that you can use with existing instant messaging accounts. The next couple of sections introduce you to the basics of using each of these instant messaging services on your Pocket PC.

AOL INSTANT MESSENGER

AOL Instant Messenger is an instant messaging service that is comparable to Microsoft's Messenger service. However, you must use the AOL Instant Messenger client application on your Pocket PC to use AOL's service. Unfortunately, instant messaging services aren't compatible with each other's software, which is why you must use a different application for each service. AOL Instant Messenger is available for free download from the AOL Instant Messenger Web site at `http://www.aol.com/aim/aim4wince.html`. After downloading and installing this application on your Pocket PC, you can begin using AOL Instant Messenger to send and receive instant messages.

To launch AOL Instant Messenger (AIM), tap AIM in the Start menu. This displays the main AIM screen, which is shown in Figure 9.12.

Figure 9.12
The main screen in AOL Instant Messenger provides access to the various areas of the AOL Instant Messenger service.

PART

II

CH

9

Figure 9.12 reveals how the main screen in AOL Instant Messenger provides access to the four main areas of the AOL Instant Messenger service:

■ Buddy List

■ Instant Message

■ News Headlines

■ Stock Quotes

Before going to any of these areas of AOL Instant Messenger, you must sign on using your AOL Instant Messenger screen name and password. To sign on, tap the Sign On button in the toolbar near the bottom of the screen. Figure 9.13 shows the Sign On dialog box, which enables you to enter your screen name and password for AOL Instant Messenger.

Figure 9.13
The Sign On dialog box in AOL Instant Messenger prompts you to enter your screen name and password.

After successfully signing on, you are shown the Buddy List, which is comparable to the contact list in MSN Messenger. In fact, two of the areas of the AOL service (Buddy List and Instant Message) are comparable to similar features in MSN Messenger. For this reason, I don't want to spend any more time focusing on them—you shouldn't have any trouble using them because you're already familiar with the same concepts in MSN Messenger. I'm more interested in pointing out aspects of AOL Instant Messenger that are different from MSN Messenger.

The News Headlines and Stock Quotes features of AOL Instant Messenger provide access to content that isn't directly related to instant messaging. To access either of these areas, tap the small button near the upper-left corner of the screen with the down arrow on it and then select News Headlines or Stock Quotes. Figure 9.14 shows the News Headlines area of AOL Instant Messenger, which provides access to breaking news stories.

To read a news story listed in the News Area, just tap it; the story then is opened as a Web page in Pocket Internet Explorer.

The Stock Quotes area of AOL Instant Messenger enables you to keep track of important investments. Figure 9.15 shows the Stock Quotes screen with a few stock quotes displayed.

Figure 9.14
The News Headlines area of AOL Instant Messenger provides access to important news stories.

Figure 9.15
The Stock Quotes area of AOL Instant Messenger provides access to important investments.

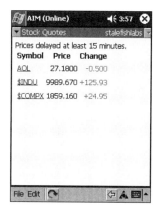

Figure 9.15 reveals how stocks and market indexes are identified solely by their ticker symbols. You can click a ticker symbol to find out more about the stock, including the company name and additional financial information. To add more stocks to the quotes list, you use only their ticker symbols; tap Preferences on the Edit menu, and then select the Stocks tab. You then enter the ticker symbol for the stock and tap the Add button to add it to the list of stock quotes.

YAHOO! MESSENGER

Yahoo! Messenger is another instant messaging service that enjoys a great deal of popularity. The Yahoo! Messenger service is similar in many ways to both MSN Messenger and AOL Instant Messenger. Like AOL Instant Messenger, you must use a special Yahoo! Messenger client application on your Pocket PC to use the Yahoo! service. Yahoo! Messenger is available for free download from the Yahoo! Messenger Web site, which is located at `http://messenger.yahoo.com/messenger/ce/downloads_ce_msgr.html`. After downloading and installing this application on your Pocket PC, you can start using Yahoo! Messenger to send and receive instant messages.

To launch Yahoo! Messenger, tap Programs on the Start menu, and then tap the Yahoo! Messenger icon. This displays the Yahoo! Messenger Sign In screen, which is shown in Figure 9.16.

Figure 9.16
The Sign In screen in Yahoo! Messenger prompts you to enter your Yahoo! ID and password.

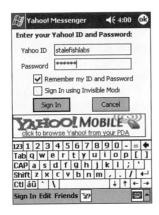

After signing on, you are given access to several interesting features of Yahoo! Messenger, including instant messaging, news headlines, stock quotes, sports scores, and weather information. Because all these features except sports scores and weather information were examined earlier when you looked at AOL Instant Messenger, I'd like to focus on the sports and weather features in Yahoo! Messenger.

To access any of the areas in Yahoo! Messenger, just select the appropriate tab near the bottom of the screen. The Sports Scoreboard tab is located one tab from the right end; when selected, it displays sports scores, as shown in Figure 9.17.

Figure 9.17
The Sports Scoreboard area of Yahoo! Messenger provides access to current sports scores.

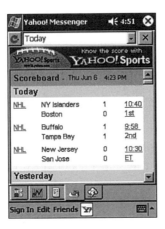

The sports scores displayed on the Sports Scoreboard in Yahoo! Messenger are determined by your personal settings on the main Yahoo! Web site. So, to customize the scoreboard, you must access the Yahoo! Web site and select personal preferences. The same thing applies to Yahoo! weather information, which is accessible via the last tab in Yahoo! Messenger. Figure 9.18 shows the Weather area of Yahoo! Messenger with current weather conditions in a few major cities.

Figure 9.18
The Weather area of Yahoo! Messenger presents current weather conditions for major cities.

Keep in mind that you can customize the type of weather information displayed by visiting the Yahoo! Web site and entering personal preferences.

TROUBLESHOOTING

PROBLEM ESTABLISHING A CHAT

I can't seem to initiate a chat with someone in my contact list, even though I know she's online in MSN Messenger.

If you've established a connection in MSN Messenger and you know someone is online, the problem is most likely that she has you blocked from chatting with her. To gain instant messaging access to her, you need to use another form of communication, such as e-mail, to request that she unblock you.

CHATTING FROM YOUR POCKET TO THE DESKTOP

I sometimes like to carry on a chat on my Pocket PC with MSN Messenger while I'm on the way to work, and I want to be able to continue the chat on my desktop PC after I arrive.

Although only one computer can be signed in to an account for chatting at any given time, you can continue a chat from your Pocket PC to your desktop PC. This is accomplished by launching Windows Messenger on your desktop PC, signing in, and then tapping the contact with whom you were chatting. On the other end of the chat, it appears as if you dropped out of the chat and then immediately returned. From the perspective of your Pocket PC, you simply are signed out of MSN Messenger.

REAL-WORLD EXAMPLE—REAL-TIME MOBILE WORKFORCE COMMUNICATION

Instant messaging is an ideal way to carry out real-time mobile workforce communication. Granted, most of us already use mobile phones for this type of communication, but as I mentioned near the start of the chapter, mobile phones can be obtrusive and downright distracting at times. For this reason, instant messaging on a Pocket PC is perfect for a mobile workforce that must stay in touch with real-time communication. If you're part of such a workforce, such as a sales or support team, take some time to try instant messaging as a convenient alternative to mobile phone calls and remote e-mail.

If you are struggling with the input inefficiencies of mobile instant messaging, consider developing a shorthand system of communication that is shared by a group. For example, you might develop acronyms or abbreviated codes that signify business processes, which helps to eliminate typing strokes. After everyone gets comfortable with the system of shorthand codes, you can communicate much more quickly via instant messaging. Of course, this system is largely dependent on your specific line of work, but it could prove useful if properly designed and implemented.

CHAPTER 10

MOBILE WEB SURFING WITH POCKET INTERNET EXPLORER

In this chapter

UNDERSTANDING POCKET WEB SURFING

With wireless Internet access now a fundamental part of Pocket PC computing, Pocket Internet Explorer has emerged as a more critical application. Web browsers have played an important role on desktop PCs for quite some time now, but their usefulness on handheld devices has been difficult to gauge, primarily because few handheld devices have had reliable network access. In the past, Pocket Internet Explorer has proven handy for synchronizing Web content to a Pocket PC and then viewing it offline. However, wireless Internet access now enables you to connect to the Internet directly and browse the Web live on your Pocket PC.

ADDRESSING THE WEAKNESSES OF POCKET IE

As a pocket version of Internet Explorer, you might expect Pocket Internet Explorer to cut a lot of corners and support only the most basic of Web technologies. Although a few important technologies are not supported in Pocket Internet Explorer, it fully supports several critical technologies, including some advanced security features. To understand the limitations of Pocket Web surfing, let's take a look at how Pocket Internet Explorer differs from its desktop counterpart. The primary Web technologies that aren't supported in Pocket Internet Explorer are

- Java applets
- HTML 4.0
- Dynamic HTML (Web scripting)
- Cascading Style Sheets (CSS)
- Animated GIF images

Java applets are special programs written in the Java programming language that run within the confines of a Web page. Although Java has become very popular and is used widely across the Web, its use on the client side of Web applications has diminished; Java is much more popular these days as a server-side component of Web applications. For client Java applets, the Java runtime engine incurs a fair amount of overhead, which is why Microsoft elected to leave it out of Pocket Internet Explorer in favor of a more streamlined application. Java applets are used on some Web sites, in which case you will find that those Web sites don't function properly in Pocket Internet Explorer because of their use of Java applets. Figure 10.1 shows a Java applet game (Connect4) that is available on my Web site at http://www.michaelmorrison.com/.

Because Pocket Internet Explorer doesn't support Java applets, you can't play this Java game on your Pocket PC. In fact, the game doesn't even show up in Pocket Internet Explorer when you view the Web page. Figure 10.2 shows the same Web page for the Connect4 game as viewed in Pocket Internet Explorer.

Figure 10.1
Online games are often created as Java applets, which enables you to play a game directly on a Web site.

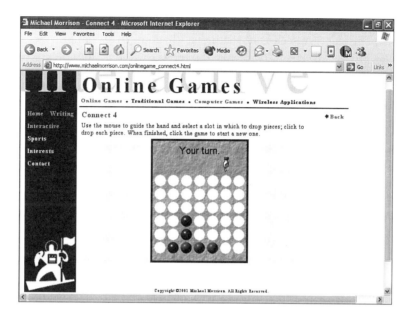

Figure 10.2
The Connect4 Java game doesn't appear in Pocket Internet Explorer because Java applets aren't supported.

Java applets aren't the only limitation of Pocket Internet Explorer. As you might know, Hypertext Markup Language (HTML) is the markup language used to describe the structure of Web pages. As of this writing, HTML 4.0 is the latest version of HTML supported in the major desktop Web browsers, including Internet Explorer. Pocket Internet Explorer supports only HTML 3.2, which puts it a little behind its desktop counterparts. Although it would be nice for Pocket Internet Explorer to support HTML 4.0, keep in mind that even Internet Explorer 5.0 didn't include complete support for HTML 4.0. Because of this, Web developers have been hesitant to build pages around the latest and greatest HTML features. For this reason, the support for HTML 3.2 isn't too big of a drawback when it comes to browsing the vast majority of Web sites with Pocket Internet Explorer.

Dynamic HTML (DHTML) is a fancy term used to describe the scripting of HTML with a scripting language such as JavaScript or VBScript. JavaScript provides a means of embedding program code directly in a Web page so you can perform interactive tasks, such as processing input from forms or performing calculations. You will likely find more Web sites that use DHTML than you will those that use Java applets, so the lack of DHTML support is somewhat more significant to Pocket Internet Explorer.

Cascading Style Sheets (CSS) is a technology being used across the Web to clean up the manner in which Web content is formatted and displayed. CSS enables you to isolate the formatting and display code for a Web page, such as the fonts and colors for each element, and place them in a separate file known as a *style sheet*. You can then apply a single style sheet to a group of Web pages to easily achieve a uniform look. Although style sheets are extremely powerful and are now being used across the Web, they still aren't supported in Pocket Internet Explorer. This isn't as bad of a weakness as it sounds, however, because most high-end Web sites include alternative formatting code that results in decent looking Web pages if CSS isn't available in a Web browser. If you refer to Figures 10.1 and 10.2, you'll notice that the formatting of the Web page in Pocket Internet Explorer looks considerably different from that in Internet Explorer. This has to do with the fact that the Web page relies heavily on CSS, which isn't supported in Pocket Internet Explorer.

The least of the missing ingredients in Pocket Internet Explorer is *animated GIF images*, which are special GIF images consisting of multiple frames that are displayed in rapid succession to give the effect of animation. In Internet Explorer, animated GIF images are responsible for adding a little pizzazz to Web pages. In Pocket Internet Explorer, on the other hand, the animated portion of these images is ignored; instead of displaying an animation, just the first frame of the animated image is displayed.

Aside from these technological differences between Pocket Internet Explorer and Internet Explorer, the other huge difference between the two browsers is the limited screen space of Pocket Internet Explorer. This might not seem like a big deal, but keep in mind that Web designers specifically target certain screen sizes when designing Web pages. The absolute minimum screen size Web designers concern themselves with is 640×480, which is four times the size of a Pocket PC screen. Most Web pages are now designed around an 800×600 screen, which is even larger. There are a couple of ways to deal with the screen size issue, which you learn about in the section titled "Getting the Most Out of Pocket Internet Explorer," later in this chapter.

PONDERING THE POSITIVES OF POCKET IE

Now that you understand the main areas in which Pocket Internet Explorer is weak, let's focus on some of its strengths. One of the most interesting technologies supported in Pocket Internet Explorer is Extensible Markup Language (XML), which is a *meta-language* used to describe specific markup languages such as HTML. XML is widely deployed across the Web as a means of structuring data and providing a uniform format for sharing data between different parts of distributed Web applications. A technology closely tied to XML and supported by Pocket Internet Explorer is Extensible Stylesheet Language (XSL), which is a special style language used to transform and render XML data for display purposes. XSL is important because it provides a means of stylizing and displaying XML data, which otherwise isn't very pretty to view.

Another positive of Pocket Internet Explorer is its support for the Wireless Application Protocol (WAP), which is the protocol used to deliver compact Web content to mobile devices such as mobile phones and pagers. WAP Web pages are created in Wireless Markup Language (WML), which is essentially an extremely scaled-down version of HTML. WAP has been around for a while and is primarily useful on devices with even more limited resources than Pocket PCs. However, enough WML content exists to make it beneficial for Pocket PCs to have access to WAP Web sites. In addition to supporting WML Web pages, Pocket Internet Explorer also supports the WMLScript scripting language and Wireless Bitmap (WBMP) images.

PART

II

CH

10

Note

WAP browsers are limited in that they can access only Web sites that are created and formatted using WML. Although Pocket Internet Explorer supports WAP, which is a good thing, it is much more flexible than pure WAP browsers in that it enables you to access normal Web sites that are based on HTML.

Because Pocket PCs are often limited to relatively low bandwidth Internet connections, it's important to minimize the amount of information transmitted and viewed in Pocket Internet Explorer. A neat feature of Pocket Internet Explorer that helps in this regard is the Hide Pictures button, which is located on the Pocket Internet Explorer toolbar. Tapping this button turns on the Hide Pictures feature, which prevents images from being downloaded and displayed. However, the outline of each image on a Web page is still displayed, and you can easily display selective images by tapping and holding on them and then selecting Show Picture. This approach to selectively displaying images provides a good trade-off between speed and usability.

Perhaps the most significant asset of Pocket Internet Explorer is its support for security features. Security is a big concern for practically all Web users because so much is at stake in terms of personal information, credit card numbers, and so on. The two mains types of security employed by Web sites are as follows:

- Secure authorization based on a user logon
- Encrypted data transfer via Secure Socket Layer (SSL)

The first security approach involves logging in to a Web site to have access to it. This approach is designed primarily to protect a Web site from unwanted users, as opposed to protecting users from giving up sensitive information. The second security approach is the one with which you are probably more familiar because it is used by practically all e-commerce Web sites. This type protects users who are transmitting sensitive data such as personal information or credit card numbers to Web sites. The sensitive information is encrypted before being transmitted and then is decrypted at the other end of the connection. This keeps the information safe should someone gain access to it while it is in transit.

Pocket Internet Explorer supports both security approaches mentioned earlier. However, unlike Internet Explorer, Pocket Internet Explorer doesn't provide any visual indication regarding the security of a site. In Internet Explorer, a small padlock icon is displayed in the status bar to let you know that a page is a secure page. Pocket Internet Explorer doesn't provide any indication of this.

→ To learn more about the security features in Pocket Internet Explorer, **see** "Feeling Secure with Pocket Internet Explorer," **p. 391**.

BROWSING WITH POCKET INTERNET EXPLORER

Unlike Internet Explorer on the desktop, which is used primarily to view Web pages while you're directly connected to the Internet, Pocket Internet Explorer is designed with offline browsing in mind. Internet Explorer includes support for online browsing, but offline browsing is much more of an issue for Pocket PC users than for desktop Internet Explorer users. Even if you have a wireless Internet service, there might still be situations where it is difficult to get online, in which case offline browsing is a viable option.

BROWSING ONLINE WITH AN INTERNET CONNECTION

Browsing online with Pocket Internet Explorer requires an Internet connection. The good news is that Pocket Internet Explorer doesn't really care about the specifics of the connection as long as it provides access to the Internet. Following are a few sample scenarios of how you might connect your device to the Internet for online browsing with Pocket Internet Explorer:

- Establish a pass-through connection with ActiveSync by connecting your Pocket PC to a desktop PC.
- Establish a wireless Internet connection by using a wireless expansion card that communicates with a wireless Internet service provider (ISP).
- Establish a wireless network connection to a LAN with Internet access by using a wireless Wi-Fi or Bluetooth expansion card.
- Use a wired dial-up modem connection by dialing an ISP using a modem expansion card.
- Use a wireless dial-up modem connection by dialing an ISP using a mobile phone that communicates with your device via Bluetooth or infrared.

These are just a few sample scenarios of how you might access the Internet for online browsing. To launch Pocket Internet Explorer, tap Programs on the Start menu and then tap the Internet Explorer icon. The initial page displayed in Internet Explorer is shown in Figure 10.3 and is actually stored on your Pocket PC.

➔ To find out more about establishing an Internet connection with your device, **see** "Creating Connections with Connection Manager," **p. 127**.

Figure 10.3
The opening page in Pocket Internet Explorer contains a variety of links for getting started with Web content.

PART

II

CH

10

The address bar near the top of the Pocket Internet Explorer application is used to enter Web page addresses (URLs) so you can visit other Web sites. If the address bar isn't visible near the top of Pocket Internet Explorer, tap Address Bar in the View menu to display it. You can then type a URL in the address bar and tap the green arrow button to the right of the address to go to the site (see Figure 10.4).

Figure 10.4
The address bar enables you to enter the address (URL) of a Web site you want to visit.

Another option for navigating to a Web site is to select the site from the list of favorites; this is accomplished by tapping the Favorites button on the toolbar. The Favorites screen is relatively empty to start with, but you can add the current Web site to the Favorites list by tapping the Add/Delete tab on the Favorites screen and then tapping the Add button. This displays the Add Favorite screen, shown in Figure 10.5. When adding a new Web site to the Favorites list, you can enter a different name for the site if you want.

Figure 10.5
The Add Favorite screen enables you to add the current Web site to the Favorites list.

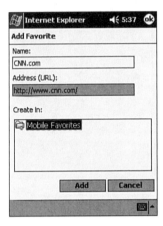

Figure 10.6 shows the resulting Favorites screen with the CNN.com Web site added as a favorite.

Figure 10.6
The Add/Delete tab on the Favorites screen provides a convenient location for managing mobile favorites.

You might notice in Figure 10.6 that the mobile favorites (links) are organized into a folder structure, much like the Pocket PC file system. This enables you to create folders for certain types of links, which provides a great deal of organization to your mobile favorites. To create a new folder, just tap the New Folder button. You also can add and delete folders just as you add and delete favorites via the Add and Delete buttons.

If you want to return to the view of mobile favorites that enables you to browse them, just select the Open tab in the Favorites window. This shows you the same list of mobile favorites, except this time you can tap any favorite to open it in Pocket Internet Explorer. You can also navigate through the folder hierarchy if you have favorites organized into sub-folders.

 If you've done a lot of online pocket Web browsing and you suspect that it might be impacting your available storage space, see "Getting Rid of Temporary Internet Files" in the "Troubleshooting" section at the end of the chapter to find out how to lighten the load in terms of cached Web content.

BROWSING OFFLINE WITH MOBILE FAVORITES

When you don't have the luxury of a live Internet connection in which to browse Web content, you can browse such content offline by downloading it to your device from your desktop PC as part of the synchronization process. This feature requires ActiveSync, which oversees all synchronization between your device and a desktop PC. It also requires that you know ahead of time which sites you want to browse. You then must save links to the Web sites in Internet Explorer on your desktop PC as mobile favorites.

CREATING A MOBILE FAVORITE

Normally, Internet Explorer favorites on your desktop are stored in the Favorites folder of Internet Explorer. When you install ActiveSync, an additional folder named Mobile Favorites is created in Internet Explorer. This folder is used to store the URLs of Web sites you want to browse offline on your Pocket PC. A new button named Create Mobile Favorite is also added to the Internet Explorer toolbar. To add a site to the Mobile Favorites folder, navigate to it in Internet Explorer and click the Create Mobile Favorite button in the toolbar. Clicking this button results in the display of a window that prompts you for the name of the Web site and the update options for the site (see Figure 10.7).

Figure 10.7
The Create Mobile Favorite window in Internet Explorer enables you to create a mobile favorite by prompting you to enter the name and update options for the mobile favorite.

The update schedule for a mobile favorite applies only if the site changes fairly often and you want to have it updated regularly. You can have the site updated daily in the morning or afternoon, or weekly. There is no need to provide update information if you don't plan on regularly retrieving site updates. The Create In button enables you to change the folder in which the site is stored. The default location is Mobile Favorites, which is where you should probably keep it unless you've created subfolders within Mobile Favorites.

PREPARING MOBILE FAVORITES FOR SYNCHRONIZATION

When you add a Web site to the Mobile Favorites folder, ActiveSync should begin synchronizing with your Pocket PC to copy the site to the device. However, you have to enable the Favorite information type in ActiveSync. To enable it, launch ActiveSync and click the Options button on the toolbar. Click the check box next to Favorite in the list to enable the synchronization of mobile favorites. You can also click the Settings button to alter the settings associated with Favorite synchronization. The Favorite Synchronization Options window is then displayed, as shown in Figure 10.8.

Figure 10.8
The Favorite Synchronization Options window in ActiveSync lets you enable and disable mobile favorites.

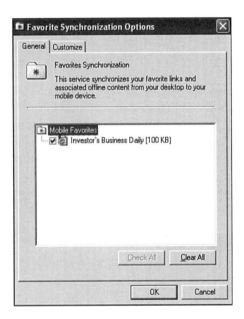

This window allows you to enable and disable mobile favorites. The Customize tab allows you to further control the synchronization of all mobile Web content by enabling and disabling the synchronization of specific types of content (see Figure 10.9).

The primary purpose of the Customize tab is to optimize offline Web content for space. When you consider that images and sounds can be quite large in terms of file sizes, you might want to disable one or both of them by clearing the appropriate check box to conserve memory space on your device. This is a personal choice and is ultimately dependent on how much Web content you synchronize and the degree to which they use images and sounds.

Figure 10.9
The Customize tab of the Favorite Synchronization Options window enables you to control the types of content synchronized.

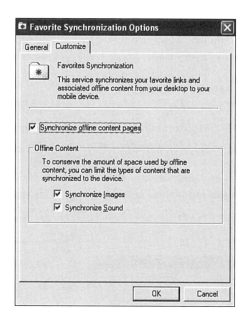

After you click OK in the ActiveSync Options window, ActiveSync immediately starts synchronizing the Web sites located in the Mobile Favorites folder. After the synchronization is complete, you can begin browsing the sites on your device. Just tap the Favorites button on the toolbar in Pocket Internet Explorer. To browse the synchronized Web site offline, simply tap it in the Mobile Favorites list. Figure 10.10 shows the Investor's Business Daily Web site as it is browsed offline in Pocket Internet Explorer.

Figure 10.10
The Investor's Business Daily Web site is a good example of a Web site you can browse offline as a mobile favorite in Pocket Internet Explorer.

It's important to understand that by default ActiveSync doesn't attempt to synchronize links to other pages from a mobile favorite. For this reason, if you tap a hyperlink in an offline Web site, Pocket Internet Explorer informs you that the page is unavailable. Of course, if you view a synchronized Web site while you happen to be connected to the Internet, the hyperlinks work just fine. In a moment, you learn how to tweak the settings for a mobile favorite so linked pages are also synchronized.

MANAGING AND CUSTOMIZING MOBILE FAVORITES

You need to understand that mobile favorites are managed on the Internet Explorer side of the synchronization equation. To organize mobile favorites, click Organize Favorites in the Favorites menu in Internet Explorer. The Organize Favorites window appears, which contains a list of all the favorites for Internet Explorer. Click Mobile Favorites in the list to focus on mobile favorites. A list of your mobile favorites appears below the Mobile Favorites folder, in which you can select and modify individual favorites. This is where you enable and disable mobile favorites for synchronization. Figure 10.11 shows how I've enabled the MSN Web site mobile favorite.

Figure 10.11
The Organize Favorites window in Internet Explorer allows you to organize and enable and disable mobile favorites.

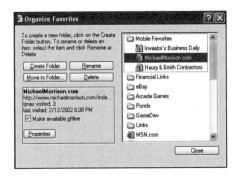

After you enable a mobile favorite, a Properties button appears that enables you to further customize the favorite. Clicking the Properties button results in the display of the Properties window, shown in Figure 10.12.

You'll notice that the Properties window includes several tabs for customizing the details of a mobile favorite. The last two tabs, Schedule and Download, are the most important because they have the biggest impact on how the Web site is synchronized. The Schedule tab enables you to customize the specifics of how a site is updated; this is the same update information you selected for a mobile favorite when you first added it to the Mobile Favorites folder. The Download tab is much more interesting in that it enables you to carefully control the amount of content synchronized for the Web site (see Figure 10.13).

The Download tab includes some powerful options for controlling the amount and types of content that are synchronized. The first option is the most dramatic in that it enables you to set the *link depth* of synchronized pages. A link depth of 1 means that Web pages directly linked from the synchronized page are synchronized as well. A link depth of 2 means that pages linked from the linked pages are synchronized, too. As you might realize, the link depth can dramatically impact the amount of content synchronized for a site.

Figure 10.12
The Properties window in Internet Explorer enables you to customize the details of a mobile favorite, such as how often the content is updated.

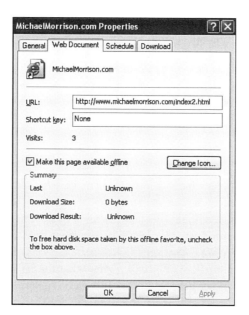

Figure 10.13
The Download tab in the Properties window enables you to carefully control the amount of content synchronized for a mobile favorite.

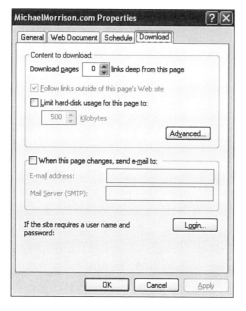

PART
II

CH

10

If you've noticed that synchronized mobile favorites are eating up your device's storage space, it might have something to do with the link depth setting in Pocket Internet Explorer. See "Saving Storage Space with Link Depth" in the "Troubleshooting" section at the end of the chapter to learn how to solve this problem.

This brings us to another important option, which enables you to limit the hard disk space for a synchronized site. This option places a cap on the size of the content synchronized for a Web site. This can be a valuable option when used in conjunction with the link depth. The default value of 500KB is a good value to use for this setting for most Web sites.

Caution

If you set the link depth to more than 1 in the Download tab, you run the risk of being overwhelmed by linked content. To avoid this problem, I highly recommend limiting the hard disk usage for a synchronized site if you set the link depth to more than 1.

The Advanced button is used to further customize the types of content synchronized for the Web site. More specifically, you can individually enable and disable images, sound, video, ActiveX controls, and Java applets, as well as hyperlinks to content other than HTML Web pages. The Java option in this case might seem confusing because I said earlier that Pocket Internet Explorer doesn't support Java. This Java option reflects the fact that Pocket Internet Explorer is designed to support several lightweight versions of Internet Explorer, including some that might support Java. The end result is that the Java setting has no impact on Pocket Internet Explorer because Pocket Internet Explorer doesn't support Java.

Note

The default values set in the Download tab are designed to include a minimal amount of content while providing a reasonable browsing experience. It's not a bad idea to try them on a few Web sites before tinkering with them too much.

USING THE AVANTGO INFORMATION SERVICE

In addition to traditional Web sites that are designed for viewing on desktop computers with full-size monitors, some Web content is specifically designed for viewing on handheld devices. AvantGo is a free information service that specializes in offering Web content in a form that is easily viewed on handheld devices, such as Pocket PCs. AvantGo content is designed for offline browsing and is therefore synchronized with your Pocket PC much like mobile favorites are.

To enable AvantGo for synchronization, launch ActiveSync and click the Options button. In the Options window, click the check box next to AvantGo to enable the synchronization of AvantGo content. No settings are available in ActiveSync for AvantGo, so after you enable the information type, you can click OK to accept it and synchronize. When the synchronization finishes, launch Pocket Internet Explorer and tap AvantGo on the main home page; if you've changed the home page already, you can go to Mobile Favorites and tap AvantGo Channels. The AvantGo home page is then displayed, which contains a list of AvantGo channels (see Figure 10.14).

Figure 10.14
The AvantGo home page contains a list of hyperlinks for the AvantGo channels that are synchronized on your device.

A *channel* in AvantGo is basically an information source, much like a Web site. However, channels differ a little from Web sites in that they are specifically designed to accommodate information that changes on a regular basis. The channels shown in Figure 10.14 are the default channels configured for synchronization with AvantGo. Following are some of the popular channels supported by AvantGo:

- The Wall Street Journal
- CNN
- Yahoo!
- New York Times
- The Weather Channel
- USA Today
- Sony USA
- CNNmoney
- CNET News
- Amazon.com
- Hollywood.com
- Fodors.com
- WIRED News

You can begin viewing the content for a default AvantGo channel by tapping any of them. However, you'll probably want to choose your own AvantGo channels, which requires you to register with AvantGo. To register, tap the word Personalize on the AvantGo home page. This displays a page that prompts you to enter an e-mail address to begin the registration process. Enter your e-mail address, and then scroll down and tap the OK button (see Figure 10.15).

PART

II

CH

10

Figure 10.15
The Personalize page in AvantGo prompts you to register by entering your e-mail address.

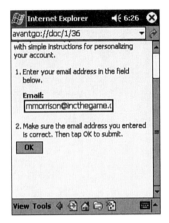

Enter your e-mail address in the AvantGo Personalize page, and you will be immediately sent an e-mail message from AvantGo that includes a hyperlink you must follow to activate your AvantGo account. Figure 10.16 shows the registration Web page you use to register with AvantGo as viewed in the desktop Internet Explorer.

Figure 10.16
Registering with AvantGo is as easy as filling out a form on the AvantGo Web site in Internet Explorer.

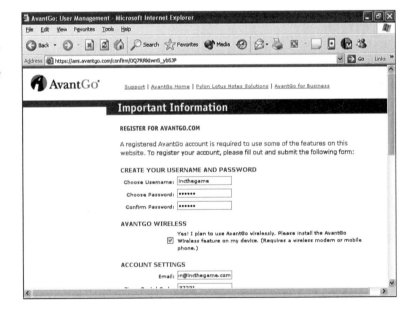

After you register with AvantGo, you're prompted to configure your handheld device profile for use in connecting with the AvantGo server. Follow the directions to configure the profile. After this is finished, you are logged on to the AvantGo Web site where you can start selecting channels for synchronization with your device. You add channels by clicking the plus sign next to each one as if you were adding it to a shopping cart. To remove channels, click the Edit button in the My Account window. Figure 10.17 shows the My Channels page, which displays a list of the selected channels, along with the respective sizes of their content.

Tip from
Michael

Although the selection and configuration of AvantGo channels in this example are shown taking place in Internet Explorer on your desktop computer, you can also use the AvantGo Channel Manager on your Pocket PC to configure channels. You access the Channel Manager by tapping Tools on the main AvantGo page and then tapping Channel Manager on the AvantGo Tools page.

Figure 10.17
The My Channels page includes a list of the AvantGo channels selected for synchronization.

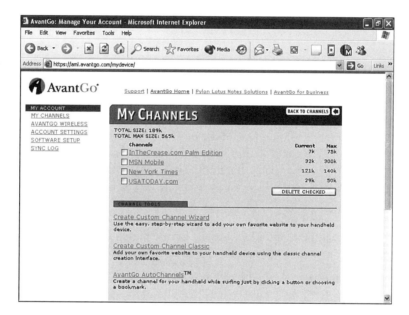

When you are finished setting up AvantGo channels, you can exit Internet Explorer. To have the new AvantGo channels synchronized with your device, open ActiveSync and click the Sync button on the toolbar. The AvantGo content is then synchronized with your device, after which you need to refresh the AvantGo home page in Pocket Internet Explorer. You're now ready to browse the new AvantGo content in Pocket Internet Explorer. Figure 10.18 shows The USA Today AvantGo channel as it is viewed in Pocket Internet Explorer.

If you decide to stop using AvantGo for some reason, you should remove it from your device entirely so that you can reclaim precious storage space. See "Cleaning Up After AvantGo" in the "Troubleshooting" section at the end of the chapter to find out how this is accomplished.

Figure 10.18
AvantGo content is tailored to the small screens of handheld devices, as the USA Today channel reveals.

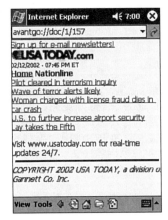

GETTING THE MOST OUT OF POCKET INTERNET EXPLORER

There are several tips and tricks that you might find useful while browsing Web sites with Pocket Internet Explorer. One of the most important tips is to use the Fit to Screen option, which scales Web pages so they fit in the Pocket PC screen a little better. The Fit to Screen option is enabled by default, but if for some reason you don't have it turned on, be sure to tap Fit to Screen in the View menu to enable it. The advantage of the Fit to Screen feature is that it reformats a Web page and resizes its images so more of the page is visible on the Pocket PC's small screen. Of course, this might not always be a good thing, especially when it comes to sites that use a lot of tricky formatting. For this reason, you might find yourself turning Fit to Screen on and off depending on the specific page you are viewing.

Another handy feature similar to Fit to Screen is Text Size, which is also located in the View menu. The Text Size feature controls the size of the text on a Web page and can be used to increase or decrease the text size; this has the effect of fitting more text on the screen or making text more readable.

Tip from
Michael

> Even with careful use of the Fit to Screen and Text Size features, you are unlikely to get most traditional Web pages to completely fit within the confines of the Pocket PC screen. Don't forget that you can use the scrollbars to move around pages that don't fit entirely in the Pocket PC screen.

Like in Internet Explorer, you can change the home page of Pocket Internet Explorer. Navigate to the page you want to use as the home page, and then tap Options in the Tools menu. Near the top of the screen you'll see a button named Use Current—tap this button to set the current Web page as the home page. Figure 10.19 shows how I've set CNN.com as the home page for Pocket Internet Explorer.

Figure 10.19
The Options window in Pocket Internet Explorer enables you to change the home page.

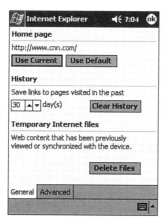

The remainder of the General tab in the Options screen enables you to adjust the amount of time recently visited URLs are stored, as well as manually clear the history list and temporary Internet files. The Advanced tab in the Options screen allows you to enable and disable cookies, images, sounds, and security warnings, as well as establish the language used in the browser.

ACCESSING WEB-BASED E-MAIL

I personally am a big fan of Microsoft Outlook as an e-mail client. It has loads of features and pretty much does everything I could ever ask for in the way of allowing me to communicate electronically through e-mail. You might have your own favorite e-mail client, which is okay, too. Regardless of which e-mail client you prefer, sometimes you simply can't use it. For example, my ISP went down a few months ago and I was stuck with no e-mail at all, which was quite painful because I'm so dependent on it. With my e-mail server out of commission, my e-mail client wasn't much use. Even so, I had a backup option that worked perfectly.

Tip from
Michael

In addition to allowing access to Web-based e-mail, Pocket Internet Explorer also serves as a useful viewer for images that are attached to traditional e-mail. If you receive an image attachment in the Inbox, you can usually tap it to view it in Pocket Internet Explorer.

I'm referring to Web-based e-mail, which is e-mail that is completely managed through a Web site, as opposed to using a client application such as Outlook. A variety of Web-based e-mail services are available, with Microsoft Hotmail being one of the leaders. The idea behind Web-based e-mail is that all you need to access it is a Web browser. You don't have to configure any POP or SMTP settings in a client application because you don't even use a client application. The simplicity of needing only a Web browser to access Web-based e-mail makes it an interesting alternative to traditional e-mail that requires a client application. Figure 10.20 shows a Hotmail e-mail account as it appears in Internet Explorer on my desktop PC.

Figure 10.20
Microsoft Hotmail is accessed purely through a Web interface, as is evident here in Internet Explorer.

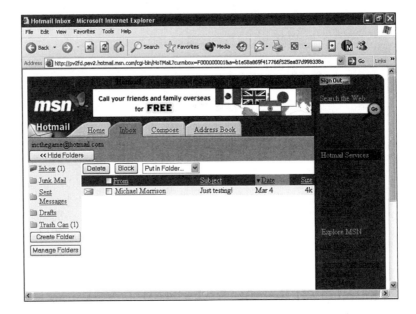

Because all that is required to access Web-based e-mail is a Web browser, it stands to reason that Pocket PCs are already equipped to handle Web-based e-mail thanks to Pocket Internet Explorer. In fact, all you have to do on your Pocket PC to access Web-based e-mail is visit the appropriate Web site for the e-mail service. In the case of Hotmail, you access the Hotmail Web site through the MSN Mobile Web site, which is located on the Pocket Internet Explorer home page; you can also directly enter the URL of the site at http://mobile.msn.com/pocketpc/. Figure 10.21 shows the MSN Mobile Web page, which includes a link to Mobile Hotmail.

Figure 10.21
The Mobile Hotmail Web site is accessible from a link on the MSN Mobile Web site.

Following the Hotmail link on the MSN Mobile Web page takes you into Mobile Hotmail, where you must log in before accessing Web-based e-mail. Similar to Instant Messenger, Hotmail requires you to have a .NET Passport to use its e-mail services. If you've already set up a Passport account, enter it in Hotmail so you can begin using it to send and receive Web-based e-mail. After you've successfully logged in to Hotmail with your Passport username and password, you can view the Hotmail Inbox, which shows any new messages you've received. Figure 10.22 shows my Hotmail Inbox with a test message sent from another one of my e-mail accounts.

Figure 10.22
The Mobile Hotmail Web site enables you to send and receive Web-based e-mail through a Web interface on your Pocket PC.

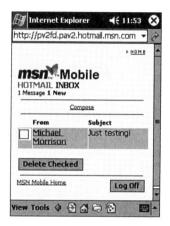

You can use the Hotmail Web interface on your Pocket PC to send and receive e-mail messages just as if it were any other e-mail client.

Tip from	
Michael	Similar to Hotmail, other types of Web-based e-mail should be accessible through Pocket Internet Explorer without any problems.

TROUBLESHOOTING

SAVING STORAGE SPACE WITH LINK DEPTH

I just synchronized my mobile favorites, and now I seem to be running dangerously low on memory on my device.

First, you need to be selective about how many mobile favorites you synchronize with your device at any given time because they can take their toll on your available storage space. However, mobile favorites usually don't start presenting a storage problem until you adjust the link depth of Pocket Internet Explorer, as was discussed in this chapter. More specifically, a link depth of more than 1 or 2 can result in an enormous amount of information being synchronized with your device, which can tax your available storage space in a hurry. Your best bet is to not go over 2 with the link depth setting, or if you must do so then limit the hard disk usage for the site so that you don't risk being overwhelmed by linked content.

GETTING RID OF TEMPORARY INTERNET FILES

I've done a fair amount of Web browsing in Pocket Internet Explorer, and I'm concerned that temporary Internet files might be taking up too much space on my device.

You're probably familiar with temporary Internet files on your desktop PC from browsing Web pages with Internet Explorer. These files include cached Web pages and related resources, as well as a history of the Web pages you've visited recently. These files take up valuable space on your device, and although you might want to keep them around for better performance, if you're running low on memory then I'd recommend clearing them out. You can do this by tapping Options on the Tools menu in Pocket Internet Explorer and then tapping the Delete Files button. To clear the history, just tap the Clear History button. You can also limit the range of the history feature by decreasing the number of days for which history links are kept.

CLEANING UP AFTER AVANTGO

I decided to stop using AvantGo, and I want to ensure it isn't wasting any space on my device.

AvantGo content is tightly integrated with ActiveSync and your Pocket PC, so removing it from your device is more involved than some other applications. To remove AvantGo and its associated content from your device, follow these steps:

1. Launch ActiveSync on your desktop PC, click the Options button, and uncheck AvantGo in the synchronization list.
2. Tap Settings on the Start menu on your device, and then tap the Connections tab.
3. Tap the AvantGo Connect icon, and then remove the AvantGo.com server from the Server settings list by tapping the Remove button.
4. Launch Pocket Internet Explorer on your device, and tap the AvantGo link on the home page. When AvantGo attempts (and fails) to load new content, it ends up cleaning up the remains of your old content. This helps to reclaim some storage space taken up by AvantGo.

REAL-WORLD EXAMPLE—TRACKING YOUR TRAVEL WITH AVANTGO

Although several travel channels are available for use within AvantGo, one channel in particular that you might find useful is Expedia To Go. Expedia To Go provides access to information on the popular Expedia travel Web site. With Expedia To Go, you can enter an entire trip itinerary and then keep tabs on your flight schedules and other pertinent information such as directions. You can access the Expedia To Go channel from the Travel section of the AvantGo channels on the AvantGo Web site at `https://ami.avantgo.com/channels/`.

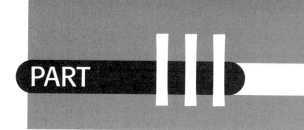

PART III

POCKET PC INFORMATION MANAGEMENT

CHAPTER **11**

ACCESSING FILES WITH FILE EXPLORER

In this chapter

USING FILE EXPLORER TO NAVIGATE FILES

The desktop application that enables you to access and manipulate files is Windows Explorer. Pocket PCs include a similar application called File Explorer that enables you to view and manipulate the file system of your Pocket PC. As you learn in this chapter, you can use the File Explorer to copy and move files back and forth between system memory and memory storage cards. Additionally, File Explorer enables you to access files on a network.

STARTING FILE EXPLORER

Unlike most of the standard applications that permanently reside in your Pocket PC's ROM, the File Explorer application isn't available from the Start menu by default. However, you can add it to the menu if you find yourself using it frequently.

→ For more information on how to add the File Explorer application to the Start menu, **see** "Tweaking the Start and New Menus," **p. 76**.

To run File Explorer, tap the Start menu and then tap Programs. In the Programs window, tap the File Explorer icon to launch the File Explorer application. The application opens, displaying the contents of the My Documents folder in main system memory, as shown in Figure 11.1.

Figure 11.1
The File Explorer application begins with the My Documents folder in view.

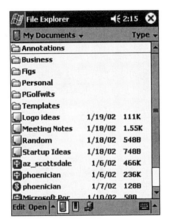

You can change the currently displayed folder by tapping the folder near the upper-left corner of the screen. This results in the display of a drop-down list from which you can select a different folder. Tapping My Device reveals the top-level folder structure of your device, which consists of the following folders by default:

- **My Documents**—Application data and related documents
- **Program Files**—Installed programs and settings
- **Temp**—Temporary files
- **Windows**—Windows settings and support files

Note

Depending on your specific Pocket PC, other default folders might exist in addition to the four mentioned here. For example, Compaq iPAQ devices include a folder named iPAQ File Store.

Of these standard folders, the one with which you are most concerned is My Documents, where you will store any files or documents you create. You can create subfolders of the My Documents folder, but it's important to keep any data files you create in this folder or a folder one level beneath it. This is necessary so that the files will be accessible from Pocket PC applications.

 If you have files stored in folders beneath the My Documents folder and are having trouble accessing them from standard Pocket PC applications, see "Finding Disappearing Files" in the "Troubleshooting" section at the end of the chapter to resolve the problem.

SORTING AND VIEWING FILES

The File Explorer application makes exploring the file system of your device and interacting with files relatively easy. You can sort the file list in File Explorer by tapping the upper-right corner of the File Explorer screen, which contains a sort method drop-down list that enables you to sort the files and folders by name, date, size, or type. Although the sort method is ultimately a personal preference, I prefer to set File Explorer so that it sorts by type, which keeps files of the same type together visually. This can be helpful if you're looking for a certain type of file, such as a Pocket Word document or an image.

When viewing files in the file list of File Explorer, be sure you pay close attention to the file size displayed to the right of the file entry. Unlike Windows Explorer, which uses the word "bytes" to identify file sizes under 1KB, File Explorer uses the letter B. It also uses the letter K to signify kilobytes (KB) and M for megabytes (MB). Even though these letters are easily distinguishable, it's a slightly different look from Windows Explorer that can go unnoticed. And don't forget that a KB is 1,024Bs and an MB is 1,024KBs.

Note

File Explorer doesn't have a Find Files feature; to find files or other information on your device, you must use the Find application that is accessible from the Start menu.

MOVING BETWEEN FILE STORAGE AREAS

Unlike Windows Explorer on a desktop PC, which typically enables you to navigate between different types of disk drives, the Pocket PC File Explorer is designed for navigating memory because Pocket PCs essentially use memory in the same manner that desktop PCs use disk drives. Even though this is different from how things are done on desktop PCs, the concept is still the same. In fact, you will understand File Explorer more quickly if you start thinking in terms of *storage areas* as opposed to memory chips or hard drives. The File Explorer is centered on three main storage areas, which are represented by three icons in the command bar along the bottom of the screen:

- My Device
- Storage Card
- Network Share

These three areas are accessible to File Explorer for exploring and manipulating files. By default, the My Device area is selected in File Explorer, which corresponds to your device's main system memory; the standard My Documents folder is located in the My Device storage area. You can always tell which storage area you're in because its icon is highlighted in the toolbar along the bottom of the screen in File Explorer. For example, Figure 11.2 shows that the Storage Card icon is highlighted when exploring files on a memory storage card.

Figure 11.2
The icons along the bottom of the screen in File Explorer enable you to navigate between storage areas, such as a memory storage card.

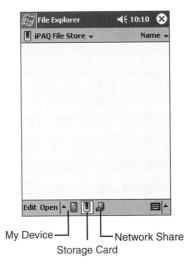

When you tap one of the storage area icons to switch to a different storage area, the folder you last visited in that storage area is automatically displayed. However, every storage area has a default folder that serves as a base for the storage area. For example, the My Documents folder is the default folder for the My Device area. You can quickly jump to the default folder when switching storage areas by tapping a storage area icon twice. Following are the various default folders for each of the storage areas:

- **My Device**—My Documents
- **Storage Card**—Root folder
- **Network Share**—Network Share prompt

As you can see, the Network Share default folder is a little different from the other two folders because it isn't fixed. Instead of being set to a specific folder, the default action for the Network Share area is to display the Network Share prompt, which asks you to enter a network folder. The reason for this behavior has to do with the fact that there really is nothing you can count on when it comes to network folders; every network is structured differently, so it's best to let the user specify what he wants to access on the network. You learn more about accessing network files later in the chapter in the section titled "Accessing Files on a Network. "

COPYING AND MOVING FILES

File Explorer makes copying and moving files from one folder to another easy between your device and desktop PC, between your device and another device, or between your device and a memory storage card. However, because the Pocket PC operating system doesn't support drag and drop, you must always use the familiar tap-and-hold technique to manipulate files. To copy or move a file from one folder to another, follow these steps:

1. Tap and hold on the file to display a menu of file options (see Figure 11.3).
2. Tap Copy to copy the file, or tap Cut to move the file.
3. Navigate to the folder in which you want the file placed.
4. Tap Edit in the lower-left corner of the screen, and then tap Paste. You can also tap and hold in the File Explorer window and then tap Paste on the pop-up menu.

Figure 11.3
Tapping and holding on a file in File Explorer presents a pop-up menu of file options.

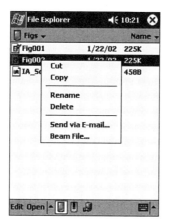

PART

III

CH

11

In addition to copying and moving individual files, you can also work with groups of files. To do this, you must tap on the first file and drag the stylus down to select additional files. Of course, this requires the files to appear next to each other in the file list. After you've selected a group of files, tap and hold on any of the files and follow the same series of steps that were just explained for copying and moving them.

Tip from
Michael

To select multiple files that aren't adjacent to each other, tap the Ctl key (Control) on the soft keyboard (Input Panel). With this key pressed, you can select and deselect individual files as part of a group using the stylus.

RENAMING AND DELETING FILES

Renaming files in File Explorer is similar to copying and moving files in that it also involves the popular tap-and-hold technique. To rename a file, tap and hold on the file and then tap Rename on the pop-up menu that appears. The name of the file then turns into an edit box, and you enter the new filename. Tapping off of the edit box commits the name change. Keep in mind that File Explorer doesn't allow you to change or even view the name of a file extension—only the first part of a filename can be changed.

Caution

There is no Recycle Bin in the Pocket PC operating system, so after you delete a file, it is gone.

 If you've tried unsuccessfully to change the file extension of a file using the File Explorer application, you might be interested in "Changing File Extensions" in the "Troubleshooting" section at the end of the chapter.

Deleting files is similar to renaming them; you tap and hold on the file and then tap Delete on the pop-up menu. Before committing to the deletion, File Explorer presents you with a confirmation box to ensure that you want to delete the file (see Figure 11.4). If you haven't changed your mind, just tap Yes and the file is deleted. On the other hand, you can tap No and nothing will happen to the file.

Figure 11.4
A confirmation box is displayed to ensure that you want to delete a file; tapping Yes follows through with the deletion, whereas No cancels it.

SENDING FILES

The File Explorer application also lets you send files to others. The two basic approaches to sending files with File Explorer are as follows:

- **E-mail**—Files are sent as e-mail attachments.
- **Infrared**—Files are sent to another device via the infrared port.

The e-mail approach to sending files involves attaching a file to an e-mail message and having it delivered through the Inbox application. If you've ever used e-mail attachments on your desktop PC, this should be familiar. The infrared approach is unique to Pocket PCs and involves sending a file over the wireless infrared port to another Pocket PC. Infrared file transfers can be extremely handy if you need to quickly share a file with someone. Generally speaking, sending files via infrared is useful if you are in physical proximity to another user who has a Pocket PC, whereas the e-mail approach is necessary if you are sending files to remote locations.

The file sending operations in File Explorer are available from the pop-up menu that appears when you tap and hold over a file in the file list. To send a file via e-mail, just tap Send via E-mail on the menu, and an e-mail message will be created with the file attached to it. You are then responsible for filling in the details of the message, such as the recipient(s), the subject, and any message to accompany the attachment. To send a file via infrared, tap Beam File on the menu and then align your device with the infrared port of another device. The devices will establish an infrared connection and then transfer the file.

→ To find out more about sending e-mail messages, **see** "Sending and Receiving E-mail," **p. 217**.

STORING FILES ON MEMORY CARDS

It's hard to discuss files and file storage without addressing memory storage cards and how they fit into the picture. If you have a memory storage card installed on your Pocket PC, it will appear as a folder named Storage Card in File Explorer beneath the My Device root folder. Some devices include additional built-in memory that is accessed independently of system memory, thereby functioning like a storage card. For example, the Compaq iPAQ H3800 series of devices includes 6MB of extra flash memory, which is accessible through a folder named iPAQ File Store, as shown in Figure 11.5.

Figure 11.5
Extra flash memory on Compaq iPAQ H3800 devices is accessed like a memory storage card through a special folder that appears beneath the My Device root folder.

The iPAQ extra memory is relevant to this memory card discussion because it functions as a nonremovable memory card. It functions independently of the main system memory. Regardless of whether we're talking about built-in extra memory or a removable memory card you can share with your digital camera, you're probably interested in learning how to store files in this storage space.

The storage space made available by a memory storage card is always associated with a folder, such as Storage Card, that resides beneath the My Documents folder. The Storage Card folder acts just like any other folder on your device, with the exception that files stored in the folder actually reside on the storage card instead of in the main system memory. If you have several storage cards or remove your card often for any reason, you must be careful about what types of files you store on it. You don't want to miss files that are on the card if you forget to carry the card with you. Many users have a single storage card that is kept in the device as long as they don't need to use a modem or some other memory peripheral. In this case, you must still be careful about what you put on the card because it won't be accessible while using a modem or other memory card, assuming your device has only one expansion slot.

→ If you're encountering a problem launching the Inbox application after removing a memory storage card, **see** "Correcting a Renamed or Deleted Attachment Folder," **p. 234**.

If you plan on using a memory card to store data files for Pocket PC applications such as Pocket Word, Pocket Excel, or Windows Media Player, you'll need to create a folder named My Documents on the card. This is necessary because Pocket PC applications are specifically designed to store files in the My Documents folder and will not see files stored elsewhere on the card. To create the My Documents folder on a storage card, follow these steps:

1. Tap the folder in the upper-left corner of the screen, and then tap My Device.
2. Tap the Storage Card folder in the file list.
3. Tap Edit in the lower-left corner of the screen, and then tap New Folder. You can also tap and hold in the File Explorer window and then tap New Folder on the pop-up menu.
4. Enter **My Documents** as the folder name.
5. Tap off the folder name to create the new folder.

The My Documents folder on the storage card can be thought of as an extension of the My Documents folder in main memory. In fact, if you use the Save Document As function in Pocket Word or the Save Workbook As function in Pocket Excel, you will have the opportunity to specify main memory or the memory card to store the file, in which case it will be stored in the respective My Documents folder.

→ To learn more about managing memory storage cards, **see** "Taking Control of Memory Storage Cards," **p. 362**.

If you don't like the idea of having all your documents and data files stored in one folder, you can create subfolders beneath the My Documents folder. For example, you could create a Pocket Word folder for Word files and a Pocket Excel folder for Excel files. Actually, the My Documents folder in main memory already includes Business and Personal folders for one possible schema of organization. In fact, it's not a bad idea to use these same names on your memory card so the folders integrate with those in main memory.

Note

Although you are free to name subfolders of the My Documents folder anything you choose, the My Documents folder itself is a necessity if you plan to access files on the memory storage card from Pocket PC applications such as Pocket Word, Pocket Excel, or Windows Media Player. Otherwise, the applications won't see any files on the card.

ACCESSING FILES ON A NETWORK

Earlier in the chapter I mentioned that the File Explorer application recognizes shared network folders as a type of storage area that can be accessed in the same manner as main memory and storage card folders on your device. This network support enables you to use File Explorer to navigate through shared network folders and perform the same file operations you've learned about throughout the chapter thus far. With Pocket PCs rapidly gaining accessibility to wireless networks, this is an incredibly powerful Pocket PC feature.

➔ To find out more about establishing a connection to a network with your Pocket PC, **see** "Creating Connections with Connection Manager," **p. 127**.

To begin working with files on a network, tap the Network Share icon near the bottom of the screen in File Explorer. You'll be presented with a dialog box that enables you to enter the path of the network file or folder you want to access (see Figure 11.6).

Figure 11.6
The Open dialog box for network sharing enables you to enter a path to a network file or folder.

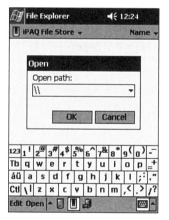

PART

III

CH

11

After entering a suitable network path, File Explorer opens the appropriate folder and enables you to view it and access files in it. One limitation of File Explorer for networking is that it doesn't allow you to open files across the network. To open a file, you must first copy it to your Pocket PC. So, you must follow the steps outlined earlier in the chapter to copy a file from a shared network folder to your device's main memory or a storage card before actually opening the file in an application.

Tip from
Michael
Many shared network folders require authentication before allowing access. In this situation, File Explorer prompts you to log in before providing access to files and folders.

You'll quickly realize that with the exception of not being able to open files directly across a network, exploring a shared network folder in File Explorer is similar to exploring files that are stored locally. This seamless integration of network file access is a new feature to Pocket PC 2002, and one that is critical in making Pocket PCs more useful in corporate environments where accessing resources on a shared network is important.

INSTALLING POCKET PC SOFTWARE

A discussion of Pocket PC file management wouldn't be complete without tackling the issue of installing Pocket PC software, which basically boils down to copying several files to your device. Fortunately, the vast majority of Pocket PC applications include installation programs that handle the details of putting files in the right places and taking care of any appropriate settings. Software installation is important because many types of interesting applications can be downloaded or purchased to expand your Pocket PC's capabilities.

Caution

Storage is a valuable and limited commodity on your Pocket PC, which usually means you have to pick and choose the software you install on the device. The massive size of desktop hard drives has spoiled many of us into installing as much software as we want with no concern about how much space it eats up. You can't get away with this when it comes to your Pocket PC, unless you've sprung for a micro hard drive card that is capable of holding gigabytes of data. Take stock of how much space you have available on your device before installing additional software.

→ To learn more about micro hard drives, **see** "Micro Hard Drives," **p. 359**.

Software is installed onto a Pocket PC in one of three ways, which is largely dependent on where the software originates:

- The software is on a CD-ROM or downloaded onto a desktop PC and is installed from a setup program that runs on a desktop PC.
- The software is downloaded onto the device or located on a memory card, and the setup program runs from the device.
- There is no setup program; the software is downloaded straight from the Web or from a desktop PC to the device.

The next few sections address the details of each of these installation approaches. It's worth pointing out that most Pocket PC applications are installed using the first approach.

INSTALLING SOFTWARE FROM A DESKTOP PC

The smoothest way to install software is to run an installation program on your desktop PC and let it do all the work. Of course, this requires your device to be connected to the desktop PC via a cradle or some other (serial/USB) cable connection. You'll also need to establish an ActiveSync connection because ActiveSync is what actually allows the installation to take place between the desktop PC and the device.

Note

Although an ActiveSync partnership is absolutely essential when synchronizing data between your desktop and Pocket PC, it is not necessary when just installing software. In other words, an ActiveSync *guest connection* is all you need to install software, not an ActiveSync *partnership*.

After establishing an ActiveSync connection, you simply run the setup program for the new application on your desktop PC. Setup programs tend to differ somewhat due to the options that are specific to each application, so I won't try to generalize the process other than to say that you'll be presented with a series of steps that outline the various options available for installing the software. After you've gone through the steps, the installation should proceed, resulting in a new icon in the Programs folder of the device. To run the newly installed program, tap Programs in the Start menu, look for the new icon, and then tap it.

PART
III
CH
11

INSTALLING SOFTWARE DIRECTLY FROM THE POCKET PC

The decision to install Pocket PC software from a desktop PC or directly from the device is not in your hands. The software publisher makes this decision when it packages the software for installation. Software designed for installation directly from your device is packaged in a file with a .cab extension. These CAB files are special compressed files similar to Zip files that are designed specifically for software distribution. You could obtain software in CAB form by downloading it off the Web or copying it straight off a CD-ROM, but the distinction is that CAB files install themselves directly onto your device.

To install software from a CAB file, copy or download the CAB file to your device and use File Explorer to open the folder in which the file is located. Tap the file, and follow the installation instructions to install the software. Similar to the desktop installation process, the CAB installation finishes by placing a new icon in the Programs folder of the device. To run the newly installed program, tap Programs in the Start menu, look for the new icon, and then tap it. Figure 11.7 shows an image viewer application called Pocket Beholder being installed via a CAB file directly on a Pocket PC.

Figure 11.7
Installing an application directly via a CAB file simply involves tapping the CAB file in File Explorer and waiting for it to install.

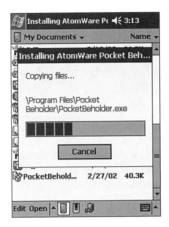

Tip from
Michael

If you install software from a memory storage card, the setup program runs directly on your Pocket PC. Typically, the setup program runs automatically when you insert the card.

INSTALLING BY COPYING AN APPLICATION FILE

The final approach to installing Pocket PC software is a more hands-on approach and doesn't involve any special setup programs. In this case, you basically are working with an executable application with an .exe or a .cef file extension that you place in a folder on your device. You could obtain the file by downloading it off the Web, copying it from a CD-ROM, or transferring it from the hard disk on your desktop PC.

The drawback to software installed in this manner is that no icon is automatically placed in the Programs folder, which means you must navigate to the file location and tap the file to run the application. Another option is to move the application to the Programs folder, which will make it more accessible. To do so, follow these steps:

1. Run File Explorer and navigate to the location of the application's executable file.
2. Tap and hold on the file, and then tap Cut.
3. Navigate to the My Device root folder.
4. Tap the Windows folder, and then tap the Start Menu folder.
5. Tap Programs to open the Programs folder.
6. Tap Edit in the lower-left corner of the screen, and then tap Paste.

Because you've moved the application file to the Programs folder, an icon for it appears next to other installed applications when you view the Programs folder via the Start menu. Keep in mind that unlike desktop Windows, which allows shortcuts to applications, the application file is actually stored in the Start folder in this example; the File Explorer application doesn't support shortcuts.

UNINSTALLING APPLICATIONS

Similar to desktop Windows, the Pocket PC operating system includes a built-in facility for uninstalling applications that have been installed. To uninstall an application from your device, just follow these steps:

1. Tap Start, and then tap Settings.
2. Tap the System tab, followed by the Remove Programs icon.
3. Select the application to uninstall, and then tap the Remove button.

Uninstalling an application removes all the application's files and related settings from your device. If you find that you aren't using an application very often, it might be worthwhile to uninstall it and free up storage space. Besides, you can always reinstall it later.

BEYOND FILE EXPLORER

If you like to push the envelope of file management, you might find that File Explorer doesn't necessarily offer enough bells and whistles to make you happy. If you find yourself wanting more in a Pocket PC file manager, some other options are available. More specifically, the following are two third-party file managers for Pocket PC that offer features beyond those included in the standard File Explorer application:

- PE File Explorer
- RESCO File Explorer

If you're satisfied using basic file management features, such as copying, moving, renaming, and sending files, you might not need to move to one of these third-party file managers. On the other hand, if you'd like functionality more in line with the desktop Windows Explorer file manager, you might want to take a look at these applications. A couple of the features supported in these applications include the ability to change the extension of filenames and support for shortcuts.

PE FILE EXPLORER

PE File Explorer is a Pocket PC file manager made by Vieka whose user interface attempts to mimic that of the desktop Windows Explorer application (see Figure 11.8). A trial version of PE File Explorer is available for free download from the Vieka Web site at http:// www.vieka.com/, where you can also purchase a full version of the software.

RESCO FILE EXPLORER

The RESCO File Explorer is a Pocket PC file manager made by RESCO that uses a hierarchical tree interface similar to Windows Explorer. This tree interface can be split into multiple panes, which is also similar to Windows Explorer (see Figure 11.9). Similar to Grundle Explorer, a trial version of RESCO File Explorer is available for free download. To download a trial version of RESCO File Explorer or download the full version, just visit the RESCO Web site at http://www.resco-net.com/.

Figure 11.8
Vieka's PE File
Explorer includes a
user interface that is
similar to the familiar
Explorer application in
desktop Windows.

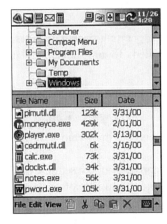

Figure 11.9
RESCO File Explorer is
a third-party file man-
ager for Pocket PC
that presents a tree
interface with multiple
panes.

TROUBLESHOOTING

FINDING DISAPPEARING FILES

*Even though I placed files beneath the My Documents folder, they aren't accessible from Pocket Word,
Pocket Excel, and other standard Pocket PC applications.*

The standard Pocket PC applications recognize files up to only one folder level beneath the
My Documents folder. For example, if you place a note in the Personal subfolder beneath
the My Documents folder, the Notes application will display it in the note list when you
select All Folders. However, if you create a subfolder named More Personal beneath the
Personal folder and place files in it, Notes will be incapable of accessing the files. This rule
applies to any Pocket PC application that stores files in the My Documents folder. To solve
the problem, just move your files around so that none are stored more than one level below
My Documents.

CHANGING FILE EXTENSIONS

I need to change the extension of a filename, but the File Explorer application doesn't seem to allow access to file extensions.

The File Explorer application doesn't enable you to view or edit the file extension of a file. Therefore, you can't change the type of a file by changing its file extension, which is a common practice in Windows Explorer on desktop PCs. If you need to change the type of a file on your Pocket PC, you must copy the file to your desktop, rename the file, and then copy it back. Optionally, you can use the Explore feature in ActiveSync to directly open a Pocket PC folder on your desktop PC and rename the Pocket PC file.

REAL-WORLD EXAMPLE—MANAGING TIMESHEETS

A lot of companies use Excel spreadsheets to keep track of employee hours, both for project management purposes and often for billing as well. Therefore, it's critical for managers to review and verify timesheets after they are turned in. For managers on the go, a unique opportunity is made possible to Pocket PCs when you consider how easily you can connect to a shared network folder, copy down a group of files, and then open those files directly on your device. A manager in this case could remotely access a special network folder that is used to store timesheet documents (in Excel format) and then use File Explorer to copy those files down to her device. From there, it's a matter of using Pocket Excel to review and signoff on each timesheet.

CHAPTER 12

E-MAIL AND THE POCKET OUTLOOK INBOX

In this chapter

THE BASICS OF E-MAIL PROTOCOLS

If you're like me, e-mail is much more than a convenience. For many computer users, e-mail has become a critical form of communication that often takes precedence over other traditional communication mediums. Pocket PCs enable you to stay in touch with e-mail while on the go. Even if you aren't a diehard e-mail user, you still might find it empowering to be able to receive e-mail messages while away from home. The Pocket PC application that facilitates e-mail is Inbox, which enables you to synchronize with Microsoft Outlook to share e-mail with your desktop computer or to connect directly with an e-mail server. The Inbox application relies on well-established e-mail protocols that enable communication with a wide range of e-mail applications and servers.

Note

Although there is no single application on your Pocket PC called Pocket Outlook, the Inbox, Contacts, Calendar, Tasks, and Notes applications are all collectively referred to as *Pocket Outlook*. Individually, these applications are sometimes referred to as Pocket Inbox, Pocket Contacts, and so on. Unlike Outlook for Windows, Pocket Outlook requires you to set up an Internet connection separately with Connection Manager, which is part of the Pocket PC operating system.

E-mail protocols are important because they govern the structure of e-mail messages and how they are delivered. Although a single protocol is used for sending e-mail messages, a couple of options are available for receiving e-mail messages from a *mail server*, which is responsible for storing and delivering mail to recipients. Following are the e-mail protocols supported by the Inbox application:

- Simple Mail Transfer Protocol (SMTP)
- Post Office Protocol version 3 (POP3)
- Internet Message Access Protocol version 4 (IMAP4)

Note

E-mail protocols impact only the Inbox application when you connect directly to a mail server to send and receive e-mail messages. When you synchronize e-mail with the ActiveSync application, no protocols are directly involved because ActiveSync communicates directly with the Inbox.

SMTP is used to send e-mail messages from the Inbox and is the only protocol available for this purpose. In other words, learn to love SMTP because it is your only option. Fortunately, SMTP is a very capable protocol and will serve your e-mail sending needs just fine.

POP3 and *IMAP4* are both used to retrieve e-mail messages from a mail server. These protocols handle the details of downloading e-mail messages from a mail server and making them available to the Inbox. Some differences exist between the protocols that will likely impact your choice of which protocol to use. However, the ultimate decision of which protocol you use might come down to which one your mail server supports. Most ISPs support POP3, so it is likely the protocol you will be forced to use unless you're connecting to a corporate mail server that supports IMAP4.

The IMAP4 e-mail protocol is more powerful than POP3 in that it provides a finer level of control over how e-mail messages are retrieved from a server and stored on your device. IMAP4 enables you to synchronize the Inbox directly with a mail server, which alleviates the issue of deciding whether to leave a copy of messages on the server or remove them after they've been retrieved. IMAP4 also supports multiple mail folders for organizing incoming e-mail automatically.

Before you get the idea that IMAP4 is the ultimate e-mail protocol, let me back up and say that POP3 is a perfectly good protocol for retrieving e-mail with the Inbox. POP3 is popular and is likely the e-mail protocol you will find yourself using because it is the only option for retrieving e-mail from many mail servers. The point to take from this discussion is that if you have the option, IMAP4 is a more powerful protocol and you should consider using it. However, in the absence of IMAP4, POP3 will serve your needs just fine. If you have a dial-up Internet service or a broadband cable modem or DSL service, you will likely use POP3; IMAP4 is typically available only in corporate environments with dedicated mail servers.

SENDING AND RECEIVING E-MAIL

The two primary actions taken with e-mail are sending and receiving e-mail messages. These are simple concepts, but a couple of different approaches are available for carrying out the specific transport of the messages:

- Send and receive e-mail messages by connecting the Inbox to an e-mail server.
- Send and receive e-mail messages by synchronizing the Inbox with a desktop computer using the ActiveSync application.

PART

III

CH

12

The Inbox application supports both of these approaches to sending and receiving e-mail messages. Although you can't use both approaches at the same time, you might find yourself relying on each of them under different scenarios. For example, you can establish a connection to a remote mail server via the Internet to send and receive messages while you're away from your desktop computer and then synchronize messages via ActiveSync when you're at home or work and have access to a desktop computer.

Connecting to an e-mail server to send and receive e-mail implies that you have some type of network connection that provides access to the server. This network connection could be a wired connection via a phone line and modem or possibly a wireless connection using a wireless network card or mobile phone. The specifics of the network connection aren't really important; for the purposes of this discussion, let's assume that you've used a modem card to connect to an Internet service provider (ISP). In reality, any Internet connection will work when it comes to connecting to an e-mail server to send and receive e-mail messages.

For example, you could use an AOL or MSN dial-up Internet service to connect using a wired modem and check e-mail.

> **Note**
>
> Establishing an Internet connection typically requires additional hardware for your Pocket PC, which is one of the main purposes of expansion slots. Generally speaking, CF and PC slots are used for connectivity accessories, whereas SD slots are used for adding storage (memory).

→ For more information on connecting your device to the Internet, **see** "Creating Connections with Connection Manager," **p. 127**.

CONFIGURING INBOX SETTINGS

After you've established an Internet connection, you're ready to configure e-mail settings in the Inbox application to communicate with a mail server. Although the process for IMAP4 isn't much different, I'm going to assume that you're using the POP3 incoming mail protocol because it is the most commonly supported protocol. Following are the pieces of information you need to configure the Inbox to connect to a mail server:

- E-mail user ID
- E-mail password
- POP3 mail server IP address
- SMTP mail server IP address

> **Tip from**
> *Michael*
>
> The POP3 and SMTP mail server IP addresses are often the same, but you should check with your ISP to make sure. You should be able to find this information on your ISP's Web site.

The e-mail user ID and password should have been provided to you by your ISP when you signed up for the service; they are often the same as your login user ID and password that you use to get online. The POP3 and SMTP mail server IP addresses are very important because they identify the actual mail servers used to send and receive e-mail messages. These server addresses should be easy to find in the documentation for your ISP service or with a quick call to the ISP's technical support. If you are already using a desktop e-mail application, such as Microsoft Outlook or Outlook Express, to access the same account, you can check the settings in it because the same server addresses had to be set up there.

→ The Pocket Outlook Inbox application can't be used to access Web-based e-mail, such as Hotmail. Because Hotmail is designed solely for access through a Web browser, you can't access Hotmail e-mail messages through the Pocket Outlook Inbox. However, you can use Pocket Internet Explorer to access a Hotmail e-mail account. To find out more about how this is done, **see** "Accessing Web-Based E-mail," **p. 193**.

If you already use an e-mail client, such as Outlook or Outlook Express, on your desktop computer, you should be able to quickly obtain all the information required to configure the e-mail settings in the Pocket PC Inbox application. In Outlook 2002, this information is available by selecting E-mail Accounts from the Tools menu, selecting View or Change Existing E-mail Accounts in the dialog box that appears, and then clicking the Next button. Then, you highlight your e-mail account and click the Change button to view its settings. You will be able to ascertain your username as well as mail server IP addresses from the Properties window that appears. Of course, your e-mail password will be masked out, so you'll have to remember it on your own or request it from your ISP.

SETTING UP A NEW E-MAIL SERVICE

Now that you know what information is required to configure your e-mail for the Inbox application, you need to fill in the blanks in Inbox to get it ready to connect to a mail server. Launch the Inbox application and tap the Services menu, followed by New Service. This starts the E-mail Setup Wizard, whose first step prompts you for an e-mail address for the new e-mail service, as shown in Figure 12.1.

Figure 12.1
The e-mail address for the new service is important because it determines where e-mail will be sent when someone replies to your messages.

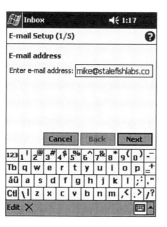

After specifying your e-mail address and tapping the Next button, the E-mail Setup Wizard attempts to automatically configure your e-mail settings based solely on the address you provided in the first step (see Figure 12.2).

To continue with the e-mail service setup, tap the Next button. You will then see the third step of the wizard, which asks you for user information, including your name, username, and password (see Figure 12.3).

PART

III

CH

12

Figure 12.2
It's worth allowing the E-mail Setup wizard to make an attempt at automatically config-uring the Inbox e-mail settings.

Figure 12.3
Your name, user-name, and password are important pieces of user information that must be entered during the third step of the E-mail Setup Wizard.

Tapping Next moves you to the fourth step in the wizard, which clarifies the type of service (POP3 or IMAP4), along with a name for the service (see Figure 12.4). Unless you know you need to use the IMAP4 protocol, select POP3 as the service type and then type a service name that identifies the e-mail service to you. The service name is purely descriptive, so you can enter any name you want.

Figure 12.4
The fourth step in the E-mail Setup Wizard prompts you for the service type and a name for the e-mail service, which should be descriptive enough for you to easily identify the service.

After entering the service type and name, tap Next to continue to the final step of the E-mail Setup Wizard, which is shown in Figure 12.5.

Figure 12.5
The final step in the E-mail Setup Wizard prompts you to enter the incoming (POP3 or IMAP4) and outgoing (SMTP) mail servers, as well as an optional domain for the service.

You should enter the POP3 mail server IP address you acquired earlier in the Incoming Mail field and then enter the SMTP mail server address in the Outgoing Mail field. The Domain property for your e-mail service should be left blank unless you are accessing a mail server on a corporate network that you know requires an e-mail domain. An *e-mail domain* is basically the name of an e-mail server that is available on the Internet. Just as a domain can identify a Web site, as in amazon.com, it can also identify an e-mail server, as in aol.com.

 If you use the Microsoft Network (MSN) to connect to the Internet, you're probably trying to set up an MSN e-mail service. See "Accessing MSN E-mail" in the "Troubleshooting" section at the end of the chapter for a couple of important tips on accessing MSN e-mail.

Note

I recommend starting out with the Domain property blank and then going back and entering a domain address only if you have problems connecting with the mail server. On the other hand, if you are accessing a corporate mail server and the Domain property is necessary, you need to get that information from your network administrator.

Caution

Although you can enter any e-mail address you want as the return address in the POP3 Service settings, you can run into a problem if your ISP compares the return address with the e-mail address it has on record for you. Although this is restrictive to users, some ISPs do this to catch junk mail (spam) senders.

Now that your new e-mail service is successfully configured, you're just about ready to try it out. However, before doing so let's take a quick moment to consider a few advanced e-mail options.

ADVANCED E-MAIL OPTIONS

Depending on your specific e-mail needs, you might want to explore the advanced options available for your new e-mail service. To do so, tap the Options button in Inbox; you'll be presented with advanced settings. The advanced e-mail settings actually consist of a shorter three-page wizard that is worth examining. Figure 12.6 shows the first step in the Advanced E-mail Setup Wizard, which specifies how e-mail is delivered.

Figure 12.6
The first step in the Advanced E-mail Setup Wizard prompts you to clarify how e-mail is delivered, including how often to check for new messages.

The default settings for the first step in the Advanced E-mail Setup will probably work out fine unless you have strong opinions about how e-mail is delivered. If you don't want messages automatically sent or downloaded, or if you want to alter the frequency between checking for new messages (15 minutes is the default), then you can do so here. The second check box in this step should be left unchecked unless you know that the outgoing SMTP mail server requires authentication for e-mail. The last setting in this step has to do with which connection settings you want to use for the e-mail service. The default setting is Default Internet Settings, which is probably what you'll want to stick with. Tapping Next takes you to the second page of Advanced e-mail settings, as shown in Figure 12.7.

Figure 12.7
You have the option of retrieving only message headers, in which case you must decide which messages to download and read, or retrieving a full copy of messages, which allows you to read all messages.

This step of the Advanced E-mail Settings wizard allows you to choose between retrieving only e-mail message headers or entire messages. Obtaining only message headers makes message retrieval much faster. If you receive a lot of messages, you can sift through the headers and download full messages for only the most important ones. If you don't have a problem with the download of e-mail messages taking a little longer, you might want to set this option to get a full copy of messages because this enables you to read the messages immediately. Tapping Next one last time takes you to the last Advanced e-mail setup step, which is shown in Figure 12.8.

PART
III

CH
12

Tip from
Michael

To download the full copy of a message when viewing the message header, tap Get Full Copy on the Edit menu. Optionally, you can tap Get Full Copy from the Services menu while viewing the list of message headers.

This final e-mail settings determines the messages that are displayed based on how old they are; you can uncheck this option to see all messages if you'd like. Tap the Finish button when you're done with this setting to finalize the new e-mail service. You're now ready to connect with an e-mail server to send and receive e-mail messages.

Figure 12.8
The last step in the Advanced E-mail Setup Wizard enables you to control how recent the messages to be displayed are.

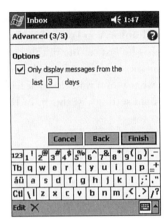

TRYING THE NEW E-MAIL SERVICE

To get started with your newly configured e-mail service, tap the Services menu and then tap Connect. If automatic sending and receiving is enabled, any messages in the Outbox folder will be delivered, whereas any new messages will be delivered to the Inbox folder.

Tip from
Michael

> The first button on the Inbox toolbar is the Connect button, which provides a quick alternative to issuing the Connect command from the Services menu.

One potential problem that might arise when you first attempt to send and receive e-mail through a mail server is a warning that you can receive e-mail messages but not send them. This is a common problem that is somewhat tricky to understand and fix. Unlike most e-mail clients, the Pocket PC Inbox attempts to access the outgoing SMTP port before it logs in to the POP3 port to see whether any e-mail messages are queued for delivery. The problem arises when your ISP performs a POP authentication, which involves checking the POP3 user ID and password before allowing access to the SMTP port. Because the Inbox attempts to access the SMTP port prior to sending the POP3 user ID and password, the authentication fails and you get the warning about not being able to send e-mail.

The good news is that after the POP3 port is accessed and the logon information (user ID and password) is sent, the SMTP port can be accessed without a problem. So, if you attempt to send and receive e-mail after the initial attempt, you will be able to do so with no problems or warnings. As described on the Pocket PC Web site, this e-mail port problem is a "chicken before the egg" dilemma in that POP3 logon information is needed to verify access to the SMTP server.

The only real workaround to the "chicken before the egg" e-mail port problem is to use a different SMTP server that doesn't use POP authentication. Keep in mind, however, that the problem doesn't keep you from being able to send e-mail—it just adds an extra step to receiving it.

CREATING A NEW E-MAIL MESSAGE

Regardless of how you actually transport e-mail messages, the task of creating a new message is pretty simple. Follow these steps to create your first "pocket" e-mail message:

1. Launch the Inbox application from the Start menu.

2. Tap New near the bottom of the screen to open a blank message (see Figure 12.9).

3. Tap To to select an e-mail recipient from your contact list, or enter an e-mail address in the edit box.

4. Tap the edit box next to Subj to enter the subject of the e-mail message.

5. Tap the body of the e-mail and enter the message.

6. Tap the Send button to queue the e-mail message for sending; this places the message in the Outbox folder.

Figure 12.9
A blank e-mail message is created when you tap the New command in the Inbox application.

PART
III

CH
12

Tip from
Michael

If you aren't too efficient at entering e-mail messages, you might consider using the My Text feature to automatically enter a commonly used phrase. Just make sure the cursor is in the body of a message, and then tap My Text on the Inbox menu. A list of commonly used phrases appears, from which you can select one that will automatically be inserted into your message. This can be a real timesaver, especially if you customize the phrases to suit your own tastes. To customize the phrases, tap Edit and then Edit My Text Messages.

At this point, the new message is in the Outbox folder, which means it is queued to be sent as soon as an opportunity arises. This opportunity is either a connection to a mail server or synchronization with a desktop mail client, such as Microsoft Outlook. ActiveSync supports e-mail synchronization only with Microsoft Outlook, but some third-party applications support other e-mail clients, such as Lotus Notes. The next few sections explore the details of transporting e-mail messages using these two approaches.

Tip from
Michael

You can spell check an e-mail message before sending it by tapping Edit and then tapping Spell Check.

SYNCHRONIZING E-MAIL WITH MICROSOFT OUTLOOK

Earlier in the chapter, I mentioned that the two main approaches to sending and receiving e-mail are connecting to an e-mail server and synchronizing with a desktop computer via ActiveSync. The synchronization approach requires that you have Microsoft Outlook installed and configured on a desktop computer. The ActiveSync application is then used to synchronize e-mail messages between Outlook and the Inbox application. During the synchronization process, e-mail messages from the Inbox folder of Outlook are transferred to the Inbox folder of the Inbox application. Additionally, e-mail messages in the Outbox folder of Inbox are transferred to the Outbox folder of Outlook, where they await delivery with your other outgoing Outlook e-mail.

Note

Pocket PC Inbox synchronization is compatible only with Microsoft Outlook versions 2000 and 2002; previous versions of Outlook are not compatible with ActiveSync and therefore aren't capable of synchronizing with the Inbox application.

E-mail synchronization must be set up in ActiveSync because ActiveSync is responsible for carrying out the transfer of messages between the desktop PC and Pocket PC e-mail applications. To set up e-mail synchronization, launch ActiveSync and click the Options button in the main toolbar. To enable e-mail synchronization, click the check box next to Inbox in the list of information types in the Options window. To fine-tune the e-mail synchronization settings, click the Settings button, which displays the Mail Synchronization Settings window (see Figure 12.10).

The main list in the Mail Synchronization Settings window shows the mail folders that are synchronized between Outlook and the Inbox application. After the list are a few options you can check or uncheck to fine-tune the manner in which messages are handled during synchronization. More specifically, the first option enables you to specify the maximum lines of text retrieved for an e-mail message. Because the Inbox already has a 5KB maximum size for e-mail messages, you might not want to change this setting. On the other hand, if you want to keep your messages extremely lean then, by all means, check the box and set the number of lines to your liking. Keep in mind, though, that the 5KB limitation applies only to the text making up the body of an e-mail message, and not to any attachments that might be included in the message.

Figure 12.10
The Mail Synchronization Settings window enables you to change the e-mail synchronization settings for ActiveSync, which enable you to fine-tune the quantity and size of messages synchronized.

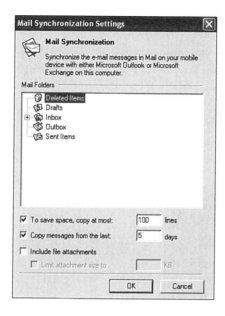

Tip from
Michael

A 5KB e-mail message contains roughly 16,000 characters, or 200 lines of 80-column text, which is a pretty sizable message by most standards.

The second option in the Mail Synchronization Settings window has to do with how recent the messages are that you want synchronized. The default setting is 5 days, which means that only e-mail messages from the last 5 days are synchronized with the Inbox. Obviously, a larger value for this setting results in more messages being transferred and stored on your device, so you must decide the precise trade-off between having access to older messages and minimizing storage space on your device.

The final option determines whether file attachments are retrieved with messages. As you probably know, file attachments are files that accompany e-mail messages. File attachments can be any type of file, such as Word documents, Excel workbooks, JPEG images, MP3 songs, or even WAV audio clips. File attachments can get quite large, so I recommend enabling attachments only if you plan on getting important files as attachments. If you want to avoid only large attachments, you can check the Limit Attachment Size To option and set a maximum file size for attachments. Later in the chapter, you learn more about handling e-mail attachments.

After you set the options like you want, the synchronization of e-mail with Outlook through ActiveSync is automatic. Depending on how you have ActiveSync set up, e-mail on your device will automatically be synchronized with Outlook whenever you connect your device to your desktop PC and any time a new message is sent or received while your device is connected.

→ For more information on ActiveSync synchronization options, **see** Chapter 8, "Using ActiveSync to Synchronize Data," **p. 145**.

PART

III

CH

12

SHARING FILES WITH E-MAIL ATTACHMENTS

E-mail attachments provide a powerful means of sharing files with people. In fact, this book is living proof of it—the chapter you are reading was originally submitted to the publisher as an e-mail attachment. In the Inbox application, it is obvious that an e-mail message has an attachment because the envelope icon next to the message header has a small paper clip attached to it. The second and third messages in Figure 12.11 have attachments, whereas the other messages do not.

Paper clip icon

Figure 12.11
E-mail messages with attachments include a small paper clip in the icon next to their headers.

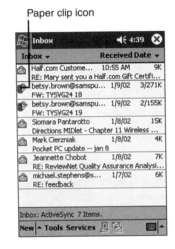

Tip from
Michael

If you have a POP3 e-mail account, the paper clip next to the mail message indicates that the attachment has already been downloaded to your device, whereas in an IMAP4 account it means that the message has an attachment but it has yet to be downloaded. When you open a message with an attachment, the icon next to the attached file or files indicates whether the file is still being downloaded.

To read an e-mail message and access its attachment, tap the message in the Inbox message list. The header and body of the message are then displayed, as is a bar along the bottom of the screen that includes the attachment (see Figure 12.12).

To open an attachment, tap the attachment icon in the bar near the bottom of the screen, which typically indicates the nature of the attachment (Word document, image, and so on). If the attachment has already been downloaded, it will be opened in the appropriate application suitable for viewing or editing it (if a suitable application is not available, the file will not open). If the attachment has not been downloaded, the Inbox begins downloading the attachment. After the download is complete, the attachment is opened in an application. If you are not connected, the attachment is flagged so that it's downloaded the next time you connect. The status of an attachment is shown by a graphical indicator that appears to the left of the attachment; no indicator means the attachment has been downloaded.

Figure 12.12
When reading an e-mail message with an attachment, the attachment is accessible in a bar along the bottom of the screen; this message actually has two attached files.

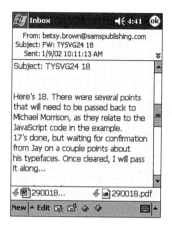

Receiving and opening attachments is easy enough, and so is creating an e-mail message with an attachment. To attach a file to an e-mail message, open the outgoing message and tap Edit on the Inbox toolbar. Then, tap Add Attachment on the Edit menu, and select the file using the Open window that appears. Another option for sending attached files is to use the File Explorer application to find a file you want to send and then tap and hold on the file. Select Send via E-mail in the pop-up menu that appears, and a blank e-mail message is created with the file attached to it. Fill out whom the e-mail is to, and send it away.

Tip from
Michael

If you want to attach a voice recording to an e-mail message, just tap the Recording button on the Inbox toolbar. The Voice Bar will appear, which enables you to record and attach a voice recording to the e-mail.

→ To learn more about the Voice Bar and how it is used to make voice recordings, **see** "Using the Voice Bar and Hand Recognition," **p. 269**.

As you probably know, e-mail attachments can sometimes be large, especially if you're dealing with multimedia files such as voice recordings or MP3 music. Rather than let your attachments hog your main system memory, you should consider using a memory storage card to house attachments. The Inbox application includes a convenient option for storing attachments on a memory card. Be sure to install a memory card first, and then follow these steps:

1. Run the Inbox application.
2. Tap Tools, and then tap Options.
3. Tap the Storage tab on the Options screen, and then check the Store Attachments on Storage Card check box (see Figure 12.13).
4. Tap OK to accept the new Inbox setting.

PART
III

CH

12

Figure 12.13
The Storage tab of the Inbox Options page enables you to specify that e-mail attachments are to be stored on a memory storage card.

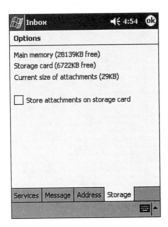

→ For more information on memory storage cards and how to install and use them, **see** "Memory Storage Cards," **p. 358**.

The only caveat to storing attachments on a storage card is that, if you remove the card, the attachments won't be accessible until the card is replaced. Although this certainly makes sense, if you have several storage cards, it can be a little confusing ensuring you have the correct card in your device for e-mail. For this reason, you should probably take advantage of this option only if you use a single storage card that you leave in your device the majority of the time. Attachments on a storage card are stored in a special, uniquely named folder on the card, which means you can still use the card to store other data.

 If the attachment folder on your storage card is somehow deleted or renamed, Inbox will report an error when you first try to run it. To solve this problem, see "Correcting a Renamed or Deleted Attachment Folder" in the "Troubleshooting" section at the end of the chapter.

MANAGING YOUR E-MAIL

The Inbox application is a full-featured e-mail client that includes standard features for managing e-mail messages. Most of the e-mail management commands are accessible from the pop-up menu that appears when you tap and hold an e-mail message (see Figure 12.14).

Following are the commands accessible from the e-mail pop-up menu, along with brief descriptions of what they do:

- **Mark As Unread**—Marks a read message as unread so that it stands out
- **Move to**—Moves a message to a different folder (deletes the original message)
- **Mark for Download**—Marks a message header or partially retrieved message so that Inbox will know to retrieve a full copy of the message
- **Reply**—Replies to a message (only the sender of the message is replied to)
- **Reply All**—Replies to a message (all addresses on the message are replied to)
- **Forward**—Forwards a message to a different e-mail address
- **Delete**—Deletes a message by moving it to the Deleted folder

Figure 12.14
Tapping and holding
an e-mail message
results in the display
of a pop-up menu full
of useful e-mail com-
mands.

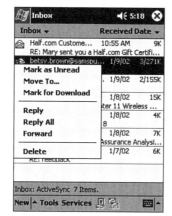

Although I describe the e-mail commands in terms of acting on a single message, all
the commands work with multiple messages if you tap and drag to select the messages
and then tap and hold to access the pop-up menu.

The Deleted folder in the Inbox application functions like the Windows Recycle Bin in that
it must be emptied from time to time to conserve space. You can easily empty the contents
of the Deleted folder by selecting Empty Deleted Items from the Inbox Tools menu. You
can also have the Deleted Items folder emptied automatically by setting the Empty Deleted
Items option in the Message tab of the Inbox Options screen, which is accessible by selecting Options in the Tools menu.

SORTING MESSAGES

Aside from issuing commands to manage e-mail messages, you can also alter the manner in
which messages are displayed in the Inbox. More specifically, a drop-down list in the upper-
right corner of the Inbox screen enables you to alter the sort order of e-mail messages.
Following are the sorting options available:

- **From**—Sorts messages alphabetically by the senders' names
- **Received Date**—Sorts messages by the received dates, with newest messages appearing
  first (this is the default sorting option)
- **Subject**—Sorts messages alphabetically by the subjects

To reverse the sorting of messages, tap the same sorting option again. For example, the
first time you tap From, the messages will be sorted alphabetically (from A to Z) by the
senders' names. Tapping From again reverses the alphabetical sort so that it goes from
Z to A.

PART

III

CH

12

WORKING WITH MULTIPLE E-MAIL SERVICES

Similar to Outlook on your desktop, the Inbox application is capable of managing multiple e-mail services. In fact, when you created the new e-mail service earlier in the chapter, you actually created it as a second service. That's because a default ActiveSync e-mail service is automatically set up when you synchronize the Inbox with Outlook. Each e-mail service on your device has an associated set of e-mail folders, such as Inbox, Outbox, Sent Items, and so on. Messages within each service are kept within their own set of folders. When you create a new e-mail message, you are creating it for delivery by a certain service. To set the service for a new message, tap the little down arrows that appear on the right edge of the screen near the subject of the e-mail. This expands the message properties to reveal the delivery service, as shown in Figure 12.15.

Figure 12.15
Tapping the little down arrows near the subject line of a new e-mail message enables you to change the delivery service for the message, which is helpful if you use several different delivery services.

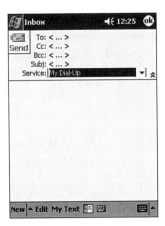

It's important to be able to navigate between folders in each of the services you have set up. To view messages associated with a particular service, you must select a folder within the service, such as the Inbox folder. To do this, just tap the drop-down list in the upper-left corner of the Inbox application, which reveals a list of all the services and folders currently active and available for use (see Figure 12.16).

Figure 12.16
Tapping the current folder results in the display of a drop-down list of e-mail folders.

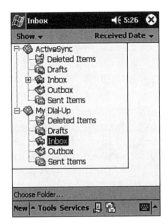

Tapping a folder in the drop-down list selects that folder in the Inbox and reveals the folder's contents. Navigating between e-mail folders and services in this manner enables you to effectively manage multiple e-mail services.

ACCESSING A CORPORATE ADDRESS DIRECTORY

A feature new to Pocket Outlook 2002 is support for LDAP, which stands for *Lightweight Directory Access Protocol*. LDAP is designed to support lightweight databases on the Internet. More specifically, LDAP makes it possible to access directory services such as corporate phone and e-mail directories. However, the idea behind LDAP is more general than simply supporting an online phone directory—any lightweight database that is generally read from more than it is written to could feasibly be accessed through LDAP. However, the initial use of LDAP is as a protocol for accessing contact information in a corporate environment.

Pocket Outlook enters the LDAP picture because it enables you to look up people on a corporate network using a directory service that supports LDAP. You must add an address book service to the Inbox application to access it as an LDAP directory. The primary benefit to doing this is that it allows you to look up e-mail recipients when composing new messages. Following are the steps required to add a new LDAP directory service to the Inbox:

1. Run the Inbox application.
2. Tap Tools, and then tap Options.
3. Tap the Address tab on the Options screen, and then tap the Add button.
4. Enter the directory name, server, and username and password if necessary (see Figure 12.17).
5. Tap OK to accept the new Inbox setting.

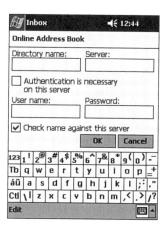

Figure 12.17
The Address tab of the Inbox Options page enables you to set up an address book for LDAP directory access.

With the LDAP directory service created, you can now start looking up e-mail recipients in the Inbox. This is accomplished when you enter the recipients for an e-mail message; just tap Edit, and then tap Check Names on the Inbox menu. The Inbox application will use the LDAP directory service you've set up to check for matches on the recipients that you entered for the message.

TROUBLESHOOTING

ACCESSING MSN E-MAIL

I followed the directions for setting up a new e-mail service for my MSN e-mail account, but it's not working.

The Microsoft Network's (MSN) e-mail server uses a special security feature that makes its e-mail a little tricky to receive using the Inbox application. The security feature is called Secure Password Authentication (SPA), and it requires you to use a special IP address for the SMTP mail server. Following are both of the mail server settings required for MSN:

- **POP3 mail server IP address**—pop3.email.msn.com
- **SMTP mail server IP address**—secure.smtp.email.msn.com

After creating and configuring the MSN e-mail service in the Inbox, you can go about sending and receiving e-mail just as you would with any other e-mail service.

CORRECTING A RENAMED OR DELETED ATTACHMENT FOLDER

Inbox reports an error when I first try to run it because it can't find the folder on my storage card for e-mail attachments. I can't even get to the Inbox options to turn off the storage card attachment setting.

When an e-mail attachment is saved to a storage card, a special folder is created on the storage card with a unique name. This name is somewhat cryptic and usually looks something like Inbox.mst*XXX.XXX*, where *XXX* is a series of numbers. If you delete this folder or format your storage card, the Inbox application generates an error because it can no longer find the folder for saving attachments. The only way to solve the problem is to re-create the missing folder, but it's unlikely that you'll remember its cryptic name with all those numbers. Although you can determine the folder name by examining the registry in your device, I prefer using a simple utility made available by Marc Zimmerman from his Web site at http://www.zimac.de/. Mr. Zimmerman's utility is available for free download and will automatically determine the name of your missing attachment folder and re-create it on a storage card. If you want to avoid repeating the attachment folder problem, you can always turn off the storage card option after you've re-created the folder and eliminated the error message.

REAL-WORLD EXAMPLE—A TRAVEL E-MAIL DIARY

The best way to get a feel for the power and flexibility of having e-mail access in the palm of your hand is to actually try using it when it is physically impossible to use traditional e-mail at your desktop. The next time you take a trip, I encourage you to make a serious effort at using the Inbox on your Pocket PC to create e-mail messages to friends and family that document your trip. For example, if you visit a park in a new city and take in a beautiful sunset, take a moment to compose a quick e-mail about the experience. Or, maybe you're away for business and go to a professional hockey game; jot down a few thoughts about the game in an e-mail to a friend who shares a common interest in the sport.

Not only is this exercise a good way to share thoughts and stay in touch with friends and family, it's also a great way to make the most of your Pocket PC. I truly believe that it's the little things in life that make living interesting, and I'm merely suggesting one way to use technology as a means of capturing and sharing some interesting events in your life when you might have otherwise never shared them.

CHAPTER **13**

USING THE POCKET OUTLOOK CONTACTS AND CALENDAR

In this chapter

MANAGING PEOPLE WITH THE CONTACTS APPLICATION

Staying in contact with friends, family, and business associates is one of the key purposes to using a handheld computer of any type, especially a Pocket PC. The standard Contacts application serves as a high-powered electronic Rolodex and synchronizes with the Contacts feature in Microsoft Outlook. The Contacts application is responsible for managing all your contacts and effectively parallels the Contacts portion of Outlook. Perhaps more importantly, the Contacts application is designed for synchronization with Outlook Contacts data, thereby enabling your desktop PC and Pocket PC to share a unified contact list. Figure 13.1 shows the Contacts application in action.

Figure 13.1
The Contacts application is responsible for managing your list of contacts.

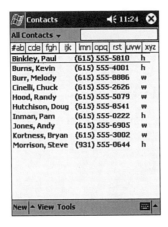

NAVIGATING CONTACTS

Contacts are displayed in the Contacts application as a list of names and related fields of contact information. Contacts in the contact list can be filtered and displayed according to the category to which they are assigned. This is a convenient way to focus on a group of contacts, but it requires you to assign categories to all your contacts for it to be useful. If you want a quicker way to navigate contacts, try clicking the small ABC tabs at the top of the contact list.

The ABC tabs at the top of the contact list enable you to jump to a section of the contact list based on the names of the contacts. For example, tapping the cde tab jumps to the first contact with a last name beginning with the letter *C*. To jump to one of the other letters in a tab, just tap the tab again. For example, to jump to contacts with last names beginning with *E*, just tap the cde tab three times. Contacts are always alphabetically sorted according to the last name of the contact. If a contact name starts with a number, it will appear ahead of names that start with a letter.

Keep in mind that you can also type in the edit box in the upper-right corner of the Contacts application to jump to contacts quickly. The difference between this approach and the ABC tabs approach is that the edit box includes both first and last names that match your criteria, whereas tabs jump only to contacts with last names that match the letter you've selected. Another difference between the edit box and ABC tabs navigation approaches is that tabs are used to move the selection cursor within the list of contacts, whereas the edit box actually filters the list. Figure 13.2 shows the results of typing *jones* in this edit box to find my friend Andy Jones.

Figure 13.2
Entering a name in the edit box near the top of the Contacts screen results in the contact list being filtered for contacts with similar first or last names.

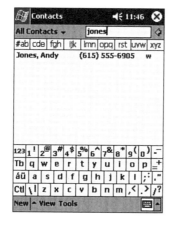

Tip from
Michael

Another quick way to find contacts is to use the Find feature that is accessible near the bottom of the Start menu. Just enter the first or last name of the contact on the Find screen, and then select Contacts as the type of data to find.

The Contacts application enables you to sort names in the contact list based on two criteria: name and company. To change the sorting of the contact list, just tap View in the Contacts menu, followed by the type of sort you want to perform. The default setting is By Name, but if you manage a lot of contacts within specific companies, you might find the By Company option to be more useful.

⚠ *If you've exhausted all the approaches to navigating the contact list, and you still feel unsatisfied, there is one more option you might consider. See "An Alternative Means of Navigating Contacts" in the "Troubleshooting" section at the end of the chapter to find out more.*

PART

III

CH

13

CATEGORIZING CONTACTS

You probably noticed that the category of contacts in the Contacts application is listed just below the Start menu; by default, the initial category includes all contacts. Although not strictly required, it is a good idea to categorize your contacts. For example, I have my contacts divided into three categories: Business, Personal, and Family. You can filter the view in Contacts to a specific category by tapping All Contacts near the top of the screen and then selecting the appropriate category from the drop-down list. Figure 13.3 shows the results of changing the category in the contact list to Personal.

Figure 13.3
You can filter the contact list in the Contacts application by changing the category of contacts displayed.

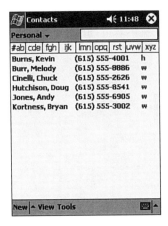

In addition to filtering categories via the drop-down list below the Start menu, you can also select multiple categories and edit individual categories by tapping More in the list. This results in the display of a category screen that enables you to select multiple categories to be filtered. You can also select No Categories to view only those contacts who aren't assigned to a category. This screen also includes an Add/Delete tab that is used to add and delete categories.

TWEAKING THE APPEARANCE OF CONTACTS

When you edit a contact in Microsoft Outlook, you can change the File As property to alter the way in which the contact is referenced. The significance of this with respect to Pocket Outlook is that the Contacts application uses the File As property as the basis for displaying synchronized contacts. In other words, by altering the File As property for a contact in Outlook, you affect the way the contact name is displayed in Pocket Outlook. After changing the File As property for a contact in Outlook, you'll need to synchronize with your Pocket PC for the changes to be reflected in the Contacts application.

Another handy feature of the Contacts application is the ability to change the contact information displayed next to the contact name. If you pay close attention, you'll notice that each contact in the contact list has a small, blue letter displayed to the right of its phone number or e-mail address. This letter identifies the piece of information to its left. For example, a letter h indicates that the information is a home phone number, a letter w indicates that it is a work phone number, and a letter e indicates that it is an e-mail address. By tapping the identification letter, you can change the piece of information displayed for the contact in the list. When you tap the letter for a contact, a drop-down list of relevant contact information is displayed from which you can select (see Figure 13.4).

Tapping a different piece of contact information in the drop-down list results in it being displayed next to the contact name. This is a useful feature because you might want to have the home phone numbers of close friends readily displayed, whereas it would probably make more sense to have the work numbers displayed for business associates.

Figure 13.4
When you tap the identification letter on the far right of the contact entry, you are presented with a drop-down list of available contact information.

Tip from
Michael

Help is always just a couple of taps away while using the Contacts application; just tap Help in the Start menu, and then tap Contacts in the Help Contents.

SYNCHRONIZING CONTACTS

You must have Contacts checked for synchronization in the ActiveSync synchronization settings for the contact information to be synchronized between Outlook and the Contacts application. To enable this setting, follow these steps:

1. Launch ActiveSync on your desktop PC.
2. Click the Options button on the main toolbar.
3. Check the Contacts item in the synchronization list to enable the synchronization of contact information (see Figure 13.5).
4. Click OK to accept the synchronization changes.

Figure 13.5
Enabling Contacts in ActiveSync allows your device to synchronize contact information with a desktop PC.

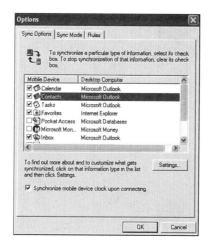

PART
III

CH

13

After you change the Contacts setting in ActiveSync, your device immediately begins synchronizing contact information.

CREATING NEW CONTACTS

Even though you will probably want to synchronize existing contacts from your desktop PC, you are still likely to create new contacts directly into the Contacts application on your device. Just follow these steps:

1. Tap New near the bottom of the screen.

2. Use the Input Panel to enter relevant contact information on the New Contact screen (see Figure 13.6).

3. Scroll down and select a category or categories for the contact by tapping Categories (see Figure 13.7).

4. Add additional text, a drawing, or a voice recording by tapping the Notes tab.

5. Tap OK to save the new contact.

Figure 13.6
Creating a new contact is as simple as entering relevant contact information on the New Contact screen.

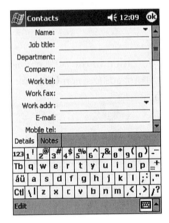

Figure 13.7
Categorizing a contact simply involves selecting one or more categories for the contact.

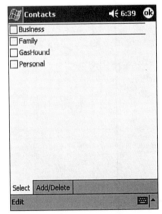

After entering a new contact, it appears in the contact list under the appropriate category. To see the details of the contact, just tap it in the list.

Tip from
Michael

> To copy, delete, send an e-mail, or beam a contact to another device via infrared, tap and hold the contact and then select the appropriate command in the pop-up menu that appears.

→ If you've installed Pocket Streets on your device, you can tap and hold a contact and then select Find on Map from the pop-up menu to find the geographic location of the contact on a Pocket Streets map. This assumes, of course, that you have the appropriate map loaded onto your device. To learn more about Pocket Streets, **see** "Getting Started with Pocket Streets," **p. 338**.

USING HARDWARE BUTTONS WITH THE CONTACTS APPLICATION

All Pocket PC devices include hardware buttons that enable you to easily launch commonly used applications. Although you can custom tailor these hardware buttons to do whatever you want, most are set by default to launch the two most commonly used Pocket Outlook applications—Contacts and Calendar. The Contacts hardware button usually is labeled with a small icon representing a contact card from a Rolodex. Try pressing the Contacts button on your device to quickly launch the Contacts application.

Tip from
Michael

> If you are already in the Contacts application, pressing the Contacts button changes the currently selected category. You can continue pressing the Contacts button to cycle through the categories of contacts.

Another hardware button, the Action button, is useful for navigating contacts. The Action button is designed as a push button that can also be rotated up and down, and it is useful in scrolling through the contact list and viewing individual contacts. The Action button is usually located on the left side of Pocket PCs, although not all devices have an isolated Action button. Instead, some devices incorporate the Action button functionality into the navigation button. Just roll the Action button up or down to scroll through the contact list. When you arrive at the contact you want to view, push the Action button and you will see the contact details just as if you had tapped it.

Note

> All Pocket PCs are required to have hardware buttons, but they are given leeway as to which applications the buttons launch. Most Pocket PCs are set up by default with hardware buttons for the Contacts and Calendar applications, along with a Start menu button, a Record button for recording voice dictations, and an Action button for scrolling and selecting items. If your device doesn't have a scrolling Action button, you

PART
III

CH
13

can use its navigation button instead. Please refer to your device's manual for more information about its default button settings.

→ To learn more about the hardware buttons available on Pocket PCs, **see** "Getting to Know the Stylus, Buttons, and Dials," **p. 34**.

CUSTOMIZING THE CONTACTS APPLICATION

You will likely find the Contacts application to be extremely usable with its default settings. Even so, at some point you might need to customize its functionality to suit your own tastes. To view the options available for customizing the Contacts application, tap Tools at the bottom of the screen, and then tap Options to open the Options screen (see Figure 13.8).

Figure 13.8
The Options screen in the Contacts application enables you to customize the application to your own preferences.

Following are the various options you can set in the Options screen of the Contacts application:

- **Show ABC Tabs**—Allows you to disable the ABC tabs that provide quicker navigation in the contact list. Disabling the tabs frees up a little screen space and enables you to see an extra name in the list, which is beneficial if you don't plan on using the tabs for navigation.

- **Show Contact Names Only**—Used to hide the additional contact information (phone number or e-mail address) displayed to the right of the contact name. Your main motive for using it would be to give the contact list a cleaner look. I personally find that seeing the contact information is more useful because it can provide a quick view of someone's phone number or e-mail address.

- **Use Large Font**—Displays the contact list in a large font for easier readability. You won't be able to see as many contacts onscreen at once, but for those of us without 20/20 vision, it might be worth the trade-off.

- **Country/Region Settings**—Contains information about your geographical location. The area code is your telephone area code, and its purpose is to automatically fill in the area code of phone numbers when entering them for contacts. This is a small time-saving feature, but it can help in terms of making data entry a little more efficient. If you are entering a new contact outside of your default area code, this feature still doesn't slow you down because the area code is the first highlighted field when you enter a phone number. This means you can begin entering a different area code, and it will automatically overwrite the default. The Country/Region setting contains your country/region and is used to fill in the country of contact addresses as another timesaving feature.

BEAMING CONTACTS VIA INFRARED

One of the most convenient features of the Contacts application is its support for beaming contacts using the infrared port on your Pocket PC. This provides a high-tech alternative to swapping business cards. Instead of trading printed paper, you align your Pocket PC with that of another person and automatically swap contact information electronically. To beam contact information to another Pocket PC via infrared, follow these steps:

1. Navigate to the contact in the contact list.
2. Tap and hold the contact entry.
3. Tap Beam Contact on the pop-up menu that appears.
4. Line up the two devices and wait for the transfer to complete (see Figure 13.9). Keep the devices aligned and within a few inches of each other throughout the transfer.

Figure 13.9 shows the Beam Contact screen as it awaits an infrared connection with another device.

Figure 13.9
Beaming contacts via infrared offers a high-tech alternative to swapping business cards.

If anyone is attempting to beam a contact to you, it also is sent during the Beam Contacts process. In other words, when you beam a contact you are actually invoking a two-way infrared communication that enables you to both send and receive contacts.

Tip from *Michael*	If you already have a contact selected in the contact list, another approach to beaming it is to select Beam Contacts from the Tools menu. This is equivalent to performing a tap and hold on the contact and selecting Beam Contact from the pop-up menu.

It's hard to imagine that infrared contact beaming will ever fully replace traditional business cards, but it definitely makes for a convenient approach to sharing contact information with other people who use Pocket PCs.

SHARING CONTACTS WITH OTHER DEVICES

In the previous section you might have been asking yourself what to do when you meet someone who uses a different type of handheld device, such as a Palm, Handspring, or Psion device. Fortunately, as of Pocket PC 2002 you now can share contacts with other devices using the Object Exchange (OBEX) standard. OBEX is a standardized communication protocol for exchanging data between different applications and computing platforms. More specific to handheld devices, OBEX provides a unified format for exchanging data and therefore enables different types of devices to share data. The Pocket PC 2002 operating system fully supports OBEX, which enables you to share information across different handheld computing platforms.

The really interesting thing about the OBEX support in Pocket PCs is that it is automatic—for example, you don't do anything differently to beam a contact to a Palm device. Similarly, you don't have to do anything special on your end of the exchange to receive a contact from a device, assuming the device also supports OBEX. The capability to share contact information with different types of devices is a huge benefit for Pocket PCs because it enables them to peacefully coexist in a world that for the moment is still heavily populated by Palm devices.

MANAGING APPOINTMENTS WITH THE CALENDAR APPLICATION

Just as it is important to keep track of contacts, it is perhaps equally important to keep up with appointments with them. The Pocket Outlook Calendar application is a flexible electronic day planner that enables you to plan your life with as much detail as you desire. Similar to Contacts, the Calendar application synchronizes with Microsoft Outlook to enable you to share personal information between your desktop PC and Pocket PC device.

→ If you don't use Microsoft Outlook on your desktop PC and you still want to synchronize contacts and appointments, **see** "Synchronizing Without ActiveSync," **p. 152**.

The Calendar application manages all date- and time-related functions of the Pocket PC. Even though it's probably obvious to you that the Calendar is ideal for keeping track of business meetings and engagements, I've also found that it is useful for keeping track of other types of scheduled commitments, such as doctors' appointments. On the entertainment side of things, you might want to consider tracking television shows you don't want to miss. If you participate in chat rooms, you might want to schedule upcoming chats. I use Calendar to schedule my hockey games.

Using Calendar Views

It's really up to you how much you want to schedule your life via Calendar. But, after you've determined which events you do want to keep track of, you then need to be able to view the calendar and see what is coming up. The Calendar application supports several views that provide different perspectives on your upcoming appointments:

- **Agenda**—Displays upcoming appointments
- **Day**—Displays appointments for the selected day
- **Week**—Displays the current week, including appointments
- **Month**—Displays the current month, including appointments
- **Year**—Displays the current year

The calendar views are important because they enable you to see what's coming in the short term and also keep long-range commitments in sight. All the calendar views have a consistent user interface in terms of calendar navigation buttons that are displayed in the upper-right corner of the screen and along the bottom of the screen in the toolbar. Figure 13.10 shows the Agenda view.

Note

The Agenda view provides the most detail when viewing appointments. At the other end of the spectrum is the Year view, which provides the least detail by not even showing appointments.

The two navigation buttons on the far right (left and right arrows) are used to move the calendar backward and forward in time. In the Agenda, Day, and Week views, these buttons move the calendar forward or backward a week. In the Month view, the buttons move the calendar forward or backward a month, and so on. The other navigation button appearing to the left of the arrows is used to take you immediately to the current date. Regardless of where you have navigated in the calendar, you can always return to the current date by tapping this button.

Figure 13.10
The Agenda view displays upcoming appointments.

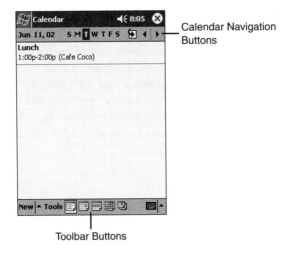

Calendar Navigation Buttons

Toolbar Buttons

Tip from
Michael

Help is always just a couple of taps away while using the Calendar application; just tap Help in the Start menu, and then tap Calendar in the Help Contents.

The row of buttons along the toolbar near the bottom of the screen is used to change the calendar views. The following views are accessible with these buttons, in order from left to right on the toolbar as shown in Figure 13.10:

■ Agenda

■ Day

■ Week

■ Month

■ Year

Although all the calendar views are useful, the Month view is particularly interesting because it uses visual icons to indicate the time commitment of each day. To switch to the Month view, tap the Month button on the Calendar toolbar. Figure 13.11 shows a Month view with several appointments that are identified with different icons.

The icons on the Month view are based on a small box that appears in the lower-right corner of each day on the calendar. Following are the meanings of these icons:

■ A dark triangle in the upper portion of the box indicates a morning appointment.

■ A dark triangle in the lower portion of the box indicates an afternoon appointment.

■ A solid dark box indicates morning and afternoon appointments.

■ A larger hollow outlined box indicates an all-day event.

Figure 13.11
The Month view uses small icons to indicate the time commitment of each day.

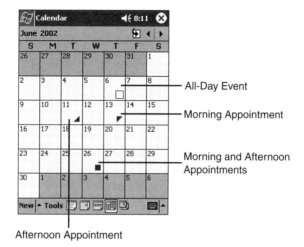

All-Day Event

Morning Appointment

Morning and Afternoon Appointments

Afternoon Appointment

Each of these different appointment icons is displayed in Figure 13.11, which should help you get a feel for how the icons visually distinguish appointment times.

CREATING NEW APPOINTMENTS

To create a new appointment, just follow these steps:

1. Tap New near the bottom of the screen.

2. Use the Input Panel to enter relevant appointment information (see Figure 13.12).

3. Select the amount of time before the appointment that you want to be given a reminder.

4. Be sure to toggle the soft keyboard if it is visible, and select any attendees for the appointment.

5. Add additional text, a drawing, or a voice recording by tapping the Notes tab.

6. Tap OK to save the new appointment.

Figure 13.12
Creating a new appointment simply involves entering relevant information about the appointment on the New Appointment screen.

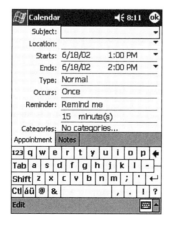

After a new appointment is entered, it appears in the list of appointments under the Agenda view. To see the details of the appointment, just tap it in the list.

Tip from Michael	To copy, delete, or send an appointment, tap and hold the appointment and then select the appropriate command in the pop-up menu that appears.

Tip from Michael	Similar to the Contacts application, the Calendar application enables you to beam appointments to another Pocket PC. To beam an appointment, tap and hold the appointment and then tap Send via Infrared on the pop-up menu that appears.

USING HARDWARE BUTTONS WITH THE CALENDAR APPLICATION

You learned a little earlier in the chapter that most Pocket PCs have a hardware button devoted to launching the Contacts application. They also usually have a hardware button—labeled with a small icon representing a calendar page—devoted to the Calendar application, making it a button push away. Please refer to your device's manual if you don't immediately see a Calendar button.

Tip from Michael	If you are already in the Calendar application, pressing the Calendar button changes the current view. You can continue pressing the Calendar button to cycle through the various views (Agenda, Day, Week, Month, and Year).

The Action button provides a quick way to navigate through the Calendar interface. Scrolling the Action button results in the current calendar view incrementing by a specific length of time. For example, in the Agenda and Day views, the Action button increments the calendar by a day. In the Week and Month views, the Action button increments the calendar by a week. In the Year view, the Action button increments the Calendar by three months. Pressing the Action button results in the creation of a new appointment if you are in the Day or Week views; otherwise, it does nothing. Keep in mind that if your device doesn't have an Action button—as is the case with Compaq iPAQ H3800 Series devices—you can press the navigation button to get the same result.

→ To learn more about the hardware buttons available on Pocket PCs, **see** "Getting to Know the Stylus, Buttons, and Dials," **p. 34**.

CUSTOMIZING THE CALENDAR APPLICATION

The Calendar application can be customized to suit your needs by tapping the Tools menu and then tapping Options. You will see the Options window, which is shown in Figure 13.13.

Figure 13.13
The Options window enables you to customize the Calendar application to your own tastes.

Here is a summary of what you can do with these settings:

- **1st day of week**—This is the first setting, and it establishes the first day of the week as either Sunday or Monday.

- **Week View**—Enables you to view a week as 5, 6, or 7 days; the 5-day view is intended to reflect a business week by excluding weekends.

- **Show Half Hour Slots**—Impacts only the Day and Week views. It adds more granularity to the views by breaking down days into half-hour blocks of time instead of hour blocks.

- **Show Week Numbers**—Applies only to the Week view. When set, it shows the week number with respect to the beginning of the year.

- **Use Large Font**—Applies to the Agenda and Day views and displays appointment information in a larger font.

- **Set Reminders for New Items**—Results in new appointments automatically defaulting to having a reminder set for a given length of time before the appointment. You can set the amount of time you need. Keep in mind that this setting is just a timesaving feature; you can still individually alter the reminder time for appointments after creating them.

- **Show Icons**—Enables and disables the display of icons in the Day view. Although the icons take up a little space on the screen, I find them useful enough to keep them enabled. If you aren't sure about using the icons, you can enable them individually or disable all of them. If an icon is surrounded by black, it's enabled; white indicates that the icon is disabled. By default, all icons are disabled, which is why they appear with a white background in Figure 13.13.

- **Send Meeting Requests via**—When you schedule an appointment with attendees, Pocket Outlook generates a meeting request, provided that the attendees use Microsoft Outlook, Pocket Outlook, or Schedule+. This results in each attendee receiving a notification of the meeting when you synchronize the Calendar application with your desktop PC or connect to an e-mail server. The default approach to sending meeting requests is to use ActiveSync, but you can change this to some other service if you so

PART
III

CH
13

desire. An example of another service is Puma Technology's Intellisync, which is used to synchronize Pocket PCs with Lotus Notes.

→ For more information on Puma Technology's Intellisync software and other alternatives to Microsoft Outlook, **see** "Synchronizing Without ActiveSync," **p. 152**.

CHANGING THE ALARM SOUND

One additional customization related to the Calendar application is the capability of changing the alarm sound that is played to signal an upcoming appointment. The following steps explain how this is accomplished:

1. Tap the Start menu, and then tap Settings.

2. Tap the Sounds & Notifications icon, and then tap the Notifications tab.

3. Select Reminders in the drop-down list of notification events.

4. Modify the relevant alarm parameters that are used to notify you of appointment reminders (see Figure 13.14).

Figure 13.14
The Sounds & Notifications settings can be modified to change the type of alarm used to notify you of appointments.

Tip from
Michael

The sound played as a reminder to signal an upcoming appointment is stored as a WAV audio file in the Windows folder of your device. You can substitute your own custom alarm by copying a WAV file to the Windows folder and then changing to the new alarm as described.

APPLYING RECURRENCE PATTERNS

When you create an appointment, you have the option of making the appointment recurring—which means it repeats according to some criteria, such as daily, weekly, or monthly. When setting a recurring appointment, the Calendar application includes several default options that are used to establish the recurrence. However, these default options might not always be what you need. In this event, you need to create a recurrence pattern that spells out exactly how your appointment repeats. The Calendar application includes a wizard to help you create recurrence patterns.

To create a recurrence pattern, follow these steps:

1. While editing an appointment, tap the combo box next to the Occurs field.
2. Tap Edit Pattern in the list of options; the Recurrence Pattern Wizard appears.
3. Set the time and duration of the appointment in the first screen of the wizard (see Figure 13.15). Then tap Next.
4. Set the recurrence of the appointment by selecting Daily, Weekly, Monthly, or Yearly and then specifying appropriate recurrence details (see Figure 13.16). Tap Next to continue through the wizard.
5. Set the start and end of the pattern in the third screen of the wizard (see Figure 13.17).
6. Tap Finish to complete the recurrence pattern.

Figure 13.15
The first screen of the Recurrence Pattern Wizard prompts you to set the time and duration of an appointment.

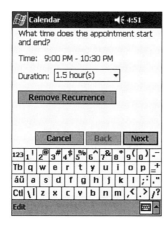

Figure 13.16
The second screen of the Recurrence Pattern Wizard prompts you to specify the recurrence of the appointment.

PART

III

CH

13

Figure 13.17
The third screen of
the Recurrence
Pattern Wizard
prompts you to set
the start and end pat-
terns of the appoint-
ment.

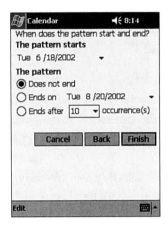

Recurrence patterns provide a great deal of flexibility in creating recurring appointments, especially when you have an appointment that doesn't adhere to the default recurrence options in the Calendar application.

 If you're having trouble creating long-term appointments that are longer than 31 days, see "Creating Long-Term Appointments" in the "Troubleshooting" section at the end of the chapter to find out how to use recurrence patterns to dodge the 31-day limitation on appointment length.

APPOINTMENTS AND THE TODAY SCREEN

As you know, the Today screen is a great starting point for assessing what is going on with the personal information you keep in your Pocket PC. One of the bands of information displayed in the Today screen contains appointments that are managed by the Calendar application. In addition to being able to turn this band on and off, you can alter its position on the Today screen and customize the types of appointments it displays. To customize the Calendar band on the Today screen, follow these steps:

1. Tap Start, and then tap Settings.
2. Tap the Today icon, and then tap the Items tab.
3. Tap the check box next to the word Calendar to enable/disable the Calendar band, or just tap the word Calendar next to the check box (see Figure 13.18).
4. Tap the Move Up and Move Down buttons to move the Calendar band around with respect to the other bands.
5. Tap the Options button.
6. Tap the Next Appointment radio button to display only the next appointment in the Calendar band, or tap Upcoming Appointments to display upcoming appointments in the Calendar band.
7. Tap the Display All Day Events check box to include all-day events in the Calendar band.
8. Tap OK in the upper-right corner, and then tap OK again.

Figure 13.18
The Today Settings window allows you to enable or disable the Calendar band, as well as change the positioning of the band with respect to other bands.

You've now customized the Calendar band of the Today screen. To see the changes, return to the Today screen and take a look at the appointments displayed.

TROUBLESHOOTING

AN ALTERNATIVE MEANS OF NAVIGATING CONTACTS

I'm not satisfied with the standard approach to navigating contacts in the Contacts application.

An intuitive approach to navigating contacts does indeed exist that involves the Action button on your device. While viewing the contact list in the Contacts application, press the hardware Action button up or down and hold it for a couple of seconds. A large letter will appear on the screen that represents the last name of a contact to which you can jump. If you continue to press the Action button up or down quickly, you can cycle through the alphabet and select a letter that will lead you to a section of the contact list. For example, cycling to the letter *H* takes you to the first contact whose last name begins with the letter *H*.

CREATING LONG-TERM APPOINTMENTS

The Calendar application won't let me create appointments that are longer than 31 days.

Although this might seem like a strange problem, there are a few scenarios where long-term appointments could prove useful. Maybe you're taking a sabbatical from work, or maybe you're a student or schoolteacher and you want to schedule the summer break as an appointment. Regardless of why you might need to create a long-term appointment, the Calendar application limits the length of appointments to 31 days to maintain backward compatibility with older versions of Microsoft Outlook. Fortunately, a workaround is available that involves creating a daily recurring appointment that stretches across the duration of the time period.

To create a long-term appointment that is longer than 31 days, just follow these steps:

1. Run the Calendar application, and tap New near the bottom of the screen.
2. Enter the subject of the appointment.
3. Select All Day as the Type of appointment.
4. Select Free or Out of Office as the Status of the appointment.
5. Tap the combo box next to the Occurs field, and select Edit Pattern in the list of options; the Recurrence Pattern Wizard appears.
6. Set the time and duration of the appointment in the first screen of the wizard so that the appointment fills up most of the day, and then tap Next.
7. Select Daily as the recurrence of the appointment, and then tap Next to continue through the wizard.
8. Set the start and end of the pattern in the third screen of the wizard.
9. Tap Finish to complete the recurrence pattern.
10. Tap OK to create the new appointment.

You have now effectively created an appointment that lasts longer than 31 days. Granted, this might not be something you need to do very often, but now you know how!

REAL-WORLD EXAMPLE—POCKET MEETING PLANNING

If you aren't already using your Pocket PC to plan meetings with the Calendar application, now is a good time to start. The next time you need to plan a meeting that involves people who all have e-mail accounts, use the Calendar application to schedule the meeting. Be sure to enter the attendees when creating the appointment, and they will automatically be notified via e-mail thanks to the integration of the Inbox, Contacts, and Calender applications in Pocket Outlook. The capability of scheduling a meeting and notifying attendees from the convenience of your Pocket PC is not only efficient, but quite convenient if you're away from your desktop PC frequently. It also keeps you from having to make phone calls to each attendee.

CHAPTER **14**

WORKING WITH THE POCKET OUTLOOK TASKS AND NOTES

In this chapter

ORGANIZING YOUR LIFE WITH TASKS

The Tasks application is the component of Pocket Outlook responsible for managing and keeping track of things you need to do. In many cases, these tasks are work related, but not always. If you have a project, chore, or some other undertaking that is currently a goal or work-in-progress, it probably qualifies as a task. When used appropriately, the Tasks application can really help you stay on track with both personal and work projects; just try to keep everything in perspective and remember that your Pocket PC is supposed to make life easier, not more complicated.

Let's get into some ideas for specific tasks you might want to manage with the Tasks application. In addition to obvious uses such as work projects, the Tasks application can help you keep up with long-term projects you don't even intend to start any time soon. Even if the projects are really just ideas, by entering them as tasks you're able to remember later that these are things you want to work on at some future time. Granted, some of these ideas might fizzle, but the worst-case scenario is that you simply delete them. The powerful thing about managing ideas as tasks is that you can have the Tasks application remind you when it's time to address a project.

Similar to Contacts and Calendar, the Tasks application is capable of being synchronized with Microsoft Outlook Tasks data. Figure 14.1 shows the Tasks application at work.

Figure 14.1
The Tasks application organizes your tasks so you can focus on completing them.

Regardless of whether you are a task-oriented person, you might still find the Tasks application useful for keeping track of projects and things to do, especially when you consider that you can carry around your task list on your Pocket PC.

CREATING NEW TASKS

As you can see in Figure 14.1, my only task is completing the writing of this chapter. This is obviously a task I've already entered. To create new tasks, just follow these steps:

1. Tap New near the bottom of the screen.

2. Use the Input Panel to enter relevant task information (see Figure 14.2).

3. Add additional text, a drawing, or a voice recording by tapping the Notes tab.

4. Tap OK to save the new task.

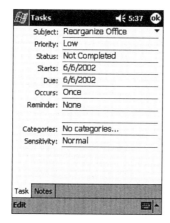

Figure 14.2
Creating a new task in the Tasks application simply involves entering the appropriate information on the New Task screen.

The new task appears in the task list immediately after you enter it. If you've specified that the task be of a high priority, a small exclamation point appears to the left of the task; the task in Figure 14.1 is a high-priority task. A low-priority task has a down arrow next to it; the new task in Figure 14.2 is a low-priority task. To see the details of a task, just tap it in the list.

Tip from
Michael

> To copy, delete, or send a task, tap and hold the task; then select the appropriate command in the pop-up menu that appears.

Tasks can be set up based on *recurrence patterns*, which are used to determine how a task repeats. Repetitive tasks might not be common for you, but if you ever need to manage one, you'll find recurrence patterns to be a big help. As an example, you might perform a quarterly review of employees, in which case you could schedule the review as a recurring pattern that occurs once every quarter. To create a recurrence pattern for a task, tap the combo box next to the Occurs field while editing the task. Tap Edit Pattern in the list of options, and then follow the steps presented in the Recurrence Pattern Wizard.

➔ For more information on how patterns are created and used, **see** the discussion of recurrence in Chapter 13, "Using the Pocket Outlook Contacts and Calendar," **p. 237**.

SPEEDING UP TASK ENTRY WITH THE ENTRY BAR

If you're the kind of person who likes to use lots of tasks to manage projects and things to do, one problem you might encounter with the Tasks application is that entering a bunch of tasks can be time-consuming. This problem is especially apparent with tasks that don't

PART
III

CH
14

require any more information than a subject. For these kinds of tasks, entering them using the Tasks application's entry bar, which is disabled by default, is much quicker. To enable the entry bar, tap the Tools menu and then tap Entry Bar. An edit box appears near the top of the screen, which you can tap and enter new tasks into without going through the detailed task creation window. Figure 14.3 shows the Entry Bar being used to enter a task.

Figure 14.3
The Entry Bar in the Tasks application enables you to directly enter and create new tasks.

Entry Bar

The two buttons to the left of the Entry Bar enable you to designate the task as being high priority (the exclamation point) or low priority (the down arrow); leaving both buttons off results in the task having a normal priority. The task isn't actually created until you tap below the Entry Bar in the main window of the Tasks application (see Figure 14.4). Keep in mind that you can still edit the newly created task if you want to alter the details. However, if you intend to create a detailed task from the start, you might as well forgo the Entry Bar and just use the New menu in the lower-left corner of the screen instead.

Figure 14.4
After tapping off the Entry Bar, a newly created task is displayed in the task list.

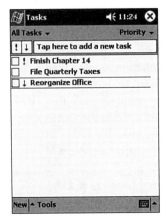

Tip from
Michael

If you want to change the priority of a task you've already created, you can tap and hold in the space between the check box and the task name in the task list where the priority icon is displayed. A pop-up menu will appear that enables you to change the priority of the task.

NAVIGATING TASKS

After you've entered some tasks and you have a task list to manage, you're ready to investigate the various navigational tools used to display the tasks. Keep in mind that tasks can be assigned to specific categories, such as Business, Personal, and so on. You can control the tasks that are displayed in the list by tapping and selecting a category in the upper-left corner of the screen (see Figure 14.5). By default, the Tasks application displays tasks in all categories, but you can select a different category to limit the tasks displayed. You can also filter the task list by distinguishing between active and completed tasks. By checking Active Tasks or Completed Tasks in the list, you limit the task list to one or the other.

Note

Just as you can with Contacts, you can share tasks with other Pocket PC users via the infrared port by tapping and holding the task and then tapping Beam Task.

Figure 14.5
Tapping the task category reveals a drop-down list from which you can filter the task list.

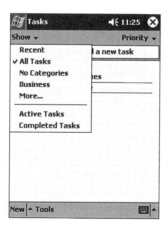

The other way to alter the display of tasks is to tap on the sort method near the upper-right corner of the screen, which displays a drop-down list of methods to use for sorting the task list (see Figure 14.6). By selecting a different sort method, you alter the order of the task list, which can be useful in determining the order in which you work on a given task. For example, I typically use the Priority and Due Date sort methods because they tell me which tasks are most important and which tasks are due or overdue.

Figure 14.6
Tapping the sort method reveals a drop-down list from which you can sort the task list by selecting a sort method.

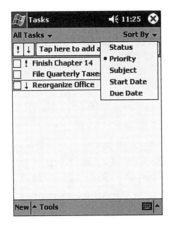

Tip from
Michael

Help is always just a couple of taps away while using the Tasks application; just tap Help in the Start menu, and then tap Tasks in the Help Contents.

USING HARDWARE BUTTONS WITH THE TASKS APPLICATION

Unlike the Contacts and Calendar applications, which are usually accessible from a conveniently labeled hardware button, the Tasks application is typically not accessible from a hardware button by default. However, reassigning a hardware button isn't too difficult if you decide you want the Tasks application to be a button press away. To reassign a hardware button on your device to the Tasks application, just follow these steps:

1. Tap Start, and then tap Settings.
2. Tap the Buttons icon.
3. Select the button you want to reassign in the list, and then select the Tasks application from the Button Assignment drop-down list (see Figure 14.7).
4. Tap OK in the upper-right corner to accept the new button assignment.

Note

Some devices enable you to launch the Tasks application with a button combination. The combination usually involves holding down the Action button and pressing one of the other hardware buttons. Check your Pocket PC's documentation to see whether a button combination exists for launching the Tasks application.

Now that you've straightened out how to launch the Tasks application with a hardware button, you might be curious about how buttons fit into using the application. The only hardware button that directly factors into using the Tasks application is the Action button, which provides a way to navigate through the Tasks interface. Scrolling the Action button moves up and down the task list, whereas pressing the Action Button is the same as tapping the currently selected task. Although this isn't necessarily an easier (or more difficult) method of navigation, it does provide you with more choices in how you use your device.

Figure 14.7
The Button Settings screen makes reassigning a hardware button to the Tasks application easy.

CUSTOMIZING THE TASKS APPLICATION

Similar to all the other Pocket Outlook applications, the Tasks application is customizable via the Tools menu. To customize the application, tap the Tools menu and then tap Options. You will see the Options window, which is shown in Figure 14.8.

Figure 14.8
The Options window in the Tasks application enables you to customize the application.

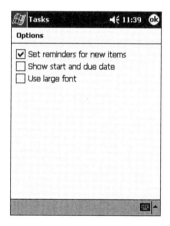

The Set Reminders for New Items option automatically sets a reminder for new tasks after you enter the due dates for the tasks. You should probably keep this setting enabled because reminders are helpful for most tasks. The Show Start and Due Date setting displays the start and due dates for a task in the task list just below the subject of the task. Although this setting results in tasks taking up more screen space, you might find it useful if you want to see more information about each task in the task list. Finally, the Use Large Font setting displays task information in a large font.

PART
III

CH
14

The Tasks application is limited in that it doesn't allow you to alter the time of task reminders. To learn about a workaround for this problem, see "Getting Specific with Task Reminders" in the "Troubleshooting" section at the end of the chapter.

An indirect customization of the Tasks application involves altering the manner in which tasks are displayed on the Today screen. Similar to the appointments created in the Calendar application, tasks can be displayed as an information band on the Today screen. Along with being able to turn the Tasks band on and off, you can alter its position on the Today screen and customize the types of tasks it displays. To customize the Tasks band on the Today screen, follow these steps:

1. Tap Start, and then tap Settings.
2. Tap the Today icon, and then tap the Items tab.
3. Tap the check box next to the word Tasks to enable/disable the Tasks band.
4. Tap the Move Up and Move Down buttons to move the Tasks band around with respect to the other bands.
5. Tap the Options button.
6. Tap the High Priority Tasks, Tasks Due Today, or Overdue Tasks check box to display the number of each task in the Tasks band (see Figure 14.9).
7. Tap the Category combo box to select a category that is used to filter the tasks displayed in the Tasks band.
8. Tap OK in the upper-right corner, and then tap OK again.

Figure 14.9
The Today Tasks Options screen enables you to customize the manner in which tasks are displayed on the Today screen.

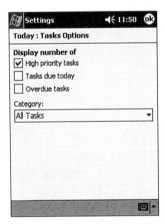

You've now customized the Tasks band of the Today screen. To see the changes, return to the Today screen and take a look at the tasks displayed.

JOTTING DOWN IDEAS WITH NOTES

Notes is probably the most flexible application included in the Pocket Outlook family of applications because the notes you create can be used to store all kinds of different information. The idea behind notes is to provide an electronic equivalent of the popular sticky paper notes you often see stuck to monitors in offices. Pocket PC notes are much more advanced than their paper counterparts in that they can include text, ink (handwriting), and voice recordings. The Notes application is responsible for supporting these various media types and providing a user interface for inputting each of them.

The interesting thing about the Notes application is that each user is likely to use it in a unique manner. Whereas I might use Notes to jot down a quick materials list for a run to the hardware store, some other user might take it a step further and include a drawing of the project to accompany the materials list just in case a substitution becomes necessary after she gets to the store. You also might be on the road and have an idea you want to document and share with an associate at work. By making a voice recording in a note and synchronizing with a dial-up connection, you can share your idea with ease.

Note

Notes entered in the Notes application are synchronized with the Notes portion of Microsoft Outlook.

The Notes application allows you to make your own voice recordings that coexist with other information within the context of a note. Pocket PC supports various audio formats for making voice recordings, which enables you to strike a balance between audio quality and storage space. To change the audio format used for voice recordings, you must go to the Options window for the Input Panel.

→ For more information about how to change the audio format used for voice recordings, **see** Chapter 3, "Navigating the Pocket PC GUI," **p. 41**.

→ For more information on how to change the options for the Input Panel, **see** "Fine-Tuning User Input," **p. 104**.

CREATING NEW NOTES

Unlike the other Pocket Outlook applications, which represent a simplified version of a Microsoft Outlook equivalent feature, the Notes application is actually a step ahead of Outlook because it supports ink (hand drawings) and voice recordings. These notes can then be attached to other types of Pocket Outlook data, such as contacts and tasks. Figure 14.10 shows the Notes application in action.

To view the details of a note, you tap it in the note list; Figure 14.11 shows an example of a note containing nothing but text.

Tip from
Michael

To copy, delete, send, rename, or move a note, tap and hold the note and then select the appropriate command in the pop-up menu that appears.

PART
III

CH
14

Figure 14.10
The Notes application displays a list of notes (just one in this case) that is logically equivalent to a stack of paper sticky notes.

Figure 14.11
A simple text note is sufficient for simple ideas, reminders, and daily to-do lists.

If you want to go beyond text and include more interesting data in a note, you might consider creating a drawing or voice recording as part of a note. To create a note, follow these steps:

1. Tap New near the bottom of the screen.

2. Use the Input Panel to enter note information.

3. Draw directly on the screen with the stylus to add drawings or handwritten text to the note.

4. Hold down the hardware voice recorder button to record a voice message and attach it to the note; the voice recording appears as a speaker icon in the note. You can add multiple voice recordings to a note if you so desire.

5. Tap OK to save the new note.

Note

While editing a note, you might notice a button that looks like a small pencil. This button is used to set the input mode to Writing, which enables you to draw graphics and handwritten text. Tapping the button a second time disables Writing mode and sets the input mode back to Typing mode.

Figure 14.12 shows a note with text, a hand drawing, and a voice recording. This example shows how I was brainstorming a logo for my game company, Stalefish Labs, and it really shows off some of the multimedia capabilities of Pocket PCs.

Figure 14.12
With support for text, hand drawings, and voice recordings, the Notes application blows away traditional paper sticky notes.

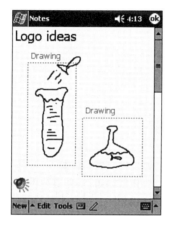

Remember that you view a note by tapping it in the note list. To listen to a voice recording in a note, tap the speaker icon that appears in the note. If multiple voice recordings are included in a note, each is identified by a different speaker icon; tapping the appropriate icon plays that particular voice recording.

MANAGING NOTES

Notes are different from other types of Pocket Outlook data because they are stored in individual files, as opposed to being stored in a database specific to a given application. This makes notes somewhat more flexible because you can access and manipulate them individually from File Explorer. By default, notes are created in the My Documents folder, but you can store them in any folder you want. The Notes application is capable of listing all the notes stored on your device regardless of the folder in which they are located. I use the word *capable* because it is possible to limit the note list to a specific folder. To do so, tap the folder in the upper-left corner of the Notes screen. A drop-down list appears that enables you to select the folder whose notes are displayed (see Figure 14.13).

PART

III

CH

14

Note

You can share notes with other Pocket PC users via the infrared port by tapping and holding the note and then tapping Beam File. Or, you can send notes as e-mail attachments by tapping Send via E-mail instead.

Figure 14.13
Tapping the note folder reveals a drop-down list that enables you to set the folders for which notes are displayed.

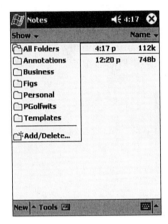

You might find it useful to create a special folder to store notes to keep your My Documents folder from getting cluttered. To create a new folder for storing notes, just select Add/Delete from the drop-down list shown in Figure 14.13. The Add/Delete Folders window appears, as shown in Figure 14.14.

Figure 14.14
The Add/Delete Folders window enables you to create, rename, and delete folders that are used to store notes.

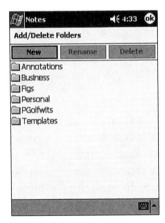

After creating any new folders you want to use to store notes, you can easily move notes between the folders by tapping and holding the note and then tapping Rename/Move. This results in the Rename/Move window being displayed, which enables you to select a folder for the note, as well as decide whether you want to store the note in the main system memory or in a memory storage card.

Tip from
Michael

You can move multiple notes simultaneously by tapping and dragging the stylus over the notes to select them, lifting the stylus, tapping and holding over the selected notes, and selecting Rename/Move from the pop-up menu that appears.

Note

When you move a note to a folder other than My Documents, the folder name appears in front of the filename when the note is synchronized and displayed in Outlook.

USING THE VOICE BAR AND HAND RECOGNITION

The note list is displayed as the main window in the Notes application and has the familiar New and Tools menus. You might have noticed an icon to the right of the Tools menu that looks like a small cassette tape. This button allows you to enable and disable the Voice Bar, which is displayed near the bottom of the screen and provides a user interface for handling voice recordings. The Voice Bar serves as an alternative to the Record button and is ultimately more flexible because it enables you to stop and play recordings, as well as change the volume of the device. The Voice Bar is automatically displayed if you use the Record button, so you have access to it without having to use the icon next to the menus. Figure 14.15 shows the Voice Bar, which is displayed near the bottom of the screen just above the menu.

Figure 14.15
The Voice Bar provides an intuitive means of recording and adding voice notations to notes.

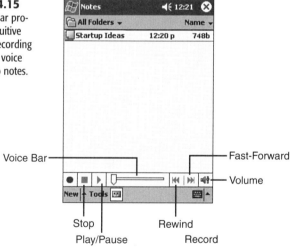

If you like to hand write information into notes but would prefer having the end result stored as text, you should try the Recognize feature in the Tools menu. To use this feature, hand write text into a note and then tap Recognize in the Tools menu. Figure 14.16 shows some handwritten text I entered into a new note.

PART

III

CH

14

Note

Although they both are a form of handwriting recognition, keep in mind that the Recognize feature for Notes is a separate program from the more powerful Transcriber utility.

→ For a refresher of handwriting recognition and the Transcriber input method, **see** "Working with Transcriber," **p. 93**.

Figure 14.16
Text that is handwritten in a note can be converted using the Recognize feature.

Figure 14.17 shows the results of using the Recognize feature to convert my handwritten text to simple text.

Figure 14.17
The end result of using the Recognize feature might not always be exactly what you expected, but in this case it worked perfectly.

Depending on your handwriting, it might not always recognize text perfectly, but it usually gets close enough that you can quickly make corrections.

Note

Help is always just a couple of taps away while using the Notes application; just tap Help in the Start menu, and then tap Notes in the Help Contents.

 If you realize that you need to add formatting to the information in a note, you will be in a predicament because the Notes application doesn't support formatting features such as fonts. However, you can convert a note into a Pocket Word document so you can add formatting. Although this isn't a standard feature of Notes or Pocket Word, there is a way to carry out the conversion without too much effort. See "Converting Notes into Pocket Word Documents" in the "Troubleshooting" section at the end of the chapter to find out how.

USING HARDWARE BUTTONS WITH THE NOTES APPLICATION

Similar to the Tasks application, the Notes application usually doesn't have a dedicated hardware button associated with it, but you can use the same technique covered earlier in the chapter to reassign a button to Notes. It's really a personal preference when it comes to determining which applications you assign to hardware buttons. Just keep in mind that typically a limited number of buttons are available for mapping, so you should pick and choose the applications you tend to use the most.

Although no default button exists for launching the Notes application, a hardware button is available that comes in handy when using Notes. I'm referring to the Record button, which enables you to quickly make voice recordings while you're working in the Notes application; the Record button provides the quickest approach to including voice recordings as part of a note.

Tip from
Michael

When recording voice, you should speak with your mouth about 4 inches from the microphone on your device.

When you make a voice recording using the Record button, the recording is stored as a wave audio file (.wav file extension) in the My Documents folder. You can access voice recordings from the Notes application or by opening the My Documents folder in the File Explorer application.

CUSTOMIZING THE NOTES APPLICATION

As you might have guessed, the Notes application is customizable via the Tools menu. To customize the application, tap the Tools menu and then tap Options. You will see the Options window, which is shown in Figure 14.18.

PART
III

CH
14

Figure 14.18
The Options window in the Notes application enables you to customize the application.

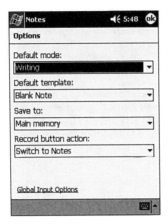

The Default Mode setting determines the input mode, which can be either Writing or Typing. Set this according to whether you prefer creating notes by hand writing with the stylus or pecking keys on the soft keyboard. The Default Template setting determines the type of note created by default. In addition to creating blank notes, the Notes application includes standard templates to help in creating commonly used notes. The default template can be set to one of these templates:

- Blank Note
- Meeting Notes
- Memo
- Phone Memo
- To Do

Figure 14.19 displays a newly created note that uses the Meeting Notes template. This gives you an idea of how templates can be useful for determining the structure of notes.

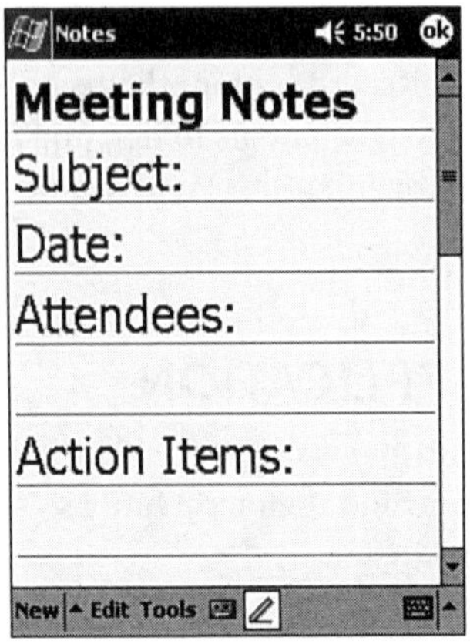

Figure 14.19
The Meeting Notes template provides a standard format for entering meeting notes.

The Save To option enables you to change the location to which notes are saved. You can choose between main system memory and a memory storage card. If you choose the Main Memory option, which is the default option, all notes are stored in the My Documents folder. The Record Button Action setting determines what happens when the Record button is pressed to make a voice recording. The default setting is for the Notes application to appear when you make a recording. This makes sense because you will likely use the Notes application to play and manage voice recordings. However, if you want to stay in the current application when you make voice recordings, you can change the setting accordingly.

TROUBLESHOOTING

GETTING SPECIFIC WITH TASK REMINDERS

The reminders for tasks always go off at 8:00 a.m. on the day the task is due, and there doesn't appear to be a way to change this reminder time.

The Tasks application doesn't provide any facility for changing the reminder time for tasks. However, if you want to have a high degree of control over when you are reminded of a task, you can create an appointment out of the task in the Calendar application. Just edit the task in the Tasks application, copy the subject of the task, and then paste the subject into the subject of a new Calendar appointment. Finally, enter a start date and time for the appointment reminder, and you will then be reminded of the task exactly when you want to be reminded.

CONVERTING NOTES INTO POCKET WORD DOCUMENTS

I've created a note that I now want to convert into a Pocket Word document so I can add formatting. Is there a way to convert a note into a Pocket Word document?

Not directly—there is no conversion utility for converting notes into Pocket Word documents, and Pocket Word isn't capable of opening notes because it recognizes only Pocket Word documents. However, you can effectively convert a note into a Pocket Word document by following these steps:

1. Open the note in the Notes application.
2. Copy the note by selecting Select All from the Edit menu and then selecting Copy from the Edit menu.
3. Run Pocket Word and create a new document.
4. Select Paste from the Edit menu to paste the note contents into the new document.

REAL-WORLD EXAMPLE—MANAGING A TEAM PROJECT

Although the Tasks and Notes applications can be very useful for managing your own tasks and keeping up with your own thoughts and notes, you also can use them to manage a team project. The next time you're involved in a project with other people, try keeping track of the project using tasks and notes on your Pocket PC. Tasks will likely be more important because you can break out each person's responsibilities and enter them as tasks. It's a good idea to use a naming system to distinguish each person's tasks, such as naming each task so it begins with the person's initials. Notes can serve as a repository for general ideas relating to the project. It's probably a good idea to create a folder using the project name that holds the notes. Granted, this project management approach might not work for large, complex projects, but you'd be surprised at what you can accomplish on your Pocket PC with a little diligence.

GETTING PRODUCTIVE WITH YOUR POCKET PC

CHAPTER 15

WORKING WITH DOCUMENTS IN POCKET WORD

In this chapter

COMPARING POCKET WORD WITH WORD

Although you might not have purchased your Pocket PC with the thought of using it to pen your first novel, the option is there. Every Pocket PC ships with Pocket Word, which is a scaled-down version of Word, Microsoft's immensely popular desktop word processor. Pocket Word is designed with mobile writing in mind and retains a core set of Word's features in a much more compact application. Pocket Word certainly doesn't include all the fancy tools and extras found in Word, but it does a good job of allowing you to create and edit formatted documents in the palm of your hand. *Formatted documents* are documents that include decorative effects such as bold and italic text, different fonts, and even embedded images. One of the most important features that did make its way into Pocket Word is a spell checker, which is critical for those of us who aren't former grade school spelling bee champions.

This chapter introduces you to Pocket Word and explores what it has to offer in terms of mobile writing. You learn about the relationship between Pocket Word and its full-grown desktop uncle, as well as some tips and tricks for getting the most out of Pocket Word.

Pocket Word uses the .psw file extension, and Word uses the .doc format. When a Word document is transferred to the Pocket PC for use in Pocket Word, it undergoes a conversion process from the .doc to .psw file extension. This conversion happens when the following takes place:

- A Word document is synchronized with Pocket Word via ActiveSync.
- A Word document is manually copied from a desktop PC to a Pocket PC device using Windows Explorer.
- A Word document is opened as an e-mail attachment using Pocket Outlook.

→ To learn more about synchronization and ActiveSync, **see** Chapter 8, "Using ActiveSync to Synchronize Data," **p. 145**.

> **Note**
>
> Pocket Word documents are automatically converted back to Word documents when they are transferred back to a desktop computer. The conversion of Word documents is handled by ActiveSync, which explains why no conversion takes place if you transfer Pocket Word documents between two Pocket PC devices. Documents stored in either Rich Text Format (.rtf files) or simple text format (.txt files) do not have to be converted to work with Pocket Word. For rich text files, this means that no formatting information is lost; text files don't include formatting information.

When a Word document is converted to Pocket Word, it retains most of its formatting but loses some important attributes. *Document attributes* are special pieces of information that describe or annotate a part of a document; examples of attributes include bold formatting, borders, and paragraph margins. It is critical to understand exactly which document attributes are retained and lost because you don't want to move files back and forth between your desktop PC and Pocket PC and unknowingly lose information. The safest way to preserve the formatting of synchronized Word documents is to use Pocket Word as a document viewer, which involves not editing or saving changes to a document after opening it. Of course, this defeats the purpose of using Pocket Word to create and edit documents. So, to safely edit Word documents in Pocket Word, you need to become acquainted with the limitations of Pocket Word and what specific information is lost in the translation from Word to Pocket Word.

Tip from *Michael*	A good way to avoid the risk of losing document attributes when working with a Word document in Pocket Word is to make a copy of the document file on your desktop PC before copying/synchronizing with your Pocket PC. You can then compare the modified file when it is converted back to Word and correct or reject any unwanted modifications. Word includes a Merge Documents utility in the Tools menu that assists in merging similar documents.

ATTRIBUTES RETAINED DURING CONVERSION

I'd like to first focus on the positive by addressing the information in Word documents that is retained when converting documents to Pocket Word. These attributes are retained throughout the Word/Pocket Word conversion process, and you can rest easy that you won't lose anything when synchronizing documents. Following are the Word document attributes that are fully supported in Pocket Word:

- Bold
- Underline
- Italic
- Strikethrough
- Bullets
- Paragraph spacing
- Paragraph alignment
- TrueType fonts (fonts must be installed on Pocket PC)

These Word document attributes are fully supported throughout the conversion process, so you can safely count on them not being altered or lost when moving documents back and forth between Word and Pocket Word.

ATTRIBUTES ALTERED DURING CONVERSION

In addition to these fully supported document attributes, some other types of document information exist that are retained in the conversion to Pocket Word but that might be slightly altered:

- **Images**—Color depth is reduced to 256 colors.
- **Indentation**—It's altered to improve readability.

- **Tables**—Formatting is lost but text is preserved.
- **Table of contents**—Formatting is lost but text is preserved.
- **Index formatting**—Formatting is lost but text is preserved.
- **OLE objects**—Objects are lost and replaced by bitmap placeholders.

Note

OLE (Object Linking and Embedding) objects are software components used throughout Windows to provide special functionality to applications. OLE allows you to embed objects such as Excel worksheets directly into Word documents.

This document information is retained in the conversion process but might not be exactly as you would expect. For example, although text is retained for document attributes, such as tables and tables of contents, keep in mind that the formatting will be lost. This means that a document converted to Pocket Word, saved, and then moved back to Word will retain table data but won't keep the table formatting. In addition to these Word attributes that are altered in Pocket Word, one Pocket Word document attribute is altered when converted back to Word. I'm referring to notes and drawings that are created in Pocket Word, which are converted to Windows metafile images when a Pocket Word document is converted to a Word document.

Note

A Windows *metafile* image is a vector image that is commonly used with clip art. Metafile images are similar in function to GIF or JPEG images, except that metafile images are particularly well suited to scalable vector images such as line art drawings and cartoons.

ATTRIBUTES NOT SUPPORTED DURING CONVERSION

At this point, you understand that some Word document attributes are fully supported, whereas some are supported with modification. To add to the confusion of this seemingly mixed support for Word document attributes, the following are some document attributes that are not supported in Pocket Word but that are restored when you convert a document back to Word:

- Margins
- Gutter size
- Paper size
- Header/footer vertical location

At this point, you might be confused as to how an attribute can *not* be supported in Pocket Word yet still be retained when a document is converted back to Word. There is actually a simple explanation: Even though Pocket Word doesn't support the functionality of these attributes, it retains them as part of the document structure. So, you wouldn't know that the attributes are there when viewing a document in Pocket Word, but they lurk just below the surface and therefore are retained when you convert a Pocket Word document back to Word.

ATTRIBUTES LOST DURING CONVERSION

Now on to the bad news! The most important Word document attributes with respect to Pocket Word are probably those that aren't supported at all, which means they are actually lost when converting documents. These attributes are as follows:

- Borders
- Shading
- Columns
- Numbered lists
- Headers/footers
- Annotations
- Footnotes
- Comments
- Revision marks
- Page setup information
- Frames
- Style sheets

Caution

Password-protected Word documents can't be converted for use with Pocket Word; you must turn off password protection to convert such documents.

You should be particularly careful when converting and editing files in Pocket Word that use any of these document attributes because they will be lost during conversion. Keep in mind that the premise behind Pocket Word is to provide a compact means of creating and editing documents. Although the preceding list might make it seem as if Pocket Word is skimping on features, the intention never was to create a full-blown desktop word processor in Pocket Word. Instead, Pocket Word is designed to facilitate word processing on the go while providing a reasonable trade-off between functionality and application efficiency.

Tip from
Michael

The safest way to ensure that no formatting information is lost when opening a Word document in Pocket Word is to use Pocket Word only as a document viewer. In other words, don't make any changes to the document in Pocket Word.

CREATING DOCUMENTS WITH POCKET WORD

To start Pocket Word, tap Programs from the Start menu and then tap the Pocket Word icon. Pocket Word first appears with a blank document opened and ready for editing. If you close this document by tapping OK in the upper-right corner of the screen, you'll see a list of Pocket Word documents that can be opened for viewing and editing. If you're using Pocket Word for the first time, you probably won't have any documents in the list. In this case, you'll probably want to create a new one, which is where you were when Word first started. To create a new document, just tap New in the lower-left corner of the screen.

→ I recommend adding Pocket Word to the Start menu if you plan to use it frequently. **See** "Tweaking the Start and New Menus," **p. 76**, if you aren't sure how to do this.

When you create a new document or open an existing document, the menu at the bottom of the screen changes to reflect commands and options available for Pocket Word:

- **Edit menu**—Contains commands used to alter the content and appearance of document data.

- **View menu**—Allows you to enable or disable the Pocket Word toolbar, as well as set the input mode and the zoom level of the document.

- **Tools menu**—Includes a variety of commands for manipulating documents, such as invoking the spell checker, performing a word count, recognizing handwritten text, sending the document via infrared or e-mail, and setting Pocket Word options. A particularly interesting command on the Tools menu is Save Document As, which enables you to save a Pocket Word document in a variety of formats, including Rich Text Format (RTF), plain text, Word 97/2000, and Word 6.0/95. The Word 97/2000 format supports saving as either a document or a template.

Caution

The standard Pocket PC applications (including Pocket Word) recognize files up to only one folder level beneath the My Documents folder. For example, if you place a Pocket Word file in the Personal subfolder beneath the My Documents folder, Pocket Word displays it in the document list when you select All Folders. However, Pocket Word will not be capable of accessing a file you placed in a folder below the Personal subfolder.

The input mode of Pocket Word is extremely important in learning to create and edit documents effectively. Following are the input modes supported in Pocket Word, which you access by tapping the View menu:

- **Typing**—Use the Input Panel to enter typed text.

- **Writing**—Use the stylus to write handwritten text.

- **Drawing**—Use the stylus to draw graphics.

- **Recording**—Use the Record button or Voice Bar to enter voice recordings.

The next few sections explore each of these modes in more detail.

TYPING MODE

You will probably rely on typing the most because it is very similar to the manner in which text is entered in other Pocket PC applications, such as Notes. In this mode, you enter text via the Input Panel (Soft Keyboard, Letter Recognizer, Block Recognizer, or Transcriber); the significance of this mode is that all data entry results in text, even if you use handwriting to arrive at the text. To try the Typing mode, tap New in the lower-left corner of the screen to create a new document, and then tap Writing in the View menu. Pocket Word displays a blank document ready for you to enter text into.

→ To learn more about the Input Panel and how it is used to enter text, **see** Chapter 5, "Making the Most of Input Methods," **p. 83**.

Entering information in Typing mode involves using the Input Panel to either handwrite characters (Character Recognizer), type characters (Keyboard), or handwrite words and sentences (Transcriber). Figure 15.1 shows some text entered into Pocket Word via the Input Panel.

Figure 15.1
Typing mode enables you to enter text via an input method on the Input Panel, such as the soft keyboard.

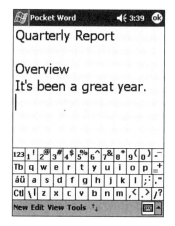

After you begin entering text, you'd probably like to format it to some degree. You can use the Edit menu to access formatting functions for formatting text you've entered. However, the most convenient way to format text is through the Pocket Word toolbar; tapping Toolbar in the Views menu enables the Pocket Word toolbar. Alternatively, next to the Tools menu you'll notice an icon with two arrows pointing up and down; tapping this icon also shows the Pocket Word toolbar. Figure 15.2 shows Pocket Word with the toolbar displayed.

The first button on the toolbar is the Format button, which displays a window containing a variety of formatting options for use with selected text. To use the Format window, select a word or group of words and then tap the Format button on the toolbar. Figure 15.3 shows the Format window and the available options.

Figure 15.2
The toolbar in Pocket Word provides convenient access to document formatting options such as the current font and text effects, including bold, italic, and underline.

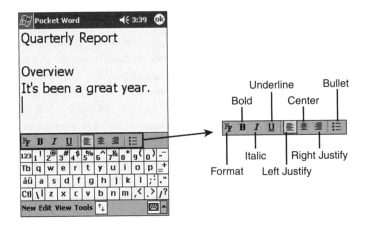

Tip from
Michael

You can find and replace text in Typing mode by tapping Find/Replace on the Edit menu.

Figure 15.3
The Pocket Word Format window provides a convenient means of formatting text.

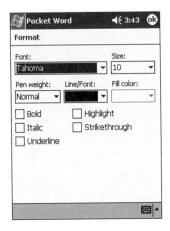

As you can see in Figure 15.3, the Format window enables you to alter the font, font size, font weight, font color, and fill color. It also offers other formatting options such as italic, underline, highlight, and strikethrough. Figure 15.4 shows how the formatting of a title is changed using the Format window.

In addition to formatting text in Typing mode, you can also alter paragraph properties. This is accomplished by tapping Paragraph in the Edit menu. This results in the Paragraph window being displayed, which provides access to paragraph settings such as the alignment and indentation of the selected paragraph or paragraphs (see Figure 15.5). The paragraph settings apply to the paragraph in which the edit cursor is currently located, regardless of whether any text is actually selected.

Figure 15.4
Just as with Word on the desktop, Pocket Word enables you to format words and sentences for impact.

Figure 15.5
The Pocket Word Paragraph window provides a means of altering paragraph properties such as the alignment and inden-tation of a paragraph.

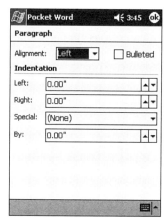

Figure 15.6 shows a paragraph of text with its left indentation set to 0.10 inches, which helps indicate that the text is associated with the "Overview" section of the document.

Figure 15.6
The left indentation of a paragraph is altered to move the para-graph over with respect to the docu-ment.

Getting back to the Pocket Word toolbar, you'll notice that to the right of the Format button are buttons for applying the bold, italic, and underline formatting properties, as well as buttons for justifying text to be either left-justified, centered, or right-justified. On the far right of the toolbar is the Bullet button, which creates a bulleted list out of a list of selected text. The interesting thing about the Pocket Word toolbar is that it changes to reflect the current input mode. The toolbar you've seen thus far applies only to Typing mode. You'll notice the toolbar change as you move between input modes in the next few sections.

Note

Although the Bullet button provides a convenient way to create bulleted lists, Pocket Word doesn't support numbered lists.

WRITING MODE

Writing input mode is different from Typing mode in that handwriting is not converted to text characters. This mode is similar to the way drawings are entered in Notes—you write on the screen with the stylus and the exact writing is retained. Lines are displayed on the screen to aid in writing lines of text. To use Writing mode, select Writing from the View menu and start writing the text. Figure 15.7 shows how I wrote text in addition to the typed text that was entered via Typing mode. Keep in mind that all text entered in Writing mode is retained as handwritten text, which is different from characters of text that are typed or recognized.

→ To find out how to create drawings in Notes, **see** Chapter 14, "Working with the Pocket Outlook Tasks and Notes," **p. 257**.

Figure 15.7
Writing mode enables you to enter hand-written text alongside typed text.

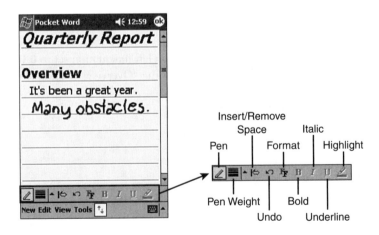

You might notice in Figure 15.7 that the toolbar has changed to reflect a different set of features for Writing mode. The button to the far left of the toolbar is the Pen button, which enables and disables the pen for writing; disabling the pen allows you to select and manipulate text. The button to the right of the Pen button is the Pen Weight button, which enables you to alter the weight (thickness) of written text. To change the weight of written text, you must disable the pen, select the text by double-tapping or dragging across it, and then tap the Pen Weight button and select a new weight. Figure 15.8 shows how the word "Many" is made thicker by changing its weight.

Figure 15.8
The Pen Weight button enables you to alter the weight of written text.

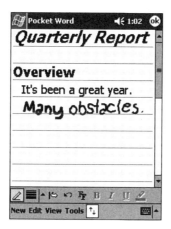

The next button on the toolbar is the Insert/Remove Space button, which is used to alter the spacing between written words. Next to that button is the Undo button, which is handy for removing poorly written text. The familiar Format button is next, which displays the Format window you saw earlier in Figure 15.3. In Writing mode, the options in the Format window impact only the weight and color of the text; fonts obviously don't apply to hand-written text.

Note

If your writing crosses three ruled lines in a single stroke, Pocket Word automatically interprets the writing as a drawing. You learn more about drawings in the next section.

To the right of the Format button are the familiar Bold, Italic, and Underline buttons. It is interesting that these buttons work with handwritten text; the ability to format handwritten text is the primary difference between handwriting text and drawings. The last button on the Writing toolbar is the Highlight button, which draws a colored highlight behind the currently selected text. This feature has an effect similar to highlighting text on paper with a yellow highlighter pen.

 If your mobile writing career is off to a slow start because you're struggling to enter text in Pocket Word, see "Struggling with Input in Pocket Word" in the "Troubleshooting" section at the end of the chapter to find out what you can do to enter text more efficiently.

DRAWING MODE

Drawing input mode is similar to Writing mode except that the emphasis is on drawing graphics. Pocket Word displays a grid of vertical and horizontal lines in Drawing mode, and it interprets strokes as discrete drawings as opposed to characters and words. The other thing that distinguishes Drawing mode from other modes is the graying of any text in the document, which is a clear indication that Drawing mode isn't about entering text information.

The toolbar in Drawing mode includes some useful drawing-related features (see Figure 15.9). The first two buttons (Pen and Pen Weight) are familiar from Writing mode, whereas the third and fourth buttons (Line/Font and Fill Color) enable you to alter the line color and fill color, respectively. The Undo button is up next, followed by the Format button, which is similar to the text-based Format button you learned about earlier. The remaining buttons are used to align, group, and ungroup drawing objects.

Figure 15.9
The Drawing mode toolbar provides convenient access to various drawing-related functions.

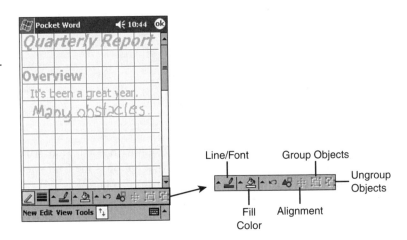

To draw graphics objects in Drawing mode, just start drawing with the stylus. You can change the thickness and color of the drawing strokes by using the Pen Weight and Line Color buttons; these changes affect the next strokes you make. You can also set the fill color of graphics using the Fill Color button, which sets the fill color of closed graphics strokes. Figure 15.10 shows a few curvy lines drawn in Drawing mode that add a little style to the quarterly report document. Granted, this probably isn't your idea of adding style to a business quarterly report, but the point is that you can easily draw graphics to appear alongside text in a document. Keep in mind that you can always create a quick drawing just to remember an idea and then later rework it on a desktop PC where you have better control.

If you tap the Pen button to turn off the pen, you can select individual strokes within the graphic image you've drawn. For example, each curvy line is an individual stroke. Figure 15.11 shows how I've selected the second line as an individual graphic object, which is indicated by the small group of squares and circles bounding the object.

PART
IV

CH
15

Figure 15.10
You can draw pictures to decorate or add impact to documents using the Draw input mode of Pocket Word.

Figure 15.11
Each stroke in a drawing is considered a discrete graphic object that can be selected and manipulated individually.

You can combine individual strokes to form a single graphic object by using the group function. You also can select multiple graphic strokes by tapping and dragging the stylus to enclose the strokes within a selection box. If you want to group all the strokes in a drawing, just tap Select All in the Edit menu. After you've selected the strokes you want to group, tap the Group button on the toolbar. You can move and resize a graphic object in Drawing mode by tapping the object to reveal a bounding box. Tap and drag in the middle of the box to move the object, or tap and drag one of the corners of the box to resize the object. You can even rotate an object by tapping and dragging on one of the sides. Figure 15.12 shows the second curvy line rotated.

Now that you have a feel for using Drawing mode to create drawings in Pocket Word, let's move on and find out how to create voice recordings in Pocket Word documents.

Figure 15.12
Rotating, moving, and even resizing graphic objects is easy in Drawing mode.

RECORDING MODE

You might not have realized that Pocket Word enables you to associate voice recordings with documents. You can think of a voice recording in a Word document as a form of annotation that is used to provide additional information about a document. Pocket Word supports voice recordings through Recording mode, which enables you to create and modify voice recordings. When you switch to Recording mode via the View menu, the Pocket Word toolbar changes to become the Voice bar, which you learned about in the previous chapter. The Voice bar serves as an alternative to the hardware Record button and enables you to stop and play voice recordings, as well as change the volume of the device. To make a voice recording using the Voice bar, just tap the Record button (red circle) on the Voice bar, wait for the beep, and begin speaking. When you're finished, tap the Stop button (black square) next to the Record button. To listen to the recording, tap the Play button (black triangle) next to the Stop button.

→ To learn more about Recording mode and the Voice bar, **see** Chapter 14, "Working with the Pocket Outlook Tasks and Notes," **p. 257**.

Tip from
Michael

As a shortcut to making voice recordings, use the hardware Record button. Hold down the button to make the recording, as opposed to using the Voice bar.

After making a voice recording, a small speaker icon is inserted into the document—tapping this icon plays the recording. Figure 15.13 shows how a voice recording icon appears in the context of a document. You don't even have to be in Recording mode to play voice recordings. If you tap the speaker icon in any mode but Drawing mode, the Voice bar will appear temporarily and the voice recording will play.

Although you probably don't typically think of a voice recording as being part of a document created in a word processor, they can nonetheless serve as a powerful means of communicating ideas beyond what appears in the text of a document.

Figure 15.13
Voice recordings are represented by speaker icons in Pocket Word documents, which can be tapped to play a recording.

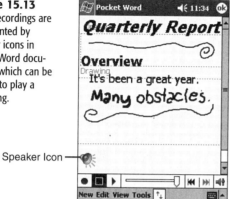

Speaker Icon

MANAGING DOCUMENTS IN POCKET WORD

The main view in Pocket Word is a document list that displays Pocket Word documents available for viewing and editing. Pocket Word includes a variety of features for managing documents; most of these features can be found in the Tools menu.

SPELL CHECKING DOCUMENTS

One of the most significant features in Pocket Word is the spell checker, which is accessible by selecting Spell Check from the Tools menu. Figure 15.14 shows the spell checker in action after it detects a problem with the misspelled word "grest," which should actually be "great."

Figure 15.14
The Pocket Word spell checker is capable of tracking down most spelling errors in your documents, and it makes the corrections available in a pop-up menu.

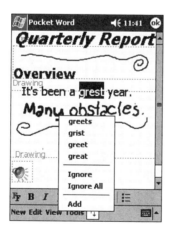

Notice in Figure 15.14 how Pocket Word offers spelling corrections in a pop-up menu. This enables you to quickly determine the correct spelling of a word and insert it into a document.

COUNTING WORDS

Another interesting Pocket Word feature accessible from the Tools menu is the word count feature, which counts the number of words in a document. Granted, a word count isn't nearly as useful as a spell check, but you might still find it handy if you do any writing that must meet a certain criteria in terms of word count. Figure 15.15 shows the word count feature used to count the words in the quarterly report document.

Figure 15.15
The word count feature enables you to quickly determine how many words are in a Pocket Word document.

Even though you might not need the word count feature on a regular basis, it can be extremely valuable in situations in which the length of a document is important. Keep in mind that many writers are paid according to the length of their writing, which means the word count feature can be used as a primitive accounting tool if you're working on a project that pays by the word.

SAVING DOCUMENTS

When you create a new Pocket Word document, the name of the document is automatically set to the first text appearing in the document. Although this approach is sufficient if you're in a hurry, it's unlikely that you'll want to allow Pocket Word to name all your documents automatically. One option to change the name of a document is the Save Document As command, which is located in the Tools menu. This command enables you to save a copy of a document under a different name.

If you don't want to make a copy of a document, you can always just rename the document. This is accomplished by using the Rename/Move command in the Edit menu. This command also enables you to move a document to a different folder or even to a memory storage card. A document can be deleted by using the Delete Document command in the Tools menu. Keep in mind that these document management features in Pocket Word can also be accomplished with File Explorer; they are provided in Pocket Word primarily for convenience. As with most standard Pocket PC applications, you can select multiple documents in Pocket Word by tapping and dragging the stylus over the documents.

→ To learn more about working with files in File Explorer, **see** Chapter 11, "Accessing Files with File Explorer," **p. 199**.

Tip from
Michael

You can perform most of the document management features of Pocket Word by tapping and holding on a document in Pocket Word's document list and then using the pop-up menu that appears. This can be often faster than navigating to a menu command.

 If you're confused about how to print a Pocket Word document without using a desktop PC, see "Printing from Pocket Word" in the "Troubleshooting" section at the end of the chapter.

The Action hardware button plays a small role in Pocket Word when it comes to document management. Scrolling the Action button moves up and down the document list, and pressing the Action Button opens the currently selected document. The only other hardware button that impacts Pocket Word is the Record button, which you learned about earlier in this chapter when getting acquainted with the Recording input mode.

CUSTOMIZING POCKET WORD

You've obviously come to realize that your Pocket PC is somewhat of a personal device in that it is designed to carry a great deal of personal information. In keeping with the idea that you can personalize various aspects of your Pocket PC to suit your individual needs, Pocket Word supports a few customization options, which are accessible via the Tools menu. To customize Pocket Word, tap Options in the Tools menu. This displays the Pocket Word Options window, which is shown in Figure 15.16.

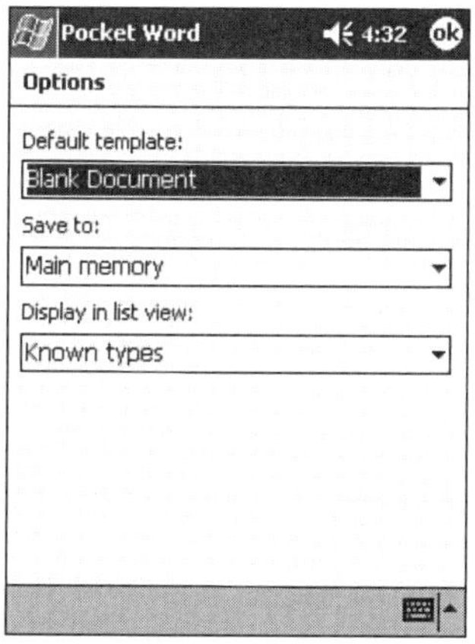

Figure 15.16
The Pocket Word Options window enables you to customize Pocket Word.

The Default Template setting determines the type of template used to create Pocket Word documents by default. In addition to creating blank documents, Pocket Word includes standard templates to help in creating commonly used documents. The default template can be set to one of these templates:

- Meeting Notes
- Memo
- Phone Memo
- To Do

Note

You might recognize the Pocket Word templates from the previous chapter when you learned about a similar set of templates for the Notes application.

The Save To option in Pocket Word enables you to change the location to which documents are saved. You can choose between main system memory and a memory storage card. If you choose the main system memory option, which is the default option, all documents will be stored in the My Documents folder in system memory.

The Display in List View option is used to determine which types of documents are included in Pocket Word's document list. The default setting is Known Types, which displays the widest range of document types. More specifically, known document types consist of Pocket Word documents, text documents, and HTML documents. Other settings enable you to limit the document list to Pocket Word and text documents or just Pocket Word documents.

SYNCHRONIZING DOCUMENTS WITH POCKET WORD

If you plan to share documents between your Pocket PC and your desktop PC, you probably should consider synchronizing documents between the two machines using ActiveSync. Synchronization enables you to share documents between your Pocket PC and a desktop PC, effectively having one copy of a given file that floats back and forth as it is edited on each machine. If you recall, ActiveSync is the desktop software that manages the connection between a Pocket PC device and a desktop PC. ActiveSync supports synchronization of Pocket Word documents by enabling you to specify documents you want synchronized between your device and desktop PC.

→ To find out more about how to synchronize files and data with ActiveSync, **see** Chapter 8, "Using ActiveSync to Synchronize Data," **p. 145**.

To synchronize Pocket Word files in ActiveSync, open ActiveSync on your desktop PC and click the Options button on the ActiveSync toolbar. This opens the Options dialog box, shown in Figure 15.17.

Figure 15.17
The ActiveSync Options window enables you to set up synchronization for Pocket Word files.

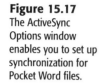

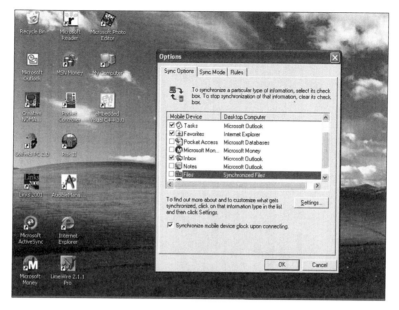

In the list of information types that can be synchronized, click Files so that the check box next to it is checked. When you click Files in the list, a message box is immediately displayed that explains about a synchronization folder that is created on your desktop PC; just click OK to continue. The synchronization folder on your desktop PC is created beneath your existing My Documents folder and is named according to the name of your Pocket PC device. More specifically, the synchronization folder is named with the device name prepended to My Documents. As an example, if my device is named Michael_PPC, the synchronization folder is named Michael_PPC My Documents. If you want to share Word documents with Pocket Word, just copy the files into this folder and they will automatically be synchronized.

Another option when it comes to determining which documents are synchronized with Pocket Word is to click the Settings buttons with Files selected in ActiveSync. This takes you to the File Synchronization Settings window, which enables you to identify specific files for synchronization (see Figure 15.18).

When you add a file to the Synchronized Files list in the File Synchronization Settings window, you effectively copy the file into the file synchronization folder; the original file is kept intact while any changes are made to the synchronized file. Upon selecting a file or files for synchronization for the first time, the Combine or Replace dialog box is displayed to clarify how you want the synchronization to proceed for Pocket Word files (see Figure 15.19).

Figure 15.18
The File Synchronization Settings window enables you to identify specific Word documents for synchronization.

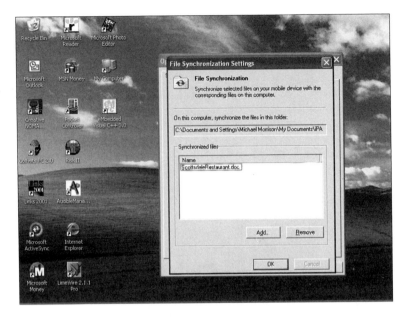

Figure 15.19
The Combine or Replace dialog box enables you to specify how synchronization should proceed for Pocket Word files.

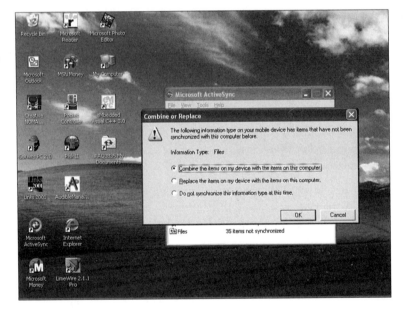

The default setting is to combine files on the Pocket PC with files on the desktop PC, which is probably your best option. Another option is to replace files on the Pocket PC with files on the desktop computer, which is primarily useful if you are using Pocket Word only to view Word documents. If you choose the replace option, keep in mind that any changes you make to documents on your Pocket PC will be lost when synchronization takes place because changed desktop Word documents will always replace the Pocket Word documents.

Therefore, the replace option should be used only in situations in which you want desktop Word documents to serve as master originals and Pocket Word documents to serve only as copies you can carry around and view.

After clicking OK in the Combine or Replace dialog box, synchronization begins and Word documents in the synchronization folder are converted and copied onto your device in the My Documents folder. Figure 15.20 shows a Scottsdale, Arizona restaurant guide I created for a friend in Word as it appears in Pocket Word after being synchronized on the device.

Figure 15.20
Most synchronized Word documents retain their looks in Pocket Word, given the obvious screen-size limitations.

Although you might have more important documents to work with than restaurant guides, this is a good example of a document that wouldn't be bad to have on your Pocket PC while traveling, especially if you're headed to Arizona. And if you wanted to update the restaurant reviews, you could do so right there at your meal and then synchronize the resulting document with your desktop computer when you return home.

TROUBLESHOOTING

STRUGGLING WITH INPUT IN POCKET WORD

I'm struggling with input in Pocket Word in that I simply can't enter text efficiently enough with the Input Panel.

If you find the Input Panel lacking when it comes to efficient text input, you should seriously consider using a keyboard with your Pocket PC. The Input Panel offers several input methods that can speed up text entry depending on your specific input abilities, but none of them compare to the efficiency of a physical keyboard. Keyboards for Pocket PCs vary from thumb-style keyboards with small buttons that you press with your thumbs to foldable full-size keyboards that are comparable to desktop keyboards. If you plan on doing any serious writing in Pocket Word, a portable keyboard of some type is a good investment. See "Keyboards" in Appendix A, "A Pocket PC Hardware Accessory Tour," for more information on available keyboards for Pocket PCs.

PRINTING FROM POCKET WORD

I want to print a document from Pocket Word without having to transfer it to my desktop PC.

You can print directly from Pocket Word, assuming you have access to a printer from your Pocket PC. One way to print Pocket Word documents is by beaming the document to a printer with an infrared port. If you have access to such a printer, just line up your Pocket PC's infrared port with the printer's port and select Beam Document from the Tools menu in Pocket Word to print the document. If you want to access a printer through a network connection, you'll need special software, such as PrintPocketCE by Field Software Products (`http://www.fieldsoftware.com/`). Regardless of how you access a printer to print Pocket Word documents, you might consider altering the margins of a document prior to printing because the default left and right margins are set to 0. To change the margins, select Paragraph from the Edit menu in Pocket Word, and then change the margin sizes, in inches.

REAL-WORLD EXAMPLE—TAKING YOUR RESUME WITH YOU

I've personally found myself in a situation in which I've met a stranger while traveling who became interested in me as a potential employee or consultant. You never know who the person next to you on an airplane might be or where an impromptu conversation might lead. For this reason, it could prove extremely valuable to have your resume available at all times. Granted, it might be a little extreme to carry printed copies of your resume everywhere you go, which is why I'm suggesting you carry an electronic version on your Pocket PC. You probably already have your resume in Word format or can easily convert it into Word format, which also makes easily getting the document into Pocket Word format easy. Pocket Word is well suited to hosting resumes because it enables you to include basic text formatting, such as different font sizes and bold and italic text. If you're fortunate enough to find yourself in a situation where someone is interested in your resume, you can either beam it to her (if she has a Pocket PC or notebook PC) or attach it to an e-mail and send it to her over a wireless network connection. Either way, you'll get the point across that you're a technically savvy candidate for the job!

CHAPTER 16

CRUNCHING NUMBERS WITH POCKET EXCEL

In this chapter

CONTRASTING POCKET EXCEL WITH EXCEL

I once had a friend whose dad liked to try to guess the exact amount of a grocery total while standing in line at the grocery store. It was pretty amazing how accurately he could guess by quickly performing a calculation as the items passed by during the checkout. My friend's dad is the kind of guy who would probably love Pocket Excel, which is the mobile version of Microsoft's powerhouse Excel desktop spreadsheet application. Similar to Pocket Word, Pocket Excel supports the basic functionality of Excel minus a lot of the fancy features. Most importantly, Pocket Excel supports the viewing and editing of Excel spreadsheets via the Excel workbook format.

This chapter introduces you to Pocket Excel and explores its feature set. You learn about the relationship between Excel and Pocket Excel, including the specific features that are supported between the two, and more importantly, the ones that aren't supported. You should leave this chapter with a solid grasp on mobile number crunching and what is possible with Pocket Excel.

If you're a user of Microsoft Excel, you'll find yourself at home with Pocket Excel; however, you will be limited to performing basic spreadsheet tasks. Although Pocket Excel supports a limited feature set of Excel, it is nonetheless quite useful when you consider that it provides spreadsheet functionality in a device a little larger than a calculator; trust me, there aren't any calculators out there that can interact with Excel spreadsheets. Not surprisingly, the biggest benefit of Pocket Excel is its support for the Excel workbook format. This enables you to carry Excel workbooks around on your Pocket PC to view and modify on the go.

In the previous chapter you learned that Word documents are converted into a special Pocket Word format whenever they are transferred to a Pocket PC. A similar conversion process takes place with Excel workbooks when they are transferred to a Pocket PC for use in Pocket Excel. The converted files are stored in a Pocket Excel format with a .pxl file extension, as compared to Excel's .xls file extension. Excel templates are converted from their .xlt file type to Pocket Excel templates with a .pxt file extension. Excel workbooks and templates are converted to Pocket Excel when any of the following situations occur:

- An Excel workbook is synchronized with Pocket Excel.
- An Excel workbook is manually copied from a desktop PC to a Pocket PC device.
- An Excel workbook is opened as an e-mail attachment using Pocket Outlook.

Note

Similar to Pocket Word, Pocket Excel documents are automatically converted back to Excel documents when they are transferred back to a desktop computer. The conversion of Excel documents is actually handled by ActiveSync, so no conversion takes place if you transfer Pocket Excel documents between two Pocket PC devices.

When an Excel workbook is converted to Pocket Excel, it retains most of its data content but is capable of losing some important information, such as functions that aren't supported in Pocket Excel. You need to understand which workbook attributes are lost in the conversion so you can avoid losing information when working with an Excel workbook in Pocket Excel. If you're concerned about losing information, I recommend using Pocket Excel as a workbook viewer, which involves not making changes to a workbook after opening it. Of course, this strategy doesn't work too well if you need to modify a workbook in Pocket Excel, which is why you might as well get acquainted with the limitations of Pocket Excel. More specifically, you need to get a handle on exactly what kind of document information is retained in the Excel/Pocket Excel workbook conversion and what kind of information is lost.

Tip from
Michael

> A good way to avoid the risk of losing workbook information when working with an Excel workbook in Pocket Excel is to make a copy of the workbook file on your desktop PC before copying/synchronizing with your Pocket PC. You can then compare the modified file when it is converted back to Excel and correct or reject any unwanted modifications.

ATTRIBUTES RETAINED DURING CONVERSION

Following is a list of the Excel workbook information that is fully supported in Pocket Excel:

- Built-in number formats
- Custom number formats
- Wrapping text
- Worksheet names (within the same workbook)

If you work with Excel workbooks that take advantage of these features, you can rest assured that no information will be lost when the workbooks are moved back and forth between Excel and Pocket Excel.

ATTRIBUTES ALTERED DURING CONVERSION

However, some workbook attributes aren't completely supported in Pocket Excel. More specifically, the following workbook attributes are retained in the conversion to Pocket Excel but might be slightly altered:

- **Formulas with arrays**—Are changed to a value
- **Formulas with unsupported functions**—Are changed to a value
- **Pivot table data**—Is changed to a value
- **Borders**—Are changed to a single line
- **Vertical text**—Is changed to horizontal text
- **Hidden names**—Are displayed

> **Note**
>
> Formulas are used in Excel to perform calculations on data residing in the cells of a spreadsheet. Most formulas are retained in Excel documents when they are converted to Pocket Excel. The exceptions to this rule are formulas with arrays and formulas that use functions that aren't supported in Pocket Excel. An *array* is simply a set of values, as opposed to a single value. So, a formula with an array acts on a set of values. Both kinds of formulas are converted to a fixed value (constant) for use in Pocket Excel, which means they cease to perform calculations.

As you can see, there are limitations to how these workbook features can be safely used within Pocket Excel. For example, most formulas are supported in Pocket Excel, which means they carry out calculations just as you would expect. However, a few advanced formulas and formulas that deal specifically with arrays are not supported and result in a constant value being inserted into the spreadsheet. You should try hard to avoid using such formulas in workbooks that will be shared with Pocket Excel because you will definitely see different results in Pocket Excel than what you would see in Excel.

ATTRIBUTES LOST DURING CONVERSION

For the purposes of successfully managing Excel workbooks in Pocket Excel, the most important Excel workbook attributes are those that aren't supported at all, in which case they are actually lost when converting workbooks. These attributes are as follows:

- AutoFilter
- Data validation
- Cell notes
- Cell patterns
- Add-ins
- Protection
- Scenarios
- Object charts
- Vertical alignment
- Text boxes
- Embedded OLE objects
- Hyperlinks
- Picture controls
- Drawing objects

If you aren't a really serious Excel user, you might not even recognize all these features. If that's the case, you probably won't have to worry too much about them. Otherwise, you should be very careful when converting and editing files in Pocket Excel that use any of these features because they will be lost completely during conversion.

CREATING WORKBOOKS WITH POCKET EXCEL

Getting started using Pocket Excel is pretty simple—just tap Programs from the Start menu, and then tap the Pocket Excel icon. Upon being launched, Pocket Excel first appears with a blank workbook open and ready to be modified. When you close this workbook, a list of Pocket Excel workbooks is displayed from which you can select a workbook to be opened for viewing and editing. If you're using Pocket Excel for the first time, you probably won't have any workbooks in the list. In this case, you can create a new one by tapping New in the lower-left corner of the screen.

→ It's a good idea to add Pocket Excel to the Start menu if you plan to use it frequently; just be sure not to overload the Start menu with too many applications. **See** "Tweaking the Start and New Menus," **p. 76**, if you aren't sure how to do this.

Upon creating a new workbook or opening an existing workbook, the menu at the bottom of the screen changes to reflect commands and options available for Pocket Excel:

- **Edit menu**—Contains commands used to alter the content and appearance of workbook data.

- **View menu**—Allows you to enable or disable the various Pocket Excel user interface bars, as well as set the currently active worksheet and the manner in which the current worksheet is viewed.

- **Format menu**—Allows you to manipulate and format cells, as well as work with rows and columns of data.

- **Tools menu**—Includes a variety of commands for manipulating workbooks, such as sorting, filtering, inserting functions and symbols, and sending the workbook via infrared or e-mail, to name a few commands. The Save Document As command on the tools menu enables you to save a Pocket Excel workbook in a variety of formats, including Pocket Excel 1.0, Excel 97/2000, and Excel 5.0/95. The Pocket Excel and Excel 97/2000 formats support saving as either a document or a template.

Caution

Similar to Pocket Word, Pocket Excel recognizes files up to only one folder level beneath the My Workbooks folder.

Figure 16.1 shows the Pocket Excel application with a new workbook opened, which looks surprisingly similar to the desktop Excel application, but on a smaller scale.

Just above the Pocket Excel menu near the bottom of the screen you'll notice a status bar. The word "Ready" in this status bar indicates that Pocket Excel isn't busy crunching numbers and is ready for you to work with the currently selected worksheet.

Tip from
Michael

If you don't see the status bar in Pocket Excel when it first starts, just tap Status Bar in the View menu to display it.

PART

IV

CH

16

Figure 16.1
The Pocket Excel application looks a lot like the desktop Excel application in that it presents rows and columns of worksheet cells.

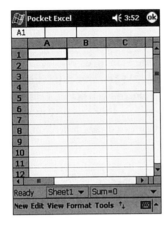

AUTOCALCULATING A RANGE OF CELLS

As you might know from using Excel, a *workbook* can contain multiple worksheets. You can view and edit only a single worksheet at a time in Pocket Excel. You select a worksheet by tapping the Worksheet button next to the status text on the status bar. This button has the name of the worksheet, Sheet1 in this case, and a down arrow on it. Next to the Worksheet button is the AutoCalculate button, which is used to perform a quick calculation on a selected range of cells in the worksheet. Tap the AutoCalculate button to select one of the following calculations (see Figure 16.2):

- **Average**—Determines the average of the cells selected
- **Count**—Determines the number of cells selected
- **Count Nums**—Determines the number of numeric cells selected
- **Max**—Determines the maximum value of the cells selected
- **Min**—Determines the minimum value of the cells selected
- **Sum**—Adds the selected cells together

Tip from
Michael

You can create custom formulas in Pocket Excel by stringing together mathematical functions such as those accessible via the AutoCalculate button.

To select cells for use with the AutoCalculate button, just tap a cell and drag the stylus over the other cells you want to select. The AutoCalculate button automatically updates to show the appropriate calculation for the cells selected. Figure 16.3 shows how the AutoCalculate button automatically calculates the sum of the currently selected cells in a sample worksheet that tracks travel expenses.

Figure 16.2
The AutoCalculate button on the Pocket Excel status bar enables you to perform calculations on selected cells such as adding, averaging, and counting the cells.

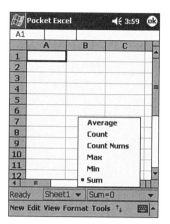

Figure 16.3
The AutoCalculate button makes performing common calculations, such as calculating sums, on selected cells easy.

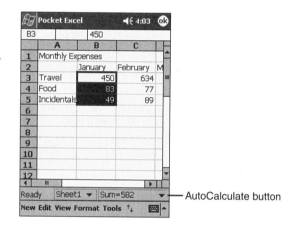

AutoCalculate button

As Figure 16.3 reveals, the AutoCalculate button is extremely handy because it gives you the ability to quickly carry out a calculation without having to actually create a formula.

Note

Pocket Excel allows you to select only a group of cells that are adjacent to each other; you can't select multiple individual cells as you can in the desktop version of Excel.

ACCESSING THE TOOLBAR

In addition to the status bar, Pocket Excel also supports a toolbar that contains various buttons for manipulating worksheets. To display the Pocket Excel toolbar, just tap Toolbar in the Views menu. Alternatively, next to the Tools menu you'll notice an icon with two arrows pointing up and down; tapping this icon also displays the toolbar. Figure 16.4 shows Pocket Excel with the toolbar displayed.

Figure 16.4
The toolbar in Pocket Excel provides convenient access to worksheet manipulation options.

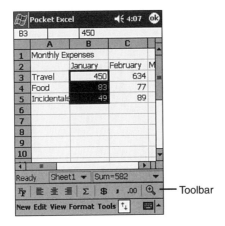

Toolbar

The first button on the toolbar is the Format button, which displays a window containing a variety of formatting options for use in formatting cells. You'll learn more about formatting cells a little later in the chapter in the section titled "Formatting Cells." Just to the right of the Format button are three buttons for setting the alignment of cells. The button next to the alignment buttons is the AutoSum button, which is used to automatically calculate the sum of a series of cells. Unlike the AutoCalculate button in the status bar, which can also calculate sums, the AutoSum button is used to create a sum and insert it into a cell in the worksheet. Next to the AutoSum button you'll find three style buttons that are used to apply common styles to selected cells. The following style buttons are included in the Pocket Excel toolbar:

- **Currency**—Displays numbers with two decimal places, a comma separator after every thousand (thousand, million, and so on), and a currency symbol (dollar sign) to the left of the number

- **Comma**—Displays numbers with two decimal places and a comma separator after every thousand (thousand, million, and so on)

- **Decimal**—Displays numbers with two decimal places

As you might have noticed, the three style buttons are progressively less detailed in the styles applied. For example, the Decimal button displays numbers with two decimal places, whereas the Comma button applies the Decimal style and also adds a comma separator after every thousand. Figure 16.5 shows how the Currency style button impacts the style of cells.

The last button on the Pocket Excel toolbar is the Zoom button, which enables you to alter the zoom level of the worksheet. Pocket Excel supports five standard zoom levels (50%, 75%, 100%, 125%, and 150%), with 100% being the default level. You can also change the zoom level by tapping Zoom in the View menu. Figure 16.6 shows how a 125% zoom level makes the worksheet easier to read, with the obvious trade-off of being able to see less information.

Figure 16.5
The style buttons on the Pocket Excel toolbar enable you to apply common styles, such as the Currency style.

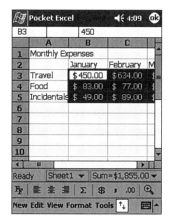

Tip from
Michael

In addition to the standard zoom levels, you can enter a custom zoom level by tapping Zoom in the View menu and then tapping Custom. The minimum and maximum zoom levels you can enter are 50% and 200%.

Figure 16.6
The Zoom button on the Pocket Excel toolbar enables you to alter the zoom level of the worksheet, although it is unlikely that you'll want to zoom a worksheet very large due to screen size limitations.

That wraps up the Pocket Excel toolbar, but it doesn't tell the whole story in terms of viewing Pocket PC worksheets. Another interesting feature in Pocket Excel is the Full Screen view, which is initiated by tapping Full Screen in the View menu (see Figure 16.7).

The Full Screen View mode is extremely helpful for getting a better perspective on a worksheet. However, it obviously results in a more limited user interface. To change back to Normal View mode, just tap the Restore button near the upper-right corner of the screen.

Figure 16.7
The Full Screen command enables you to view the worksheet with slightly more screen space due to the fact that the toolbar, status bar, and row and column headers are hidden.

FORMATTING CELLS

Pocket Excel includes several formatting options that can be used to format cells. To format cells, first tap and drag to select the cells you want to format, and then tap Cells in the Format menu. The Format button on the Pocket Excel toolbar can also be used to format selected cells. This results in the display of the Format Cells window, which is shown in Figure 16.8.

Figure 16.8
The Font tab of the Format Cells window is used to select font options for cells.

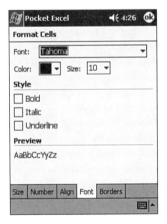

You'll notice in Figure 16.8 that the Format Cells window contains several tabs, and the Font tab is selected by default. The Font tab enables you to alter the font, font color, font size, and font style of the current selection, as well as see a preview of the new font setting. Other tabs in the Format Cells window enable you to alter other aspects of cells, such as the cell size, number format, alignment, and borders. The Size tab, which is shown in Figure 16.9, is used to set the size of cells in the worksheet.

Figure 16.9
The Size tab of the Format Cells window is used to alter the size of cells.

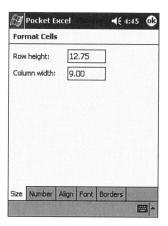

The Number tab in the Format Cells window is used to alter formatting that is specific to numerical data. This tab includes several categories of number types, each of which has its own formatting options. Figure 16.10 shows the formatting options for numeric currency data.

Figure 16.10
The Number tab of the Format Cells window is used to alter the formatting of numeric data, such as currency, which impacts the number of decimal places shown as well as how negative numbers are displayed.

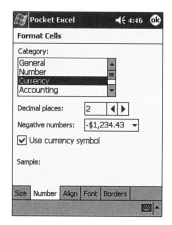

The Align tab is used to tweak the alignment of cells, as shown in Figure 16.11.

The last tab in the Format Cells window is the Borders tab, which enables you to create visual borders around cells. Borders are useful for dividing and calling out information in worksheets. Figure 16.12 shows the Borders tab, which in this case is being used to provide a visual cue for the worksheet's title by adding borders along the left, right, and bottom of the cells, as well as a gray fill color.

Figure 16.11
The Align tab of the
Format Cells window
is used to alter the
horizontal and verti-
cal alignment of cells.

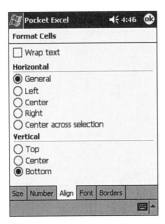

Figure 16.12
The Borders tab of
the Format Cells win-
dow is used to create
visual borders around
cells, as well as
change the back-
ground color of cells.

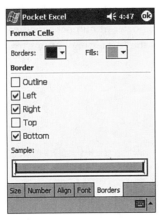

Whereas the Format Cells window enables you to alter the appearance of cells, other features in Pocket Excel enable you to manipulate the structure and content of cells. For example, you can insert and delete cells using the Insert Cells and Delete Cells commands in the
Format menu. You can also hide entire rows or columns of cells using the Hide command,
which is located in the Row and Column submenus of the Format menu. Hidden rows and
columns are retained in a worksheet but are hidden from view. In addition, the Unhide
command can be used to show hidden rows and columns. One final cell formatting option is
the AutoFit feature, which is used to automatically size cells to fit their contents. You can
enable this feature by tapping AutoFit in the Row or Column submenu of the Format menu.

Tip from
Michael

To select a hidden row or column, tap Go To from the Tools menu and then enter a reference that is in the hidden row or column. The most likely reference is the row number (displayed to the left of the worksheet) or column letter (displayed above the
worksheet).

Pocket Excel enables you to assign a name to a cell or group of cells, which is useful when creating formulas. To name a cell, select the cell and then tap Define Name in the Tools menu. This displays the Define Name window, which allows you to enter a name for the selected cell (see Figure 16.13).

Figure 16.13
The Define Name window is used to create and assign names to cells, which allows you to reference cells in formulas.

To name the cell, enter the name and tap the Add button. If there are any other names in the workbook, they will appear in the list of names shown in the Define Name window. You can assign any of the names to a cell, and you can assign a list of names to a list of cells by tapping the Paste List button.

> **Note**
>
> The name of a cell has no direct relation to the value of the cell; the name is simply used to reference the cell in formulas.

USING PANES

If you want to look at a worksheet from several perspectives, you'll probably find panes to be a useful feature of Pocket Excel. To provide different views on the same worksheet, Pocket Excel enables you to split the worksheet into multiple panes. This is accomplished by tapping Split in the View menu. A splitter bar will appear between the two panes, which you can tap and drag with the stylus to alter the pane sizes. Figure 16.14 shows two panes divided by a splitter bar.

> **Note**
>
> Pocket Excel allows a maximum of four separate panes divided by splitter bars. The panes are adjusted by tapping and dragging the splitter bar. In most cases, it is helpful to have only two panes visible at almost any given time because of the limited screen space on Pocket PCs.

Figure 16.14
Pocket Excel enables you to divide a worksheet into multiple panes separated by splitter bars, which gives you several views on the data in the worksheet.

As you move around within a worksheet using the scrollbars, both of the panes change to reflect the selection point in the worksheet. If you want to keep one of the panes focused on a particular section of the worksheet, you can freeze it. To *freeze* a pane, tap Freeze Panes in the View menu. This results in the top pane freezing, while the bottom pane changes to show the remainder of the worksheet. This can be a little confusing at first because the splitter bar disappears, but when you scroll around, it becomes apparent that the bottom pane is the only pane moving. To unfreeze the panes, tap Unfreeze Panes in the View menu. You can also remove the splitter bar, and therefore the extra pane, by tapping Remove Split in the View menu.

WORKING WITH FORMULAS AND FUNCTIONS

It can certainly be beneficial to simply use Pocket Excel as a means of entering tabular data, but formulas and functions are the Pocket Excel features that really enable you to do some interesting things with worksheet data. *Formulas* are used to perform calculations on cells, whereas *functions* are standard mathematical operations used within formulas. Pocket Excel includes a Formula box near the upper-right corner of the screen that is used to enter formulas. To create a formula, you must first select a cell with which the formula is associated; this is the cell in which the formula result will appear. In other words, the result of the formula calculation is stored in the selected cell.

After selecting a cell, you create a formula by entering an equal sign (=) followed by the formula in the Formula box. Although you can reference cells in a formula by entering their names, you can also specify cells by tapping them on the worksheet; to specify a range of cells in a formula, tap and drag over the cells. Figure 16.15 shows a formula that performs a simple calculation on a cell in the worksheet.

This formula calculates the average travel expenses for the first quarter of the worksheet, which involves adding the travel values for the three months and dividing by three. The resulting average is then displayed in the selected cell after entering the formula.

Figure 16.15
The Formula box enables you to enter formulas that perform calculations on other cells.

 If you're having trouble figuring out how to graph data in a Pocket Excel worksheet, see "Graphing Pocket Excel Data" in the "Troubleshooting" section at the end of the chapter to find out about the graphing limitations of Pocket Excel and what you can do to get around them.

Although it's fine to create your own formulas as was done in the previous example, it's a good idea to use functions whenever possible to avoid reinventing the wheel. The standard AVERAGE() function is particularly useful in this example. To select a function while editing a formula, tap the fx button to the left of the Formula box. This displays the Insert Function window, which provides a list of functions (organized by category) that can be used in formulas (see Figure 16.16). If you spend some time in this window, you'll see that Pocket Excel supports a surprising number of functions.

Figure 16.16
The Insert Function window provides a list of categorized functions available for use in formulas.

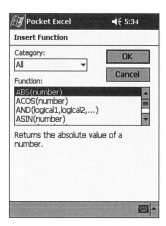

Figure 16.17 shows the travel expenses averaging formula modified to use the AVERAGE() function, as selected in the Insert Function window. Pay close attention to the Formula box, which shows how the AVERAGE() function is now being used instead of averaging the cells manually.

Figure 16.17
Functions can eliminate the need to create custom formulas, and can therefore save time and reduce errors.

Because functions can save you time and energy in creating your own formulas, it's worth taking some time to get acquainted with the functions built into Pocket Excel.

INTERACTING WITH WORKBOOKS IN POCKET EXCEL

Pocket Excel's Tools menu includes a variety of features for interacting with workbooks. Because the features found in the Tools menu act on the current workbook, you must create a new workbook or open an existing one for the commands to appear in the menu. The first of these features has to do with how Pocket Excel workbooks are saved. When you create a new Pocket Excel workbook, the name of the workbook is automatically set to the word Personal followed by a number, such as Personal1. One option to changing the name of a workbook is the Save Workbook As command, which is located in the Tools menu. This command enables you to save a copy of a workbook under a different name.

A simpler option is to just rename the workbook instead of making a copy of it. This is accomplished by using the Rename/Move command in the Edit menu. This command also enables you to move a workbook to a different folder or a memory storage card. A workbook can be deleted by using the Delete Workbook command in the Tools menu. Understand that these workbook management features in Pocket Excel can also be accomplished with File Explorer; they are provided in Pocket Excel as a convenience. As with most standard Pocket PC applications, you can select multiple workbooks in the Pocket Excel workbook list by tapping and dragging the stylus over the workbooks.

→ To learn more about working with files in File Explorer, **see** Chapter 11, "Accessing Files with File Explorer," **p. 199**.

Tip from
Michael

You can perform most of the workbook management features of Pocket Excel by tapping and holding on a workbook in Pocket Excel's workbook list, which is displayed when no workbooks are open. This can often be faster than navigating to a menu command.

If you're concerned about storing sensitive information in a Pocket Excel workbook, see "Securing Pocket Excel Workbooks" in the "Troubleshooting" section at the end of the chapter to find out how to password-protect individual workbooks.

Pocket Excel workbooks typically consist of multiple worksheets. You learned earlier in the chapter how to switch between worksheets via the status bar. You can also switch to different worksheets by tapping Sheet in the View menu, followed by the worksheet you want to view. To add or remove worksheets, tap Modify Sheets in the Format menu. Doing so displays the Modify Sheets window, shown in Figure 16.18.

Figure 16.18
The Modify Sheets window enables you to rename, insert, delete, and reorder worksheets.

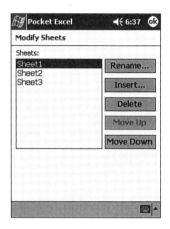

Speaking of buttons on the Modify Sheets window, a different kind of button exists that can be used to manipulate workbooks in Pocket Excel. I'm referring to the hardware Action button, which is the only hardware button that directly impacts Pocket Excel. Scrolling the Action button moves up and down the workbook list, whereas pressing the Action button opens the currently selected workbook. Within a workbook, you also can scroll the Action button to move up and down cells; pressing the button closes the workbook.

CUSTOMIZING POCKET EXCEL

Similar to most Pocket PC applications, Pocket Excel is customizable to some degree. You can begin customizing Pocket Excel by closing any open workbooks and then tapping Options in the Tools menu. This displays the Pocket Excel Options window, which is shown in Figure 16.19.

Note

The Pocket Excel Options window is available only when you don't have a workbook open. In other words, you won't be able to find the Options command in the Tools menu if you have a workbook open.

Figure 16.19
The Pocket Excel Options window enables you to customize Pocket Excel.

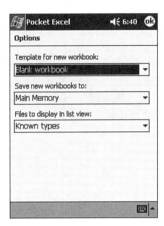

The Template for New Workbook setting determines the type of default template used to create Pocket Excel workbooks. In addition to creating blank workbooks, Pocket Excel supports standard templates to help in creating commonly used workbooks. The only standard template included in Pocket Excel is the Vehicle Mileage Log template, which helps in keeping track of mileage on a vehicle while traveling. You can also create your own templates in Excel and use them in Pocket Excel by copying them to the My Documents folder on your device.

The Save New Workbooks To option enables you to change the location to which workbooks are saved. You can choose between main system memory and a memory storage card. If you choose the main system memory option, which is the default option, all workbooks will be stored in the My Documents folder in main memory.

The last option, Files to Display in List View, is used to determine which types of workbooks are included in Pocket Excel's workbook list. The default setting is Known Types, which displays the widest range of workbook types. The other setting enables you to limit the workbook list to just Pocket Excel workbooks.

SYNCHRONIZING WORKBOOKS WITH POCKET EXCEL

As with many other types of files that you probably work with on your desktop PC, Pocket Excel workbooks can be synchronized with your desktop PC by using ActiveSync. ActiveSync supports Pocket Excel synchronization by enabling you to specify workbooks you want synchronized between your device and desktop PC. To synchronize Pocket Excel files in ActiveSync, open ActiveSync and click the Options button on the ActiveSync toolbar. This results in the Options dialog box being displayed, which you saw in Chapter 15, "Working with Documents in Pocket Word," while synchronizing Word documents.

→ To find out more about how to synchronize files and data with ActiveSync, **see** Chapter 8, "Using ActiveSync to Synchronize Data," **p. 145.**

In the list of information types that can be synchronized, click Files. When you begin synchronizing Excel files with Pocket Excel, you'll place them in a special synchronization folder on your desktop PC that is located beneath your existing My Documents folder. Just as with synchronized Word documents, the synchronization folder for Pocket Excel is named with the device name prepended to My Documents, such as Michael_PPC My Documents.

Another synchronization option is to click the Settings buttons with Files selected in the ActiveSync list. This takes you to the File Synchronization Settings window, which enables you to identify specific files for synchronization. When you add a file to the Synchronized File list in the File Synchronization Settings window, you effectively copy the file into the file synchronization folder; the original file is kept intact while any changes are made to the synchronized file. Upon selecting a file or files for synchronization for the first time, the Combine or Replace dialog box is displayed so you can clarify how you want the synchronization to proceed for Pocket Excel files. After selecting a synchronization approach and clicking OK, synchronization begins and Excel workbooks in the synchronization folder are converted and copied onto your device in the My Documents folder. Figure 16.20 shows a spreadsheet I created in Excel as it appears in Pocket Excel after being synchronized on the device.

Figure 16.20
Most synchronized Excel workbooks retain their looks in Pocket Excel, given the obvious screen-size limitations.

Granted, recreational hockey stats might not be your idea of an important Excel worksheet, but we all have our priorities! Regardless of how you choose to use Pocket Excel, it's quite handy to be able to synchronize worksheets between Pocket Excel and Excel.

TROUBLESHOOTING

GRAPHING POCKET EXCEL DATA

I can't seem to figure out how to graph data that I have stored in a Pocket Excel worksheet.

Unfortunately, Pocket Excel doesn't include any graphing capabilities so you can't graph worksheet data without using a third-party application. However, such applications do exist, and they make graphing Pocket Excel data very easy. One such application is Pocket AutoGraph by DeveloperOne (`http://www.developerone.com/pocketpc/`). Pocket AutoGraph supports several types of graphs, including bar, column, line, pie, scatter, and stock graphs. Although Pocket AutoGraph doesn't include the graphing capabilities of the desktop Excel application, it nonetheless provides a good solution for graphing worksheet data on your Pocket PC.

SECURING POCKET EXCEL WORKBOOKS

I've created a Pocket Excel workbook that contains sensitive data, and I want to protect it from prying eyes in case my device falls into the wrong hands.

Unlike other standard Pocket PC applications, Pocket Excel includes a built-in security feature that allows you to password-protect individual workbook files. To set a password for a workbook, select Password on the Edit menu, and then enter and verify a password. Then, close the workbook; it will now be password-protected so that you must enter the password to open the workbook. To learn more about securing your Pocket PC with file encryption and employing other security measures, see Chapter 20, "Beefing Up Your Pocket PC's Security."

REAL-WORLD EXAMPLE—KEEPING SCORE

Maybe you were thinking that a good real-world example of Pocket Excel is keeping up with business expenses or tracking a sales quota over the course of a year of business. Even though these are certainly good examples of practical business uses for Pocket Excel, I suspect many Pocket PC users will find Pocket Excel quite useful for keeping up with sports scores and statistics. Whether it's your golf handicap or your child's basketball team statistics, Pocket Excel is excellent for sports because it enables you to enter data as it is being generated at the sporting event. In the case of golf, you can keep up with rounds just as you use a traditional golf scorecard; just create a golf worksheet once and then reuse it each time you play. The great thing about Pocket Excel is that its calculation features can be used to automatically keep up with your handicap. For an even more impressive approach to keeping track of golf with your Pocket PC, see "Hitting the Links with Your Pocket PC" in Chapter 24, "Playing Around on Your Pocket PC."

CHAPTER 17

MANAGING MONEY WITH YOUR POCKET PC

In this chapter

MONEY FOR POCKET PC AND MICROSOFT MONEY

If the idea of keeping track of your finances on your Pocket PC sounds interesting, then you're bound to like Money for Pocket PC, which provides mobile access to Microsoft Money data. The last two chapters introduced you to pint-sized versions of the popular Microsoft desktop applications Word and Excel. Money for Pocket PC is a little different from Pocket Word and Pocket Excel in that it isn't really intended for use as a standalone Pocket PC application. Even though Pocket Word and Pocket Excel can be synchronized with Word and Excel, they still function more or less as independent applications in which you can view and edit files from your Pocket PC. Money for Pocket PC can also be used as such an application, but that's not where you will realize its true benefits. Money for Pocket PC is designed to provide a quick view of your most important financial accounts, as well as a convenient place to enter transactions while on the go.

> **Note**
>
> The terminology in this chapter is very important when it comes to distinguishing Money on the Pocket PC from its desktop counterpart. The Pocket PC version of Money is known as Money for Pocket PC, whereas the desktop application is simply called Money. So, when I refer to Money or Money 2002, I'm always referring to the desktop application. The Pocket PC version of Money will be consistently referred to as Money for Pocket PC.

Money for Pocket PC is not the ideal application to use as the sole means of managing personal finances; desktop applications such as Money 2002 and Quicken offer significantly more features and are relatively inexpensive. What Money for Pocket PC offers is the capability to view and enter financial data from anywhere because you can carry it around in your pocket. If you already use personal finance software on your desktop PC, you probably realize the significance of being able to enter transactions and manage accounts while away from your desktop computer.

The point is that Money for Pocket PC is really more of a companion for Money 2002. You are much better served using it in conjunction with the desktop Money application. Money 2002 excels at financial analysis, of which Money for Pocket PC is virtually devoid. This is not to criticize Money for Pocket PC—it merely demonstrates its supporting role. Following are the three main tasks for which Money for Pocket PC proves most useful:

- Entering financial transactions
- Reviewing account balances
- Tracking investments

Note

> Money for Pocket PC is compatible with two versions of Microsoft Money: 2001 and 2002. However, you must use the appropriate version of Money for Pocket PC with each version of Money. Money for Pocket PC is freely available online from Microsoft, or updates are available if you'd prefer using the previous version that is compatible with Money 2001. You learn more about downloading and installing Money for Pocket PC in the next section.

Unlike Pocket Word and Pocket Excel, which you might or might not decide to synchronize with their desktop counterparts, synchronizing Money for Pocket PC with Money 2002 is a must if you use Money 2002. In fact, you should synchronize Money for Pocket PC with Money 2002 before you ever even run it because trying to preserve information you've entered in Money for Pocket PC prior to synchronization is difficult.

PART

IV

CH

17

Caution

> Entering transactions into Money for Pocket PC prior to synchronizing with Money 2002 is problematic because the synchronization with Money 2002 should take place on a blank Pocket PC Money database. In other words, Money for Pocket PC shouldn't have any transactions entered into it prior to synchronization. Any transactions entered prior to synchronization that you want to keep should be reentered on Money 2002 before synchronizing.

→ For more information on synchronization and Pocket Word, **see** "Synchronizing Documents with Pocket Word," **p. 294**.

→ For more information on synchronization and Pocket Excel, **see** "Synchronizing Workbooks with Pocket Excel," **p. 316**.

Note

> Money for Pocket PC is not directly compatible with Quicken. However, you can import a Quicken file into Money 2002 and then synchronize with Money for Pocket PC.

SETTING UP MONEY FOR POCKET PC

Some Pocket PCs include Money for Pocket PC on the CD-ROM that accompanies the device. However, no devices include it directly in the hardware's memory. Knowing this, you'll have to either install Money for Pocket PC from a CD-ROM or download and install it from your local hard drive. It is also available for free download from Microsoft at http://www.microsoft.com/MOBILE/pocketpc/downloads/money.asp. Regardless of whether you install Money for Pocket PC from a CD-ROM or from a downloaded file, it's important that you already have the desktop Money application installed on your desktop computer before installing Money for Pocket PC.

→ For more information on connecting your device to a desktop PC, **see** "Connecting to Your Desktop PC," **p. 45**.

→ To learn more about installing Pocket PC software, **see** "Installing Software from a Desktop PC," **p. 209**.

SYNCHRONIZING FOR THE FIRST TIME

As I'm sure you've guessed, ActiveSync is the software responsible for synchronizing Money for Pocket PC with Money. Before performing the synchronization for the first time, you need to set up synchronization settings for Money for Pocket PC.

> **Caution**
>
> You can synchronize Money only between one desktop PC and one Pocket PC. If you have two Pocket PC devices, you can't synchronize between the two of them from a single desktop. Likewise, you can't synchronize from two desktop PCs with a Pocket PC device. This synchronization restriction applies only to Money for Pocket PC and Money; other types of data synchronized via ActiveSync aren't affected.

Money data is automatically synchronized the first time you synchronize your device with ActiveSync after installing Money for Pocket PC. You might want to tweak the synchronization options for Money for Pocket PC, in which case you must click the Options button on the ActiveSync toolbar. The list of information types in the Options window includes an entry for Microsoft Money, which is checked by default to enable the synchronization of Money data. If you click the Settings button, you can fine-tune the options regarding the Money data that is synchronized. This displays the Money Synchronization Settings window, which is shown in Figure 17.1.

Figure 17.1
The Money Synchronization Settings window enables you to specify the exact Money data that is synchronized, including specific accounts.

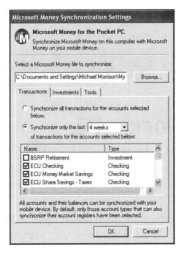

TWEAKING SYNCHRONIZATION SETTINGS

The first option in the Money synchronization settings enables you to select a different Money 2002 file for synchronizing with Money for Pocket PC. Money 2002 stores all your financial information in a special file with a .mny file extension. If several people in your household use Money 2002, you might have multiple Money files and need to be sure to look for the one that applies to you. Below the file setting is a tabbed view that displays the Transactions tab initially. This tab enables you to specify the accounts that are synchronized, as well as the transactions for the accounts. You have the option of synchronizing all transactions for the accounts or specifying a number of weeks of data to synchronize. The default setting of 4 weeks is a good place to start, but you can adjust this to suit your needs (between 1 and 52 weeks). The list near the bottom of the window takes its information from Money 2002 and enables you to choose the accounts you want to synchronize.

Note

Although you can synchronize all the data in Money 2002 if you choose, it is important to assess how much information you're synchronizing so as not to waste Pocket PC resources. The main use of Money for Pocket PC is in entering and maintaining current transactions, which probably means you can get by without synchronizing your entire financial history. Remember that large data files will inevitably slow down Money for Pocket PC.

By default, ActiveSync enables only accounts that support an account register in Money for Pocket PC. This includes the following account types:

- Cash
- Checking
- Savings
- Credit Card
- Line of Credit

Other account types can be synchronized with Money for Pocket PC, but you won't be able to add or view transactions with the account; the account balance is all that is retained. This is totally acceptable for some accounts, such as Investment accounts, because you probably care only about the balance anyway.

The second tab in the Money Synchronization Settings window is the Investments tab, which enables you to select the individual investments that are set up in Money 2002 (see Figure 17.2). You can choose whether to synchronize all investments or just the ones selected in the list.

Figure 17.2
The Investments tab in the Money Synchronization Settings window enables you to select investments for synchronization, which you can later update online through their ticker symbols.

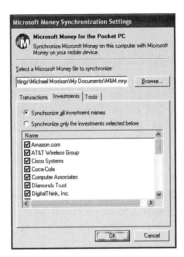

The third Money Synchronization Settings tab, Tools, enables you to manage the data that is synchronized with Money (see Figure 17.3). This tab is especially helpful if your Money for Pocket PC data doesn't appear to be properly synchronized with Money on your desktop computer. The Sync All button is used to force a full synchronization of all your mobile Money data again, whereas the Delete All button removes all Money data from your device. The last option on the Tools tab is a check box that gives ActiveSync permission to remember your Money password so it doesn't have to be entered each time you synchronize Money for Pocket PC.

Figure 17.3
The Tools tab in the Money Synchronization Settings window enables you to synchronize and delete all your Money data in one swoop.

Note

Microsoft Money 2002 takes advantage of Microsoft's .NET Passport service to provide unified user identification across multiple applications and Web sites. This is important because your Passport password is your Money 2002 password, which is the same password used to synchronize Money for Pocket PC. To learn more about the .NET service, including how to sign up for it, see the section "Signing Up for a .NET Passport" in Chapter 9.

After analyzing and setting appropriate Money for Pocket PC synchronization options, click the OK button to accept the settings and return to the ActiveSync Options window. Clicking OK again in the Options window enables ActiveSync to get to work synchronizing Money data based on the new synchronization settings. Depending on how much data you've selected for synchronization, ActiveSync will churn for a few moments synchronizing Money data on your Pocket PC.

Caution

Be careful not to turn off your Pocket PC or otherwise interrupt the synchronization of Money data. Doing so can cause the Money for Pocket PC database to get corrupted, which requires you to delete the Pocket PC partnership and set up Money for Pocket PC again to fix it.

Note

If you open a different file in Money 2002, it doesn't affect the synchronization in Money for Pocket PC. However, if you select a different Money file for synchronization in ActiveSync, the existing data in Money for Pocket PC will be replaced.

With the Money for Pocket PC synchronization settings successfully altered to suit your needs, you can move on to actually keeping track of your finances with Money for Pocket PC. If, on the other hand, you entered data into Money for Pocket PC prior to synchronizing for the first time, you should pay close attention to the next section.

SYNCHRONIZING PREEXISTING MONEY FOR POCKET PC DATA

Earlier in the chapter, I mentioned that you shouldn't enter data into Money for Pocket PC prior to synchronization if you plan to synchronize later because no straightforward way exists to synchronize Money for Pocket PC data that was entered prior to setting up Money synchronization.

However, you can do it. During the initial Money synchronization, ActiveSync expects one of the Money files (Money 2002 or Money for Pocket PC) to be empty of any data. Because you've entered data in Money for Pocket PC, neither of the files is empty, which presents a problem. By performing the following steps, you will create a temporary Money 2002 file that is empty, thus circumventing the problem:

1. Create a new Money 2002 file, and set it as the Money synchronization file in ActiveSync.

2. Synchronize Money for Pocket PC with the new Money 2002 file, which will enter your Money for Pocket PC data into Money 2002.

3. Export the Money 2002 data to a QIF (Quicken Interchange Format) file.

4. Open your original Money 2002 file, and import the data from the QIF file.

5. Set the original Money 2002 file as the Money synchronization file in ActiveSync.

Keep in mind that this is an issue only when initially synchronizing Money data. Also keep in mind that you can avoid the hassle of performing this trick if you synchronize Money for Pocket PC with Money 2002 prior to entering any financial data in Money for Pocket PC.

USING MONEY FOR POCKET PC

With Money for Pocket PC properly synchronized and full of Money 2002 data, you're almost ready to start using it to enter transactions and monitor accounts and investments. However, before doing so you might want to consider setting a password for the application that keeps your financial data from prying eyes in case someone gets his hands on your Pocket PC. This password applies only to Money for Pocket PC and is completely different from any password you might be using with Money 2002. The Money for Pocket PC password is purely a precaution to keep people from being able to access Money data on your Pocket PC. To set a password for Money for Pocket PC, tap Password in the Tools menu. You'll be prompted to enter a password, after which you'll have to enter it each time you run Money for Pocket PC.

→ To find out how to use a password to protect your device, **see** "Password-Protecting Your Pocket PC," **p. 62**.

 Another potential security issue related to Money for Pocket PC is the account information that is automatically displayed on the Today screen. To find out how to control exactly what Money information is displayed on the Today screen, see "Controlling Money Account Information on the Today Screen" in the "Troubleshooting" section at the end of the chapter.

MANAGING YOUR FINANCES WITH THE ACCOUNT MANAGER

With a little financial security in place, you can get started working with accounts and managing your finances. To launch Money for Pocket PC, tap Programs on the Start menu and then tap the Microsoft Money icon. Money for Pocket PC begins by displaying the Account Manager screen, which contains a list of the accounts that are set up for use in it (see Figure 17.4).

Note Just in case you're curious about the Money data used throughout this chapter, the account names, transactions, and amounts are entirely fictitious.

Figure 17.4
The Account Manager screen displays a list of accounts set up in Money for Pocket PC, along with their respective balances.

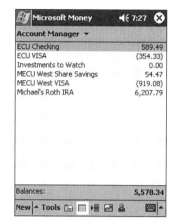

To create a new account, tap New near the lower-left corner of the screen. To find out more about an account, just tap the account in the account list. Figure 17.5 shows the Account Register screen, which is displayed when you tap an account that supports an account register in Money for Pocket PC, such as a checking account.

Figure 17.5
The Account Register screen displays a list of transaction entries in an account, including the date, amount, and payee for the transaction.

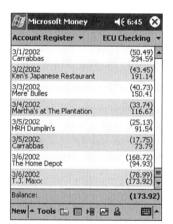

ENTERING TRANSACTIONS WITH THE ACCOUNT REGISTER

The Account Register screen resembles a register used to enter transactions in your checkbook and is a simplified version of the Money 2002 account register. To edit an individual transaction, just tap it in the list. To enter a new transaction, tap New in the lower-left corner of the screen. Figure 17.6 shows a transaction being edited.

PART

IV

CH

17

Tip from

Michael

Most of the fields used to enter and edit transaction information use the AutoComplete+ feature, which automatically enters data based on previously entered information. This helps to significantly speed up the entry of common transactions.

Figure 17.6
When editing a transaction, you can modify information such as the type, account, payee, date, and amount of the transaction.

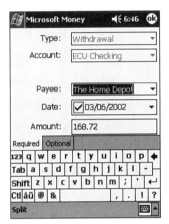

You'll notice in the transaction that the Required tab is initially selected; this tab reflects information that is required for the transaction to be considered complete, which includes the type of transaction, account for the transaction, payee, date, and amount. The Optional tab is used to enter additional information that isn't as critical to the transaction. Figure 17.7 shows the Optional tab information for the transaction.

Tip from

Michael

If you need to perform a quick calculation while entering a transaction, just tap Calculator in the Tools menu to launch the Pocket PC Calculator.

Figure 17.7
Enter optional information while editing a transaction.

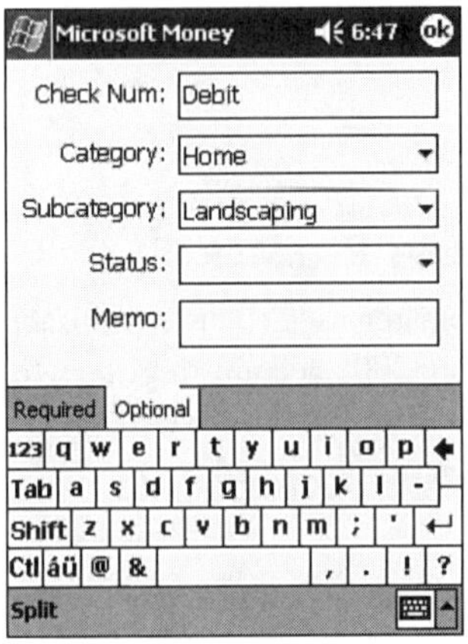

The Optional tab includes optional fields such as the check number. I like to categorize transactions in Money, so I use the Category and Subcategory fields whenever possible. The Status field is used to signify whether a transaction has been cleared, reconciled, or voided. Finally, the Memo field is used to provide additional information about the transaction. Tapping OK in the upper-right corner of the screen commits the changes to the transaction and returns you to the Account Register screen.

MANAGING CATEGORIES, INVESTMENTS, AND PAYEES

Back in the Account Register screen (refer to Figure 17.5), you'll notice two drop-down lists near the top of the screen. In the upper-right area of the screen is a drop-down list that enables you to select an account; all the accounts set up for synchronization with Money for Pocket PC are shown in the list. The list on the upper-left enables you to choose from the following screens to manipulate Money data:

- Account Manager
- Account Register
- Categories
- Investments
- Payees

PART

IV

CH

17

Tip from
Michael

The Account Manager, Categories, Investments, and Payees screens are also accessible via toolbar buttons along the bottom of the screen in Money for Pocket PC.

You've already learned about the Account Manager and Account Register screens, so let's move on to the others. To access the Categories screen, tap the upper-left drop-down list and then tap Categories. Figure 17.8 shows the Categories screen, which contains a list of all the categories used in Money for Pocket PC.

Figure 17.8
The Categories screen contains a list of all the categories.

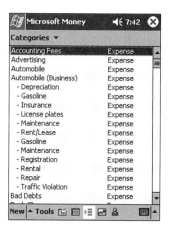

To create a new category, tap New near the lower-left corner of the Categories screen. To edit a category, just tap it in the category list. Figure 17.9 shows a category being edited.

Figure 17.9
When editing a category, you can modify information such as the name and type of the category.

To accept the changes to the category, tap OK in the upper-right corner of the screen. Categories are an important part of both Money 2002 and Money for Pocket PC, so it's important to categorize transactions whenever possible.

You access the Investments screen by tapping the upper-left drop-down list and then tapping Investments. Figure 17.10 shows the Investments screen, which contains a list of the investments being tracked in Money for Pocket PC.

Figure 17.10
The Investments screen contains a list of the investments being tracked in Money for Pocket PC, and includes the ticker symbol, number of shares owned, and current share price for each investment.

The total market value for all the investments is displayed at the bottom of the screen. To add a new investment, tap New near the lower-left corner of the screen. To edit an investment, just tap the investment in the list of investments. Figure 17.11 shows an investment being edited.

Figure 17.11
Editing an investment simply involves modifying its pertinent information; this can be useful in situations where the ticker symbol changes or when you need to adjust the number of shares due to a stock split.

Editing investments is pretty straightforward in that you enter information such as the name, ticker symbol, last price, and number of shares held for the investment. Tap OK in the upper-right corner of the screen to commit the changes to the investment. Notice that there is no reference to how much was paid for an investment or any commissions paid. This keeps you from being able to determine the performance of an investment, which is not the role of Money for Pocket PC; you should use Money 2002 for analytical purposes.

Note

There is a difference between an investment and an investment account. Although you can edit investments, you can't add or remove transactions for an investment account.

Back in the Investments screen, you might have noticed several buttons to the right of the Tools menu. Most of these buttons correspond to menu options, such as Account Manager, Categories, and Investments, but the last button on the right is unique in that it enables you to update investment quotes online. The Update Quotes button is handy for keeping tabs on your investments while traveling with your Pocket PC. You need an Internet connection to retrieve the quotes, but a modem or an Ethernet card makes this an easy task. You can also update the quotes via ActiveSync if your device is connected to your desktop computer.

→ For more information on how to get online with your Pocket PC, **see** "Creating Connections with Connection Manager," **p. 127**.

Tip from
Michael

If you don't have access to an Internet connection, you can manually update investment prices by editing the investment and entering a share price directly in the Last Price field.

The last Money for Pocket PC screen to address is the Payees screen, which enables you to customize the payees used throughout this application. Similar to being able to add and edit categories in the Categories screen, you can add and edit payees in the Payees screen, which is shown in Figure 17.12.

Figure 17.12
The Payees screen contains a list of all the payees used in Money for Pocket PC.

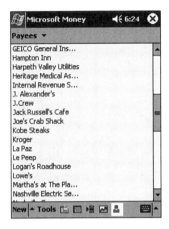

To create a new payee, tap New near the lower-left corner of the Payees screen. To edit a payee, just tap it in the payee list. Figure 17.13 shows a payee being edited.

Figure 17.13
When editing a payee, you can modify information such as the name, address, phone number, and account number of the payee.

Although you might sometimes find it useful to edit payees via the Payees screen, I typically enter new payees by just entering them when I enter a transaction for them. Money for Pocket PC automatically adds the new payee to the payee list, in which case you can edit the details later if necessary using the Payees screen.

CUSTOMIZING MONEY FOR POCKET PC

Money for Pocket PC includes a few options that can be customized to alter the way the application works. You can customize it by tapping Options in the Tools menu. This displays the Microsoft Money Options window, which is shown in Figure 17.14.

Figure 17.14
The Money for Pocket PC Options window enables you to customize it by selectively using the AutoComplete, AutoFill, and Large Font features.

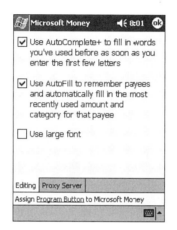

The first check box in this window enables the AutoComplete+ feature, which automatically fills in Money information when entering transactions and payees. This is a useful feature, and I've never encountered a scenario where it would be beneficial to disable it. The second check box fills in recently used amounts for categories and payees when entering new transactions. This feature can save you time if you repeatedly enter transactions of the same amount to the same payee. Similar to AutoComplete+, I haven't encountered a scenario where AutoFill is a hindrance, even if it doesn't always enter a suitable amount.

The final option in Money for Pocket PC allows you to enable large fonts, which makes text in the various screens easier to read. The small font setting is the default and is used in the figures you've seen throughout this chapter. I personally prefer the small font setting because it gives Money for Pocket PC a cleaner look that is capable of fitting more information on the screen, but if you find large fonts easier to read then by all means change the setting.

Another tab in the Money for Pocket PC Options window, named Proxy Server, is shown in Figure 17.15. This setting is useful if you are on a network that requires a proxy server for accessing the Internet. A *proxy server* is an application that serves as an intermediary between computers on a network and is often used to cache files for improved performance and filter information passing between computers. If you do require a proxy server, this information is necessary so that Money for Pocket PC can update investment quotes from the Internet.

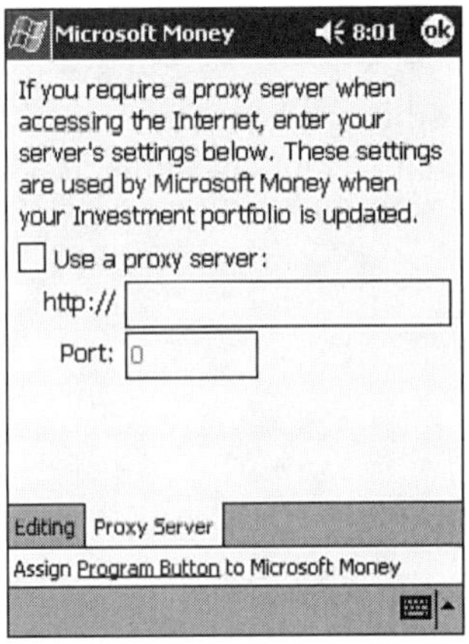

Figure 17.15
The Proxy Server tab in the Money for Pocket PC Options window enables you to set a proxy server for accessing the Internet, which is important if you plan to retrieve investment quotes online and your network requires a proxy server.

| Microsoft Money | 8:01 | OK |

If you require a proxy server when accessing the Internet, enter your server's settings below. These settings are used by Microsoft Money when your Investment portfolio is updated.

☐ Use a proxy server:
  http://
  Port: 0

| Editing | Proxy Server |

Assign Program Button to Microsoft Money

If you require a proxy server, you'll definitely want to enter the relevant information in this window to update investment quotes in Money for Pocket PC. You should be able to obtain this information from your network administrator.

KEEPING MONEY FOR POCKET PC RUNNING SMOOTHLY

Even though it's true that Money 2002 for Pocket PC is considerably more reliable than earlier versions when it comes to synchronizing with Money 2002, it's important to use caution when synchronizing Money data so you avoid corrupting the Money for Pocket PC database. Money for Pocket PC is, for some reason, more susceptible to synchronization problems than other Pocket PC applications, which is why you should try to follow a few rules when it comes to synchronizing Money data. Following are some suggestions for keeping Money for Pocket PC running smoothly:

- Do not disconnect your device during synchronization.
- Do not use Money 2002 on your desktop PC while your device is synchronizing.
- Avoid using Money for Pocket PC while your device is connected to your desktop PC.

Note

You'll know if you have a corrupt Money for Pocket PC database because a message will be displayed when you try to run the application and you won't be allowed to access any Money data on your device.

If you follow these suggestions, you will greatly reduce the risk of having problems with Money for Pocket PC.

⚠ *If the Money for Pocket PC database somehow gets corrupted, you won't be able to run Money for Pocket PC or access your Money data on the device. To find out how to restore a corrupted Money for Pocket PC database, see "Repairing a Corrupt Money for Pocket PC Database" in the "Troubleshooting" section at the end of the chapter.*

BEYOND MONEY FOR POCKET PC

As you know, Money for Pocket PC is designed only for synchronization with data stored in Microsoft Money 2001 or 2002. If you use different personal finance software, such as Quicken, you'll find that Money for Pocket PC isn't very useful. Of course, you can export Quicken data and then import it into Money, but this still requires you to continue using Money instead of Quicken, which might not be ideal for everyone. If you're a diehard Quicken user, there aren't any really good alternatives to Money for Pocket PC at the time of this writing. LandWare, the maker of Pocket Quicken for Palm devices, plans to have a version of Pocket Quicken for Pocket PC by the third quarter of 2002, so at least a solution is in the works.

If you're leaning more toward a complete financial software package for your Pocket PC, as opposed to a scaled-down application that synchronizes with your desktop computer, a few options are available. Following are a few commercial financial software packages for Pocket PC that are full-featured enough to use in lieu of a desktop application:

- **Cash Organizer**—Available at `http://www.inesoft.com/`
- **PoQuick Money**—Available at `http://www.mastersoftmobilesolutions.com/`
- **PocketMoney**—Available at `http://www.catamount.com/`

These applications are primarily useful if you don't intend to use a desktop financial application such as Microsoft Money or Quicken. If you prefer to handle most of your personal finances on your desktop computer and use your Pocket PC only for entering mobile transactions, you'll probably be better off using Money for Pocket PC (for Money users) or the upcoming Pocket Quicken (for Quicken users).

TROUBLESHOOTING

REPAIRING A CORRUPT MONEY FOR POCKET PC DATABASE

When I run Money for Pocket PC, it complains that the Money database is corrupted.

If your Money for Pocket PC database somehow gets corrupted, you'll need to clear your device of all Money data and then resynchronize with Money. The bad news is that you'll lose any unsynchronized data that has been entered on your device. Following are the steps required to repair the Money for Pocket PC database:

1. Connect your device to your desktop PC and establish a connection with ActiveSync.
2. Click the Options button in the ActiveSync toolbar to display the ActiveSync Options window.
3. Click Microsoft Money in the list, and then click the Settings button to display the Money Synchronization Settings window.
4. Click the Tools tab, and then click the Delete All button to remove all Money data from the device.

5. Click the Sync All button to synchronize all Money data with the device.

6. Click the OK button to accept the synchronization settings, and then click OK again to get out of the Options window.

7. Wait for the synchronization to finish, and then run Money for Pocket on your device to access the newly synchronized Money data.

CONTROLLING MONEY ACCOUNT INFORMATION ON THE TODAY SCREEN

I'm concerned about the fact that Money for Pocket PC account information is displayed on the Today screen. How do I control what account information is displayed?

By default, all Money for Pocket PC account balances are displayed on the Today screen when you install and synchronize Money for Pocket PC. If you want to remove some or all of this information from the Today Screen, follow these steps:

1. Tap Start, and then tap Settings.

2. Tap the Today icon, and then tap the Items tab.

3. Tap Money in the list of Today items, and then tap the Options button (uncheck the Money item if you want to eliminate all Money information from the Today screen).

4. Tap to check and uncheck the account and investment information you want to appear on the Today screen.

5. Tap OK twice in the upper-right corner to accept the Today screen changes.

REAL-WORLD EXAMPLE—A ONE-WEEK MONEY FOR POCKET PC TRIAL

Most users of desktop financial applications fall into one of two camps: those who keep up with receipts and enter them into a financial application and those who ignore receipts and wait to enter transactions when they see what appears on their monthly statements. Regardless of which transaction entry style you use, I challenge you to experiment with using Money for Pocket PC to streamline the process of entering transactions into Microsoft Money. More specifically, commit to spending one week carrying around your Pocket PC as if it was your paper check register. However, instead of just entering checks, go ahead and take the time to enter checks, debits, credits, and any other mobile transaction that impacts an account you have set up in Money.

The purpose of this one-week trial period is to show you how useful Money for Pocket PC can be when you give it a chance. It simply isn't enough to use Money for Pocket PC just to track account balances without entering transactions.

CHAPTER 18

NEVER LOSE YOUR WAY WITH POCKET STREETS

In this chapter

GETTING STARTED WITH POCKET STREETS

If you're the kind of person who likes to plan every trip down to the most intricate detail, then you'll probably welcome the idea of Pocket Streets, a software mapping system that runs on your Pocket PC. Even if you aren't such a detailed person, Pocket Streets can still be useful because it alleviates the hassle of thumbing through paper road atlases to find out where you're going. In fact, a Pocket PC running Pocket Streets in many ways is the ultimate road atlas because it is interactive. Not too many printed road atlases enable you to zoom in and out, and there definitely aren't any that enable you to navigate based on specific points of interest, such as restaurants or historic landmarks. Or maybe you're interested in seeing only bowling alleys and movie theatres? That's not a problem because Pocket Streets allows you to enable or disable points of interest at will. Not only that, but with the proper GPS hardware, Pocket Streets enables you to pinpoint yourself on a map.

POCKET STREETS AND DESKTOP MAPPING APPLICATIONS

Pocket Streets is designed for use with a desktop mapping application such as Microsoft Streets & Trips. Because desktop mapping applications run on a desktop PC, they don't have to concern themselves too much with storage limitations. Pocket PCs, on the other hand, don't have this luxury. Because maps can get fairly big due to the large amount of information contained in them, creating smaller maps using a desktop mapping application will probably be useful. Creating maps involves taking an existing map in a desktop mapping application and selecting a region (sub-map) that is exported into a map suitable for use with Pocket Streets. Pocket Streets is compatible with the following desktop mapping applications:

- Microsoft Streets & Trips 2002
- Microsoft MapPoint 2002 North America
- Microsoft MapPoint 2002 Europe
- Microsoft AutoRoute 2002 Europe

Although you will probably want to use one of these mapping applications to create maps for Pocket Streets, you can also download maps for free. For example, you can download maps for most of the major cities in the United States and many cities across Europe. Later in the chapter you learn how to download maps, but keep in mind that the capability of creating custom maps in a desktop application is very significant. This is important primarily because, with a desktop mapping application, you can zoom in on a map and export only the exact portion of the map that you plan to use with Pocket Streets, which can save a significant amount of storage space. Maps can be quite large, so minimizing their size is an important consideration when using them with Pocket Streets.

Tip from
Michael

Given the fact that maps can take up a considerable amount of storage space, it's a good idea to store maps on a memory storage card. In fact, you could buy a small capacity storage card (16MB, for example) for very low cost and use it only for map storage.

Note

You might notice that the version of each of the desktop mapping applications mentioned is 2002, which is necessary for compatibility with Pocket Streets 2002, the current version of Pocket Streets. Maps created in older versions of Microsoft's desktop mapping applications are not compatible with Pocket Streets 2002.

If you've used previous versions of Pocket Streets, you might be surprised to find that Pocket Streets 2002 is not included on the CD-ROM that came with your Pocket PC. This is because Microsoft decided to stop giving away Pocket Streets with Pocket PCs and instead now bundle it with desktop mapping applications. So, all the previously mentioned desktop mapping applications now include Pocket Streets 2002. The remainder of the chapter assumes that you've acquired Pocket Streets 2002 along with a compatible desktop mapping application.

INSTALLING POCKET STREETS

Although Pocket Streets is a powerful and useful application, it is not included in the ROM of your Pocket PC like other standard applications such as Word and Excel. Instead, you must install Pocket Streets from a desktop PC. Pocket Streets is included with all of Microsoft's desktop mapping applications, such as Microsoft Streets & Trips 2002. When you install Streets & Trips onto your desktop PC, you are given the option to also install Pocket Streets on your Pocket PC. Of course, your device must be connected to the desktop PC for Pocket Streets to be installed.

To begin installing Pocket Streets, you first need to connect your device to the desktop PC via a cradle or some other connection (USB, serial, Bluetooth, and so on). You also must establish a connection via the ActiveSync software because ActiveSync is responsible for handling communication between the desktop PC and the device. ActiveSync automatically establishes a connection with your device when you connect it to your desktop PC. With an ActiveSync connection established, you should begin installing the desktop mapping application, being sure to look for the option to also install Pocket Streets. Figure 18.1 shows the Pocket Streets installation option that appears as part of the Microsoft Streets & Trips 2002 installation procedure.

→ For more information on connecting your device to a desktop PC, **see** "Connecting to Your Desktop PC," **p. 45**.

If you continue with the installation, Streets & Trips is installed on your desktop PC and Pocket Streets is installed on your Pocket PC. The last step of the process displays the Setup Complete window, which includes a check box that enables you to view the Read Me file for Pocket Streets upon completing the installation. I encourage you to accept this setting and read the file because it typically contains late-breaking information regarding Pocket Streets. Click the Finish button to complete the setup and view the Read Me file. Pocket Streets is now installed and ready to use on your Pocket PC.

PART

IV

CH

18

Figure 18.1
You install Pocket Streets 2002 to your Pocket PC during the Microsoft Streets & Trips 2002 installation procedure.

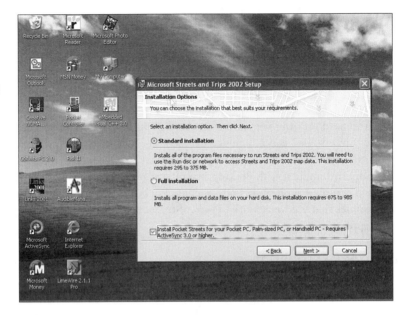

OBTAINING MAPS FOR POCKET STREETS

If you're the impatient type, you've probably already run Pocket Streets to see how it works. Unfortunately, you found out that Pocket Streets isn't very useful without a map, and no map is installed to your device by default. You must download or create a map for use with Pocket Streets to start using it. Because maps can take up a lot of space, it's important to be selective about the maps you store on your device for use with Pocket Streets. The good news is that maps are easy to obtain. You can acquire maps for Pocket Streets in the following two ways:

■ Download them from the Web.

■ Create them using a desktop mapping application.

The next few sections explain how to use these two approaches to obtain maps for Pocket Streets.

DOWNLOADING MAPS

The quickest way to get started with Pocket Streets is to download a map from Microsoft's Pocket Streets Web site, which is located at http://www.microsoft.com/pocketstreets/. From this Web site, you can download maps for specific cities around the world by first selecting the country and then the city. The map sizes vary according to the size of the city, but overall the maps available for download are reasonable sizes because they are limited to individual cities. Figure 18.2 shows the map download page of the Pocket Streets Web site, which reveals how to select a country and state for selecting a city map.

Because downloadable Pocket Streets maps target specific cities, they might not always serve your needs if you require a map for a road trip between cities. If you need a map that includes a route from one point to another, you'll probably be better off creating your own map from a desktop mapping application.

Figure 18.2
Microsoft's Pocket Streets Web site enables you to download individual city maps for Pocket Streets 2002, which you can then use to navigate around a city.

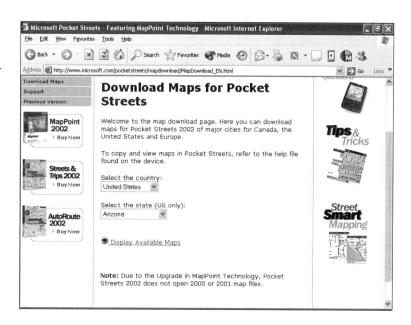

After clicking Display Available Maps, you are presented with cities you can click to download relevant maps. The size of each map is displayed next to the city so that you'll know how much storage you need on your device, as well as how large of a file you're about to download. Figure 18.3 shows the Arizona city maps available for download.

Pocket Streets maps (.mps files) are usable only in Pocket Streets and therefore aren't capable of being viewed in a desktop mapping application such as Microsoft Streets & Trips. However, several popular desktop mapping applications, including Microsoft Streets & Trips, are capable of generating .mps maps for use in Pocket Streets.

After you decide on a city map to download, just click it and follow your Web browser's directions for saving the map file to your hard disk. After the map file finishes downloading, use ActiveSync to copy the file from your desktop hard disk to the My Documents folder of your Pocket PC. The map is now ready to be viewed in Pocket Streets 2002. We'll get into the specifics of that a little later in this chapter in the section "Navigating with Pocket Streets."

Figure 18.3
This list of city maps for Arizona is a good example of how the Pocket Streets Web site includes the size of each map so you can assess device storage requirements.

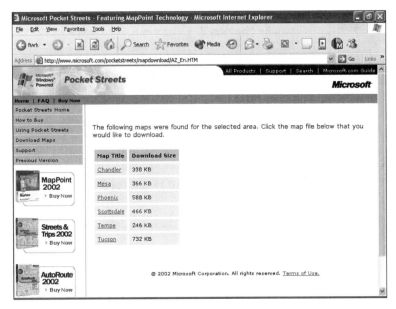

 *Pocket Streets requires maps to be stored in the My Documents folder to access them. See "Locating Missing Maps" in the "Troubleshooting" section at the end of the chapter if you've copied a map to your device and it doesn't appear in Pocket Streets.*

You can download and view as many maps as you want in this manner—just be careful not to overdo it in terms of using up precious device memory. Keep in mind, too, that you can always store maps on your desktop PC and copy them to your Pocket PC on an as needed basis.

CREATING YOUR OWN MAPS

If you want a little more control over the maps you use with Pocket Streets, you probably should consider creating your own. Don't worry, this doesn't involve renting a helicopter or performing any kind of geological surveys. Creating maps for Pocket Streets is simple because it involves using a desktop mapping application to select and export a region of an existing map. For example, you might need the map for only a particular part of a city, in which case the entire city map is unnecessary. In this situation you can use a desktop mapping application to select the exact area of the map you want to create and then export it for use in Pocket Streets.

The remainder of this section focuses on using Microsoft Streets & Trips 2002 to create maps for Pocket Streets. If you are using one of the other desktop mapping applications, the process should be very similar. Keep in mind that the focus of this chapter is on using Pocket Streets, so my intention is to cover just enough of Microsoft Streets & Trips to create maps for use with Pocket Streets. I encourage you to experiment and learn more about your desktop mapping application of choice if you so desire, but for the purposes of this chapter I'm covering only the bare essentials.

To get started, launch Streets & Trips by clicking its icon in the Start menu's Programs folder. If you've elected to install Streets & Trips so that it pulls map data off a CD-ROM, you'll need to insert the CD-ROM when you run the application. Streets & Trips displays a Start screen that gives you quick access to its most useful features. The best way to start in Microsoft Streets & Trips 2002 is to type a location in the Location bar near the top of the screen, which finds a place in the United States by default.

As an example of how to find a place, let's plan a trip to visit the Phoenician Resort in Scottsdale, Arizona. Entering **Phoenician Resort** in the Location bar and pressing Enter (or clicking the Find button) results in the Find window appearing with a list of location matches. In this case, the correct match is the fourth item in the list (see Figure 18.4). Notice the small icon to the left of the item in the list of matching places. This icon indicates that the Phoenician Resort is a hotel; many icons are used throughout Microsoft Streets & Trips to represent various types of places.

Figure 18.4
The Find window comes up with a match for the Phoenician Resort in Scottsdale, Arizona; notice the little hotel icon to the left of the hotel name, as well as other icons such as restaurants.

Hotel icon

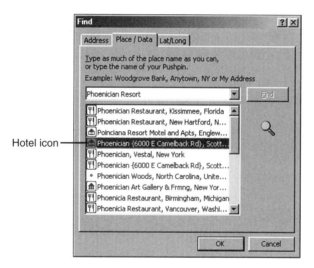

Clicking the OK button in the Find window results in Microsoft Streets & Trips changing the map to view the selected place. Figure 18.5 shows the Phoenician Resort selected in the center of a map of Scottsdale, Arizona.

At this point, you're ready to create a map for Pocket Streets, but it's important to select only the part of the map that you absolutely need in order to limit the size of the map. To do so, click the mouse and drag to create a box around the portion of the map you want to use. After you've selected the portion of the map you're interested in, you can right-click inside the box and select Export Map for Pocket Streets from the pop-up menu. Alternatively, you can select Export Map for Pocket Streets from the Tools menu. When you initiate the Pocket Streets map creation by issuing this command, a window is displayed that indicates the size of the resulting map (see Figure 18.6).

Figure 18.5
After you select a place on the map with the Find window, the map automatically zooms and centers itself on the place.

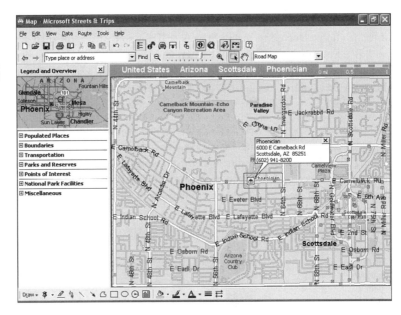

Maps you create for Pocket Streets can get large if you aren't careful. See "Dealing with Large Custom Maps" in the "Troubleshooting" section at the end of the chapter to find out how to keep maps down to a reasonable size.

Figure 18.6
The size of maps is very important given the limited storage available on Pocket PCs, which is why Pocket Streets informs you of the map size when you attempt to create a new map.

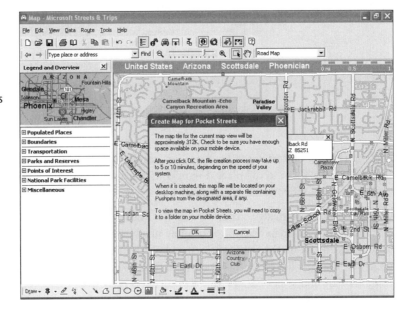

Map files exported for use with Pocket Streets have the file extension .mps. Pushpins can be defined within a map, in which case an additional file is created with a file extension .psp. *Pushpins* are used to mark locations on a map and are covered in the next section, "Navigating with Pocket Streets."

You are given the option to confirm or reject the map at this point because a large map would likely prove cumbersome on a Pocket PC. In this case, the map is 312KB, which is reasonable given the storage capability of Pocket PCs; I would try to avoid map files over 1MB or 2MB unless you're using a memory storage card. Clicking the OK button in this window results in you being prompted to enter a filename and location for the map on your desktop PC. The filename and location are entirely up to you, but you can save time copying the file to your Pocket PC by saving it directly in your synchronization folder. After you provide a filename for the map, Microsoft Streets & Trips 2002 starts exporting the map for Pocket Streets. This can take a few minutes, depending on the size of the map.

Now that the map file is created, all that is left to do is copy it to your Pocket PC using ActiveSync. If you exported the file to your synchronization folder, it will automatically be copied to your Pocket PC upon synchronization with ActiveSync. Otherwise, you must manually copy it over with ActiveSync. Keep in mind that maps must be placed in the My Documents folder or a folder one level beneath My Documents for Pocket Streets to have access to it.

PART

IV

CH

18

NAVIGATING WITH POCKET STREETS

With a map or two stored on your Pocket PC, you're ready to take Pocket Streets for a spin. To launch Pocket Streets, tap Programs in the Start menu, and then tap the Pocket Streets icon. Depending on how many maps you have on your device, Pocket Streets will start by showing a map or an Open window. In this case, Pocket Streets opens the Phoenician map created in the previous section (see Figure 18.7).

Figure 18.7
The most recently displayed or downloaded map is shown by default when you run Pocket Streets.

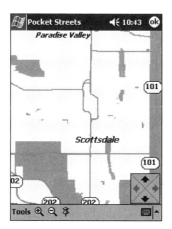

As you can see in Figure 18.7, the map has lost a lot of detail in the conversion from Microsoft Streets & Trips to Pocket Streets. Even so, a lot of information is still present, as you'll soon see.

Along the bottom of the screen in Pocket Streets is the menu, which is used to navigate and manipulate maps. The Tools menu contains various features for finding addresses and places, as well as managing pushpins and controlling the map view. Next to the Tools menu are two Zoom buttons, which enable you to zoom in and out of a map. If the road or location you want to see isn't fully in the window, you can use the scroll buttons in the lower-right corner of the screen (up, down, left, and right) to bring it into view.

The last icon on the menu is the Pushpin icon, which enables you to create a pushpin that is used to remember a location on the map. Although you can tap anywhere on the map and create a pushpin, I usually find it better to find a place and then create a pushpin for it. To do this, tap Tools near the lower-left corner of the screen, and then tap Find Place. A screen appears that enables you to enter the name of a place to find. After entering the name of the place to find, tap OK in the upper-right corner of the screen to find matching places. Figure 18.8 shows the only match returned when trying to find the Phoenician Resort in Scottsdale, Arizona.

Tip from
Michael

You don't have to enter the complete name of a place to find it. In fact, if you aren't sure of the name of a place, you're more likely to find it if you enter a partial name.

Figure 18.8
To find a place in Pocket Streets, you must first enter its name.

If several matches exist for the place you entered, you will have the option of selecting a place from a list. Otherwise, you'll be immediately returned to the map, where the place you're looking for is now highlighted. Figure 18.9 shows the Phoenician Resort displayed on the map.

Figure 18.9
After you find a place, the map is automatically zoomed and centered to show the place.

Pushpin

It's a good idea to mark a place with a pushpin so you can easily find it again. Pocket Streets maintains a list of pushpins that you can use to find places after you've marked them. To convert the Phoenician Resort place into a pushpin, tap the Pushpin button in the menu at the bottom of the screen, and then tap the caption on the map that says Phoenician {6000 E Camelback Road}. Figure 18.10 shows the window that appears, which enables you to customize the specifics of the pushpin.

PART

IV

CH

18

Figure 18.10
Creating a pushpin involves entering the name of the pushpin, along with optionally providing a note and selecting a different visual symbol.

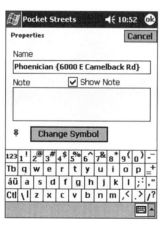

When you create a pushpin from an existing place, as in this example, the name of the pushpin will already be filled out. You have the option of accepting it or changing it to something else. You can also enter a note to go along with the pushpin. Every pushpin is represented on the map by a visual symbol, which you can change by tapping the Choose Symbol button. The default symbol for a pushpin is a yellow pushpin image, which is suitable in most cases. Ultimately, the visual appearance of a pushpin is a personal preference. Figure 18.11 shows the various pushpins you can use to visually mark a place on a map.

Note

Notes are used to add comments and additional information to pushpins, such as a description of a location.

Figure 18.11
Pushpins can have different visual symbols to help make spotting them on a map easier.

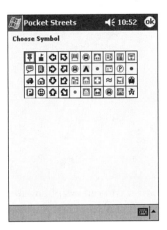

After entering information regarding the new pushpin, tap OK to create it. The pushpin symbol is then displayed along with the caption on the map where the place is located.

Note

Pushpins are stored in files with a .psp file extension. It is very important for pushpin files to be stored in the same folder as the maps to which they belong. Pocket Streets automatically stores pushpin files in the proper location, but if you ever copy pushpin files from a desktop mapping application, be sure you place them in the same folder as the .mps map file on your device.

After a pushpin has been created, you can then use it to quickly find a location on the map. This can be handy for finding the location of a place with respect to a zoomed-out map. For example, the Zoom Full command zooms out the map as far as possible, which gives you a large view of the map. To access this command, tap Tools followed by Map, and then Zoom Full. Figure 18.12 shows the Phoenician Resort pushpin as viewed with the map zoomed out.

The Tools menu contains some other commands you might find useful. One of the more interesting features of Pocket Streets is the ability to view points of interest on the map, such as restaurants, hospitals, and ATMs. You can selectively enable and disable certain types of points of interest by tapping Points of Interest on the Tools menu. Figure 18.13 shows how the various points of interest are enabled and disabled.

Figure 18.12
Pushpins help you see places within the big scheme of things when a map is zoomed out.

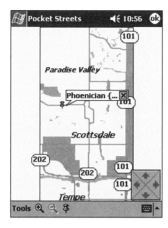

Figure 18.13
If you want to target a specific type of point of interest, such as museums or parks, Pocket Streets enables you to selectively view points of interest according to their type.

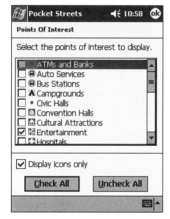

To see how powerful points of interest can be, I navigated to a different area of Scottsdale that is a little more commercial than the immediate area surrounding the Phoenician Resort. Figure 18.14 shows an area known as Old Town Scottsdale that includes several restaurants and hotels. Notice in Figure 18.14 that a hotel is denoted by a hotel symbol, whereas the restaurant (Jacqueline's Market Place) southwest of it is denoted by a restaurant symbol. You can view the name of a point of interest by tapping its symbol.

Note

When several points of interest are too close together for Pocket Streets to display their distinct symbols, a special symbol is displayed that looks like three overlapping boxes. If you zoom in further, you will be able to see the individual symbols. If it isn't possible to zoom any further, you can tap the symbol to see a list of the multiple points of interest.

Figure 18.14
Points of interest are identified on the map with special icons, as the restaurant in this figure reveals.

If you plan on hitting several destinations on a single trip, you will probably want to carry along several maps. If you have several maps stored on your Pocket PC, you'll need to use the Maps submenu of the Tools menu to manage them. In addition, some other commands are available for working with maps in this menu. The Close command is used to close a map, which returns you to the Pocket Streets map list where you can open a different map. The Copy Map command copies the current map view so that it can be pasted into other Pocket PC applications, such as Notes or Pocket Word.

The last command on the Map submenu is the Map Styles command, which enables you to alter the background color of the map (light or dark), as well as the street detail (less detail or full detail). The default settings are Light Background and Less Street Detail, which are acceptable. If you don't mind the map updating a little more slowly, the Full Street Detail setting is nice because it shows much more detail when zoomed out on a map. Figure 18.15 shows how the Full Street Detail setting adds more interest to the Phoenician map even when you aren't zoomed in completely.

Figure 18.15
The Full Street Detail setting adds much more interest to maps when zoomed out, although it does result in them updating a little more slowly.

USING GPS WITH POCKET STREETS

Although Pocket Streets can be useful in keeping you from getting lost, you might want to consider taking things a step further. I'm referring to the combination of Pocket Streets with Global Positioning System (GPS) hardware. GPS is an advanced tracking system that enables you to pinpoint your location on a map. In terms of Pocket Streets, imagine a pushpin that tracks your position on a map as you travel. The main requirement is a Pocket PC GPS receiver, which communicates with satellites in orbit and provides positional data that is used by Pocket Streets to show your location. Using the data provided by these satellites, a GPS receiver can determine its exact location, direction, and speed.

If you currently don't have a GPS receiver and you're considering getting one, the following are some GPS receivers designed specifically for use with Pocket PCs:

- **Pretec CompactGPS**—http://www.pretec.com/
- **Pocket Co-Pilot GPS**—http://www.pocketcopilot.com/
- **Destinator GPS**—http://www.destinator1.com/
- **Pharos GPS**—http://www.pharosgps.com/
- **Teletype GPS**—http://www.teletype.com/

In addition to a GPS receiver, you also need a software update for Pocket Streets to use GPS with Pocket Streets. This update is available for free download from Microsoft at http://www.microsoft.com/pocketstreets/using/download.htm. This software update adds GPS functionality to Pocket Streets, which enables Pocket Streets to recognize and communicate with a Pocket PC GPS receiver. With the Pocket Streets update and a GPS receiver, you can update your position on a map roughly every 15 seconds.

> **Note**
>
> With the update installed, Pocket Streets 2002 will work with any GPS receiver that is compliant with the National Marine Electronics Association (NMEA) 0183 standard, version 2.0 or later. This standard specifies the protocol used to communicate positional information over a GPS connection.

After installing the Pocket Streets update, a new GPS item appears on the Tools menu, as shown in Figure 18.16.

To use GPS with Pocket Streets, just tap Track Position from the new GPS menu. It might take a few minutes for the GPS receiver to obtain your position, but eventually the map will change to reflect your current location, as shown in Figure 18.17.

PART
IV
CH
18

Figure 18.16
The new GPS item on the Tools menu provides access to GPS-related features in Pocket Streets.

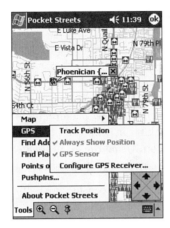

Figure 18.17
The circle with crosshairs in Pocket Streets shows your current location as determined by the GPS receiver.

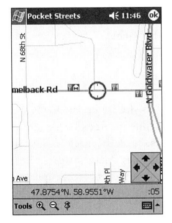

TROUBLESHOOTING

OBTAINING POCKET STREETS 2002

Pocket Streets 2002 doesn't appear to be on my Pocket PC, and I can't find it on the CD-ROM that came with my device. How do I get Pocket Streets?

Pocket Streets 2002 is not included in the ROM of Pocket PCs, and it doesn't ship on the CD-ROM that comes with Pocket PCs. Pocket Streets 2002 is only available bundled with desktop mapping applications. So, you must purchase a desktop mapping application, such as Microsoft Streets & Trips 2002 or MapPoint 2002, to get Pocket Streets 2002.

LOCATING MISSING MAPS

I copied a map to my Pocket PC, and for some reason it won't appear when I run Pocket Streets. Where did it go?

Map files must be placed in the My Documents folder of your device or in a folder one level beneath the My Documents folder. Otherwise, Pocket Streets won't be capable of finding the map. If you've copied a map to some other location on your device, you must move it to My Documents or one of its immediate child folders.

DEALING WITH LARGE CUSTOM MAPS

The custom maps I create are too large to store on my device. Is there a way to make them smaller?

The only way to make a map file smaller is to make the map itself smaller. In other words, you need to select a smaller region when you're creating the map in a desktop mapping application. It's important to carefully consider the use of each map you store on your device; also, make sure you don't generate maps any larger than you need.

REAL-WORLD EXAMPLE—PLANNING A TRIP WITH POCKET STREETS

Planning a trip with Pocket Streets can be quite useful in terms of charting destinations and ensuring you never get lost. One way to plan a trip with Pocket Streets is to make a list of all your points of interest, which can include hotels, restaurants, parks, and so on. For each point of interest, create a pushpin in Pocket Streets, which makes navigating to the location on the map easier. With all the pushpins in place, you can rest easy knowing your trip is planned out and that you won't have trouble getting from place to place.

If you want to take things a step further, you can use a desktop mapping application, such as Streets & Trips, to calculate the distance and travel time between each point of interest. Although Pocket Streets doesn't enable you to calculate this type of information, you can enter it into the notes for each pushpin before you leave and still have it accessible from within Pocket Streets. For the utmost in nerd travel, take along a GPS receiver so you can track your movement between points of interest in Pocket Streets.

SAFEGUARDING YOUR POCKET PC

CHAPTER 19

FINDING STORAGE FOR YOUR INFORMATION

In this chapter

POCKET PC INFORMATION STORAGE OPTIONS

As you probably know, storage is critical in any computing environment. Without plenty of storage for applications and data, computers wouldn't be of much use. Desktop PCs these days have the luxury of relatively inexpensive memory and disk drives, which means they rarely run into storage problems. When it comes to handheld devices, however, storage presents a unique problem because practical size and economic limitations exist that make including generous storage space difficult in such small devices. Pocket PCs deal with this problem in a variety of ways, but the overall solution involves expansion of some sort. In other words, you must consider expanding the storage options for your Pocket PC at some point if you find yourself outgrowing the built-in storage space.

The most obvious way to expand the storage capabilities of a Pocket PC is to purchase a *memory storage card*, which is an expansion card containing memory that is extremely valuable for storing data and add-on applications. Because memory storage cards are an industry standard, they can be interchanged with other devices, such as digital cameras and MP3 music players. Closely akin to a memory card is the *micro hard drive*, which is a tiny hard disk drive packaged like a memory storage card. From your device's perspective, there is no difference between the two other than the fact that a micro hard drive has significantly more space.

Memory storage cards and micro hard drives are two expansion options for you to consider, but others are also available. Following are the various options to investigate when considering how to expand the storage capabilities of your device:

- Memory storage card
- Micro hard drive
- The Digital Wallet
- Virtual hard drive

The next few sections explore each of these storage options in more detail and give you some perspective on how to compare each solution and select which one is right for your needs.

→ To learn more about Pocket PC memory and storage cards, **see** "Understanding Memory," **p. 27**.

MEMORY STORAGE CARDS

Memory storage cards consist of PCMCIA (PC), CompactFlash (CF), SecureDigital (SD), and MultiMedia Card (MMC) storage cards, each of which provides a means of increasing the available storage space of Pocket PCs. Memory storage cards are currently available in sizes ranging from 8MB to 1GB, depending on the manufacturer. The primary manufacturers of memory storage cards are Kingston Technology, Pretec, SanDisk, and Lexar. You should check the documentation for your device and see what type of expansion slot it has to determine what type of storage card to buy. CF cards are by far the leading solution for Pocket PCs, but PC cards and SD cards also factor into the equation. Compaq is the first

Pocket PC manufacturer to adopt an SD slot as its only built-in expansion option in the H3800 series of devices. Compaq also offers an expansion sleeve that enables you to use PC and CF cards.

Tip from
Michael

> You can use CF cards with computers and devices that have only a PC card slot by using a PC card adapter. This adapter accepts a CF card and is sized for PC card slots.

Another deciding factor when it comes to selecting a memory storage card is whether you can use it with multiple devices. If you have a digital camera that uses CF cards, you probably should get a CF card for your Pocket PC in case you ever want to share the memory between the two devices. In fact, this can be quite handy because you can take pictures; slide the memory card into your Pocket PC; and then view, edit, and e-mail the pictures. In addition to storing photographic images, memory storage cards are great for storing other types of memory-hungry data, such as MP3 or WMA music, which could also be interoperable with MP3 music players.

 Although you can share memory storage cards with several devices, including digital cameras, dealing with the file system created by some devices can be tricky. If you have trouble finding the image files on a storage card you're sharing with a digital camera, see "Locating Images on a Shared Memory Card" in the "Troubleshooting" section at the end of the chapter.

Note

> If you want to be able to access memory storage cards directly from a desktop PC, you can purchase a storage card reader/writer. These devices support PC, CF, and SD cards and typically attach to your desktop PC via a Universal Serial Bus (USB) port. With such a device, you can basically access a memory storage card as if it were a local disk drive.

Regardless of what type of memory storage card you use, the fundamental premise is that you're plugging a card into your device that will expand the amount of storage you have available for data and add-on applications. In this way, memory storage cards in Pocket PCs function as the logical equivalent of hard disk drives in desktop PCs. However, memory storage cards rely on nonvolatile memory chips, not a physical disk drive, to store information. Speaking of hard drives, some hard drives are in fact available for Pocket PCs that closely resemble memory storage cards.

MICRO HARD DRIVES

I just made the analogy that expansion memory in a Pocket PC plays the same storage role as a hard disk drive in a desktop PC. You can forgo a memory storage card and install a miniature hard drive in your Pocket PC. These hard drives are known as micro hard drives and are currently manufactured by IBM, Toshiba, and Kingston Technology.

PART

V

CH

19

IBM Microdrive cards are tiny hard drives embedded in CF cards that can be used to expand the storage of Pocket PCs. Unlike CF memory cards, Microdrive CF cards are designed around the CompactFlash Type II standard, which means the cards are slightly thicker (5mm thick) than the Type I memory cards (3.3mm thick). This also means you must have a Pocket PC that supports Type II cards. Toshiba and Kingston micro hard drives are packaged as Type II PC cards and therefore require a Type II PC card slot on your Pocket PC.

The big advantage micro hard drives have over memory storage cards is price; as of this writing, IBM Microdrive cards are roughly half the price of CF memory cards when you consider the price per megabyte (MB) of storage. Micro hard drives are also available in considerably larger sizes than memory storage cards. For example, IBM Microdrives are currently available in sizes up to 1GB, whereas Toshiba's micro drives are reaching sizes of 20GB! One drawback to micro hard drives is that they (like any hard disk) are slower to access than memory chips. Even so, the speed issue with micro hard drives is not a deal breaker—they are speedy enough to use without too much of a wait problem.

Even with the advantages of micro hard drives versus memory storage cards, one noticeable downside does exist. Micro hard drives put a heavier drain on the main Pocket PC battery. The degree to which this drain affects your specific device varies according to the normal battery life, condition of the battery, and so on. Fortunately, Pocket PC 2002 imposes higher requirements on battery life, so newer Pocket PCs have relatively long-lasting batteries. Even so, it's important to understand that you'll get a shorter runtime when using a micro hard drive. However, the dramatically increased storage space just might be worth it!

Caution

Micro hard drives are considerably more fragile than memory storage cards and therefore must be handled with much more care. This shouldn't pose a problem while a micro hard drive is installed in your device, but you need to be very careful when handling them outside of a device.

THE DIGITAL WALLET

If the idea of using a hard disk drive with your Pocket PC sounds interesting, you might like the Digital Wallet by Minds@work, which is essentially a standalone hard disk drive you use to store information for mobile use. Unlike micro hard drives, you don't access files stored on a Digital Wallet in real-time as you're using your Pocket PC. Instead, you move files to the Digital Wallet to free up space on your device and then copy them back later as you need them. The idea is that you might need access to much more information than you can fit on your device, so you store a bunch of stuff on your Digital Wallet and carry it along with you. When you need something that is stored on the Digital Wallet, you just copy it over to your device. A Digital Wallet is capable of storing up to 20GB of data, which is a hefty chunk of storage space.

To move information back and forth between your Pocket PC and a Digital Wallet, you typically use a memory storage card. So, you copy files to a memory storage card or a micro hard drive and then plug that card into the Digital Wallet. After the files have been safely stored away in the Digital Wallet, you can clear the memory card and conserve space. It's worth pointing out that the Digital Wallet does include a USB port, so any Pocket PCs with USB ports can access the Digital Wallet directly and forego using a memory card to transfer information. Currently, few Pocket PCs include a USB port, but that's likely to change eventually.

The fact that the Digital Wallet doesn't connect directly to most Pocket PCs is likely a turn-off for some users. However, consider the unique problem of needing access to a significant amount of data while away from a desktop PC or notebook PC with a CD-ROM. The Digital Wallet is ideal in this scenario because it serves as a standalone storehouse whose storage space you can leverage against available device memory. The Digital Wallet might not be for everyone, but it offers a unique solution to a real problem. To learn more about the Digital Wallet, visit the Minds@work Web site at `http://www.mindsatwork.net/`.

VIRTUAL HARD DRIVES

You now understand that you can increase your device's storage space by adding expansion memory, a plug-in micro hard drive, or a standalone hard drive. These are all solutions that involve purchasing additional hardware for your device, some of which can be quite expensive. Another option is available that doesn't require any new hardware at all. I'm referring to *virtual hard drives*, which are online file repositories where you can store and access files remotely through a wireless connection. Now that Pocket PCs have gone wireless on a large scale, the concept of virtual hard drives is not only realistic, but quite practical.

The idea behind a virtual hard drive is similar to that of the Digital Wallet in that there is information that you can't fit in your device's memory that you want to have access to while away from your desktop PC. It obviously doesn't help to copy the information to a Zip disk or a writeable CD-ROM because your Pocket PC has no way of accessing such storage media. A virtual hard drive solves this problem by allowing you to access files over the Internet. You simply use the File Transfer Protocol (FTP) or a Web-based interface to copy files from your Pocket PC or desktop PC to a virtual hard drive site on the Internet. When you need access to the files, you just establish an Internet connection with your device and download whichever files you need. Virtual hard drives truly provide a ubiquitous storage medium for Pocket PCs that is limited only by the bandwidth of your Internet connection speed and the size of your virtual hard drive account.

Several companies offer virtual hard drive storage solutions, but many of them are not compatible with Pocket PCs. The reason for this is because you use Pocket Internet Explorer to access the Web-based interface for accessing files on your virtual hard drive, and not all services have a Web interface suitable for Pocket Internet Explorer. So, understand that you'll have to work from within the constraints of Pocket Internet Explorer when managing files on a virtual hard drive because everything takes place through a Web interface. Following are a few of the more popular virtual hard drive providers, along with their Web addresses:

- **My Docs Online**—`http://www.mydocsonline.com/`
- **FreeDrive**—`http://www.freedrive.com/`
- **Xdrive**—`http://www.xdrive.com/`

Each of these virtual hard drive providers offers its own unique approach to supporting Web-based file storage and retrieval. For example, My Docs Online is capable of being used in conjunction with the popular AvantGo information service to provide a means of archiving and accessing Web-based content. FreeDrive, on the other hand, offers several interesting features that are a little more consumer oriented. For example, you can create online photo albums by storing photos on a FreeDrive virtual hard drive. Additionally, FreeDrive provides a CD burner service called Burn It! that involves FreeDrive burning you a CD-ROM of your virtual hard drive contents for a small fee. Xdrive is geared a little more toward the corporate crowd by offering workgroup-based virtual hard drives. Xdrive is also unique, at least on the desktop side of things, because it is designed so that your virtual hard drive can be accessed via Windows Explorer on your desktop PC as drive X. In other words, your virtual hard drive appears alongside your physical hard drive(s) and is identified by the letter X.

→ To find out more about the AvantGo information service, **see** "Using the AvantGo Information Service," **p. 188**.

Now that you have a basic idea of what is capable with virtual hard drives, you can explore the services further and see which one might be right for you. A little later in the chapter, in the section titled "Using a Virtual Hard Drive," I show you how to set up and use a virtual hard drive with your Pocket PC over the Internet.

TAKING CONTROL OF MEMORY STORAGE CARDS

The beauty of memory storage cards is that you plug them into your device and you're ready to go. There is no complex installation procedure or tricky configuration settings—you don't even have to go through any type of plug-and-play device detection as you would on a desktop PC. This reveals one of the enormous benefits of handheld computing—the simplicity of a closed environment. When I say *closed environment*, I simply mean that you are limited in terms of how you can mix and match Pocket PC hardware. For example, you can't buy a different graphics or sound card, and you can't even add memory directly at the board level as you can with a desktop PC. The way to add memory to a Pocket PC is through memory storage cards, which are virtually idiot-proof.

FORMATTING A NEW MEMORY STORAGE CARD

When you first insert a new memory storage card into your device, it will need to be formatted. A dialog box automatically appears when a new card is inserted, and you are given the opportunity to format the card (see Figure 19.1).

Figure 19.1
The Pocket PC operating system prompts you to format a new memory card upon inserting the card into your device.

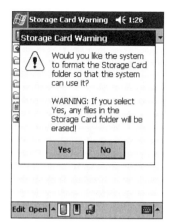

If you tap Yes in this dialog box, the memory card is formatted. This takes a few seconds, after which another dialog box is displayed that notifies you of how much free space is available on the storage card (see Figure 19.2). In this case, my 32MB SD storage card has 29MB of usable space; the file system accounts for the missing 3MB of space.

Figure 19.2
This notification clarifies exactly how much space is available on a freshly formatted memory storage card.

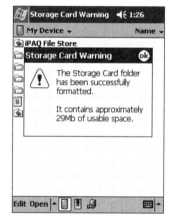

PART
V
CH
19

MANAGING MEMORY WITH FLASH FORMAT

You probably noticed that no options related to the formatting of the storage card are available. Additionally, what happens if you want to reformat a storage card later to clear everything off and get a fresh file system? The default action of the Pocket PC operating system is to allow you to format a storage card only when it detects that the card is unformatted. It's clear that it would be nice to exert a little more control over the formatting and management of storage cards, and fortunately there is an application that gives you this control.

It's called Flash Format by CNetX and is basically a memory management tool that enables you to peer behind the curtain of memory cards to see what's going on. More specifically, you can view the current memory allocation of a memory card, as well as detect and repair errors. Of course, the primary purpose of Flash Format is to provide a means of formatting memory cards with exacting control; you can control the file system, control the cluster size, and have a My Documents folder automatically created when formatting a memory card with Flash Format.

Note

If you aren't interested in the extra features of Flash Format beyond simply formatting memory storage cards, you might want to check out Format Flash Card by PDA Resources. This application also enables you to format memory storage cards and is available from the PDA Resources Web site at http://www.pdaresources.com/formatflashcard.htm.

Flash Format is available online from the CNetX Web site at http://www.cnetx.com/format/. You can purchase the software online or download a free evaluation copy. After installing Flash Format, you might be surprised to find that it isn't located in the familiar Programs folder of your device. Instead, Flash Format is accessible from your device Settings. Just tap Settings in the Start menu, and then go to the System tab. There you'll see a Flash Format icon, which you can tap to launch Flash Format. Figure 19.3 shows the Info tab of Flash Format, which is the default tab displayed when you run Flash Format.

Figure 19.3
The Info tab of Flash Format provides general information about a memory storage card, such as the total storage capacity and the amount of storage in use.

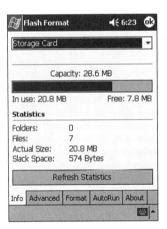

The Info tab is purely an informational tab, providing statistics such as a storage card's capacity, memory in use, and number of files and folders. The Advanced tab is a little more interesting because it delves into the details of how a storage card is structured (see Figure 19.4).

Figure 19.4
The Advanced tab of Flash Format includes information such as the type of file system used by a memory storage card, as well as the number of heads and cylinders on the card.

The Advanced tab begins by listing the number of heads and cylinders present on the storage card and then moves on to tell you about the specifics of the file system. In this example, the storage card is using a FAT16 file system with a sector and cluster size of 512 bytes. If the technical details of a storage card aren't too terribly interesting to you then you might find the Verify and Repair button near the bottom of the screen to be more intriguing. Tapping this button results in Flash Format performing a verification on the storage card, after which the Status indication near the bottom of the Advanced tab changes to 0k.

The Format tab in Flash Format is used to format a memory storage card based on very specific settings. Figure 19.5 shows the various settings available when formatting a storage card via the Format tab.

PART
V

CH
19

Figure 19.5
The Format tab of Flash Format enables you to format a memory storage card based on very specific settings, such as the file system and cluster size of the storage.

The format options in Flash Format give you the ability to change the file system and cluster size for a storage card, along with several other interesting things, such as creating a backup of the FAT and automatically creating a My Documents folder on the card. To carry out the format, just tap the Format button near the bottom of the screen.

The last tab of interest in Flash Format is the AutoRun tab, which enables you to set the AutoRun feature for a memory storage card. With AutoRun enabled, your storage card automatically runs a certain application or opens a certain document (MP3 music file, eBook, and so on) whenever the card is inserted into a device. Figure 19.6 shows the AutoRun tab with an MP3 music file set to play whenever the storage card is inserted into the device.

Figure 19.6
The AutoRun tab of Flash Format enables you to set an application or document to be run or opened automatically when a memory storage card is inserted into a device.

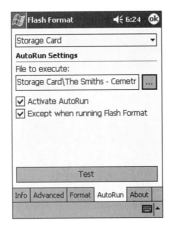

To test the AutoRun setting, just tap the Test button near the bottom of the screen. To accept the AutoRun setting, tap OK in the upper-right corner of the screen. After you set up AutoRun, the specified application or document is automatically invoked any time the storage card is inserted into a device.

 If you change out memory storage cards frequently and get tired of having a document opened or an application executed every time you insert a storage card, see "Undoing AutoRun on Your Memory Storage Card" in the "Troubleshooting" section at the end of the chapter.

USING A VIRTUAL HARD DRIVE

Earlier in the chapter you learned how virtual hard drives provide a means of storing information that can be accessed remotely from the Internet. The emphasis in the earlier discussion was on the viability of virtual hard drives as compared to other storage options. Now I'd like to spend a moment demonstrating exactly how to use a virtual hard drive with your Pocket PC. Although you can use several different virtual hard drive services with your device, I opted to use My Docs Online for demonstration purposes.

UPLOADING FILES TO A VIRTUAL HARD DRIVE

The first step in using any virtual hard drive is to establish a user account with the virtual hard drive service provider. In this case I'm using My Docs Online, whose Web site is located at http://www.mydocsonline.com/. To get started with My Docs Online, you must register for an account, which is very inexpensive. For example, as of this writing it costs $9.95 per quarter for a 50MB virtual hard drive with My Docs Online.

After establishing an account, you can upload files to the virtual hard drive for wireless access with your Pocket PC. Figure 19.7 shows a file being uploaded through the My Docs Online Web-based interface.

Figure 19.7
My Docs Online provides a Web-based interface that enables you to browse your local hard drive and upload files to the virtual hard drive.

The file in this example is a JPEG image that was taken at a Halloween party. As you upload files to the virtual hard drive, they appear in your My Files folder that is displayed on the My Docs Online Web site, as shown in Figure 19.8.

PART

V

CH

19

Figure 19.8
The My Files folder is used to store files on your virtual hard drive at My Docs Online.

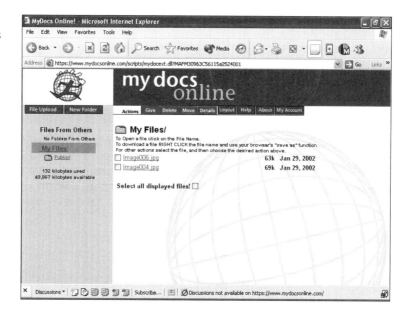

The My Docs Online Web interface includes familiar commands for moving and deleting files, among other things. After you get comfortable with using the Web interface on your desktop PC, you're ready to take a stab at accessing it wirelessly from your Pocket PC.

ACCESSING A VIRTUAL HARD DRIVE

To access a virtual hard drive from your Pocket PC, you must establish an Internet connection of some sort and then open the Web interface for the virtual hard drive. The Internet connection can be a wireless connection, wired LAN connection, or cradle connection through ActiveSync and a desktop PC. In other words, the specifics of the Internet connection don't really matter as long as you can browse the Web. Figure 19.9 shows how Pocket Internet Explorer is used to log in to the My Docs Online Web site from a Pocket PC.

→ For more information on Pocket Internet Explorer and how it's used to browse the Web, **see** "Getting the Most Out of Pocket Internet Explorer," **p. 192**.

Figure 19.9
You must first log in to a virtual hard drive service before accessing the hard drive.

After logging in, you're presented with a view of the My Files folder on your virtual hard drive. Unfortunately, most virtual hard drive Web sites use an interface consisting of multiple frames, which is quite annoying given the limited screen size of Pocket PCs. Figure 19.10 shows what I'm talking about—the My Docs Online Web interface consists of four frames!

Tip from
Michael

If you don't mind doing a lot of scrolling around, you can set Pocket Internet Explorer so that it displays the My Docs Online Web interface at full size. Just uncheck the Fit to Screen menu item on the View menu. Although this setting makes the Web page quite large relative to the size of your device screen, it eliminates the problem of multiple frames being cramped.

Figure 19.10
The My Docs Online Web interface consists of four frames, which can be difficult to navigate in Pocket Internet Explorer due to the limited screen size of Pocket PCs.

To solve the frames problem in My Docs Online, you need to tap and drag the horizontal frame divider up so that the upper two frames are reduced to nothing. This improves the usability of the site because the lower two frames are the only two you really need to use to access files. In the lower two frames, tapping and dragging the vertical divider so that the right frame is larger than the left is helpful. Figure 19.11 shows the Web interface with the frames adjusted for better viewing.

Figure 19.11
You can improve the usability of the My Docs Online Web interface by adjusting the frame dividers to provide more space for the most important frames.

PART

V

CH

19

Now you can clearly see the available files in the right frame of the Web interface. To access a file, just tap it. Figure 19.12 shows one of the image files I uploaded to the virtual hard drive being viewed in Pocket Internet Explorer.

As you can see, the My Docs Online virtual hard drive is very easy to use even if its Web interface isn't perfectly suited for Pocket PCs. Other virtual hard drives work in a similar manner, so you shouldn't have any trouble using a different service if you decide it works out better for your needs.

Figure 19.12
To access a file on the virtual hard drive, such as an image, just tap it in the right frame of the Web interface.

WORKING WITH COMPRESSED ZIP FILES

I've already mentioned several times throughout the book how important it is to keep a tight reign on the size of data files you store on your device. If you recall, this has to do with the fact that Pocket PCs have a limited amount of memory. Granted, you've learned in this chapter that expanding your device's storage capabilities is easy by using a memory storage card, micro hard drive, Digital Wallet, or virtual hard drive, but the fact remains that memory is a Pocket PC resource you should guard carefully.

Desktop PCs have long used a technique known as *compression* to minimize file sizes. A compression application takes a file and compresses it into a smaller format that can later be expanded back to its original size and format. The most popular compression format on desktop PCs is called Zip, and it was popularized by the application WinZip. The Zip format enables you to compress one or more files into a special file known as a *Zip archive*. Zip archives, or Zip files, are regularly used to exchange files through e-mail because e-mail attachments are limited in terms of size.

→ If you use a memory storage card to store e-mail attachments, and the attachment folder on your storage card is somehow deleted or renamed, Inbox will report an error when you first try to run it. To solve this problem, **see** "Correcting a Renamed or Deleted Attachment Folder," **p. 234**.

Although Pocket PCs don't include built-in support for the Zip format, you can use a third-party Zip application to access and manipulate Zip files on your device. One such application is HandyZIP by CNetX, the makers of Flash Format, which you learned about earlier in the chapter. This might sound like an ad for CNetX, but I can assure you I have no affiliation with them; they just happen to be the maker of two very useful Pocket PC utilities. Getting back to HandyZIP, it enables you to work with Zip files on your Pocket PC and includes common Zip file functions such as adding and inserting files, removing files, and extracting files.

Note

You can compress any file with HandyZIP, but not all files benefit from being compressed. For example, JPEG images are already compressed, so you're unlikely to see them shrink much at all when placed in a compressed Zip file.

HandyZIP is available for purchase from the CNetX Web site at http://www.cnetx.com/ HandyZIP/. You can also download a free evaluation version of the application from this Web site. After installing HandyZIP, you can begin using it by launching it directly from the Start menu. Figure 19.13 shows the main screen of HandyZIP, which lists all the Zip files stored on your device.

Figure 19.13
The folder list of HandyZIP initially shows all the Zip files stored on your device.

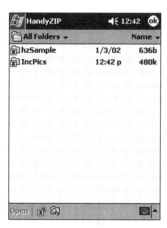

Figure 19.13 shows I have two Zip files stored on my device. To open a Zip file and view its contents, all you have to do is tap the file in the list. Figure 19.14 shows the contents of the IncPics Zip file as viewed in HandyZIP.

Figure 19.14
HandyZIP displays the contents of a Zip file in a manner very similar to File Explorer's file list.

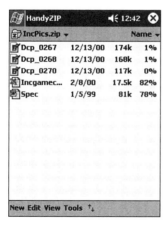

PART
V

CH

19

The file list in HandyZIP reveals that the IncPics Zip file contains five files: three images, a Pocket Excel workbook, and a Pocket Word document. If you look to the right of each file entry, you'll see a percentage that indicates to what degree the file was compressed from its original size. In this case, the Excel workbook file was compressed the most (82%), whereas the first image was compressed the least (0%). One of the most useful features of HandyZIP is the capability of opening compressed files directly from within a Zip file; to do so, just tap the file in the HandyZIP file list. Figure 19.15 shows the Spec Pocket Word document opened in Pocket Word.

→ To find out more about Pocket Word documents, **see** "Managing Documents in Pocket Word," **p. 291**.

→ To find out more about Pocket Excel workbooks, **see** "Interacting with Workbooks in Pocket Excel," **p. 314**.

Figure 19.15
Tapping a file in the HandyZIP file list opens the file, which in this case is a Pocket Word document.

In addition to opening and extracting files from a Zip file, you can also add files by selecting Add Files from the Tools menu. The Tools menu also contains an Options command that enables you to tweak the options relating to how Zip files are handled in HandyZIP. Speaking of options, you can change the manner in which compressed files are displayed in the file list by using the View menu. Figure 19.16 shows the file list view changed to Large Icons, which helps to more clearly reveal the types of files in a Zip archive.

In this example I demonstrated how to access a Zip file already stored on a device. Keep in mind that HandyZIP is perhaps even more useful for opening Zip files that arrive as e-mail attachments through the Inbox application. The good news is that you interact with attached Zip files in the same manner as the locally stored Zip file you just saw.

Figure 19.16
The View menu enables you to change the manner in which files are displayed in the HandyZIP file list, such as whether they are displayed as a detailed list or as icons.

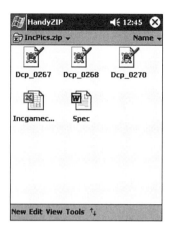

TROUBLESHOOTING

UNDOING AUTORUN ON YOUR MEMORY STORAGE CARD

Every time I insert a memory storage card my device begins playing music. How can I turn this off?

The AutoRun feature of memory storage cards enable you to designate a document to open or an application to run upon inserting a card into your device. In this case you have set the AutoRun feature for a storage card so that it plays an MP3 or WMA music file. To turn off this functionality, run Flash Format, which you learned about in this chapter, and tap the AutoRun tab. Uncheck the Activate AutoRun check box to disable the AutoRun feature.

LOCATING IMAGES ON A SHARED MEMORY STORAGE CARD

I'm sharing a memory storage card between my Pocket PC and digital camera, and I'm having trouble finding image files on the storage card when I insert it in my Pocket PC.

Some digital cameras create a seemingly strange file system on a memory storage card that can be a little confusing at first. Rest assured that image files are definitely on the card—you might just have to navigate through the file system in File Explorer on your Pocket PC to find them. Keep in mind that all image files on your device are displayed in File Explorer with a special image icon clearly indicating that the files are images. You can tap most images and quickly view them in Pocket Internet Explorer.

REAL-WORLD EXAMPLE—BACKING UP TO A VIRTUAL HARD DRIVE

One of the most common uses of a virtual hard drive is in storing backups of important files. Keep in mind that virtual hard drives are unique in that they are in a physically remote location. This makes them ideal for backups because they are immune to things such as fire, floods, and other disasters that tend to physically destroy data. In terms of Pocket PCs, virtual hard drives enable you to back up data that you might need while traveling.

For example, consider the situation in which the main battery of your device malfunctions and you lose memory, or maybe you lose your device and have to buy a new one. With a backup of important files available on a virtual hard drive, you can easily solve the problem.

This type of backup typically involves manually selecting files and adding them to a backup Zip file. You don't want to perform a normal Pocket PC backup because it requires ActiveSync and a desktop PC to restore. Instead, use HandyZIP to create a Zip file, and then add all the important files to this Zip file. After uploading the Zip file to a virtual hard drive, you can rest easy knowing that important files are easily accessible should anything go wrong while you're on the road.

CHAPTER **20**

BEEFING UP YOUR POCKET PC'S SECURITY

In this chapter

UNDERSTANDING POCKET PC SECURITY

I think it's safe to say that Pocket PCs have gone beyond high-powered PDA status and are now rapidly being integrated into the corporate environment as networked handheld computers. This is a significant shift in the use and perception of Pocket PCs because it poses new challenges for Pocket PC users and those who come into contact with them. More specifically, after you start to look at a Pocket PC as part of a larger network of computers, security becomes a significant issue. Whether interfacing with a corporate network or the Internet at large, a single Pocket PC could potentially serve as the weak link in an otherwise secure environment.

There are a variety of ways that security enters the picture with Pocket PCs. First is the issue of losing valuable, maybe even confidential, data by simply misplacing your device or someone stealing it. Although notebook computers have a similar weakness, Pocket PCs are smaller than notebooks so they are much easier targets for theft. Their compact sizes also make Pocket PCs much easier to misplace. When you consider that your data is lost with your device, it is clear that some measure of security needs to be in place for Pocket PC users who carry around sensitive information. This information can range from sensitive corporate documents to your personal financial account numbers—both of which could be extremely damaging in the wrong hands.

Aside from the dangers of losing your device or having it stolen, plenty of security risks also are involved in the normal operation of a Pocket PC. For example, any computer connected to a network is potentially at risk for hackers breaking in and causing problems. Even if your device isn't necessarily a worthy target in the minds of hackers, it could be used as a gateway into a larger network. The security of a network is really only as strong as its weakest link. Given the limited processing power and memory resources of Pocket PCs, it stands to reason that they will be the weak links in most corporate environments. This is only the case, however, if you decide to ignore the security implications of using a Pocket PC on such a network. Fortunately, ways are available to avoid your device being a unique threat to your network.

Following are four principle areas of Pocket PC security, which can be combined to help establish a level of defense for your device that acts to significantly minimize the risks of security leaks and attacks:

- Antitheft devices
- User authentication
- Data encryption
- Secure communications

The next few sections explore each of these areas of Pocket PC security in more detail. It's important to focus on all four facets when considering a strategy for protecting your device and computers with which your device is potentially networked.

Note

Another facet of Pocket PC security is antivirus software, which is used to detect and eliminate rogue applications. Chapter 21, "Protecting Against Pocket Viruses," is devoted solely to Pocket PC viruses and antivirus software, so I won't mention them anymore in this chapter.

ANTITHEFT DEVICES

It might sound painfully obvious, but avoiding theft is one of the best security measures you can take with your Pocket PC. You could glue your device to a large concrete block, but there are better ways to discourage others from attempting to steal your device. For one, the Kensington PDA Saver security device works with most Pocket PCs and is useful in situations in which you are using your device in one place for a while. This device uses a galvanized steel cable that anchors your device to an immovable object, such as a desk. The cable connects to your device through the stylus cavity; it plugs into the stylus cavity and then provides an additional cavity to store the stylus. PDA Saver is available directly from Kensington at http://www.kensington.com/.

I understand that anchoring a Pocket PC to a desk might not be the ideal antitheft solution for everyone. A simpler solution is to purchase a compact carrying case for your Pocket PC that enables you to carry the device everywhere you go. The idea is to keep your device near you at all times, which will go a long way toward keeping it from being stolen. If you're looking for a more high-tech option than simply keeping close tabs on your device, you might want to wait for a device tracker, which is supposedly in the works. A device tracker will work similarly to the LoJack system used to track vehicles and prevent theft. More specifically, the LoJack system relies on a radio beacon that is capable of being tracked by police to find stolen cars. Such a system would potentially enable you to track down a stolen handheld computer. Unfortunately, details for this new system are sketchy as of this writing, so I can't offer much more than a heads-up that it will hopefully be available soon.

→ To find out more about Pocket PC carrying cases, **see** "Carrying Cases," **p. 488**.

Tip from
Michael

Regular backups of your Pocket PC can serve as a form of insurance because they enable you to restore your system on a new device should something happen to yours.

PART
V
CH
20

Although it won't work if your device is stolen, another interesting option exists for possibly recovering a Pocket PC in the event that you lose it. I'm referring to online services such as StuffBak, which serves as an online "lost and found" that connects people with their lost valuables. To use StuffBak, you order and receive special labels that include information about how to return a lost item to its rightful owner. By sticking these labels to your valuables, you give finders the ability to return the items; StuffBak acts as the middleman in the return. Furthermore, you can even offer a reward for the return of an item, which can significantly improve the chances of getting it back. To learn more about StuffBak, visit its Web site at http://www.stuffbak.com/.

USER AUTHENTICATION

Although you might have bonded with your Pocket PC and feel like it knows you, unfortunately you can't count on an electronic device to hold a human bond and recognize you. However, there are ways to identify yourself to your device, even if it isn't driven by love or emotion. I'm referring to *user authentication*, which involves identifying yourself to your device through some type of password or other means. The idea is that access should be provided only to authenticated users. This same approach is used by ATMs when dishing out cash—only authenticated users can access their accounts and withdraw money. In the case of Pocket PCs, only an authenticated user can access the device.

The most obvious form of user authentication is the power-on password employed by the Pocket PC 2002 operating system. Under this scheme, you must enter a password upon powering up a device, and you can't access any part of the device until successfully entering the password. Three levels of user authentication are available for use with Pocket PCs:

- No password
- Four-digit PIN
- Strong password

The first level of authentication is really the absence of authentication because no password allows anyone to access your device. However, if you don't store critical information on your device or don't travel very often, you might be okay with this security level, even if you don't use it all the time. A more practical security level involves using a four-digit PIN code, which is just four numbers that must be entered to access your device. This security level is along the same lines of ATM access.

The good thing about the PIN code approach is that you can enter it very quickly, so it doesn't get in the way too much. If you really want to protect others from being able to access your device, a strong password is in order. A *strong password* is an alphanumeric password that is at least seven characters long; this option is without a doubt the best for corporate users who carry sensitive information on their devices.

In addition to the built-in password approach to user authentication, some other options are available that you might consider if you want to take matters a step further. I'm referring to *biometrics*, which are authentication techniques that involve reading or measuring some part of the human body as a means of uniquely identifying users. For example, the most commonly used biometric authentication involves scanning your fingerprint. Hollywood has also shown us retinal scanners that examine your eye for unique features, but I'm not sure how practical those would be for Pocket PCs. However, fingerprint and handwriting authentication devices are already available for Pocket PCs, as you will learn later in the chapter.

DATA ENCRYPTION

You've now learned how to avoid having your device stolen and how to limit access to your device if it should fall into the wrong hands. Let's now focus on what happens if both of those security approaches fail. Your last line of defense lies in *data encryption*, which involves converting important data into a format that cannot be understood and that can be converted into a meaningful form only with a special software key. Data encryption software enables you to encrypt files, folders, and memory storage cards, and even create special encrypted databases that contain smaller pieces of confidential data such as credit card numbers. The Pocket PC 2002 operating system doesn't include any built-in data encryption tools for encrypting individual files and folders, but several third-party options are available that will likely serve your data encryption needs. You learn more about these options a little later in the chapter in the section titled "Putting Data Encryption to Work."

> **Note**
>
> Although the Pocket PC 2002 operating system doesn't include any data encryption tools, it does include support for data encryption through the Microsoft Crypto API. The Crypto API (Application Programming Interface) is a library of low-level cryptography utilities that can be used by programmers to develop encryption applications. The Crypto API enables developers to more easily create Pocket PC applications that support data encryption.

SECURE COMMUNICATIONS

Although the Pocket PC 2002 operating system doesn't include built-in encryption features for files and folders, it does include encryption support for secure communications thanks to Pocket Internet Explorer and Secure Sockets Layer (SSL). *Secure communications* refers to the capability to access and share information over a network connection securely. You're probably somewhat familiar with secure Web sites because they enable you to buy goods and services online without the risk of someone stealing your credit card number. Anytime you see a little icon of a padlock in the lower-right corner of your desktop Web browser, you are viewing a secure Web page. This typically means that the Web browser is using SSL to encrypt information sent back and forth through the Web connection. Toward the end of this chapter, in the section titled "Feeling Secure with Pocket Internet Explorer," you learn more about the SSL support built into Pocket Internet Explorer.

Another facet of secure communications built into the Pocket PC 2002 operating system is support for virtual private networks (VPNs). A *VPN* is a private network, usually in a corporate environment, that relies on the Internet to facilitate connections between remote computers. A VPN is different from a truly private network in that it involves Internet connections. Of course, security is a big concern with VPNs because you are relying on the Internet to communicate between remote computers. VPNs solve the security problem primarily by using firewalls and encryption. Another important facet of VPNs is *tunneling*, which is a networking solution that enables you to layer communication protocols over each other. Tunneling is essentially what allows a private network to communicate with another private network using the Internet as the go-between.

I didn't really intend for this discussion to become a tutorial on VPNs, but I wanted to ensure that you had at least a basic understanding of them because they definitely factor into the Pocket PC 2002 security features. For example, the Pocket PC 2002 operating system includes support for Point-to-Point Tunneling Protocol (PPTP), which is a popular tunneling protocol used by VPNs. Although it's not important for you to understand how PPTP works, it is important to understand that PPTP and VPNs enable you to carry out secure communications on corporate networks with your Pocket PC.

REVISITING THE POWER-ON PASSWORD

Before getting into advanced Pocket PC security techniques such as data encryption and biometric authentication, we need to cover the basics and make sure you have the most obvious form of security in place. I'm referring to the power-on password, which helps to ensure that you're the only person to have access to your device. I know that someone could possibly look over your shoulder or otherwise acquire your PIN code or password if you're careless with it, but the fact remains that the power-on password is a simple and effective security measure.

> **Caution**
>
> Try to avoid setting a password for your device that is directly linked to public information about you, such as your birth date or anniversary. Even the most inexperienced hacker can gain access to your device if you use a password that is too obvious.

Fortunately, if you've been following my advice throughout the book you've already set a password. For this reason, I won't go into the details of how to set a password for your device because you can just refer to Chapter 4, "Personalizing Your Pocket PC." However, I would like to reiterate a point regarding the power-on password that you might not have taken too seriously back in Chapter 4. You can set an *active period* for the power-on password that determines how long your device must sit idle before requiring the password to be reentered. Figure 20.1 shows the Password Settings screen, which enables you to set the active period for the power-on password. To access this setting, tap Start followed by Settings, and then tap the Password icon.

→ For more information on setting a password for your device, **see** "Password-Protecting Your Pocket PC," **p. 62**.

Figure 20.1
The active period for the power-on password is set on the Password Settings screen and is useful in adding an extra degree of security to your device.

EXPLORING DATA ENCRYPTION OPTIONS

Earlier in the chapter you learned that data encryption involves converting sensitive information into an unrecognizable format that can be recovered only with a special password or key. The sensitive information can consist of files; folders; or individual pieces of data such as credit card numbers, Social Security numbers, or bids for a business proposal. The Pocket PC 2002 operating system doesn't directly include any features for encrypting specific files, folders, or pieces of data, but several third-party applications provide this very functionality:

- PocketLock
- Sentry 2020
- FileCrypto for Pocket PC
- PassKey
- The Safe
- Cryptographer for Windows CE
- SmartPass CE

The next few sections explore these data encryption applications in more detail and help you get acquainted with what each has to offer in terms of Pocket PC security.

Tip from Michael	Although not all data encryption software allows you to target specific folders for encryption, one approach to isolating encrypted data is to use encryption solely with a memory storage card. You then store sensitive information on the storage card only, which is kept encrypted at all times.

POCKETLOCK

PocketLock is an application created by Applian Technologies that enables you to encrypt a file or folder using a numeric PIN code or an alphanumeric password. PocketLock provides a relatively simplistic approach to data encryption, but it works quite well if you have simple needs in the area of encryption. A desktop version of PocketLock is also available, which enables you to synchronize and share encrypted files between your desktop PC and Pocket PC. To find out more about PocketLock, visit the PocketLock Web site at
`http://www.applian.com/pocketpc/pocketlock/`.

PART V

CH 20

SENTRY 2020

SoftWinter's Sentry 2020 is another data encryption application that enables you to encrypt files and folders. Sentry 2020 allows you to create *containers*, which are basically archives containing one or more encrypted files. The neat thing about Sentry containers is that they appear as folders in the standard File Explorer application, which is a pretty slick integration of data encryption into File Explorer. The integration of Sentry 2020 data encryption into the Pocket PC file system makes it a very intuitive application to use. Similar to PocketLock, SoftWinter makes available a desktop version of the Sentry 2020 application.

To find out more about Sentry 2020, stop by the SoftWinter Web site at `http://www.softwinter.com/`, or just read on because I put Sentry 2020 through its paces a little later in the chapter.

FILECRYPTO FOR POCKET PC

If you want to extend the encryption capabilities of your device to also include e-mail, you might like FileCrypto for Pocket PC by F-Secure Corporation. Similar to the other encryption applications you've learned about, FileCrypto supports the encryption of files and folders. However, FileCrypto adds to this support the capability to encrypt e-mail messages, as well as files and folders on memory storage cards and micro hard drives. To learn more about FileCrypto, you can visit the F-Secure Corporation Web site at `http://www.europe.f-secure.com/`.

PASSKEY

Maybe you don't need to encrypt entire files and folders and instead simply need to encrypt specific pieces of important information. If this is the case then you might be interested in PassKey by Application Development Studio. PassKey is basically an encrypted information manager that enables you to store small pieces of information in an encrypted database. PassKey is ideal for safely storing information such as Web site passwords and registration information, among other things. For more information on PassKey, visit the Application Development Studio Web site at `http://www.appstudio.com/`, or continue reading because I demonstrate how to use PassKey a little later in the chapter.

THE SAFE

Another application that provides an encrypted database for storing important pieces of information is The Safe by Softwarebu[um]ro Mu[um]ller. The Safe is similar in function to PassKey in that it supports the encryption and storage of small pieces of information, such as serial numbers and passwords. One interesting feature of The Safe is that it enables you to break down the database into categories so that information can be grouped. To find out more about The Safe, visit its Web site at `http://www.sbm.nu/englisch/windowsce/thesafe/`.

CRYPTOGRAPHER FOR WINDOWS CE

Removable storage cards are an obvious concern when it comes to security and data encryption. Paragon Software's CryptoGrapher for Windows CE is specifically designed to encrypt and protect data stored on memory storage cards. CryptoGrapher automatically encrypts any data written to a storage card and then decrypts the data when it is read. One feature of CryptoGrapher that I found interesting is how it destroys the contents of a storage card if the encryption key is entered incorrectly more than 25 times. This is a stop-gap measure designed to thwart a hacker who is repeatedly trying to break the security of your device. You can learn more about CryptoGrapher for Windows CE by visiting its Web site at `http://www.penreader.com/WinCE/CryptoGrapher.html`.

SMARTPASS CE

Perhaps the most advanced of all the encryption applications I've covered is SmartPass CE by V-ONE. SmartPass is actually a client application designed for use with VPNs. It includes support for advanced corporate security features such as encrypted terminal server access. Given SmartPass's slant toward corporate users, it isn't necessarily for everyone. However, its feature set appears to be unmatched in the Pocket PC marketplace. The only potential drawback to SmartPass is that it requires the SmartGate Server, which is also available from V-ONE. To learn more about SmartPass CE and the SmartGate Server, stop by the V-ONE Web site at `http://www.v-one.com/`.

PUTTING DATA ENCRYPTION TO WORK

Now that you have an understanding of what is available in terms of Pocket PC data encryption applications, I'd like to take some time to show you how a couple of them work. This will not only help you get a feel for how data encryption on the Pocket PC works from a practical level, but it will also get you more acquainted with a couple of the applications mentioned in the previous sections. Keep in mind that the next two sections aren't intended to steer you toward one application or another—all the data encryption applications mentioned previously are both adequate and useful, so please take the time to investigate and decide exactly which application best suits your needs.

ENCRYPTING FILES AND FOLDERS

Earlier you learned that Sentry 2020 by SoftWinter is a data encryption application that integrates with File Explorer to enable you to create and manage encrypted archives, also known as containers. Sentry 2020 is easy to use and makes data encryption a simple part of using your Pocket PC. You can download an evaluation copy of Sentry 2020 from the SoftWinter Web site at `http://www.softwinter.com/`. After downloading and installing Sentry 2020, you begin using the application by creating a new container in which to store encrypted files and folders. To do this, just tap New on the File menu for the application. You are presented with the New Container screen, which is shown in Figure 20.2.

Figure 20.2
The New Container screen in Sentry 2020 enables you to create a new container for storing encrypted files and folders and allows you to set the size of the container as well as the level of encryption used.

PART

V

CH

20

Creating a new container involves specifying a name for it, a size, the type of encryption used, the location of its key, a password, and a timeout period. The default settings are probably acceptable if you don't know for certain what you have in mind for the container, although you might want to increase the size if you plan on storing several files or folders. If you tap the small ellipsis to the right of the container (volume) name, you can specify the name and location of the container, as shown in Figure 20.3.

Figure 20.3
A Sentry 2020 container can be stored in main memory, on a storage card, or in built-in Flash ROM if your device has it available.

After establishing the new container parameters, you simply tap OK in the upper-right corner of the screen to create the container. You then are prompted to format the container so it can be used to store encrypted files and folders (see Figure 20.4). You must format a container before you can use it, so formatting isn't really an option you can decline.

Figure 20.4
Sentry 2020 prompts you before formatting a newly created container; just tap Yes to continue with the formatting.

The new container is formatted very quickly, after which another dialog box appears that informs you of the new container size (see Figure 20.5). This is important because it lets you know how much space you have for storing encrypted data. Keep in mind that you set this size when you created the container earlier.

Figure 20.5
A dialog box in Sentry 2020 informs you of a successful format, as well as the size of the new container folder.

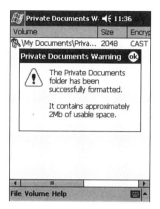

Now that the container is successfully created and formatted, it appears to your device as another folder in the file system. Check out Figure 20.6 to see what I mean—notice that the Private Documents container appears as a folder alongside other normal folders on the device.

Figure 20.6
The Private Documents encrypted container appears alongside other normal folders on the device and is distinguishable by a small icon on the folder.

If you look at Figure 20.6 closely, you'll notice that the Private Documents container folder has a little graphic on the folder icon that distinguishes it from other folders. In fact, this graphic is the same one that appears on the Storage Card folder. This tells you that the device views the Private Documents container folder as a separate physical storage location, which is the same way it perceives memory storage cards.

PART

V

CH

20

Note

You might have also noticed in Figure 20.6 that the iPAQ File Store folder has a graphic on its folder icon to designate it as a separate physical storage location. This folder corresponds to the built-in Flash ROM storage area on Compaq iPAQ devices. Most Pocket PC 2002 devices have a similar storage area for storing information that you don't want to lose in the event of a power loss, although each manufacturer names the folder differently.

To encrypt a file and safely store it in the Private Documents folder, you just need to copy or move the file to the Private Documents folder using File Explorer. Figure 20.7 shows a couple of files I've placed in the Private Documents folder.

Figure 20.7

Placing files in an encrypted container simply involves copying or moving them to the container folder using File Explorer; the files in this figure are encrypted because they are stored in the encrypted folder.

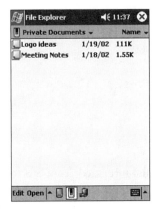

You've now placed some files in an encrypted container, but you've probably noticed that you can still access the files just as though they were in any other folder. To actually invoke the security of Sentry 2020, you must dismount the container folder. Do this by tapping and holding the folder in Sentry 2020 and then selecting Dismount from the pop-up menu. After dismounting a container, its folder no longer appears in File Explorer and all access to its contents is revoked.

To access a container's contents again, you must mount the container by tapping and holding and then selecting Mount. Of course, you'll have to enter the password for the container to successfully mount it. The container folder again appears in File Explorer after the container is successfully mounted. This process of mounting and dismounting containers is what enables you to manage encrypted archives and then seal them off for safekeeping.

SAFELY STORING SENSITIVE INFORMATION

Encrypting files and folders is one approach to data encryption on Pocket PCs. Another approach involves encrypting smaller pieces of information and storing them in an encrypted database. An application that enables you to carry out this type of encryption is PassKey by Application Development Studio. You can download an evaluation copy of PassKey from the Application Development Studio Web site at http://www.appstudio.com/. After downloading and installing PassKey, you can use the application to safely store passwords, registration information, and other important pieces of data. To add a piece of information to PassKey, just tap New on the File menu for the application. You are presented with the New Passkey screen, which is shown in Figure 20.8.

Figure 20.8
The New Passkey screen enables you to create a new passkey to be encrypted and stored by the PassKey application.

As you can see, a passkey consists of very little information: a name, a user ID, a password, registration information, and notes. In the example in Figure 20.8, I'm using the passkey to store only a user ID and password, but you could also include registration information such as a serial number, and notes about a piece of data. After a passkey is created, it appears in the main list in the PassKey application, as shown in Figure 20.9.

Figure 20.9
The main screen in the PassKey application consists of a list of passkeys, which in this case contains only one passkey.

To actually protect the passkeys stored in the PassKey application, you must set a startup password for the application, which is done by selecting Options from the Tools menu. Figure 20.10 shows the PassKey Options screen, which enables you to set a startup password for the application.

If you set a startup password for the PassKey application, you'll be prompted for the password the next time you run the application. Keep in mind that the application must be closed and removed from memory for the startup password to enter the picture. In other words, if you want to secure the passkeys you've stored in PassKey, be sure you manually close the application—don't just rely on the Pocket PC operating system to remove it from memory.

→ To recap how to manually close applications, **see** "Memory Management and Closing Applications," **p. 56**.

PART
V

CH
20

Figure 20.10
The PassKey Options screen enables you to enter a startup password that is used to protect passkeys stored by the application.

GOING SCI-FI WITH BIOMETRIC AUTHENTICATION

If you've ever seen a spy movie then you're no doubt familiar with the concept of biometric authentication. Okay, maybe the fancy term wasn't used, but the idea of analyzing a body part for uniqueness is not all that new. The most reliable biometric throughout recent history is the fingerprint; it is easily accessible, is fairly easy to read, and guarantees uniqueness. Fingerprints aren't the only biometric applicable to Pocket PCs, however. Your signature is also something highly unique to you, which makes it a candidate for biometric authentication.

Note

A pen or pencil isn't technically part of the human anatomy, but the gesture used to sign your name nonetheless falls within the realm of biometric authentication.

Currently, two products are on the market for Pocket PCs that use biometric authentication:

- PINprint Pilot for Windows CE
- Sign-On for Pocket PC

The next two sections take a look at these biometric authentication products in more detail and help to provide you with an understanding of how they work.

Note

In case you're wondering, other biometric authentication approaches are in use beyond fingerprint scanning and signature analysis. In fact, seven fundamental approaches to biometric authentication exist, which roughly correspond to different parts of the human anatomy: fingerprint, hand, face, voice, iris, retina, and signature. Fingerprint scanning is currently the most popular biometric authentication approach. Compaq and Acer both offer notebook PCs with fingerprint-scanning hardware and software included, whereas Microsoft has plans to incorporate biometric authentication capabilities into future versions of Windows.

PINprint Pilot for Windows CE

PINprint Pilot for Windows CE is a hardware device used to read a fingerprint and compare it to an authenticated user's fingerprint to grant access to a Pocket PC. The fingerprint reader is powered by two AAA batteries and is capable of being used wirelessly via an infrared port. PINprint Pilot can store up to 16 fingerprints, which means it can provide authentication for up to 16 different users. A neat feature of PINprint Pilot is that it can be used to limit access to the entire device or specific files and folders. PINprint Pilot is manufactured by Applied Biometrics and can be found on the Web at http://www.appliedbiometrics.net/.

Sign-On for Pocket PC

If you don't like the idea of using special hardware for carrying out biometric authentication, you might consider the Sign-On for Pocket PC application by Communication Intelligence Corporation. Sign-On for Pocket PC is a log-on security utility that uses a signature as a means of authenticating users. When you consider the fact that signatures have long been used as a means of executing legal documents, it makes a lot of sense to authenticate users via a signature. If you're concerned about someone being able to learn and duplicate your signature to beat the security, understand that Sign-On not only factors in the shape of a signature, but also analyzes the rhythm and timing of the strokes used to make the signature.

You can download an evaluation version of Sign-On for Pocket PC from the CIC Web site at http://www.cic.com/products/signon/. After installing Sign-On on your device, running it results in the display of a Welcome screen that gives you a chance to enable Sign-On authentication. Keep in mind that you run the Sign-On application by tapping Settings on the Start menu and then tapping the Sign-On icon. Figure 20.11 shows the Welcome screen of Sign-On, which also warns you about performing a backup of your device before enabling Sign-On. This is a legitimate precaution because it is technically possible to have difficulty accessing your device if you can't get Sign-On to recognize your signature. I encourage you to follow this advice and perform a backup just in case you have trouble with Sign-On.

Figure 20.11
The Welcome screen of Sign-On gives you a warning about backing up your device before enabling Sign-On, which is important just in case you have trouble with your signature and get locked out of the device.

To get started using Sign-On, you must go through a quick enrollment procedure on your device to establish a signature. Figure 20.12 shows the first screen of the enrollment procedure, which prompts you to sign your name.

Figure 20.12
Accurately signing your name is an important part of the Sign-On enrollment procedure.

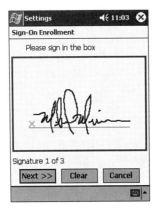

You are actually prompted to sign your name three times, which allows Sign-On to determine small variances in your signature. People rarely sign their names exactly the same each time, but common aspects of a signature can be detected. These common signature parameters are what Sign-On is analyzing as you sign your name multiple times. After signing your name three times, Sign-On prompts you for a password, which is really a four-digit PIN code (see Figure 20.13). This code is important because it enables you to change your signature later, and it can even be used in conjunction with the signature for authentication purposes.

Figure 20.13
Sign-On uses a PIN code password to enable you to make changes to your signature and also to provide a higher level of sign-on security if desired.

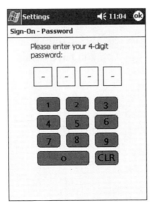

After entering the PIN code password for Sign-On, you're ready to begin using Sign-On as a biometric authentication service. Before doing so, however, you should use the Test button on the main Sign-On application screen to test your signature and ensure that Sign-On is accurately detecting it—you wouldn't want to get locked out of your device with a bad signature. After you're comfortable that your signature is working okay, you can enable Sign-On, tap OK in the upper-right corner of the screen, and then turn off your device to test it. Figure 20.14 shows a signature entered in Sign-On, which is used to gain entry into the Pocket PC.

Figure 20.14
With Sign-On enabled, you are presented with a Sign-On screen anytime you power up your device, which requires a signature before providing access to the device.

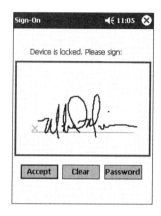

> Until you get comfortable with signature authentication, you might be worried about Sign-On not recognizing your signature and locking you out of your device. See "Avoiding Signature Lock-Out" in the "Troubleshooting" section at the end of the chapter for some tips on how to avoid this.

Accessing your device is just a matter of accurately signing your name. If you make a mistake or feel as if you didn't sign your name properly, tap the Clear button and try again. After you're comfortable with the signature, tap Accept and hopefully Sign-On will recognize you. In the event that you have trouble accessing your device via signature, you can tap the Password button to bypass the signature and log on with Sign-On's four-digit password. The default setting in Sign-On enables you to bypass the signature authentication with the password, but you can easily eliminate this option after you get comfortable by using the Prefs tab in the Sign-On application. It's worth noting that Sign-On for Pocket PC is also available for your desktop PC, which enables you to employ the same user authentication approach on your Pocket PC and desktop PC.

FEELING SECURE WITH POCKET INTERNET EXPLORER

Earlier in the chapter I mentioned that a popular form of security employed on the Web is called SSL, which stands for Secure Sockets Layer. SSL is used to encrypt data sent over a Web connection and is in wide use, especially in e-commerce applications such as online shopping carts. Pocket Internet Explorer fully supports SSL, which includes 128-bit encryption for secure Web sites. Secure Web sites that use SSL can take advantage of either 40-bit encryption or 128-bit encryption. 128-bit encryption is more desirable because it results in considerably stronger protection because of the larger encryption keys. Pocket Internet Explorer supports both 40-bit and 128-bit encryption via SSL. The benefit to this security support in Pocket Internet Explorer is that you can browse and shop the Web with as much security on your Pocket PC as you have on your desktop PC.

PART
V

CH
20

Some Web sites require a user ID and password before allowing access. See "Accessing Password-Protected Web Sites" in the "Troubleshooting" section at the end of the chapter to learn more about how these Web sites impact Pocket Internet Explorer.

Unlike desktop Web browsers, which use a little padlock icon in the status bar to clearly identify secure Web pages, Pocket Internet Explorer doesn't have enough screen real estate to spare for this type of information. To check whether you're viewing a secure Web page, select Properties from the View menu. Figure 20.15 shows the properties for the default Pocket Internet Explorer home page, which is not a secure Web page.

Figure 20.15
The default Pocket Internet Explorer home page is not a secure Web page, as is evident by viewing its properties.

You can easily identify a secure Web page on the Properties screen by taking a look at the protocol, which is set to Secure Hypertext Transfer for secure Web pages. Additionally, the Properties screen explicitly says the page is secure next to the word Security near the bottom of the property information for the page. In this example, it is clear that the page isn't secure because the words Not Secure appear in this location. The only drawback to secure Web sites and Pocket Internet Explorer is that Pocket Internet Explorer does not notify you when you enter a secure site. However, you are notified when leaving a secure site, which is certainly more important if you're entering sensitive information.

TROUBLESHOOTING

AVOIDING SIGNATURE LOCK-OUT

I'm using Sign-On for Pocket PC, and I'm worried about it not recognizing my signature and locking me out of my device.

First of all, understand that Sign-On for Pocket PC requires you to enter your signature three times when enrolling, which helps to establish an "average" signature that factors in variances in how you sign your name. Sign-On also includes a test feature that allows you to test your signature and ensure it is successfully recognized before turning on sign-on protection. It is very important to test your signature a few times and ensure it is recognized without any problems.

Another way to get comfortable with Sign-On is to initially use the Signature or Password option, which enables you to circumvent the sign-on signature with a numeric PIN code. As you get more comfortable with the sign-on procedure, you can eventually set this option to Signature Only or perhaps even Signature and Password for the utmost in sign-on security. To access these settings, go to the Prefs tab in the Sign-On application. Remember, to get to the Sign-On application, you must tap Settings on the Start menu and then tap the Sign-On icon.

ACCESSING PASSWORD-PROTECTED WEB SITES

My corporate intranet requires me to log in with a user ID and password before allowing access. How do I perform such a login using Pocket Internet Explorer?

Similar to the desktop Internet Explorer, Pocket Internet Explorer fully supports password-protected Web sites that require a login. When you visit a Web site that requires a login, Pocket Internet Explorer automatically displays a prompt for entering the user ID and password and also gives you a chance to save the login information for subsequent visits to the site. To summarize, there is really no difference in visiting a password-protected site with Internet Explorer on the desktop versus Pocket Internet Explorer.

REAL-WORLD EXAMPLE—IMPLEMENTING A POCKET PC SECURITY PLAN

Regardless of how serious or casual a Pocket PC user you are, you should develop a security plan for your device. Take some time to assess the realistic risks associated with your device and the data you store on it. Using the security knowledge you gained in this chapter, put together a plan that addresses these risks. Make a determination regarding which security measures serve your needs the best, and then take the necessary steps to put the security in place. Even if it's just purchasing a good carrying case and a StuffBak label, every bit of effort you put toward improving the security of your Pocket PC can make a big difference.

If you're a corporate user, I encourage you to go to the next level and use some combination of user authentication and data encryption software. Hopefully, this chapter has given you enough of a knowledge base regarding which types of security tools are available so that you can quickly put a security plan into action. The money spent on security software will likely be well worth the peace of mind in knowing that your sensitive Pocket PC data is secure.

CHAPTER 21

PROTECTING AGAINST POCKET VIRUSES

In this chapter

A QUICK VIRUS PRIMER

The very concept of this chapter might surprise you a little because there hasn't been a lot of talk in the media about the prospect of viruses on handheld computers. There have simply been no known viruses to target Pocket PC devices, and very few to target other handhelds such as Palm devices. However, it is likely only a matter of time before viruses enter the picture with handhelds because they are linked to desktop and laptop PCs, as well as a variety of networks including both the Internet and private corporate networks. The reality is that your Pocket PC could act as the carrier for a virus that is intended to do damage to your desktop PC and other computers on your network.

Before I get into the specifics of how viruses factor into the Pocket PC equation, it's worth taking a moment to get acquainted with viruses in general and to learn a little about how they work. Viruses have been around virtually since the dawn of personal computers in one form or another and were originally created as a means of exploring the inner workings of computer hardware in operating systems. The earliest viruses weren't so much harmful as they were annoying, and they were created more in the spirit of pranks. However, viruses eventually matured into a form of cyberterrorism that could be used to destroy data, divulge secrets, and bring companies to their knees.

Thus far I've used the term *virus* to loosely describe a computer program with malicious intent. Although this is accurate in a general sense, the term *virus* actually refers to a specific type of malicious program. In fact, three fundamental types of malicious programs are capable of attacking a computer system: viruses, trojans, and worms.

VIRUSES

A *virus* operates by infecting files on a computer when a program is run that contains the virus. The idea behind a virus is that it propagates itself by infecting files that continue to carry the virus and then infect more files. Similar to some human viruses, the most dangerous computer viruses have the capability of spreading quite rapidly. Viruses can be fairly harmless and just annoy you with pop-up messages, or they can be destructive and destroy data. The Jerusalem virus is one of the most famous viruses to date and is also one of the earliest viruses to cause problems on a wide scale. The virus was named after one of its victims, Jerusalem University, and was quite malicious in that it destroyed files on infected computers.

TROJANS

Trojans are malicious programs masquerading as something other than what they are, similar to the famous Trojan Horse that allowed Greek soldiers to sneak into the city of Troy in the Trojan War. You typically run a trojan under a false pretense, and only after it's too late do you realize the problem. Trojans have been used to allow unauthorized access to computers, which enables prying eyes to view sensitive information. Trojans can also be more directly destructive by destroying files or erasing disk drives. For example, the BackOrifice trojan is a notorious example of a trojan that provided unwarranted access to user information, system passwords, files, and corporate networks.

WORMS

Worms are viruses and trojans that cause problems simply by propagating themselves rapidly. For example, the Melissa worm caused quite a stir a few years ago when it brought numerous e-mail servers to a screeching halt due to overloads. Worms propagate at an amazing rate because they are designed to reproduce and pass themselves along every chance they get. Worms are kind of like a virus equivalent of a pyramid marketing scheme in which every person tells two people, and then they tell two people, and so on. Before long, everyone has been "touched" and systems break down due to nothing other than information overload.

ASSESSING THE RISKS OF HANDHELD VIRUSES

A few viruses have already surfaced on Palm devices. The Phage virus was one of the first Palm viruses to have the capability of infecting applications and replicating itself. The first handheld trojan also appeared on Palm devices. This trojan, known as Liberty, posed as a Game Boy emulator application, which made it an appealing download. There is, in fact, a Game Boy emulator named Liberty, but in this case the program turned out to be a trojan that erased files. Liberty wasn't necessarily an advanced trojan by any means, but it proved that handheld computers are no more immune to viruses, trojans, and worms than any other computers.

Although a large-scale virus has yet to attack handheld computers, the risks are substantial when you look at the sheer number of devices in use. Market research firm International Data Corp. expects more than 60 million wireless handheld device users with Internet access to exist in the United States in 2003. Many of these devices will be full-blown handheld computers such as Pocket PCs, which will likely have connectivity to a desktop PC and possibly a corporate network. Where there is connectivity, there is the risk of spreading viruses.

Another chunk of the 60 million devices will be smart phones, which are now incorporating the same hardware and software of handheld computers, thereby blurring the idea of what constitutes a handheld computer. For example, Handspring's new Treo communicators are smart phones that run the Palm operating system. It's literally becoming possible to spread viruses through your telephone! If you're finding this hard to believe, consider the fact that Telefonica, a Spanish telecommunications provider, was attacked by a virus that used the text messaging capabilities of mobile phones. The virus, known as Timofonica, clogged the Telefonica cellular network by jamming it with a barrage of text messages.

→ To learn more about the relationship between Pocket PCs and smart phones, **see** "The Convergence of Pocket PCs and Mobile Phones," **p. 14**.

PART

V

CH

21

Note

The word *timo* in Spanish means prank, which helps to explain the name of the Timofonica virus that attacked the Telefonica wireless phone network.

It's really only a matter of time before viruses become an issue for Pocket PCs, and not just because they are popular. You must consider the fact that viruses are just like any other software—they are limited only by the hardware and operating systems on which they run. In the case of Pocket PCs, the hardware and operating system is significantly more advanced than Palm devices and most smart phones, which makes Pocket PCs better targets for virus writers. If you're an aspiring virus writer, please don't take this as a suggestion—I'm just pointing out the obvious fact that Pocket PCs are the most powerful handheld computers available and therefore provide the most opportunities for creating malicious programs.

Of course, Pocket PCs still are limited when compared to desktop PCs, which makes it a little tougher on virus writers. For example, let's revisit the famous Melissa virus that made us all scared to open e-mail a few years ago. This virus was written as a Microsoft Word macro that was delivered via e-mail as part of an attached Word document. When the infected Word document was opened, the embedded macro jumped into action and sent the same infected Word document as an e-mail to the first 50 people in the user's Outlook address book. The key to this virus working was the macro capabilities of Word, which are non-existent in Pocket Word on Pocket PCs. So, we can safely eliminate viruses of the Melissa ilk right away when it comes to Pocket PCs.

→ For more information on the differences between Pocket Word and Word, **see** "Comparing Pocket Word with Word," **p. 277**.

This brings us to the important point that it is ultimately software features that give viruses opportunities to strike. The macro functionality in Word is actually a quite powerful feature that enables you to develop custom programs that run inside Word to carry out tasks such as intelligent mail merges. It took a crafty virus writer to turn this feature into a liability for Word users. So, it is an inevitable consequence that features and complexity in software create opportunities for virus writers. Generally speaking, the more complex a software system is, the more opportunities there are for virus writers to exploit unforeseen weaknesses. For this reason, Pocket PCs aren't as good of targets for viruses as are desktop PCs. On the other hand, they are better targets than Palm devices.

The wireless networking capabilities of Pocket PCs offer an opportunity for viruses. As an example, consider the fact that Bluetooth enables Pocket PCs to communicate wirelessly as long as they are within about 30 feet of each other. Although the Bluetooth applications require you to actively establish a Bluetooth connection, there is no reason applications won't eventually have roaming capabilities, where they automatically make connections as you move in range of other Bluetooth devices. If this scenario were to play out, you could literally "catch" a virus by passing someone on the street who is using an infected Bluetooth device. Hopefully, I've painted an exaggerated scenario here, and Bluetooth networking will be more controlled than this. However, Bluetooth is still new enough that it's hard to tell how everything will pan out when millions of Bluetooth devices are floating around out there.

In addition to Bluetooth, the 802.11b wireless networking standard, also known as Wi-Fi, poses another potential virus risk to wireless Pocket PCs, as do wireless phone networks. Wi-Fi is roughly similar to Bluetooth except that its range extends to about 100 yards.

The good news is that a Wi-Fi connection is more akin to a standard wired network connection, which typically involves a higher degree of security than Bluetooth. You can pretty much approach a Wi-Fi network connection involving a Pocket PC with the same caution that you treat a wired network connection.

→ For more information on Bluetooth and Wi-Fi wireless networking, **see** "Evaluating Networking Options," **p. 111**.

SPREADING THE DISEASE

Now that you understand the potential risks associated with Pocket PC viruses, it's worth looking into some specifics regarding how Pocket PC viruses might spread. Equally important are the ways in which viruses can't spread on Pocket PCs. For example, you learned earlier in the chapter that Pocket PCs don't include any type of macro feature such as the one found in Microsoft Word, which was ultimately responsible for the troublesome Melissa virus. So, you don't have to worry too much about Pocket Word infecting your e-mail and spreading a virus to your friends and co-workers.

Another possible misconception with respect to Pocket PC viruses has to do with desktop PC viruses. For example, let's say you just found out that your desktop PC has become infected with a virus, and you're now worried that it could have spread to your Pocket PC. You dispel any worries because it is technically impossible for the same virus to infect both a desktop PC and a Pocket PC. This has to do with the fact that Pocket PCs use completely different processors than desktop PCs and therefore run entirely different machine code. In other words, an application (including a virus program) must be specifically compiled for a desktop PC or a Pocket PC, but not both at the same time. Even so, it is certainly possible for a desktop PC to be used as a means of planting a Pocket PC virus on your device, but the virus in this case is a Pocket PC virus, not a desktop PC virus. More importantly, desktop antivirus software would probably never detect such a program because the program isn't causing any harm to your desktop computer. So, although a single virus can't infect your desktop PC and your Pocket PC at the same time, it can certainly travel between them.

Caution

Don't assume that just because you have antivirus software installed on your desktop PC that it will protect your Pocket PC as well. A desktop PC can still unknowingly serve as a transport mechanism for a Pocket PC virus, in which case the virus will likely fly below the radar of the desktop PC's antivirus software.

→ For more details on Pocket PC processors, **see** "Processors: The Brains of the Outfit," **p. 25**.

While we're on the subject of virus misconceptions, you might have some concern over the fact that information can be beamed to your Pocket PC wirelessly via the infrared port. Keep in mind that you are always given the option to accept files that are sent to you as part of the standard beaming process, which is the only way a virus could be spread. This keeps viruses from being capable of automatically transmitting themselves from one device to

PART
V
CH
21

another using the infrared port. As long as you're careful about what you allow to be sent to your device via the infrared port, you're unlikely to ever receive a virus through it. If you're receiving beamed information other than standard Pocket PC data, such as contacts and notes, be sure you know what you're getting before you open any files. Keep in mind that trojans work by making you think they are one thing, even though they are quite another.

 The best way to avoid a problem with viruses is to actively prevent them. To find out how to reduce the risks of getting a virus on your Pocket PC, see "Preventive Medicine for Pocket Viruses" in the "Troubleshooting" section at the end of the chapter.

One final point to make in regard to virus risks for Pocket PCs has to do with memory storage cards. In the early days of desktop PC viruses before computers were heavily networked, the primary manner in which viruses spread was through floppy disks. If you copied a file to a disk and passed it along to a friend or co-worker, he ran the risk of a virus entering his system through the disk if the file was infected. In many ways, memory storage cards are the equivalent of floppy disks for Pocket PCs. Granted, Pocket PC storage cards hold much more data than traditional floppy disks, and storage cards aren't typically passed around in the same manner, but the risk is still the same.

Caution

Try to be extremely careful about sharing memory storage cards with other people. As soon as someone inserts your memory card into her device, the card is susceptible to being infected by a virus.

→ To find out more about how to use memory storage cards, **see** "Memory Storage Cards," **p. 358**.

Note

The process of sharing files by copying them to a floppy disk and handing it off to someone else was often referred to jokingly as a "sneaker net" because you had to physically walk over and give the person the disk.

The best way to minimize the risk of getting a virus through a memory storage card is to avoid swapping cards with other people. If for some reason you must share storage cards with friends or co-workers, an antivirus software package for your Pocket PC will serve as a safety net should you encounter an infected storage card. Speaking of antivirus software, the next section takes a look at what is currently available for keeping your Pocket PC virus free. Before getting into that, however, let's cap off this discussion with a set of rules that will help you avoid getting a virus on your Pocket PC:

- Use reputable antivirus software, and update the signatures frequently, particularly after you hear of a major virus attack.

- Be sure that all desktop PCs you connect to also employ some form of virus protection.

- Never install a program unless you know and trust the source.

- Never open e-mail attachments unless you not only trust the sender, but are expecting the file attachment as well. Just ask anyone who opened one of those unexpected ILOVEYOU files for further verification on this suggestion.

- Share files via your infrared port only with users you trust and who preferably also use some type of Pocket PC virus protection.

You can think of this set of guidelines as the computer equivalent of washing your hands and taking vitamin C supplements—they will go a long way toward keeping your Pocket PC (and your desktop PC) free of viruses.

POCKET PC ANTIVIRUS SOFTWARE

As I'm sure you know, antivirus software has become a standard component of most desktop computer systems. Viruses are simply too prevalent and too dangerous to not employ some degree of protection. Fortunately, most desktop antivirus software packages do a great job of catching and resolving viruses. Unlike its desktop counterpart, Pocket PC antivirus software is still in its infancy. Antivirus software makers have yet to figure out the best solution for detecting viruses given the limited processing capabilities of Pocket PCs. For this reason, a few different approaches are currently being taken to address the needs of Pocket PC users who desire virus protection.

The most logical approach to virus detection on Pocket PCs is to carry it out the same way it is handled on desktop PCs; a special program runs in the background on your device and looks for suspicious activity among other programs. The problem with this approach, though, is that Pocket PCs don't have much spare processing power or memory to enable such a program to carry out its job. Another approach is to place the burden of scanning a device for viruses on a desktop PC. In this scenario, your desktop PC uses ActiveSync to monitor files and memory on your device and check them for viruses. Although this approach certainly removes much of the processing burden from your device, it has the significant disadvantage that it works only while your device is connected to a desktop PC.

Note

The Pocket PC 2002 operating system is designed with virus detection in mind–Microsoft built an antivirus programming interface into Pocket PC 2002 that enables antivirus software developers to more easily create virus detection software.

Even though viruses have yet to strike Pocket PCs, several antivirus software packages are available, each of which has its own unique approach to combating rogue applications. Following are the commercial antivirus software packages currently available for Pocket PCs:

- McAfee VirusScan for Pocket PC
- InoculateIT for CE

PART
V

CH
21

- PC-cillin for Wireless
- F-Secure Anti-Virus for Pocket PC

The next few sections introduce you to each of these antivirus software packages and arm you with enough information to decide which antivirus solution is right for your needs.

 If you think you've fallen prey to a Pocket PC virus, see "Inoculating an Infected Pocket PC" in the "Troubleshooting" section at the end of the chapter to find out what to do.

McAFEE VIRUSSCAN FOR POCKET PC

You probably recognize McAfee as one of the heavy hitters in the desktop antivirus arena. McAfee has taken its considerable skill with virus prevention and detection and used it to create a Pocket PC version of its popular VirusScan application, which is called VirusScan for Pocket PC. VirusScan for Pocket PC doesn't run on your Pocket PC. Instead, it is integrated with ActiveSync to carry out a virus scan through your desktop PC's connection to your Pocket PC. This dodges the processor and memory limitations of Pocket PCs by putting the virus scanning task on a desktop PC. Of course, the drawback to this approach is that you have no virus protection when your device is away from your desktop PC. The idea is that you get a virus scan every time you synchronize with your desktop PC, which is fairly regularly for most users. So, even though you don't have full-time virus protection with this approach, it could be sufficient if you synchronize your device regularly.

You can purchase VirusScan for Pocket PC directly from the McAfee Web site at http:// www.mcafee.com/. Because VirusScan runs entirely on your desktop PC and interacts with your Pocket PC through ActiveSync, it doesn't install anything on your device. This causes synchronization to be a little slower, but it isn't too bad when you consider that a virus scan is taking place.

PC-CILLIN FOR WIRELESS

If you decide you want a more robust antivirus solution than the synchronization-only approach taken by VirusScan for Pocket PC, you might consider PC-cillin for Wireless by Trend Micro. PC-cillin for Wireless runs directly on your device and can be called on to scan for viruses at any time. Unlike desktop antivirus applications, PC-cillin does not run in the background, constantly watching for potential viruses. Although this might sound like a drawback to using the software, this design actually results in PC-cillin putting less of a processing burden on your Pocket PC because it runs only when you need it.

PC-cillin for Wireless is easy to use, requiring little effort to perform a virus scan. The main screen of PC-cillin gives you the option to scan your device, view the virus scan log, or view information about detected viruses (see Figure 21.1).

To start a virus scan, just tap the Scan button. Another screen appears that shows the status of the virus scan, along with the total number of files scanned and the number of viruses found (see Figure 21.2).

Figure 21.1
The main screen of PC-cillin presents you with a series of buttons for performing antivirus tasks.

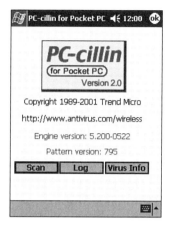

Figure 21.2
Performing a virus scan with PC-cillin simply involves waiting for the application to sift through the files on your device looking for viruses.

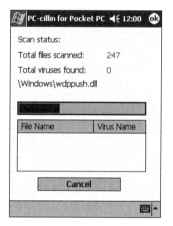

Perhaps the most compelling argument for using PC-cillin for Wireless is that it is available for free from the Trend Micro Web site at http://www.antivirus.com/wireless/. Trend Micro also plans to offer virus updates for PC-cillin for Wireless, which makes it a legitimate contender in the Pocket PC virus software market.

F-SECURE ANTI-VIRUS FOR POCKET PC

Another Pocket PC antivirus solution worth mentioning is F-Secure Anti-Virus for Pocket PC, which takes a similar virus scanning approach as PC-cillin by residing locally on your device. F-Secure Anti-Virus enables you to perform a virus scan on demand and can be set up to monitor and scan memory storage cards that are inserted into your device. You also can configure F-Secure Anti-Virus to perform a virus scan upon startup, which might be desirable for some users. F-Secure Anti-Virus for Pocket PC is available for purchase from F-Secure at http://www.europe.f-secure.com/wireless/.

PART

V

CH

21

TROUBLESHOOTING

PREVENTIVE MEDICINE FOR POCKET VIRUSES

Knowing that prevention goes a long way toward avoiding problems associated with viruses, what can I do to reduce the risks of getting a virus on my Pocket PC?

Along with using antivirus software, the best way to avoid getting viruses on your Pocket PC is to be very careful about the software and files you run on your device. Whether you are installing downloaded software or copying a file given to you by someone, it's important to know the exact source of anything you store on your device. If at all possible, stick with *trusted applications*, which are applications published by reputable companies you can trust. As long as you're obtaining software directly from the publisher or a reputable retailer, you shouldn't have any problems.

A secondary solution to minimizing the problems brought on by viruses is to regularly back up your device. If you make regular backups, you'll be covered even if a virus should strike. Unlike a desktop PC, which typically has layers and layers of installed software, you can reset a Pocket PC to its factory settings and then restore a backup pretty quickly, which essentially rolls back your system to its state prior to the virus strike.

INOCULATING AN INFECTED POCKET PC

My Pocket PC has a virus; what should I do?

The first step to take in assessing whether you have a virus is to install antivirus software and perform a virus scan. If, for some, reason your device won't boot up, you will likely have no option but to perform a soft reset and hope for the best. If this fails, a hard reset might be your only option. This no-win situation comes about because Pocket PCs, unlike desktop PCs, don't really have a means of circumventing the standard bootup procedure. On a desktop PC you can always boot from an emergency disk and perform a virus scan from there. Of course, the boot code in a Pocket PC is in ROM, so there is little chance that a virus could realistically keep your device from booting because the boot code cannot be modified.

Keep in mind, however, that hackers have always seemed to find ways to exploit weaknesses in computers, and Pocket PCs will likely be no different. The best defense against a potential virus is to make regular backups of your device so you can safely perform a hard reset if a virus should ever put your device into an unrecoverable state. A hard reset is pretty much guaranteed to solve the problem, but you'll lose data if you haven't backed up.

REAL-WORLD EXAMPLE—GET PROTECTED

It's safe to say I've burdened you with enough theory and speculation on pocket viruses in this chapter. Therefore, it's now time to shift into the practical and do something about protecting your Pocket PC from virus attacks. Spend some time considering your unique needs when it comes to virus protection and assess which, if any, antivirus software package is best suited to your needs. For example, do you regularly operate your device in a networked environment with a lot of other computers, or does it connect only with an isolated desktop computer for synchronization? Additionally, do you rely on a handful of built-in applications for your mobile computing needs, or do you regularly install and use shareware and other third-party applications? And finally, do you regularly receive e-mail attachments on your device? If so, you'll definitely have more significant virus issues to consider.

This chapter has outlined some usability guidelines for minimizing your exposure to Pocket PC viruses. The only remaining step is to determine whether an antivirus software package exists that meets your needs—if so, start using it. Even though no known Pocket PC viruses have surfaced yet, it's just a matter of time until one does, and you'd probably rather learn about it from an antivirus application than learn about it too late.

Fun with Your Pocket PC

CHAPTER 22

READING eBOOKS WITH READER

In this chapter

READER AND THE EBOOK REVOLUTION

Although most people probably take them for granted, when you think about it, a library card is pretty powerful. On a small card that you can fit in your wallet or purse, you have access to hundreds of thousands of books. Everyone is amazed by the capacity of CD-ROMs and DVDs, but we've always had access to tons of information via our library cards. Admittedly, it takes more effort to go check out a book than to search a CD-ROM, but the point is that often a lot of useful information gets overlooked because the methods for getting it are becoming antiquated. Now, imagine a library card that not only allows you easy access to an information source as vast as a library, but also stores the books themselves and provides an interface for reading them. The Microsoft Reader application for Pocket PC provides this functionality because it enables you to store and read books on your Pocket PC.

The idea of reading books on computers is nothing new. However, as anyone who uses computers regularly can attest, reading text on the screen takes longer than reading printed text does. My profession dictates that I read a lot of technical documentation that is typically in electronic form, so I have a real appreciation for the difference between reading screen text versus printed text. Even so, the benefits of electronic publishing are huge: No printing means information can be made available much more quickly, and it results in a savings to consumers. Both publishers and readers benefit from the move to electronic publishing; the significant obstacles have been the difficulty in matching screen typography with that of the printed page and the more practical issue of making eBooks as rugged and convenient as printed books.

Microsoft researchers have been trying to figure out the exact reasons the typography in printed books is ideal for reading. We often take them for granted, but the physical structure of books, along with the typography used for the text, has evolved over several centuries. Microsoft engineers developed a technology called ClearType, which draws on the superior typography of books to provide an immersive reading experience for computers. This technology was designed for Microsoft Reader and results in a book-style interface that is simple yet elegantly useful. Although Reader's success is ultimately measured by how little you notice that it is a software application imitating a book, there are clearly still some hurdles to leap before people start clearing out their bookshelves.

Even if you're sold on the technical merits of Microsoft Reader, the availability of eBooks is another important factor in ushering in the eBook revolution. It is true that we are witnessing an industry shift, but we are still at the front end of this shift. It still might be a while before you can go into a bookstore and leave with a CD-ROM full of books, but many new books are being released in both print and eBook form. Also, the push by some prominent authors, such as Stephen King, to explore new electronic distribution methods will certainly spur on the shift toward electronic book publishing. Stephen King embarked on a project to publish a book purely through electronic channels, and although the project ultimately failed, we will likely look back on it someday as a milestone in the evolution of electronic book publishing.

The good news for eBooks is that they are already widely available online from established booksellers. For example, take a stroll through the eBooks section of Amazon.com at http://www.amazon.com/ or the Barnes and Noble Web site at http://ebooks.barnesandnoble.com/. You'll find that the vast majority of recently published books are available as eBooks, with more on the way.

UNDERSTANDING CLEARTYPE

Before getting any deeper into the details of eBooks and how they are used with Reader, it's worth taking a moment to explore the technology behind the Reader application. I'm referring to ClearType, which is a text rendering technology that simulates the appearance of text on a printed page when reading eBooks on your Pocket PC. Many studies have been carried out that validate the problems associated with reading text on a computer screen. There are a variety of reasons the printed page is a superior "technology" for displaying printed text, but perhaps the most significant is the sharpness between printed letters and the page on which they appear. ClearType is designed to simulate improvement on the sharpness of text on the Pocket PC display.

ClearType works by taking advantage of the physical makeup of LCD displays. More specifically, a single pixel on an LCD display consists of three vertical stripes, or *subpixels*, that represent the red, green, and blue color components of the pixel (see Figure 22.1). So, even though your eyes perceive a single pixel as being a solid color, it actually consists of three vertical bands of color. ClearType manipulates these individual color bands to help improve the sharpness of text.

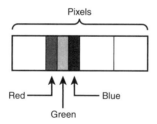

Figure 22.1
Each individual pixel on an LCD display actually consists of three vertical bands of color, also known as subpixels.

By manipulating the three subpixels that comprise each pixel on a display, ClearType effectively triples the horizontal resolution of the display. In other words, instead of having 240 pixels with which to work (the Pocket PC display is 240×320), ClearType works with 720 subpixels (3×240). Therefore, ClearType is capable of altering individual subpixels to change the appearance of adjacent pixels, and ultimately it can provide better contrast between text and the background. Because contrast is the name of the game with ClearType, it works considerably better on black-and-white graphics—black text on a white background or white text on a black background. The Reader application simulates printed pages in a book by rendering black text on a white background.

To better understand how subpixels take part in improving the appearance of text, let's take a look at an example. Figure 22.2 shows the letter *M* as it should appear on a Pocket PC display. Given the limited resolution (240×320) of the Pocket PC display, rendering the letter with the degree of accuracy shown in the figure is very difficult. In fact, the second image in the figure shows how the letter would be rendered in the absence of ClearType, which is quite chunky indeed! Notice, however, that the rendered image is comprised of subpixels that could be used to improve the appearance of the letter. Now look at the third image in the figure, which shows how ClearType alters individual subpixels to dramatically improve the appearance of the rendered letter.

Figure 22.2
By looking at a rendered letter up close, you can see how ClearType uses an interesting technique of varying the shades of pixels to make the letter look more like printed text.

The letter *m*
as it should
appear

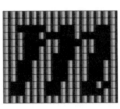

The letter *m*
rendered
without
ClearType

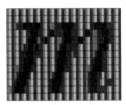

The letter *m*
rendered
with ClearType

Admittedly, this might have been more than you wanted to know about ClearType, but it is an extremely important technology as we push toward a future filled with electronic media. Paper is certainly here to stay, but technology will continue to lead us toward eBooks and other forms of electronic media that replace traditional media whenever possible.

CREATING A LIBRARY OF eBOOKS

The availability of eBooks is obviously critical to the success of the Pocket PC as an electronic reading device. In an attempt to deal with the copyright issues associated with eBooks, Microsoft is using its .NET Passport service as a means of validating eBooks for Reader. This means you have to set up a Passport account to obtain and read most eBooks with Reader. More specifically, the majority of eBooks available for purchase require Passport authentication to ensure that you are indeed the person who purchased the eBook.

Although the whole .NET Passport authentication scheme could be viewed as somewhat of a hassle, the issue of copyright protection is a very real problem that is difficult to solve without the cooperation of users. In the case of Reader, your cooperation involves accepting Microsoft Passport as a means of managing eBook rights. It doesn't cost anything to set up and use a Passport account, and you'll likely find it useful in other situations, such as when using Hotmail and MSN Messenger. So, before you learn how to download and read books in Reader, let's quickly take a look at how to activate Reader so you can access premium content.

→ To learn more about .NET Passport and its role in MSN Messenger, **see** "Signing Up for a .NET Passport," **p. 162**.

ACTIVATING READER

To use your Passport account to view eBooks that have digital rights associated with them, you must *activate* your device. Activation is a process of tying your .NET Passport account to your physical device. The first time you run Reader it is made very clear that you must activate your device to access premium eBook titles. Figure 22.3 shows what I'm talking about.

Figure 22.3
The first time you run Reader on your Pocket PC you are given a warning about the importance of activation.

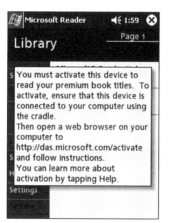

If you plan on purchasing any eBooks for use with Reader, you'll have to activate your device. The good news is that activating Reader is not difficult at all. In fact, the task is handled automatically by Microsoft through a special Web site located at http:// das.microsoft.com/activate/. When you visit this Web site, you are prompted to sign in to your Passport account, as shown in Figure 22.4.

Be sure your device is connected to your desktop PC and that an ActiveSync connection has been successfully established; then sign in to your Passport account. After successfully signing in, you are presented with a button labeled Activate My Pocket PC. Clicking this button starts the activation process, which is entirely automatic. You'll see a progress meter that slowly fills as the activation process is carried out.

Figure 22.4
Microsoft's Pocket PC Activation Web page prompts you to sign in to your Passport account or create a new Passport account if you don't have one.

⚠ *A bug exists in the Pocket PC Activation Web page that can make activating your device difficult if you already have a Passport account. To find out how to get around this bug, see "Problems Activating Reader" in the "Troubleshooting" section at the end of the chapter.*

With your device successfully activated, you're now ready to get online and go on an eBook shopping spree!

ACQUIRING EBOOKS

The only book installed by default on Pocket PCs is Reader Help, which is accessible in Reader even if you haven't activated it. Unless you're the type of person who enjoys reading manuals cover to cover, you'll probably want to find some more interesting reading than Reader Help. Fortunately, the CD-ROM that accompanies your Pocket PC includes several eBooks, many of which you'll recognize as literary classics:

- *Little Women* by Louisa May Alcott
- *Peter Pan* by J. M. Barrie
- *Kai Lung's Golden Hours* by Ernest Bramah
- *Wuthering Heights* by Emily Bronte
- *Secret Garden* by Francis Hodgson Burnett
- *Tarzan of the Apes* by Edgar Rice Burroughs
- *Innocence of Father Brown* by G. K. Chesterton
- *My Bondage and My Freedom* by Frederick Douglass
- *Study in Scarlet* by Arthur Conan Doyle
- *Riders of the Purple Sage* by Zane Grey

- *Legend of Sleepy Hollow* by Washington Irving
- *Three Men in a Boat* by Jerome K. Jerome
- *Call of the Wild* by Jack London
- *The Prince* by Machiavelli
- *Captain Blood* by Raphael Sabatini
- *Unbearable Bassington* by Saki (H. H. Munro)
- *Treasure Island* by Robert Louis Stevenson
- *Dracula* by Bram Stoker
- *Tom Sawyer* by Mark Twain
- *Around the World in 80 Days* by Jules Verne
- *The Time Machine* by H. G. Wells
- *Importance of Being Earnest* by Oscar Wilde
- *Encarta Pocket Dictionary* by Bloomsbury Publishing

As you can see, this is quite an impressive list of books—hopefully, you'll take the time to transfer some of them to your Pocket PC and try them in Reader. All these books are located on the CD-ROM that came with your Pocket PC. It's worth noting that none of these books require you to activate Reader, so you could forego activation if these books sufficed for your entire eBook library. However, you'll no doubt want to expand your literary reach beyond this list, which is why I guided you through the activation process in the previous section.

Regardless of whether you're looking for additional freebies or are ready to purchase a few eBooks online, you can visit several Web sites to download and purchase eBooks:

- **Microsoft Reader**—http://www.microsoft.com/reader/read/
- **Amazon.com**—http://www.amazon.com/
- **Barnes and Noble**—http://pocketpc.barnesandnoble.com/pocketpc/
- **CyberRead**—http://www.cyberread.com/
- **Fictionwise**—http://www.fictionwise.com/
- **Peanut Press**—http://www.peanutpress.com/
- **Powells.com**—http://www.powells.com/ebookstore/mreader.html
- **Slate eBooks**—http://slate.msn.com//?id=117506
- **University of Virginia eBook Library**—http://etext.lib.virginia.edu/ebooks/

The Microsoft Reader Web site includes several free eBooks you can download, along with links to other eBook sites. The Amazon.com and Barnes and Noble Web sites both include a large selection of eBooks for purchase, as do the other online bookstores listed. Slate is an online magazine edited by Michael Kinsley that tackles all kinds of topics, usually social or political in nature. Slate is unique in that it was the first periodical to be offered in eBook format.

This means that you can download articles from Slate; more specifically, you can download an entire week of Slate articles as a single eBook or pick and choose articles to create a custom eBook. The eBook support in Slate makes your Pocket PC not only capable of allowing you to read books, but also capable of giving you a virtual magazine subscription.

Now that you know about several sources for acquiring eBooks, I want to focus on how to purchase and download an eBook. As an example, I purchased and downloaded *The Constitution of the United States of America, 1787*, from Amazon.com, and I received an eBook file named ConstitutionofUnitedStatesofA[1].lit. The file format used to store eBooks uses a file extension of .lit, which explains the filename. When you purchase or download an eBook, you receive a file with a .lit extension—this is the file you must copy to your Pocket PC.

You might be curious as to how I received the file after making the purchase. The way it works with Amazon.com is that after making the purchase, you receive an e-mail, which directs you to your Digital Library at Amazon.com. The Digital Library includes links that enable you to download any eBooks you've recently purchased. Figure 22.5 shows the Digital Library at Amazon.com with a couple of books available for me to download.

Figure 22.5
Amazon.com's Digital Library serves as a virtual library for downloading purchased eBooks.

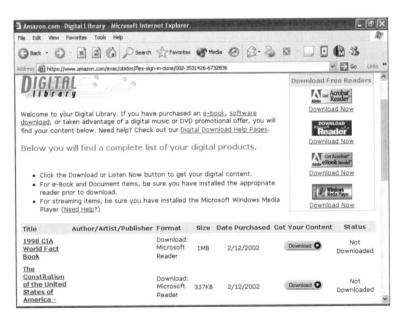

To download eBooks from Amazon.com's Digital Library, you simply click the Download image to the right of each book. Downloaded books are automatically stored in the My Library folder on your desktop PC, which is located just beneath the all-important My Documents folder. If you have Microsoft Reader installed on your desktop PC, a downloaded eBook automatically is opened for reading. For example, Figure 22.6 shows *The Constitution of the United States of America, 1787*, opened in the desktop version of Reader.

Figure 22.6
The desktop version of Reader enables you to read eBooks on your desktop or notebook PC and has a user interface similar to the Pocket PC version of Reader.

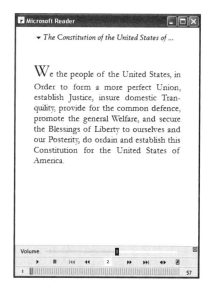

Note

The desktop version of Microsoft Reader is available for free download from the Microsoft Reader Web site at http://www.microsoft.com/reader/. This version of Reader is virtually identical to the Pocket PC version except that you can view eBooks in much larger fonts because of the higher resolutions afforded by desktop monitors.

TRANSFERRING AN EBOOK TO YOUR DEVICE

After you've downloaded an eBook to your desktop PC, copying it to your device for viewing in Reader is simple. In fact, transferring an eBook from your desktop PC to your Pocket PC is really no different from transferring any other file. To copy an eBook file to your Pocket PC, follow these steps:

1. Connect your device to your desktop computer.
2. Navigate to the My Documents\My Library folder in Explorer on your desktop PC.
3. Launch ActiveSync on your desktop PC, and click the Explore button.
4. Use Explorer on your desktop PC to drag the eBook file (.lit file extension) to the ActiveSync Explorer window.

After the eBook is copied to your Pocket PC, it is ready for viewing in the Reader application; Reader automatically locates all eBooks stored on your device. Figure 22.7 shows *The Constitution of the United States of America, 1787*, opened in Reader on a Pocket PC.

Figure 22.7
The Pocket PC version of Reader enables you to read eBooks on your device; just because a document is in the eBook format doesn't necessarily mean it is a traditional book, as this example of the United States Constitution demonstrates.

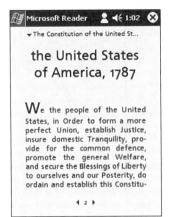

Although you might not think of it as casual reading, I encourage you to read the Constitution on your Pocket PC. It's not a bad document to be familiar with when you consider that it lays the groundwork for the rights of all Americans.

MANAGING eBOOKS IN READER

In addition to providing a user interface for reading individual eBooks, the Reader application also enables you to manage a library of eBooks that are stored on your device. To launch the Reader application, tap Programs on the Start menu, and then tap the Microsoft Reader icon. Following a brief title screen, the main screen displayed in the Reader application is the Library, which is a list of all the eBooks installed for use with Reader (see Figure 22.8).

Figure 22.8
The Library displays all the eBooks installed for use with Reader and allows you to quickly select a book for reading.

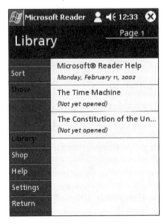

You'll notice to the left of the books is a vertical toolbar of commands. These commands are used to do useful things such as sorting the list of books by any one of the following criteria: title, author, last opened, book size, and date acquired. The Library enables you to delete books when you are finished with them, which is a good idea because books take up valuable device memory. Fortunately, individual books aren't too large in terms of memory, but there's still no reason to leave a book around that you aren't planning to read any time soon; you can always store it on your desktop PC and copy it back to your Pocket PC later. As an example, H.G. Wells's *The Time Machine* takes up about 230KB of memory. To delete a book from your device, tap and hold on the book in the Library and then tap Delete in the pop-up menu that appears.

Note

If you have more books installed than will fit on the Library screen, Reader automatically divides the book list into pages. You can then flip through the pages of the Library much as you flip through a book.

If you were previously reading a book in Reader and then try to delete it, Reader might refuse the deletion. This is because Reader still has the book open and therefore doesn't want you to delete the file. If this happens, try opening a different book and then deleting the original book. Another option is to close the Reader application, launch it again, and then delete the book in the Library.

→ To recap how to close applications, **see** "Memory Management and Closing Applications," **p. 56**.

READING EBOOKS

To read an eBook in the Reader application, just tap the name of the book in the Library. You will then see the cover image for the book, followed by the cover page; just tap the title of the book on the cover page to begin reading. Near the upper-left corner of the screen you'll see the title of the book, which actually invokes a drop-down list when you click it (see Figure 22.9).

Figure 22.9
The drop-down list of commands in Reader provides a convenient means of navigating throughout the application.

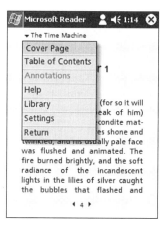

The commands in this list are used to navigate through Reader. More specifically, these commands provide access to the Cover Page and Table of Contents for the book, along with annotations and Reader help. A Library command is also available, which takes you back to the Library. The Settings command enables you to alter the settings of Reader. And finally, the Return command takes you to the last screen displayed. These commands are accessible from anywhere in a book and are useful in getting around Reader.

NAVIGATING THE READER USER INTERFACE

Several of the commands I just mentioned are accessible from the cover page of a book. Another command that can be found on the cover page is the Go To command, which enables you to quickly move around within a book. You can tap these Go To links to go to specific areas of a book:

- **Table of Contents**—The table of contents for the book
- **Most Recent Page**—The most recently read page of the book
- **Begin Reading**—The first page of the book's text
- **Furthest Read**—The furthest read page of the book
- **Annotations**—A list of all the annotations (highlights, bookmarks, notes, and drawings) for the book
- **About This Title**—General information about the book
- **Cover Image**—The cover image of the book

These standard links are handy navigational aids when it comes to moving around in a book and managing any annotations you've entered. You learn how to annotate a book a little later in the chapter in the section titled "Examining Annotations." The Furthest Read link is especially useful for returning to the furthest page you've read in a book. Even though you can set bookmarks wherever you want in a book, the Furthest Read link functions as an automatic bookmark.

Perhaps the most interesting thing about Reader is the simplicity of its user interface. Keep in mind that Microsoft's goal with Reader was to closely simulate the simplicity of the printed page. This involved eliminating as much clutter as possible, reducing the page of a book to text and a few small user interface elements. The drop-down list in the upper-left corner of the screen is easily identifiable because it shows the name of the book. The other important user interface element on each page of a book consists of navigation buttons for turning the page. In the middle near the bottom of the screen appear the page number and arrows for turning forward or back a page. In addition to tapping the right arrow to move forward a page, you can also tap the page number itself to move forward. For even more control over page navigation, tap and hold on the page number. This displays a pop-up menu that enables you to navigate to a specific page number or jump to the last page of the book.

Tip from
Michael

I've found that the page navigation buttons in Reader can be annoying because they are so small that several taps are often required to turn the page. A more efficient way to turn the page is to use the Action button or navigation button. You can rotate the Action button up and down to turn pages backward and forward or tap different sides of the navigation button to achieve a similar result. This button is located in different places on different devices; to find out more about the hardware buttons available on Pocket PCs, see "Getting to Know the Stylus, Buttons, and Dials" in Chapter 2.

Note

Unlike printed books, pages in Reader books aren't fixed in terms of the content they contain. This is apparent when you alter the font size used to display books in Reader, which results in books having more pages because less text can be fit on each page. You learn how to change the font size a little later in the section titled "Customizing Reader."

SEARCHING FOR TEXT IN EBOOKS

While reading a book in Reader, you can search for text that appears in the content of the book. To search for additional occurrences of a given word, tap the word on the screen and a pop-up menu appears. Tapping Find in the menu opens a small Find window that enables you to change the word you are trying to find, along with specifying whether you want to find the first occurrence in the book or the next occurrence (see Figure 22.10). You can also search for phrases by tapping and dragging over the phrase, in which case the same pop-up menu appears.

Figure 22.10
The Find window enables you to search for words and phrases in an eBook.

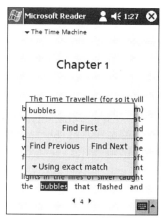

Tip from
Michael

By default, the Find feature in Reader attempts to find an exact match for the word or phrase for which you are searching. You also can search for an approximate match of the word or phrase. You do this by tapping Using Exact Match in the Find window and then tapping Using Approximate Match in the pop-up menu that appears.

Text that is found using the Find feature is highlighted on the page on which it is found. To close the Find window, tap outside of it. If the Find feature has moved you to another location in the book and you want to return to the page where you first started the search, tap the drop-down list in the upper-left corner of the page and then tap Return. In addition to finding text, you also can copy text to the Clipboard by tapping it and then tapping Copy Text on the pop-up menu. After you copy text in this manner, it is on the Clipboard and available for pasting into other Pocket PC applications.

When you're finished reading a book, the best thing to do is to return to the Library. This usually results in Reader releasing the book, which enables you to delete the book if you want. If you leave a book open in Reader, you won't be allowed to delete it from memory. Keep in mind that you return to the Library by tapping the title of the book in the drop-down list near the upper-left corner of the page and then tapping Library.

EXAMINING ANNOTATIONS

The Reader application supports several approaches to providing additional information about a book while reading it. Information you add to a book for your own use is generally referred to as *annotations* and includes the following types of information:

- Bookmarks
- Highlights
- Text notes
- Drawings

The next few sections examine each type of annotation and how they fit into Reader. You also find out how to explore and manage all the annotations for a particular eBook.

BOOKMARKS

Bookmarks are extremely useful if you want to mark a specific page so you can return to it later. To create a bookmark, tap or highlight a word or phrase on a page and select Add Bookmark from the pop-up menu that appears (see Figure 22.11). Even though a bookmark identifies an entire page, it is important to associate specific text with a bookmark because Reader uses it to help identify the bookmark. For example, you might want to select the beginning of a sentence when creating a bookmark so that the bookmark is easily recognizable if you later view it in annotations. You learn more about annotations later in this section.

After you create a bookmark, a small, colored icon appears in the right margin of the page. You can delete the bookmark by tapping the icon and then tapping Delete in the pop-up menu that appears. When you are viewing any page other than the page identified by the bookmark, the bookmark appears as a small, colored box in the right margin; tapping the box takes you to the bookmarked page. Each bookmark you create automatically takes on a different color to distinguish them from one another.

Figure 22.11
A bookmark is created by selecting a word or phrase and then tapping Add Bookmark in the pop-up menu that appears.

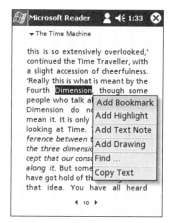

HIGHLIGHTS

Whereas bookmarks are useful for marking important pages, *highlights* are used to mark important text. Highlighting in Reader works very much like a highlighter pen in a traditional printed book. To highlight a word or phrase, tap and drag to select the text; then tap Add Highlight in the pop-up menu. Highlights can be deleted only from the Annotations Index, which you learn about in a moment.

TEXT NOTES

In some cases, a highlight just doesn't provide enough information about a word or phrase in a book. Have you ever caught yourself taking notes by writing in the margin of a book? If so, you'll find text notes in Reader to be the perfect tool for attaching information to a word or phrase. To attach a text note to a word or phrase, tap and select the text and then tap Add Text Note. A note entry window appears, which you can use to enter a text note that is associated with the selected text in the book (see Figure 22.12).

Figure 22.12
Text notes are associated with words or phrases in a book by entering text in a special note entry window.

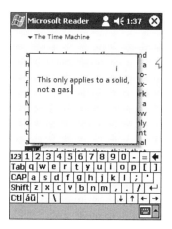

After entering a note, a special icon appears in the left margin of the page next to the text to which the note is attached. Unlike the icons for bookmarks, which appear on all pages, note icons appear only on the page in which they are associated. You can access all notes for a book from Annotations. You can delete notes from Annotations by tapping and holding the note icon on a page and then tapping Delete in the pop-up menu that appears.

DRAWINGS

The last type of annotation supported in the Reader application is *drawings*, which are drawn by hand and associated with text in a book. To add a drawing to a book, tap and select a word or phrase and then tap Add Drawing in the pop-up menu that appears. A small toolbar then appears along the bottom edge of the screen that includes three buttons for editing a drawing:

- **Done**—Finishes the drawing
- **Change Color**—Changes the color of the drawing stroke
- **Undo**—Undoes the previous drawing stroke

Creating a drawing is as simple as drawing on the screen with the stylus. Keep in mind that the drawing appears on top of the page of text, although you can toggle the display of the drawing if it gets in the way of the text. You can make as many drawing strokes as you want and change the color of each stroke by tapping the Change Color button at the bottom of the screen. When you're finished with the drawing, tap the Done button. Figure 22.13 shows a drawing being edited in Reader.

Figure 22.13
Creating a drawing in Reader is as simple as drawing on the screen with the stylus.

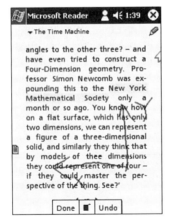

After creating a drawing, you'll notice a small pencil-shaped icon in the upper-right corner of the page. Tapping this icon toggles the display of the drawing on the page. You can tap and hold the pencil icon to display a pop-up menu of options for editing and deleting the drawing.

MANAGING ANNOTATIONS

The Reader application provides a central location to view and edit drawings and other annotations. I'm referring to the Annotations page, which is accessible from the drop-down menu near the upper-left corner of the page that appears when you tap the title of the book. Figure 22.14 shows the Annotations page for *The Time Machine*, which includes a listing of all the annotations associated with the book.

PART

VI

CH

22

Figure 22.14
Annotations groups all the annotations for a book into one convenient list with icons that distinguish between the various kinds of annotations.

You can identify annotations by the special icons displayed to the left of each annotation, as well as the text that is associated with each. You can see in the Annotations page how the text associated with an annotation is important because it becomes the name of the annotation. You can change the name of an annotation by tapping and holding on the annotation and then tapping Rename in the pop-up menu that appears. You can also delete an annotation by tapping Delete in the same menu. Tapping an annotation immediately takes you to the page containing the annotation.

The Annotations page enables you to sort annotations by using the Sort command that appears to the left of the list of annotations. To alter the sort order of the annotation list, tap the Sort command and then tap one of the sort criteria (By Type, By Page Number, By Date Created, or By Last Modified). To alter the annotations that are displayed, tap the Show command and then tap the filter criteria (Show All, Show Highlights Only, Show Bookmarks Only, Show Drawings Only, or Show Text Notes Only).

CUSTOMIZING READER

The Reader application includes several settings you can modify to alter the manner in which you read eBooks. The Reader settings are accessible by tapping Settings on the drop-down list that is accessible from the title of each book. The settings for Reader are divided across multiple pages, which you access much like an eBook. Three pages of settings exist, which correspond to the following categories:

- Screen settings
- Annotations off/on
- Font settings

Screen settings consist of visual guides that help you navigate through eBooks in Reader. If you really want to streamline the user interface, you can turn them off, but I think they're worth keeping on. The Annotations settings enable you to turn off individual types of annotations. Unless you use tons of annotations and they get in the way, you probably won't need to change these settings. Finally, the Font settings enable you to alter the size of the font used to display eBooks. This is a very important setting that you should consider changing to suit your own unique viewing needs. I personally don't mind the default setting, which is the smallest font size, but if you have trouble reading small text then by all means change the setting.

→ One other setting that isn't directly related to Reader but that nonetheless impacts how it displays books is the brightness setting for your device's screen, which can impact how well you see text in Reader. For more information on how to adjust the brightness of the screen, **see** "Extending the Backlight and Power," **p. 79**.

CREATING YOUR OWN eBOOKS

The most common use of Microsoft Reader clearly is to read published works that you would otherwise read in printed form. However, another use of Reader exists that doesn't get as much attention—self-publishing! That's right, you can create your own eBooks for use with Reader. This could include creating eBooks of personal essays and poetry, or it could be something more practical such as business proposals and white papers you want to share with prospective clients. Technically, you could even sell your own eBooks from your own Web site and effectively become your own publisher.

The software required to create eBooks for Microsoft Reader is called ReaderWorks by OverDrive. The Standard edition of ReaderWorks is available for free download from the ReaderWorks Web site at http://www.readerworks.com/. The more advanced ReaderWorks Publisher software package is available for purchase from the same Web site, along with several other high-powered e-publishing packages. Assuming you've downloaded and installed the ReaderWorks application, let's examine what it takes to create an eBook that can be read in Reader on your Pocket PC.

The ReaderWorks application starts with a Quick Start window, which gives you options regarding how to start using the application. Accepting the default option of creating a Blank ReaderWorks Project is sufficient for creating most eBooks. Upon selecting this option, the ReaderWorks application opens with an empty project, as shown in Figure 22.15.

Figure 22.15
The ReaderWorks application initially opens and displays the source files for an empty project.

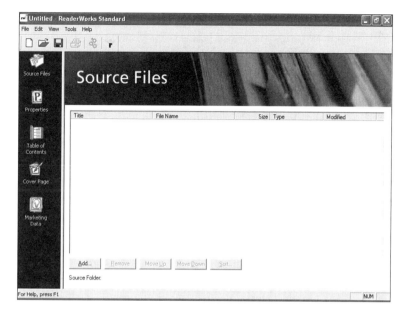

Source files in ReaderWorks are the original documents and resources that go into a finished eBook. Examples of source files include text documents, HTML documents, and image files. For the purposes of this example, I'm adding a single source file to the project by clicking the Add button located near the bottom of the window. You are then given a chance to browse and locate the file on your hard drive. After locating the source file, it is added to the source file list.

In addition to specifying source files that drive the content of eBooks, ReaderWorks enables you to alter specific aspects of an eBook. For example, clicking the Properties icon along the left side of the application window switches to a Properties view that enables you to edit properties of the eBook. The list of properties you can edit is extensive, but some of the ones you can edit include Title, Author, and Subject. Additional icons along the left side of the application window enable you to provide further details about an eBook by creating a table of contents, adding a cover page, and providing marketing data. Many of these detailed aspects of an eBook are editable only in the ReaderWorks Publisher edition, which is available for purchase from the ReaderWorks Web site.

To generate an eBook file (.lit file) in ReaderWorks, either click the Build eBook button (gear icon) in the application toolbar or select Build eBook from the File menu. Initiating the build process results in the display of the Build eBook Wizard, shown in Figure 22.16.

Figure 22.16
The ReaderWorks
Build eBook Wizard
steps you through the
process of creating an
eBook by first
prompting you for the
filename of the
eBook.

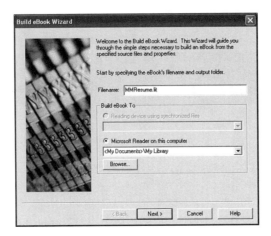

Although the Build eBook Wizard is implemented through a wizard user interface, the necessary information required to build the eBook is all gathered in the window shown in Figure 22.15. You must clarify the filename of the resulting eBook, along with the location in which the eBook is to be stored on your desktop computer. Clicking the Next button creates the eBook.

After creating an eBook, you must copy the .lit file from your desktop computer to your Pocket PC to view it in Reader. Figure 22.17 shows the cover page of my resume eBook as viewed in Microsoft Reader on a Pocket PC.

Figure 22.17
The cover page of a
custom resume eBook
that was created by
ReaderWorks.

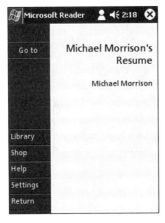

LISTENING TO AUDIBLE BOOKS

Although certainly not as popular as printed books, many books are available as audio books on tape or CD and are convenient for people who find listening easier than reading. Pocket

PART
VI
CH
22

PCs support a more advanced equivalent of audio books by allowing you to listen to eBooks using Reader. Reader supports audio eBooks, also known as *audible books*. One popular online retailer of audible books is Audible.com, which is located on the Web at http://www.audible.com/. Audible.com is an online bookstore for audible books in electronic form. In addition to books, however, Audible.com also offers audible versions of periodicals such as *The Wall Street Journal*, *Forbes*, and *Fast Company*. There is even a weekly comedy series by Robin Williams available. Audible.com offers an interesting range of audio content that expands the media appeal of Pocket PCs considerably.

INSTALLING THE AUDIBLE SOFTWARE

The first time you purchase an audible book from Audible.com, you must install a special desktop application for managing audible books. This free application is called AudibleManager, and it greatly simplifies the task of copying audible books to your Pocket PC. In addition to the desktop AudibleManager application, you must also download and install a free audible book player, AudiblePlayer, on your Pocket PC. Technically, you can listen to audible books using Windows Media Player, but the AudiblePlayer application is much better suited to listening to audible books.

The most important part of the AudibleManager/AudiblePlayer installation procedure is configuring the applications for use with your specific Pocket PC. Figure 22.18 shows the part of the AudibleManager setup routine that requires you to specify the type of general device you'll be using to listen to audible books.

Figure 22.18
The AudibleManager setup routine requires you to specify the type of general device you plan on using to listen to audible books.

You should select Pocket PC from the list of devices and then select the specific Pocket PC device in the next window that appears. From there, the installation of the AudibleManager and AudiblePlayer applications continues without you having to do anything but sit back and wait. AudibleManager is the software used on your desktop computer to manage and transfer audible books to your Pocket PC. The AudibleManager application should automatically launch when the installation finishes.

USING THE AUDIBLEMANAGER APPLICATION

The AudibleManager application includes a lot of functionality for managing audible books. It's somewhat beyond the scope of this chapter to delve into the details of the AudibleManager application. Instead, I want to focus on how to access audible books and transfer them to your Pocket PC. The main window in AudibleManager contains a list of the audible books stored on your desktop PC and initially contains a sample audible book that welcomes you to AudibleManager as well as any audible books you've already purchased. You can select a book and click the Play button on the toolbar to listen to it on your desktop PC. Figure 22.19 shows the AudibleManager application with a couple of audible books listed.

Caution

Because computer audio files can get fairly large, it's important to consider space issues on your Pocket PC before purchasing audible books for it. Audible books can easily weigh in at several megabytes (MB), with some exceeding 10MB.

Figure 22.19
The Ayn Rand audible book *Anthem* in AudibleManager is being copied to a Pocket PC for listening.

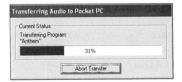

Note

Audible.com supports various audio quality levels—numbered 1, 2, 3, and 4—in order of increasing quality (and file size). When you download a book, you must specify in which quality you want the book.

You might notice in Figure 22.18 that one of the audible books is actually being transferred to a Pocket PC. More specifically, the book *Anthem* by Ayn Rand was purchased and downloaded from Audible.com, after which it became available in the AudibleManager application. Transferring the audible book to a Pocket PC is as simple as selecting the book in the list and clicking the Add to Pocket PC button on the AudibleManager toolbar. The progress window in Figure 22.18 details the progress of the file transfer. Keep in mind that the transfer can take some time because of the large size of most audible book files.

 If you find yourself with an enormous audible book that won't fit on your device, See "Minimizing the Size of Audible Books" in the "Troubleshooting" section at the end of the chapter for a simple solution to the problem.

LISTENING TO AN AUDIBLE BOOK WITH AUDIBLEPLAYER

When the file finishes transferring, you are ready to launch the AudiblePlayer application on your Pocket PC to listen to the audible book. To listen to the book, tap Programs on the

Start menu and then tap the AudiblePlayer icon. Figure 22.20 shows the Ayn Rand audible book *Anthem* opened in AudiblePlayer.

Figure 22.20
The Ayn Rand audible book *Anthem* opened in AudiblePlayer for listening.

Instead of the normal eBook options, you'll notice that AudiblePlayer includes controls more akin to Windows Media Player that are used to control the playback of the audible book. You can use various buttons to move forward and backward in the audible book, as well as pause and play the book. You can also create bookmarks, which are handy for returning to specific locations within an audible book.

TROUBLESHOOTING

PROBLEMS ACTIVATING READER

I have a Passport account, but the Pocket PC Activation Web page won't seem to let me activate my device.

This problem has to do with the fact that the Pocket PC Activation Web page doesn't respond well if you already have cookies stored on your computer that are related to Passport. The solution is to remove the offensive cookies, which can be tricky. To remove the problematic cookies in Internet Explorer, follow these steps:

1. Select Internet Options from the Tools menu.
2. Click the Settings button near the middle of the Internet Options dialog box.
3. Click the View Files button.
4. Select and delete each of the following files in the Explorer window that appears, where *YourName* is your full name:

   ■ *YourName*@passport.com
   ■ *YourName*@passporttest.com

- Cookie:*YourName*@das.microsoft.com/
- Cookie:*YourName*@passport.com/
- Cookie:*YourName*@passport.com/ppsecure

5. Close all browser windows, and then reopen Internet Explorer and try the activation procedure again at http://das.microsoft.com/activate/.

If you're using Netscape Navigator, follow these steps to solve the problem:

1. Close all browser windows.
2. Use Notepad to open the text file \Program Files\Netscape\Users*YourName*\ cookies.txt.
3. Delete all lines in the file that start with passport.com and das.microsoft.com.
4. Reopen Netscape Navigator and try the activation procedure again at http://das.microsoft.com/activate/.

Because tracking down all the offending cookies can be tedious, another solution is to delete all the cookies for your Web browser. Although this approach certainly works, it can be a hassle if you have lots of login information stored in cookies for Web sites you regularly visit.

MINIMIZING THE SIZE OF AUDIBLE BOOKS

I purchased and downloaded an audible book, but it takes up way too much memory on my device.

The audible books available from Audible.com can be downloaded in four audio quality levels; the higher the quality, the larger the resulting file. If your device doesn't have an exorbitant amount of expansion memory, I recommend starting out with the lowest-quality audio format when downloading audible books. You can always go back and get a higher-quality version if the low-quality version isn't acceptable to your ears.

REAL-WORLD EXAMPLE—DISSEMINATING BUSINESS DOCUMENTS

If you're part of a mobile workforce that uses Pocket PCs in everyday business, you're in a perfect position to take advantage of Reader. Reader is an ideal application for sharing business documents among a group of people who you might otherwise have trouble reaching with printed materials. For example, you could create a white paper for a new technology as a Reader eBook and then e-mail the eBook to every member of your sales team, even if they're all on the road. They can retrieve the attached eBook from the Inboxes on their Pocket PCs and then open it in Reader.

CHAPTER 23

MULTIMEDIA AND VIDEO IN YOUR POCKET

In this chapter

DIGITAL MULTIMEDIA CONTENT AND POCKET PCS

In addition to being very capable productivity tools, Pocket PCs are also surprisingly effective as entertainment devices. One of the most exciting features of Pocket PCs that arouses interest in even the most die-hard PDA purists is its support for playing digital music. With music available in digital form, you can move it around just like any other file on your computer and then listen to it on your Pocket PC using Windows Media Player. Windows Media Player, with its support of several digital music formats, effectively turns a Pocket PC into a high-tech Walkman, which adds significantly to its allure as a mobile computing device. As practical as it is to edit Word documents, check your e-mail, and enter financial transactions, kicking back and listening to music is a luxury many of us appreciate while traveling.

To use Windows Media Player as a digital Walkman, you must first download digital music files into your Pocket PC. You can also store digital music on memory storage cards, in which case you just insert a card to have the music available to Windows Media Player. You then have the option of either playing the music through the standard Pocket PC speaker or plugging headphones into the headphone jack. Windows Media Player makes listening to digital music using your Pocket PC easy. Except for the rugged construction of some traditional portable audio players, you're likely to find yourself using Windows Media Player and your Pocket PC as the primary means of listening to music on the go.

Tip from
Michael

The speaker on most Pocket PCs isn't quite adequate for playing high-quality audio, so you might want to use a pair of headphones if you're serious about your music.

Unlike a traditional Walkman, Windows Media Player is designed to support the playback of audio in several digital audio formats. I use the word "audio" instead of "music" because you can also use Windows Media Player to listen to sampled audio and voice recordings. Following are the types of digital multimedia formats supported by Windows Media Player:

- MP3 (MPEG Audio Layer 3)
- WAV (Waveform audio)
- Windows Media Audio
- Windows Media Video
- ASF Streaming Multimedia

You might have noticed that I sneaked a video format into this list of multimedia formats. This is significant because Windows Media Player is actually very adept at playing video. By supporting several audio and video formats, Windows Media Player is kind of like a portable Walkman that can play 8-track tapes, cassettes, CDs, mini-discs, and even DVDs. Because no such Walkman exists in the real world, in some ways you can think of a Pocket PC with Windows Media Player as the ultimate Walkman.

Before getting into the details of how to use Windows Media Player to play audio and video, it's worth taking a moment to learn a little more about the various multimedia formats. The next few sections examine each of the formats supported by Windows Media Player in more detail and provide you with some insight regarding their strengths and weaknesses.

MP3 AUDIO

PART
VI
CH
23

You are probably familiar with the first two types of digital audio. MP3 files have been greatly popularized as the standard format for digital music and form the basis of popular music-sharing applications such as LimeWire, Morpheus, and the one that started it all, Napster. MP3 is also the format used in Walkman-style digital audio (MP3) players, such as the Creative Labs Nomad players, Diamond Multimedia's RIO players, and Apple's innovative iPod. The popularity of MP3 is largely due to the fact that it compresses audio into more manageable file sizes than prior digital audio formats, such as WAV. When referring to the Pocket PC's capability to play digital music, you will often hear people refer to it as an "MP3 player" because MP3 is the digital music format with which most people are familiar.

WAV AUDIO

The WAV format is a digital audio format that has been around for quite a while and is known more for sampling sounds than for storing music. WAV is the standard audio format used in the Windows operating system. For example, all the Windows system sounds you hear while working within Windows are actually WAV sounds. The WAV format doesn't employ any type of compression to optimize file size and therefore is not very efficient at storing long pieces of audio. Nevertheless, it is still used frequently and serves as a convenient format for sharing short pieces of sampled audio, such as voice recordings.

WINDOWS MEDIA AUDIO AND VIDEO

Windows Media Audio and Video are relatively new multimedia formats created by Microsoft that are intended to provide a more efficient alternative to MP3 audio and MPEG video. Windows Media Audio uses a different compression scheme to further whittle down the size of digital audio files beyond the capabilities of MP3. Although MP3 is currently the industry standard for storing digital music, Windows Media Audio is steadily growing in popularity as users realize the benefits of its improved compression. Similarly, Windows Media Video is designed to provide better performance when storing and playing videos.

Note

Unlike the MP3 audio format, the Windows Media Audio format supports the Secure Digital Music Initiative (SDMI) and Digital Rights Management (DRM), both of which require you to have an electronic license to listen to a licensed audio file. DRM is designed to prevent the piracy of copyrighted audio.

If you've downloaded an audio or video file and are having trouble getting it to play in Windows Media Player on your device, it might be a licensed file that you haven't properly unlocked. See "Playing Licensed Multimedia Content" in the "Troubleshooting" section at the end of the chapter to find out how to play licensed audio and video.

ASF STREAMING MULTIMEDIA

ASF (Advanced Systems Format) is a multimedia format designed to support streaming multimedia, which typically involves a media object being transmitted over a network connection such as the Internet. The ASF format is particularly useful for listening to music or watching videos over an Internet connection, in which case the streaming benefits are very apparent. The streaming support in ASF enables music or video to begin playing before the entire file is transferred. This is an important feature for audio and video that is played over the Internet because it typically takes a little while for the relatively large files to transfer.

ASF is actually the underlying format used by Windows Media Audio and Video. However, I want to describe them separately because you will often see Microsoft make the distinction between Windows Media Audio files (.wma), Windows Media Video files (.wmv), and ASF files (.asf). The true distinction between these file types has to do with the underlying compression scheme (MP3, Windows Media Audio, and so on) used to shrink multimedia content into a smaller size. Because ASF enables you to stream a media object across a network connection, as opposed to waiting for the entire clip to download, both Windows Media Audio and Video have streaming capabilities.

WORKING WITH DIGITAL MULTIMEDIA CONTENT

Although multimedia content might seem a little mysterious given that it can involve audio, video, or a mixture of the two, it's important to understand that multimedia content is like any other data on your Pocket PC. More specifically, most multimedia content is stored as files you can copy and move around the same way you move other files, such as Pocket Word documents and Notes documents. I use the word "most" because some types of multimedia content you obtain directly through a network connection, in which case the content doesn't correspond to a local file. This kind of multimedia content is known as *streaming content* because it comes across a network connection as a steady stream of information. The significance of streaming content is that it doesn't require you to download a complete file before you can start experiencing it.

Streaming content is not only a convenience for experiencing multimedia content more quickly over a network, but it is also a necessity in some situations. For example, you can use Windows Media Player to listen to live Internet radio stations. Because a radio broadcast is a continuous broadcast, there is no way you could break it down into files for downloading without significant breakups in the transmission. This is an ideal application of streaming content because it enables you to receive the broadcast as a steady stream of audio data. It also eliminates the need to store a huge file on your device, which is a side benefit.

Of course, streaming content isn't the ideal solution for every multimedia problem. What if you want to use your device more as a traditional Walkman and listen to a few songs while waiting in an airport? Clearly, there needs to be some type of storage going on; otherwise, the songs wouldn't be readily available for listening. In this case, it makes more sense to store Windows Media Audio or MP3 files on your device and listen to them with Windows Media Player. When listening to a file in this scenario, no streaming is taking place because you're listening to the content directly from a file stored on your device.

The point I'm trying to make with this discussion is that Windows Media Player provides a high degree of flexibility when it comes to how you experience multimedia content. This flexibility ultimately boils down to the multimedia formats supported by Windows Media Player, which you learned about in the previous section. Let's take a moment to find out how to work with multimedia content in a few of these formats.

PART
VI
CH
23

COPYING MULTIMEDIA FILES WITH EXPLORER

The most straightforward way to work with multimedia content on your Pocket PC is to simply copy multimedia files from your desktop PC to your Pocket PC as if they were any other files. Because MP3 is such a widely used music format, your first experience with Windows Media Player might involve listening to MP3 music tracks on your device. Just copy the MP3 files over to your device, and you're ready to go. To transfer MP3 music files from your desktop PC to your Pocket PC, you must follow these steps:

1. Launch Explorer on your desktop PC, and navigate to the folder containing your MP3 music files.

2. Launch ActiveSync on your desktop PC, and click the Explore button to explore the My Documents folder of your device.

3. Select MP3 files on your desktop PC, and drag them to the My Documents folder on your device.

Keep in mind that you can also store multimedia files on a memory storage card, which helps free up your main system memory. Figure 23.1 shows an Explorer view of the My Documents folder on a memory storage card that now stores a few MP3 music files.

After the music files have been transferred to the My Documents folder on your device or storage card, you're ready to start listening to them in Windows Media Player. Although I've used MP3 as the media type for this example, you can copy multimedia files in any of the supported formats and they will be fully accessible to Windows Media Player. However, if you don't like the idea of using Explorer to move multimedia files between your desktop PC and Pocket PC, you can accomplish the same task using Windows Media Player on your desktop PC.

Figure 23.1
This memory storage card contains a few freshly copied MP3 music tracks, which are now available for playback on the Pocket PC.

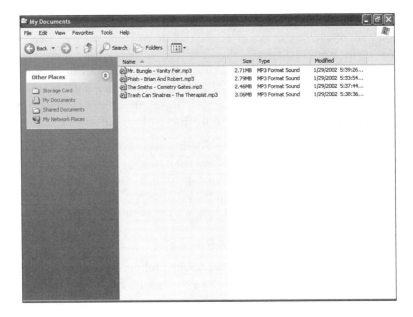

USING WINDOWS MEDIA PLAYER TO COPY MULTIMEDIA FILES

Windows Media Player for your desktop PC also supports the copying of multimedia files from a desktop PC to a Pocket PC. In fact, this approach to sharing multimedia content with your device is in many ways better than the last approach because Windows Media Player organizes your multimedia files according to a variety of parameters. For example, you can organize music according to genre, artist, or song title, to name a few options. This makes quickly finding tracks much easier, as opposed to sifting through a list of files in Explorer.

Caution

This discussion assumes that you're using Windows Media Player 8 or greater. It's important that you have version 8 or greater of Windows Media Player; otherwise, you might not have access to features mentioned in this section. You can download the latest version of Windows Media Player from Microsoft at `http://www.microsoft.com/windows/windowsmedia/players.asp`.

When copying multimedia files to your device, you need to determine exactly where you want the files to go. For example, memory storage cards serve as great locations to store digital music and videos because they often provide more storage than your main system memory, and they are removable, which means you could devote a storage card solely to music. Windows Media Player enables you to specify exactly where multimedia files are to be copied. It's generally a good idea to keep the files in the My Documents folder of the storage location you decide to use (main system memory, storage card, and so on).

To use Windows Media Player to share multimedia files with your Pocket PC, follow these steps:

1. Launch Windows Media Player on your desktop PC.
2. Click Copy to CD or Device on the left side of the Windows Media Player window.
3. In the left pane of Windows Media Player, navigate to the multimedia files you'd like to copy.
4. Click the check box next to each file you'd like to copy to your device.
5. In the right pane of Windows Media Player, click the drop-down list below Music on Device and select your device or storage card in the list of options.
6. Click the My Documents folder on the device or storage card.
7. Click Copy Music in the upper-right corner of the window to copy the multimedia files.

PART

VI

CH

23

 If you're having trouble accessing your Pocket PC from within Windows Media Player on your desktop PC, see "Getting the Desktop Windows Media Player to Recognize Your Device" in the "Troubleshooting" section at the end of the chapter for a simple solution.

Figure 23.2 shows two Windows Media Audio files being copied between Windows Media Player on a desktop PC and a memory storage card on a Pocket PC.

Figure 23.2
The desktop Windows Media Player makes copying music tracks and other multimedia files to a Pocket PC easy—you just check off each file and wait for it to copy.

To verify that the Windows Media Audio files were copied over properly, you can always view the storage card again in Explorer (see Figure 23.3).

Figure 23.3
The two new
Windows Media
Audio files now
appear on the storage
card when viewed in
Explorer.

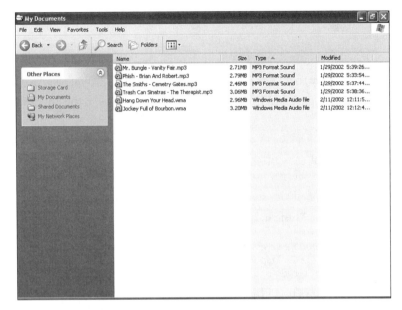

Note

You might be wondering at this point how to access streaming multimedia content over a network. Because this doesn't involve copying files, you have to use Windows Media Player on your device to connect to a specific Web site and access the streaming content. You learn exactly how to do this a little later in the chapter, in the section titled "Playing Streaming Multimedia Content."

TAKING ADVANTAGE OF PLAYLISTS IN WINDOWS MEDIA PLAYER

You now have a pretty good understanding of how to get multimedia files onto your device for listening and viewing with Windows Media Player. Believe it or not, that was the hard part—playing multimedia content in Windows Media Player on your device is not only easy, but also pretty fun. As you know, Windows Media Player is a standard Pocket PC application built into system ROM. It has a user interface that should be familiar to anyone who has used a CD player or VCR. To run Windows Media Player, tap Windows Media in the Start menu. If you've placed any audio files in the My Documents folder on the device or on a memory storage card, one of them will appear as the currently selected track in Windows Media Player upon it being launched. Figure 23.4 shows the music track "Vanity Fair" as the selected track in Windows Media Player.

Figure 23.4
The Windows Media Player user interface has a feel reminiscent of a CD player, with familiar buttons for Play, Stop, Pause, and so on.

The user interface in Windows Media Player consists of the name of the currently selected track near the top of the screen. Below that is the main Windows Media Player window, followed by the status of the player. Below that is a timeline of the current track as it is being played. You can tap and hold the circular control on this timeline and drag it to move around within a track. The buttons along the bottom of the screen perform familiar media control functions such as Play, Stop, Next Track, and Previous Track; to the right of these buttons is a sliding volume control. You can use these buttons at any time to play, pause, stop, and otherwise control the currently selected audio or video content.

Tip from
Michael

If you get serious about using your Pocket PC as a music player, you might want to consider using a special device called SoundFeeder, which enables you to wirelessly transmit the audio output of your Pocket PC to a radio frequency. SoundFeeder is manufactured by a company called Arkon and can be found online at `http://www.arkon.com/sf.html`. Using SoundFeeder, you can transmit audio from your Pocket PC to any stereo with an FM receiver, including a car stereo!

The Tools menu includes a Properties command that enables you to view additional information about the currently selected track. This results in the display of the Properties window, which is shown in Figure 23.5.

The Select command that appears next to the Tools menu displays the Windows Media Player Playlist, which is a listing of the tracks currently queued for play (see Figure 23.6). You can create multiple playlists that include different songs arranged in a specific order. The default playlist is Local Content, which includes all the songs stored on your device. Technically, Local Content isn't a playlist that you can edit and modify like other playlists—it's just a way of providing a view of all multimedia content available for playback on your device.

Figure 23.5
The Properties window displays additional information about the currently selected audio track including the title, album, artist, and storage location, among other information.

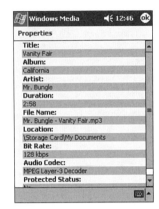

Note

The Playlist automatically updates whenever you add new multimedia content to your device. This includes plugging in a memory storage card that has audio or video stored on it—the content on the storage card is combined with the content already stored on the device.

Figure 23.6
The Playlist screen in Windows Media Player displays the currently active playlist, which is Local Content by default.

You add and modify playlists by tapping the name of the current playlist and then tapping Organize Playlists from the menu that appears. You also use this menu to choose between playlists when you have more than one. Selecting Organize Playlists from the menu reveals the Organize Playlists screen, which enables you to create and manage playlists. To create a new playlist, just tap the New button on the Organize Playlists screen. You are then prompted to enter the name of the playlist, as shown in Figure 23.7.

After entering the name of the new playlist, you are then given the chance to select which audio and video files you want to include in the playlist (see Figure 23.8).

Figure 23.7
The first step in creating a new playlist is to enter its name, which can be as descriptive as you want.

Figure 23.8
Selecting audio and video files for inclusion in a playlist simply involves checking them off a list.

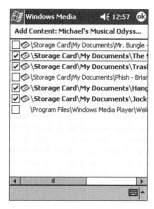

After you've confirmed your playlist selections and tapped OK, the new playlist appears in Windows Media Player in place of the previous Local Content playlist. Notice in Figure 23.9 that Michael's Musical Odyssey consists of the four audio tracks that were selected in Figure 23.8.

Figure 23.9
Playlists appear in the main Windows Media Player window where they provide a means of playing an exclusive list of content.

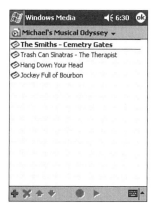

In Figure 23.9, you'll notice that a toolbar appears along the bottom of the screen that enables you to manipulate content in the list; this is how you modify an existing playlist. The Add Content button (the plus sign) is used to add content to the currently selected playlist, whereas the Remove Content button (the red X) is used to remove content from the list. The Move buttons, which are represented by up and down arrows, are used to move content up and down to change the order of the playlist. Finally, the Play button is used to play the currently selected content.

PLAYING STREAMING MULTIMEDIA CONTENT

As you learned earlier in the chapter, streaming content is content that is delivered as a stream of data over a network connection. Given the wireless capabilities of Pocket PCs, streaming multimedia content will likely emerge as one of the killer applications for Pocket PCs because it enables you to listen to live Internet radio and watch streaming videos. Bandwidth is really the only limitation when it comes to the streaming capabilities of Pocket PCs. If you can get a fast enough wireless network connection, there's no reason you can't watch streaming television on your device.

ACCESSING STREAMING CONTENT WITH POCKET INTERNET EXPLORER

The key to accessing streaming content on Pocket PCs is the relationship between Windows Media Player and Pocket Internet Explorer. Windows Media Player has limited features for navigating to find streaming content, which is why Pocket Internet Explorer is so important. Fortunately, the two applications are designed to work together to solve this very problem. Knowing this, you'll often use Pocket Internet Explorer to find streaming content and then use Windows Media Player to view or listen to it.

The best place to start when it comes to streaming content is Microsoft's Windows Media Web site, which is located at `http://www.windowsmedia.com/`. Figure 23.10 shows Pocket Internet Explorer tuned to the Windows Media Web site.

Figure 23.10
Microsoft's Windows Media Web site is the best place to start for finding streaming content to play on your device.

As you can see, the Windows Media Web site has recommendations on the home page and has sections devoted to Radio and Video. Figure 23.11 shows the Radio section of the Web site, which provides access to several Internet radio broadcasts.

Figure 23.11
The Radio section of the Windows Media Web site provides access to several Internet radio broadcasts you can listen to on your device.

Following a link to a live radio broadcast results in the radio content being streamed through Windows Media Player. Although the content you hear is digital audio, the effect is that of listening to a radio station on a traditional stereo. Figure 23.12 shows National Public Radio (NPR) News being played in Windows Media Player, even though there isn't much identifiable about NPR in the figure.

Figure 23.12
Catching up on the latest news is easy when you use Windows Media Player to listen to up-to-the-minute radio news.

 If Windows Media Player is having trouble accessing streaming content, you might need to tweak its network settings to accommodate your specific network connection. See "Accessing Streaming Content with Windows Media Player" in the "Troubleshooting" section at the end of the chapter for more information on changing network settings in Windows Media Player.

Not all the links in the Radio section of the Windows Media Web site link to pure audio content, however. For example, the MSNBC News link leads to a streaming video clip of the latest news stories. In addition, a Video section of the Web site offers numerous streaming video clips for you to try. Figure 23.13 shows a news video clip being played in Windows Media Player.

Figure 23.13
If you prefer news with video images, you can use Windows Media Player to play video news updates.

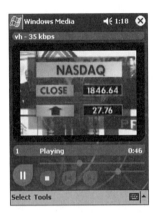

Depending on the speed of your network connection, video clips can offer a more immersive experience than a purely audio radio broadcast. However, most video clips aren't continuous feeds, unlike live radio broadcasts.

ADDING WEB FAVORITES IN WINDOWS MEDIA PLAYER

If you've played around with Windows Media Player much, you might have noticed that it has an Add Web Favorite command on the Tools menu. This command is used to store links to streaming content on the Internet so you can easily access them later; it's basically the Windows Media Player equivalent of Pocket Internet Explorer's Web site Favorites. To add a favorite to Windows Media Player, just select Add Web Favorite from the Tools menu. After adding the favorite media link, you can access it as a playlist from within Windows Media Player. Figure 23.14 shows the various playlists set up on my device, two of which are links to streaming media content (NPR Hourly News and MSNBC News).

You can organize and manipulate streaming media playlists just as you would with custom playlists that link to local multimedia files. Of course, most streaming Internet playlists consist of only one media object, especially if the object represents a live feed such as a radio station. The nice thing about handling streaming media content as playlists is that it enables them to integrate directly into the framework of Windows Media Player. In other words, you can manage local content and streaming Internet content without too much regard for where they are physically located.

Figure 23.14
Playlists in Windows Media Player enable you to manage local content and streaming Internet content without regard for where they are physically located.

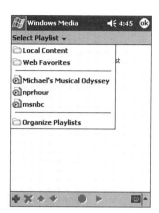

PART

VI

CH

23

CUSTOMIZING WINDOWS MEDIA PLAYER

Like most Pocket PC applications, Windows Media Player can be customized for your individual tastes. One personalization technique enables you to alter the look and feel of the user interface. This is accomplished through special graphical looks called *skins*. Windows Media Player skins are roughly similar to the schemes used to alter the look of the Windows desktop. However, skins go a bit further by actually altering the number and positions of buttons in the Windows Media Player user interface.

Another customization technique for Windows Media Player involves assigning functions to your device's hardware buttons. For example, you might assign the Play and Pause functions to the up and down motion of the Action button. These button mappings apply as long as Windows Media Player is active in memory.

The next couple of sections explore Windows Media Player personalization using both skins and hardware button mapping.

SKINNING WINDOWS MEDIA PLAYER

Skins are special "looks" that can be applied to Windows Media Player to give it a different look and feel. They are a great way to personalize your Pocket PC and are freely available for download from Microsoft's Windows Media Web site. A skin consists of a group of bitmap files and a text file with a .skn file extension that includes organizational information about the skin. Because skins consist of multiple files that are named similarly, you should place each skin in its own folder to keep them separated. You can download skins from Microsoft's Windows Media Player for Pocket PC Web page at `http://www.microsoft.com/windows/windowsmedia/download/pocket.asp`. Each skin is packaged in a self-extracting Zip file. When you extract a skin, allow it to unzip to the folder it suggests because you will copy this entire folder directly to your Pocket PC.

To install a skin on your Pocket PC, copy the skin folder from your desktop PC to the Windows Media Player folder on your device; this folder is named `Program Files\Windows Media Player`. To copy the skin folder, you can use the Explore feature in ActiveSync to navigate to the Windows Media Player folder and then copy the skin folder over from your desktop PC. After the skin folder is copied, you can set the skin in Windows Media Player using the Skin Chooser. To select a skin with the Skin Chooser, tap Settings in the Tools menu, followed by Skin Chooser. Figure 23.15 shows the Skin Chooser in action.

Figure 23.15
The new skin Silver is selected in the Skin Chooser, which will make it the skin used by Windows Media Player.

After selecting a new skin, the look of Windows Media Player immediately changes to reflect the newly selected skin. Figure 23.16 shows how the Silver skin impacts the look of Windows Media Player.

Figure 23.16
The Silver skin changes the look of Windows Media Player.

As you can see, skins change not only the graphical look of Windows Media Player, but also the size and location of the buttons and track information. Some skins have an overly simplified look and feel, which might not seem appealing at first, whereas other skins rely on the use of complex graphics.

Tip from
Michael

Another customization option for Windows Media Player involves the manner in which video is played back. If you aren't satisfied with the size of video displayed in Windows Media Player, you can choose to have video played in full screen. Additionally, you can even specify that video is to be rotated and viewed in landscape mode where you hold your device sideways; this is a great option for movies, which are typically much wider than they are tall. Landscape mode roughly corresponds to the shape of a television screen, which is the size of most video clips. To set either of these options, tap Settings in the Tools menu of Windows Media Player, followed by Audio & Video.

CUSTOMIZING HARDWARE BUTTONS

Another neat Windows Media Player customization is mapping hardware buttons to Windows Media Player functions. You perform this mapping by tapping Settings in the Tools menu of Windows Media Player, followed by Buttons. This displays the Button Mapping screen, which is shown in Figure 23.17.

Figure 23.17
The Button Mapping screen enables you to map Windows Media Player functions to Pocket PC hardware buttons, which can dramatically improve the usability of Windows Media Player.

Figure 23.17 shows the hardware buttons and combinations to which you can associate Windows Media Player functions. Following are the functions available for the associations:

- Play/Pause
- Play
- Pause
- Stop
- Next Track
- Previous Track
- Mute
- Volume Up
- Volume Down
- Screen Toggle

To map a function to a button, select the function in the drop-down list and then press the desired button on the device. The Button Mapping list in the Options window reflects the mapping. To unmap a button, tap and hold over the button in the list and then tap Unmap This Button.

Note

Button mappings created within a specific application, such as Windows Media Player, override device-wide button mappings as long as the application is in memory. After the application closes, the mappings return to their normal functions. Device-wide button mappings are created and modified by tapping Settings in the Start menu and then tapping the Buttons icon. Button mappings made on this screen apply to the entire system, not just a specific application.

Button mappings are very personal and will likely vary a great deal among different people. A few mappings I suggest are to map the Volume Up and Volume Down functions to the Up and Down buttons, which correspond to rotating the Action button up and down. One other useful mapping is to map the Screen Toggle function with the Action button. The Screen Toggle function turns off your device's screen, which helps conserve battery life. After all, you don't necessarily need the screen on while you're listening to music.

GETTING SERIOUS WITH POCKET PC VIDEO

At this point in the book, you certainly realize that a Pocket PC is capable of many things right out of the box, but you might be surprised to find out that besides excelling at digital video playback, it also excels at digital video recording. It really isn't too much of a leap when you consider that a Pocket PC has a great viewfinder (screen) and a lot of storage options (memory)—two requirements of any decent digital camera. All that's missing is the actual camera hardware, which can be placed conveniently on an expansion card. It's pretty amazing, but you can get a digital camera card that plugs into your Pocket PC and enables you to take digital pictures and record short videos.

CAPTURING DIGITAL VIDEO

Turning your Pocket PC into a digital camera is as simple as purchasing a special PC or CF card that includes camera hardware. Several manufacturers are now making such camera cards, but Casio gets credit for being the first. The Casio camera card is a CF card that slides into the top of your Pocket PC using the CF slot. The camera lens rests on top of the device and can be rotated to shoot forward or backward. The Casio camera card uses a 350,000-pixel CCD with a focal range of 30.7" in Normal mode and 3.9" in Macro mode. The camera supports the JPEG file format for still images and Casio's CMF file format for short videos. The camera card relies on the Pocket PC's main system battery for power and puts a considerable drain on it. You should expect your battery life to drop sharply while using the camera.

Caution

The Casio CF camera card currently works only with Casio Pocket PCs. Fortunately, other manufacturers are quickly entering the marketplace with camera cards for other devices. For example, HP currently offers a camera card for its Jornada line of Pocket PCs.

→ For more information about digital camera cards for your Pocket PC, **see** "Digital Camera Cards," **p. 486**.

Note

The CMF file format is based on the popular MPEG1 video format. You can view CMF videos on your desktop PC by using Casio's Mobile Video Player application. Casio offers utilities for converting from popular video formats into the CMF format, but currently there is no way to convert from CMF to another format.

Although the Casio digital camera card is admittedly much more suited to taking still digital photographs than it is capturing digital video, it nonetheless demonstrates the fact that Pocket PCs are highly capable of capturing digital video. I'm not so sure you can count on this accessory to replace your video camera just yet, but the seed has been planted for manufacturers to consider the prospects of video capture with Pocket PCs. Because you probably won't rely solely on your Pocket PC to create videos, it's worth exploring what can be done in terms of acquiring and watching videos other than streaming videos. The next section tackles this challenge.

WATCHING VIDEOS IN OTHER FORMATS

Earlier in the chapter you learned about the video capabilities of Windows Media Player and how it can be used to view streaming video content over a wireless network connection. I want to clarify that streaming video content doesn't represent the only option to viewing video in Windows Media Player. You also can download or copy video files onto your Pocket PC and play them back just as you play back MP3 or Windows Media Audio music tracks. This approach makes more sense for certain types of video, especially movies. Of course, the video files must be in a format supported by Windows Media Player, which basically means Windows Media Video or ASF.

You will often run into video files that aren't in the Windows Media Video or ASF formats, in which case you must rely on specialized media players. One such media player is the ActiveSky Media Player, which plays videos in the proprietary SKY format. Even though the ActiveSky player supports only a proprietary video format, several content providers offer interesting video content in the SKY format. One of these content providers is Atom Films (http://www.atomfilms.com/), which is a Web-based film house that offers short films and animations for download. Content is the name of the game when it comes to media players, so I recommend checking into the available content for each player when deciding which one to use.

Another popular media player for both desktop PCs and Pocket PCs is the Macromedia Flash Player, which enables you to watch Flash animations. Macromedia offers a Flash player for Pocket PC, which is available for free download at `http://www.macromedia.com/shockwave/download/alternates/`. A great deal of Flash content is available for download, and the great thing is that it doesn't take up much space. The previously mentioned Atom Films Web site contains lots of really interesting Flash movies you can download and carry around for viewing on your device.

Tip from *Michael*	Because of the relatively large size of most videos, you should store them on a memory storage card if you have one. Just be sure to create a My Documents folder on the card if it doesn't already exist, and then place the video in it.

TROUBLESHOOTING

PLAYING LICENSED MULTIMEDIA CONTENT

I purchased and downloaded a digital music file, and I can't get it to play in Windows Media Player on my device.

If you have trouble with a particular music or video file you've downloaded, the file is probably licensed. *Licensed content* is copyrighted content distributed in a locked form, and it requires an electronic license to be unlocked and played. Prior to being unlocked, licensed content is encrypted so that you can't play it. When you purchase licensed content, you are actually purchasing a license to play the content. The licensing aspect of licensed content is involved when you first purchase the content. You must use the license to unlock the content file, after which you can play the content as frequently as you want without ever having to hassle with the license again. After you've gone through the licensing process, working with licensed content is no different from working with unlicensed content.

The Windows Media Audio and Video formats support *digital rights management (DRM)*, which means you might have to obtain an electronic license before being able to play the content. This license should have been provided when you first purchased and downloaded the content. Windows Media Player fully supports licensed content, so you shouldn't have any problems after you properly obtain an electronic license for a multimedia file.

GETTING THE DESKTOP WINDOWS MEDIA PLAYER TO RECOGNIZE YOUR DEVICE

I'm trying to share multimedia content between my desktop PC and Pocket PC using Windows Media Player on my desktop PC. However, Windows Media Player on my desktop PC won't recognize my device.

The desktop Windows Media Player application doesn't always detect your device when you connect it to your desktop PC. The problem reveals itself when you try to share multimedia content between your desktop PC and Pocket PC. You should be able to view your device in the Music on Device drop-down list in Windows Media Player, but it doesn't always show up. The simple fix for this problem is to click the Music on Device drop-down list and then press the F5 key on your desktop keyboard, which forces Windows Media Player to look for devices. As long as your device is connected to your desktop PC and visible to ActiveSync, it should appear in the list and you can start sharing content between it and your desktop PC.

ACCESSING STREAMING CONTENT WITH WINDOWS MEDIA PLAYER

I keep trying to access streaming content over a network connection with Windows Media Player, but it complains that it can't access the content.

You need to double-check the network requirements of your specific connection to ensure that you are connecting properly. This primarily includes any proxy settings required for the network. Keep in mind that wireless network connections aren't always the most stable connections, so you might encounter legitimate connection problems even if your network settings are properly configured. Just be sure to try accessing streaming content a few times before you go changing network settings. If you determine that you do need to tweak the network settings for Windows Media Player, you can do so by tapping Settings in the Tools menu, followed by Network.

REAL-WORLD EXAMPLE—KEEPING TABS ON THE WORLD

One of the most compelling benefits of Windows Media Player is the ability to couple its streaming video capabilities with the wireless Internet. This combination of technologies enables you to keep up with world affairs and critical world events even if you aren't near a television. As an example of how this could have been extremely useful, my wife was traveling during the September 11th terrorist attacks and didn't have access to a television to find out any specifics about was going on. Because newspapers couldn't help her in terms of delivering up-to-the-minute news, she could have benefited from using Windows Media Player on a Pocket PC to tune in and watch wireless video feeds of what was going on.

CHAPTER **24**

PLAYING AROUND ON YOUR POCKET PC

In this chapter

POCKET PC: A GLORIFIED GAME BOY?

When you consider the advanced hardware and bundled productivity software that comes standard with Pocket PCs, you probably don't think too much about the capabilities of the devices as mobile gaming machines. However, Pocket PCs are ideally suited to run mobile games that you might otherwise play on a portable game system such as a Nintendo Game Boy Advance. Granted, the Pocket PC operating system includes Solitaire, which can certainly help kill time while waiting in a dentist's office, but some incredibly slick games are available for Pocket PC that will force you to view it in a different way. In fact, several popular desktop PC games have been ported over to Pocket PC, with many others on the way.

Nintendo's Game Boy Advance is the hands-down market leader when it comes to portable video game systems. Some pretty interesting and exciting games are available for the Game Boy Advance, which helps to explain its success. However, you might be surprised to learn about the hardware that goes into these devices. More importantly, it might come as a surprise to find out how much more powerful the hardware in a Pocket PC is when compared to Game Boy Advance hardware. To understand what I'm talking about, consider the basic technical details of the Game Boy Advance:

- **Processor**—32-bit ARM running at 16MHz
- **RAM**—256KB
- **Screen**—240×160 with 32,768 colors

If you recall the technical specifics of Pocket PCs, you probably see where I'm headed with this. If not, take a look at a similar list of technical details for the popular Compaq iPAQ H3800 series Pocket PC:

- **Processor**—32-bit Strong ARM running at 206MHz
- **RAM**—64MB (that's megabytes, not kilobytes!)
- **Screen**—240×320 with 65,536 colors

As you can see, comparing the technical capabilities of a Pocket PC with that of a Game Boy Advance is way past the apples and oranges analogy. These are two very different machines that admittedly are designed for different purposes. Or, so we think. Why should a device with the technical capability to serve as a killer portable game machine not be exploited as such? The truth is Pocket PCs have more than enough horsepower to be a dominant portable game platform. However, a few obstacles must be overcome before Pocket PCs gain any appeal as pure gaming machines. The primary problem is price— Pocket PCs are still three or four times the upper limit the average consumer would be willing to pay for a portable game device. In addition to being much more expensive than pure portable game machines such as the Game Boy, game developers have only recently started taking the Pocket PC seriously as a target platform for modern games. However, in the past year we've finally seen some popular desktop games ported to Pocket PC, so perceptions are definitely changing.

The remainder of this chapter is devoted to painting a clear picture of the Pocket PC game industry. In addition to learning about the various games available, you also gain some insight into the companies that are developing the games. Pocket PC gaming is still in an evolutionary phase in which game developers are experimenting with the possibilities of what can be done on a mobile device with wireless network access. It's quite likely that entirely new types of games will eventually emerge as developers and players alike figure out how to make the most of Pocket PC technology. Pocket PCs might have a ways to go to give Nintendo a run for its money, but it will be fun to watch the Pocket PC platform grow as a serious base for gaming.

Note

If you finish this chapter and decide that you haven't learned enough about Pocket PC games, or if you'd just like to have another resource for learning about Pocket PC gaming in general, I encourage you to visit the Pocket Gamer Web site at `http://www.pocketgamer.org/`. There you'll find game reviews, discussion boards, press releases for new games, and links to other game Web sites.

PART
VI

CH
24

MAKING THE MOST OF FREEBIES

Quite a few commercial games are on the market that you can purchase online or buy at a retail store. However, why would you want to buy a game when some really fun free games are available? The truth is you will probably still want to buy a few games because some amazing games are available for the Pocket PC. However, before you run out and spend a bunch of money on games, I encourage you to try a few free games and see whether you like them. Following are a few free games I've found that I can safely recommend:

- Solitaire
- Cubicle Chaos
- TankZone 2000
- Sega Virtual Game Gear

Okay, I know, Solitaire came with your Pocket PC so it's not really fair to call it a free game. On the other hand, I couldn't help but mention it because Solitaire is jokingly considered one of the primary applications that made the Microsoft Windows operating system so successful. If it was possible to chart how many lost hours of productivity Solitaire has caused in offices around the world, the toll would be staggering. Now mobile slackers of the world can rejoice in having Solitaire on their Pocket PCs.

Tip from
Michael

Anyone who has played Solitaire can attest to the fact that it is quite addictive. If you find yourself in a rut where you simply cannot win, you might find this tip uplifting. Launch Solitaire and then invoke the soft keyboard in the Input Panel. On the soft keyboard tap the Control key, tap the Shift key, and then tap New near the bottom of the screen in Solitaire to start a new game. You will be dealt a "perfect" hand of Solitaire that has the cards grouped so you can easily win!

The other three games I listed are not included on your Pocket PC, but they are available for free download on the Web. The next few sections introduce you to these games and guide you to the Web sites where you can download them. Before you download and install a bunch of games on your device, you need to understand that every application installed on your Pocket PC (including games) takes up valuable memory, so be careful to ensure that you plan on using any applications you install. In regard to games, this means that you should make sure you really plan on playing a game before wasting memory on it. Of course, you can always install a game and remove it later if you don't like it or if you get tired of it.

 If you find your device running noticeably more slowly after playing certain games, see "Combating Device Slowdown from Games" in the "Troubleshooting" section at the end of the chapter.

CUBICLE CHAOS

Next to Pong, one of the original classic home video games that comes to mind for most people is Breakout. Breakout is a game that involves a row of bricks across the top of the screen and a small bar on the bottom of the screen. You control the bar and use it to keep a ball bouncing up and down around the screen. Each time the ball hits a brick the brick is destroyed; the object is to eventually clear all the bricks. You lose when you miss the ball with the bar and it falls off the bottom of the screen. The game gets more difficult with each new level as the bricks lower and the ball moves more quickly.

Cubicle Chaos is a contemporary remake of Breakout that uses an office metaphor instead of bricks, bars, and balls. The premise of this game is that you fling balls at fellow co-workers in an attempt to collapse their cubicles. Having personally witnessed a co-worker getting beaned in the head with a Koosh ball at a previous job, I can certainly appreciate the premise of this game. In Cubicle Chaos, you sit at your desk along the bottom of the screen (the bar) and slide back and forth deflecting the bouncing ball. Your co-workers sit at their desks (the bricks) in various cubicle formations around the screen. The object of the game is to hit your co-workers and rid the office of them and their cubes. You can download Cubicle Chaos for free from Microsoft at `http://www.microsoft.com/mobile/pocketpc/downloads/cubiclechaos.asp`.

> **Note**
>
> Cubicle Chaos is also included in Microsoft's Games PocketPak, which you learn about in the section "Games PocketPak," later in the chapter.

Figure 24.1 shows the bouncing ball at work destroying fellow employees and their cubicles in Cubicle Chaos.

You control the desk-roving employee in Cubicle Chaos by tapping and dragging the stylus back and forth across the screen. Your only goal is to keep the bouncing ball alive by constantly deflecting it with the employee and his desk. Various items will fall on occasion when you destroy a fellow employee's desk; some of these items give you extra powers, whereas some of them cause strange things to take place that hinder you. All the effects brought on by falling items are temporary.

Figure 24.1
The Cubicle Chaos game in action.

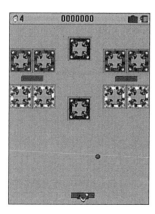

TANKZONE 2000

Another classic video game is Battlezone, which was a very popular arcade game and is still highly regarded among arcade collectors. The original Battlezone game was a vector game, which means its graphics consisted of lines as opposed to individual pixels on the screen. Battlezone was a first-person tank game where you drove your tank around and attempted to blow up other tanks without getting blown up yourself. TankZone 2000 is a Pocket PC take-off of the original Battlezone game that was developed by Stellar Metrics, the maker of several Pocket PC productivity applications. TankZone 2000 is available for free download from Stellar Metrics at http://www.stellarmetrics.com/Software/tankzone.htm.

Figure 24.2 shows a game of TankZone 2000 with an enemy tank targeted for attack.

Figure 24.2
TankZone 2000 is a take-off on the classic vector tank battle game Battlezone.

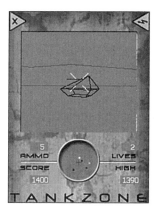

SEGA VIRTUAL GAME GEAR

Earlier in the chapter I compared Pocket PCs to the Game Boy Advance portable game system. Although the Game Boy and Game Boy Advance systems have dominated the portable game market for years, other systems have given them competition. One of these systems was Sega's Game Gear, which is basically a portable version of the once popular Sega

Master System home video game system. If your memory is fuzzy on the Sega home video game system, it was made popular by the game Sonic the Hedgehog, which was Sega's answer to Nintendo's immensely popular Super Mario Brothers games. Although Sonic the Hedgehog has diminished significantly in popularity since Sega's heyday, it is still a memorable game that has its place in video game history.

The question you're probably asking is what does this history lesson of Sega video games have to do with Pocket PCs? The answer is that a software company called Synovial created a Sega Game Gear emulator named Virtual Game Gear that runs on Pocket PCs. An *emulator* is a software application that simulates a hardware device, which in this case is a portable game device. What this means for you and me is that we can play games originally made for the Sega Game Gear system on our Pocket PCs. Because Virtual Game Gear exactly simulates the hardware in a Game Gear, you literally run the exact same game code on your Pocket PC that was stored on Game Gear game cartridges.

Although it might be exciting to think about playing Sega games on your Pocket PC, there is a catch with Virtual Game Gear in that it isn't officially available for purchase. Synovial worked out a deal with Compaq to ship Virtual Game Gear on the CD-ROM accompanying iPAQ H3800 series Pocket PCs, but beyond that there is currently no way to get your hands on the Virtual Game Gear software. This is unfortunate because it really is a unique piece of software that gives you the capability of playing some interesting games. I included mention of Virtual Game Gear in this freebies section because, if you own an iPAQ H3800 series Pocket PC, you have free access to Virtual Game Gear on the CD-ROM that came with the device.

The following games are included with the Virtual Game Gear application:

■ Sonic the Hedgehog

■ Sega 4-in-1

■ Baku Baku

Sonic the Hedgehog is obviously the most significant of these games because it enjoyed such commercial success in its original release. Figure 24.3 shows Sonic the Hedgehog being played on a Pocket PC through the Virtual Game Gear emulator.

Figure 24.3
Sega's classic action game Sonic the Hedgehog can be played on your Pocket PC thanks to the Virtual Game Gear emulator.

Synovial is expected to release additional games that you can purchase and play on the Virtual Game Gear emulator. For now, the three games that come with the emulator are a good start.

MICROSOFT'S TAKE ON POCKET GAMING

Even prior to the release of Microsoft's Xbox home video game system, Microsoft had shown a strong interest in being a player in the computer and video game marketplace. Microsoft has developed, licensed, and published several bestselling computer games, and with the Xbox it is now a serious console game contender. Knowing this, it shouldn't come as too much of a surprise to find out that Microsoft is also pushing the Pocket PC operating system as a realistic gaming platform. In fact, Microsoft is currently one of the leading developers of Pocket PC games, with no less than three bundled game packs:

PART
VI
CH
24

- Entertainment PocketPak
- Games PocketPak
- Arcade PocketPak

These three game packs include a wide variety of Pocket PC games ranging from traditional card and tile games to take-offs on familiar video game classics to exact remakes of classic arcade games. The next few sections examine these game packs and show you exactly which games Microsoft has to offer.

ENTERTAINMENT POCKETPAK

Microsoft's Entertainment PocketPak is a bundle of Pocket PC games that lean more toward card games and turn-based strategy games. Most of these games rely on little or no animation and are primarily designed so that they can be played quickly. Following are the games that are included in the Entertainment PocketPak:

- Blackjack
- Chess
- Cinco
- Freecell
- Hearts
- Minesweeper
- Reversi
- Sink The Ships
- Space Defense
- Taipei

You probably recognize most of these games because virtually all of them are recreations or take-offs of classic games. One of my favorite games in the bunch is Hearts, which is a deceptively tricky card game that you might have played on a desktop PC. Hearts is my favorite computer card game because it is so much fun trying to pull one over on the other players. The Pocket PC version of Hearts is just as much fun and even supports two human players via an infrared connection between devices. Figure 24.4 shows a game of Hearts between a human player (Todd) and four computer players.

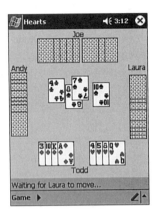

Figure 24.4
This game of Hearts involves a human player (Todd) and four computer players.

If you want something more traditional than Hearts, there is always Chess, which is a game that needs no introduction. The Pocket PC version of Chess enables you to play against the computer or against another human player. However, unlike Hearts, you don't play against another player with two devices connected via infrared. Instead, you just share the same device and take turns making moves. Admittedly, this is more cumbersome than the infrared approach, but it does alleviate the need for two devices. Figure 24.5 shows the early stages of a game of Chess.

Figure 24.5
This game of Chess is still in its early stages.

Other games in the Entertainment PocketPak that deserve an honorable mention are Sink The Ships and Space Defense. Sink The Ships is a take-off on the traditional Battleship game in which you attempt to sink your opponent's ships by firing torpedoes on a grid. Space Defense is a take-off on the classic Missile Command arcade game that graced many arcades in the early 1980s.

To learn more about Microsoft's Entertainment PocketPak or to purchase it online, stop by its Web site at `http://www.microsoft.com/mobile/pocketpc/downloads/entpack.asp`.

GAMES POCKETPAK

Microsoft's Games PocketPak is geared more toward the office crowd in that every game is themed around some part of an office environment. The game bundle consists of five games, each of which is uniquely different from the others:

- Cubicle Chaos
- Fire Drill
- Killer Commute
- Stock Scramble
- Task Master

Cubicle Chaos should be familiar to you from earlier in the chapter when you found out how to download it for free from Microsoft. The other games in the bundle are similar to Cubicle Chaos in that they are relatively simple action games with an office theme. Fire Drill is one of my favorites in this bundle. It involves controlling a little guy who must run around an office putting out fires. Fire Drill employs a top-view scrolling approach to provide a view of a highly combustible office. When you extinguish all the fires in one level, they spread to another and get more aggressive; your work is never done in Fire Drill. Figure 24.6 shows the Fire Drill hero busy at work putting out fires with his fire extinguisher.

Figure 24.6
The hero in Fire Drill never gets to rest because he must continually douse this highly combustible office.

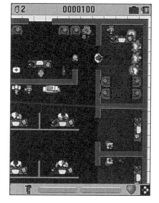

Other games in the Games PocketPak include Killer Commute, which is a take-off on the immensely popular Frogger arcade classic. Unlike Frogger, though, in Killer Commute you must guide a little person to work by dodging lots of obstacles, including dogs, people, and cars.

Stock Scramble is somewhat of a throwback to a popular trend in arcade games where you guide a character around multiple levels connected by ladders. Donkey Kong comes to mind as a popular game that fit this trend. In Stock Scramble, you must dodge several bosses who are wandering around, as opposed to a gorilla like in Donkey Kong. The idea in Stock Scramble is to grab up stock options without your bosses catching you.

Task Master is a take-off of the ingenious game Lemmings that rocketed into popularity on desktop PCs several years ago. In Lemmings you have to control a line of marching creatures so that they don't march themselves to a certain death. This involves building bridges, digging tunnels, and generally being creative to solve their transportation needs. Task Master takes the same approach as Lemmings, except in this case you're guiding employees around obstacles such as photocopiers and water coolers.

To find out more about the Microsoft Games PocketPak or to purchase it online, visit its Web site at http://www.microsoft.com/mobile/pocketpc/downloads/gamespak.asp.

ARCADE POCKETPAK

The last of Microsoft's three game packs is the closest to my heart because it brings back my youth spent in video game arcades. Ask just about anyone over 25 to name the single most popular arcade game of all time, and the answer will likely be Pac-Man. Together with Asteroids and Space Invaders, Pac-Man is responsible for separating quite a few people from their hard-earned quarters. Microsoft obviously wanted to tip its hat to the golden age of video game arcades when it decided to make Pac-Man a part of the Arcade PocketPak.

Note   To learn more about classic arcade games, I strongly encourage you to visit the Killer List of Videogames (KLOV) Web site at http://www.klov.com/. KLOV serves as a information repository for every arcade game ever made and includes a lot of interesting background information on popular arcade games.

Ironically, even though Pac-Man is likely the most recognized maze game ever created, Ms. Pac-Man is actually held in higher regard by game players. This probably explains why Microsoft added Ms. Pac-Man to the mix. If you then throw in Dig-Dug, you have the Arcade PocketPak, which consists of the following games:

- Pac-Man
- Ms. Pac-Man
- Dig-Dug

The Arcade PocketPak enables you to relive 1980 in the comfort of the twenty-first century by playing Pac-Man, Ms. Pac-Man, and Dig-Dug on your Pocket PC. Figure 24.7 shows how Pac-Man on the Pocket PC is identical to its historical arcade counterpart.

Figure 24.7
Pac-Man for the Pocket PC is true to its historical arcade counterpart in every way.

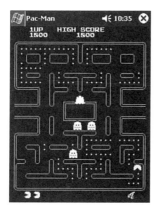

PART

VI

CH

24

For more information on the Arcade PocketPak or to purchase it online, stop by its Web site at `http://www.microsoft.com/mobile/pocketpc/downloads/arcadepak.asp`.

SURVEYING THE POCKET GAMING LANDSCAPE

If you're concerned that Microsoft is the only show in town when it comes to Pocket PC games, I'm happy to report that the Pocket PC game marketplace is growing quite rapidly. Although Microsoft has some interesting offerings in its bundled game packs, some companies are taking things a step further by migrating popular desktop PC games to the Pocket PC. In fact, some games already are available on the Pocket PC that I wouldn't have dreamed could be played on a mobile device as recently as a year or two ago.

In this section of the book I introduce you to some of these companies, along with the games they have to offer. I'm not a game reviewer, and I don't intend to present a review or in-depth analysis of each game. Instead, I want to paint the current state of the Pocket PC game industry in broad strokes. I'll leave it up to you to investigate these companies and their games further. Just consider this a guided tour of some of the best games available for Pocket PCs.

ZIOSOFT GAMES

ZIOSoft is a game development company that is quickly establishing itself as the heavy-hitter in the Pocket PC game community. Not only has it developed some original games of its own, but it has proven itself quite adept at licensing and porting existing desktop PC games over to the Pocket PC. For example, the best-selling city simulator SimCity 2000 was ported to the Pocket PC by ZIOSoft. Following are some of the ZIOSoft games currently available, all of which directly target the Pocket PC platform:

- SimCity 2000
- Metalion
- ZIOGolf
- Space Tactics
- Chopper Alley
- Pocket Bass Pro
- Pocket Athlete
- Ultima Underworld
- Need for Speed: High Stakes
- Tiger Woods PGA Tour
- Expresso Run

As you can see, some of these games are Pocket PC versions of successful desktop PC games. For example, Ultima Underworld, Need for Speed: High Stakes, and Tiger Woods PGA Tour are all established desktop PC games that have been ported to the Pocket PC platform. In addition to these crossover games, Metalion is a new game created solely for the Pocket PC that represents a significant step forward in the evolution of Pocket PC games. Figures 24.8–24.10 show some of the more popular ZIOSoft games in action.

Caution

If you're a huge fan of a desktop PC game that has been ported to Pocket PC, you might want to approach the Pocket PC version with guarded optimism. Not every game scales well to the limited screen and processing resources of Pocket PCs, so you don't always find the same game-play experience in a game on a Pocket PC as compared to its desktop counterpart.

Figure 24.8
ZIOSoft's SimCity 2000 brings the popular desktop PC city simulator to the Pocket PC.

Figure 24.9
Metalion represents one of the first Pocket PC shoot'em-up games with truly impressive graphics and speed.

Figure 24.10
Space Tactics brings multiplayer net-worked strategy gam-ing to the Pocket PC.

To learn more about ZIOSoft and its Pocket PC games, stop by the Pocket PC section of its Web site at `http://www.ziosoft.com/html/pocketpc/pocketpcindex.html`.

HEXACTO GAMES

Hexacto is a relatively new game company based in Montreal, Canada, and it is focusing solely on Pocket PC games. Its Bounty Hunter 2099 Pinball game has received exceptional reviews from the Pocket PC community, and its two sports games—Tennis Addict and Soccer Addict—are very impressive given that sports games are particularly tricky to develop for portable game systems. Following are the games currently offered by Hexacto:

- Bounty Hunter 2099 Pinball
- FullHand Casino
- Bob The Pipe Fitter
- Tennis Addict
- Soccer Addict
- Slurp
- Lemonade Inc.

Figures 24.11 and 24.12 show a couple of Hexacto's games in action, which reveals its attention to graphic detail.

Figure 24.11
Bounty Hunter 2099 Pinball is one of the first, and quite likely the best, pinball game for the Pocket PC.

Figure 24.12
Bob The Pipe Fitter is an addictive, yet simple, puzzle game with very nice graphics.

To find out more about Hexacto and its games, visit the Hexacto Web site at http://www.hexacto.com/.

JIMMY SOFTWARE GAMES

Jimmy Software gets credit for being the first game company to directly target the Pocket PC. Jimmy Software began as one guy (Jimmy) working with Windows CE back in 1997 and has created several freeware utilities that have been very popular. When Jimmy realized there was virtually no competition in the Windows CE game market, he switched his focus to games and apparently hasn't looked back. The Jimmy Software development team is responsible for some of the most innovative games to appear on Pocket PCs. Following are some of the most popular Jimmy Software games available for Pocket PCs:

- Turjah and Turjah II
- Saffron

- JimmyARK
- FireFrontier
- Boyan and Boyan's Crystal
- RallyCE
- PocketRunner
- CrossWord

Turjah and Turjah II are perhaps the most noteworthy of the Jimmy Software games; they are space shoot'em-up games with excellent graphics, music, and sound effects. Another popular game from this lineup is FireFrontier, which is a shoot'em-up that employs a top-view approach of presenting a maze full of tanks and other futuristic vehicles of war. You control a tank and basically drive around blasting everything that moves. Boyan is yet another Jimmy Software shooting game, except in it you control a small spaceship and blast aliens as they drift from the bottom to the top of the screen hanging onto balloons. The idea is to keep the aliens from getting to the top of the screen, where they will join forces and create a great deal of havoc. Figures 24.13–24.15 show off some of Jimmy Software's more popular titles.

Figure 24.13
Turjah II is an award-winning vertical shooter that is a must-have for any serious Pocket PC gamer.

Figure 24.14
FireFrontier is an exciting tank game that pits you in a battle against a variety of enemy vehicles.

Figure 24.15
Boyan is a simple shooting game with a strange cast of cartoon characters and compelling graphics.

To learn more about Jimmy Software and its Pocket PC game offerings, visit the Jimmy Software Web site at `http://www.jimmysoftware.com/`.

FLUX GAMES

Similar to Jimmy Software, FLUX is a game company that solely targets the Pocket PC platform with its games. FLUX offers several unique games that are establishing interesting genres of Pocket PC games. For example, The Mark is a game in which you play the role of a sniper who targets villains from atop buildings. Another game that goes in a completely different direction is Power Grip, which is the only Pocket PC bowling simulation game currently available. Following are some of the more interesting games offered by FLUX:

- The Mark
- Power Grip
- Black Jack
- Fishing Fishing

To learn more about FLUX and its games, visit the FLUX Web site at `http://www.flux2game.com/`. From there, you can download trial versions of the games, as well as purchase them online.

MONKEYSTONE GAMES

Even though Pocket PCs are still cruising beneath the radar of the video game industry at large, several game insiders believe Pocket PCs represent a significant opportunity for game developers. Monkeystone Games is a new game company founded by game insiders who, before starting Monkeystone Games, played a role in developing hit games such as Quake, Doom, Wolfenstein 3D, Duke Nukem, and Age of Empires, to name a few. Monkeystone Games currently has only one Pocket PC game on the market—Hyperspace Delivery Boy—but the game is significant because it is a genuinely unique game that was designed from the ground up for Pocket PCs.

Hyperspace Delivery Boy is part adventure game, part action game, and part puzzle game, and it is surprisingly fun. Figure 24.16 shows some of the action in Hyperspace Delivery Boy.

Figure 24.16
Hyperspace Delivery Boy offers a unique mix of adventure, action, and puzzles in a Pocket PC game.

PART
VI

CH
24

To learn more about Monkeystone Games and Hyperspace Delivery Boy, visit the Monkeystone Games Web site at `http://www.monkeystone.com/`.

CAPCOM GAMES

The Pocket PC game companies I've mentioned thus far are fairly new companies whose focus is solely on mobile games. However, these aren't the only types of companies interested in the Pocket PC platform. In fact, one of the major players in the arcade game industry has released several of its classic arcade games for the Pocket PC platform. I'm referring to Capcom, which was founded in Japan in 1979 and is responsible for several popular arcade games, such as Street Fighter, Resident Evil, and the Mega Man series. Capcom is also the creator of several classic arcade favorites, such as Ghosts 'N Goblins and Commando. These classics are what Capcom has now focused on with its Pocket PC development efforts. Following are the Pocket PC games currently offered by Capcom:

- Ghosts 'N Goblins
- Commando
- Legendary Wings
- 1942
- Section Z

For more information on Capcom and its line of classic Pocket PC games, visit the Pocket PC section of the Capcom Web site at `http://www.capcom.com/pc.xpml`.

HITTING THE LINKS WITH YOUR POCKET PC

Throughout this chapter, I've introduced a variety of video games that can be played on your Pocket PC. All these games technically qualify as "virtual games" because they are played entirely within the confines of your device. However, a Pocket PC can also be used as a tool to enhance your experience within a game in real life. One game in which Pocket PCs can come in handy is golf, which involves careful scorekeeping to establish a handicap and track your progress. Pocket PCs are ideal devices for this type of mobile bookkeeping because they enable you to quickly enter information on the go, store it in a reliable format, and then analyze it later.

Siscosoft's Pocket Golfwits is a powerful golf recordkeeping application that enables you to tap to record each shot you take on a digital map of the course you are playing. You can specify how the shot was hit (slice, hook, and so on), as well as the club used to hit it. This information can be valuable in improving your game when you consider that each and every shot is documented in detail.

Note

Course maps for Pocket Golfwits are available for download from the Siscosoft Web site at http://www.siscosoft.com/. If a course isn't available, you can request Siscosoft to create a map for it or create the map yourself using a special tool available from Siscosoft.

Pocket Golfwits can be used as a standalone application, but it is particularly powerful when coupled with the desktop Golfwits application. Pocket Golfwits includes many of the same features as its desktop counterpart, but the desktop application is easier to use when it comes to analyzing your play. Figure 24.17 shows the Golfwits desktop application with a hole displayed that has been played.

Notice in Figure 24.17 that the left side of the screen contains a graphical rendering of a golf hole. Lines and points are displayed to indicate the location of each shot that was made to complete the hole. The right side of the screen includes a wealth of interesting statistics regarding the specifics of the shots made during the round. Figure 24.18 shows Pocket Golfwits, which displays only the left side of the desktop application's view because of the limited screen space.

The real power of Pocket Golfwits is that you can keep your golf score without ever entering numbers or doing any math. You enter everything visually by tapping on a map of the course, which is incredibly intuitive. Pocket Golfwits is then capable of determining a great deal of information about your game from the visual data you provide it. As an example, Figure 24.19 shows the Hole Review view in Pocket Golfwits, which provides a written summary of a hole based on the data that was entered graphically.

Figure 24.17
The Golfwits desktop application is a full-featured golf record-keeping and analysis tool.

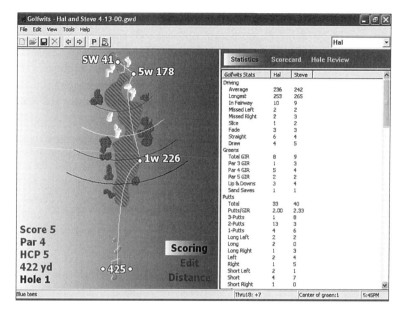

Figure 24.18
The Pocket Golfwits application is a great companion to the desktop application and makes keeping a detailed record of your golf rounds easy.

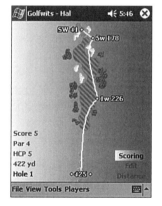

Figure 24.19
The Hole Review view in Pocket Golfwits provides a great written record of a hole, even though you don't have to type anything.

There are clearly significant benefits to using Pocket Golfwits for the golfer who wants to keep up with his game. It solves a need that is well-suited to Pocket PCs, and it does so in a manner that doesn't add any technical hassle. No one wants to fool with gadgets while trying to enjoy themselves outdoors. Keeping score in Pocket Golfwits is not much different from writing down numbers on a scorecard, and you end up with much more information at the end of the day. For more information on Golfwits, visit the Siscosoft Web site at http://www.siscosoft.com/.

 If you play a golf course that isn't currently available for Golfwits, see "Unmapped Courses and Golfwits" in the "Troubleshooting" section at the end of the chapter to find out what to do about it.

Tip from *Michael*	You can make voice recordings and associate them with different holes in Pocket Golfwits. This is a great way to add any extra commentary about a particular hole.

TROUBLESHOOTING

COMBATING DEVICE SLOWDOWN FROM GAMES

My device seems to noticeably slow down after playing certain games. How can I speed things back up?

This problem has to do with the fact that the Pocket PC operating system doesn't close applications when you tap the X in the upper-right corner of the screen. Instead of being closed, applications are typically just minimized. Although this works fine for most applications, games tend to hog a lot of memory and processor resources, so they can really tax the system if they're left minimized. So, if you find your device slowing down after playing a game or two, go into your device settings and manually close the games if they are still running.

If you notice that some games are playing slowly, you might be able to speed them up by adjusting the manner in which memory is allocated on your device. Select Settings from the Start menu, select the System tab, and then tap the Memory icon to access the memory settings for your device. Drag the slider bar to the left to allocate more memory for running programs, which can help the performance of some games that are highly memory intensive.

→ To recap how to manually close all applications that are running, **see** "Memory Management and Closing Applications," **p. 56**.

UNMAPPED COURSES AND GOLFWITS

My favorite course isn't available for Golfwits. How can I still use the application to keep track of my golf game?

One question you might have in regard to Golfwits and Pocket Golfwits is course availability. Obviously, the applications are useful only if you can obtain courses that you play.

Siscosoft currently has several thousand courses available with many more in the works; new courses are being released on a regular basis. All the courses are freely available from the Siscosoft Web site. If you're antsy and can't wait for Siscosoft to get around to creating a map of your favorite course, you can map it yourself using the Mapwits software. Mapwits enables you to construct golf course maps for use in Golfwits. You can also send Siscosoft information about your course and have them map it for you, although this will take longer than doing it yourself.

REAL-WORLD EXAMPLE—IMPROVING YOUR GOLF GAME

If you're like most of the amateur golfing world, you no doubt struggle to improve your game. One problem most golfers face is the inability to accurately track their game and focus on their weaknesses. For example, you might go to the driving range regularly and still find yourself shooting bad scores because your short game is out of whack. The Golfwits application you learned about in this chapter enables you to target weaknesses in your golf game because it doesn't just keep up with a score for each hole—it keeps up with each individual shot. I encourage you to try using Golfwits for a while and see whether it doesn't help you target problems in your golf game. It might not make you a better golfer overnight, but it can at least clue you in as to how you should be practicing.

APPENDIXES

APPENDIX **A**

A POCKET PC HARDWARE ACCESSORY TOUR

In this appendix

POCKET PC HARDWARE ACCESSORIES

As I'm sure you've realized, Pocket PCs are incredibly powerful devices straight out of the box. However, their power, flexibility, and usability can be greatly improved with the addition of a few choice hardware accessories. Many of these accessories come in the form of CF, SD, or PC cards that plug into standard slots, whereas others are designed to operate through the infrared port on your device. This appendix explores some of the more interesting Pocket PC hardware accessories currently available. The accessories are broken down into the following categories:

- Storage
- Communication
- Multimedia and I/O
- Carrying cases
- Pointing tools

The remainder of this appendix explores hardware accessories in each of these categories and why you might find them useful with your Pocket PC.

STORAGE

Because memory is a limited resource in all Pocket PC devices, additional storage is likely the most useful hardware accessory you'll purchase. The most popular accessory for expanding the memory of Pocket PCs is the CF memory card, which is a CF card containing flash memory that is extremely valuable for storing data and installed applications. Some devices include an SD slot, as opposed to a CF slot, in which case you'll have to use the newer SD memory cards. Because CF and SD memory cards are industry standards, they can be interchanged with some digital cameras and MP3 music players. CF cards are considerably cheaper than SD cards simply because they've been around longer, but SD prices will surely drop as they continue to gain acceptance.

Another interesting type of storage accessory available for Pocket PCs is the micro drive, which is a tiny hard disk drive embedded in a CF or PC card. Both IBM and Toshiba manufacture micro drives. The big advantage micro drives have over memory cards is price; as of this writing, micro drives are roughly half the price of most memory cards when you consider the price per megabyte (MB) of storage. Micro drives are also available in considerably larger sizes than memory cards. The drawbacks to micro drives are that they are slower to access and tend to drain batteries more quickly than memory cards. Even so, if you require large amounts of storage, the upside to micro drives might just outweigh the negatives.

MEMORY CARDS

CF memory cards are currently available in sizes ranging from 8MB to 1GB, depending on the manufacturer. The cards themselves weigh approximately one-half ounce and are the size of a matchbook. CF memory cards are designed according to the CompactFlash Type I standard, which means they are usable on the widest range of Pocket PC devices; some Pocket PC devices support only CompactFlash Type I cards. One compelling reason to use CF memory cards is because they are compatible with many popular digital cameras. If you own a digital camera that uses CF memory cards, you can take pictures; slide the card into your Pocket PC; and then view, edit, and e-mail the pictures. In addition to storing photographic images, CF memory cards are great for storing other types of memory-hungry data, such as MP3 or WMA music.

SD memory cards are relatively new to the Pocket PC memory wars and are therefore more limited in terms of size; they're also more expensive than CF cards. However, SD cards are extremely small and lightweight, which gives them an advantage in terms of mobility. Their incredibly small size and lack of weight makes SD cards quite durable. The "Secure" in the name Secure Digital implies that SD cards include some type of security feature. This security feature has to do with keeping track of licenses for licensed content such as digital music and eBooks. It eventually might allow book and music publishers to use SD cards as a distribution medium.

Following are some of the major manufacturers of CF and SD memory cards:

- **Kingston Technology**—`http://www.kingston.com/`
- **Pretec**—`http://www.pretec.com/`
- **SanDisk**—`http://www.sandisk.com/`
- **Lexar Media**—`http://www.lexarmedia.com/`

Micro Drives

If you plan on using your Pocket PC as a portable jukebox or you other excessive storage needs, you might want to forego a memory storage card and install a micro drive in your Pocket PC. Unlike CF memory cards, micro drive CF cards are designed around the CompactFlash Type II standard, which means the cards are slightly thicker (5mm thick) than the Type I cards (3.3mm thick). This also means that you must have a Pocket PC that supports Type II cards. The IBM Microdrive CF cards are currently available in 170MB, 340MB, and 1GB. Toshiba micro drive cards are available as PC cards, and they come in much larger sizes: 2GB, 5GB, 10GB, and 20GB.

Keep in mind that all micro drive cards put a heavier drain on the main Pocket PC battery. The degree to which this drain affects your specific device varies according to the normal battery life, condition of the battery, and so on. Regardless of the specifics, you'll get a shorter runtime when using a micro drive card. However, the dramatically increased storage just might be worth it!

Check out the following links for more information on the IBM and Toshiba micro drives:

- **IBM Microdrive**—`http://www.storage.ibm.com/hdd/micro/`
- **Toshiba**—`http://www.toshiba.com/taecdpd/products/hdd.shtml`

APP

A

COMMUNICATION

Communication comes in a close second to storage as the most useful type of Pocket PC hardware accessory. Communication accessories include wired modem cards, wireless modem cards, infrared modems, digital phone cards, local area network (LAN) cards, and GPS receivers. As this list reveals, many options are available when it comes to communicating with a Pocket PC.

WIRED MODEM CARDS

Wired modem cards are CF or PC cards that typically include tiny 56Kbps (kilobits per second) embedded modems. To use such a modem card, you insert the card into your device and then plug in a telephone cable. Then, it's just a matter of establishing a dial-up modem connection, which enables you to use the modem to connect to an ISP or some other dial-up network. Wired modem cards are relatively power efficient, so you don't have to worry too much about them draining the battery of your Pocket PC.

A variety of wired modem cards are available on the market, and the primary difference between them is size. For example, the Casio modem card is the same size as a CF memory card with an additional connector cable attached to it for plugging in a phone line. The Compaq, Pretec, and Targus cards are larger, and include the phone-line connector on the modem itself. If you're looking for a modem that can be safely tucked away inside your Pocket PC, the Casio modem is a winner. However, it does require you to keep track of the connector cable, which could get lost. The Compaq, Kingston, and Pretec modems are larger and protrude from the CF card slot, but they are self-contained so there is nothing to worry about losing.

Following are some links you can follow to learn about each of the wired modem cards:

- **Casio CF Modem**—http://www.casio.com/accessories/
- **Compaq 56K CF Fax Modem**—http://www.compaq.com/products/handhelds/pocketpc/options/modems.html
- **Pretec CompactModem**—http://www.pretec.com/
- **Targus Pocket Modem 56K V.90**—http://www.targus.com/

WIRELESS MODEM CARDS

If you're looking for the utmost in connectivity flexibility, wireless modem cards might be for you. The primary offerings in the wireless modem card market are the Sierra Wireless AirCard 300 and AirCard 510, which are basically wireless CF modem cards designed to work on mobile phone networks. The AirCard 300 can be used on Cellular Digital Packet Data (CDPD) networks such as AT&T Wireless, Verizon, and GoAmerica, whereas the AirCard 510 is designed for use on a Code Division Multiple Access (CDMA) network such as Sprint PCS. Both of the AirCards are PC cards, and each has a small antenna it uses to reach the network. The Enfora Pocket Spider is another wireless modem card that is also designed for CDPD networks. Unlike the AirCards, though, the Pocket Spider is a CF card, which makes it more accessible to some Pocket PCs.

The principle drawback to wireless modems at the moment is their slow maximum speed of 19.2Kbps. However, when you consider the flexibility of being able to surf the Web and check e-mail from virtually any location, the speed is something you might be able to accept. To learn more about the AirCard 300 or AirCard 510, visit the Sierra Wireless Web site at `http://www.sierrawireless.com/ProductsOrdering/handhelds.html`. To find out more about the Enfora Pocket Spider, visit the Enfora Web site at `http://www.enfora.com/`.

INFRARED MODEMS

You might not have realized that you can use the infrared port on your device to establish a wireless network connection. This is possible through an infrared modem that communicates with your device via a wireless infrared connection. A good example of an infrared modem is the Psion Infrared Travel Modem, which communicates with a Pocket PC at speeds up to 56Kbps using the infrared port. In other words, the modem sits next to your Pocket PC and doesn't involve any physical connection to the device. The infrared modem approach taken by Psion has several advantages:

- No wires are connected to your Pocket PC.
- Expansion slots are kept free for other accessories, such as memory cards.
- There is minimal power drain on the Pocket PC battery.

The Travel Modem operates on two AA batteries or an optional power adapter, which explains why it doesn't eat into the Pocket PC battery. This is probably a benefit for most Pocket PC users, but it does mean you have to concern yourself with buying new batteries when the modem goes dead, or possibly invest in rechargeable batteries. Expect a fresh set of AA batteries to be good for around four to six hours of continuous online use.

The obvious downside to the Travel Modem is that it has to be physically positioned next to a Pocket PC so their infrared ports line up. Depending on how you are accustomed to using your Pocket PC, this might not be a big deal. At times, it would probably be beneficial to have the convenience of a CF or PC modem card that is physically attached to the device, although at other times the Travel Modem would probably work just fine. One argument that cannot be refuted is the benefit of not having to give up an expansion slot for the Travel Modem. To learn more about the Psion Travel Modem, visit `http://www.psion.com/connect/tmmenu.htm`.

DIGITAL PHONE CARDS

If you like the convenience of your digital mobile phone and would like to have the same convenience with Pocket PC connectivity, a digital phone card is probably for you. Digital phone cards basically enable you to use your mobile phone as an external modem for your Pocket PC. Digital phone cards typically connect to a Pocket PC via a CF slot and then connect to a mobile CDMA or GSM phone using a special cable. You must use a digital

APP

A

phone card that is compatible with your specific mobile phone. Following are a couple of digital phone cards currently available for use with Pocket PCs:

- **Socket Digital Phone Card**—http://www.socketcom.com/
- **Xircom CompactCard GSM**—http://www.xircom.com/

WIRED LAN CARDS

If you need to connect your Pocket PC to a local area network, you might be interested in a wired LAN card, which is essentially a compact Ethernet card for Pocket PCs. As an example, Socket Communications makes a popular wired LAN card that is a CF Type I card. This card includes a removable RJ-45 cable that enables you to connect your device to a 10BASE-T Ethernet network. Additionally, a rugged version of the Ethernet card is available that includes a fixed cable with a reinforced connector for use in industrial applications. Keep in mind that wired LAN cards require a physical (wired) connection to a network. Following are a few of the wired LAN cards available for Pocket PCs:

- **Pretec CompactLAN**—http://www.pretec.com/
- **Socket Low Power Ethernet CF Card**—http://www.socketcom.com/
- **Targus Low Power CF Ethernet Card**—http://www.targus.com/

WIRELESS LAN CARDS

Wireless LANs have become a very popular networking solution in the past couple of years thanks to Wi-Fi networking hardware, which is based on the 802.11b wireless networking standard. If you use a Wi-Fi wireless LAN at work or at home, you'll probably find that connecting your Pocket PC to the network is incredibly tempting. Fortunately, this is easily accomplished with a wireless LAN card. One such card is made by Socket Communications and is available as a CF card. Accessing a LAN wirelessly is as simple as plugging in the CF wireless LAN card and getting to work. One huge benefit of this networking approach is that it enables you to synchronize via ActiveSync as long as you're within a few hundred feet of the wireless base station. To find out more about the Socket Wireless LAN Card, go to http://www.socketcom.com/.

BLUETOOTH NETWORKING

Another type of wireless communication possible with Pocket PCs is through Bluetooth, which is a peer-to-peer wireless communication standard. Bluetooth is designed to allow individual devices to communicate with one another and hopefully cut down on the number of wires running around the typical office and home office. A few Pocket PCs currently ship with built-in Bluetooth support, which is pretty neat, but if you aren't so lucky to have built-in Bluetooth, you still have options. For example, Compaq offers a Bluetooth expansion sleeve that includes not only a CF card slot, but also a Bluetooth wireless radio for Bluetooth communication. To find out more about this expansion sleeve, visit http://www.compaq.com/products/handhelds/pocketpc/options/wireless_packs.html.

If you don't have a Compaq Pocket PC then the Bluetooth expansion sleeve obviously isn't an option. Fortunately, Socket Communications offers the Bluetooth Card, which is a CF card designed primarily as a means of connecting a Pocket PC to a mobile phone for wireless Internet access. Visit the Socket Communications Web site at `http://www.socketcom.com/` to learn more about its Bluetooth Card.

GPS RECEIVERS

Another area of Pocket PC communication that might not be so obvious to you is global positioning, which enables you to determine where you are geographically positioned on the Earth. A global positioning system (GPS) receiver is capable of pinpointing your coordinate, which can then be fed into Pocket Streets to show you exactly where you're located on a map. Although this might sound a little like science fiction, it is very much a reality. Following are some of the GPS receivers currently available for use with Pocket PCs:

- **Pretec CompactGPS**—`http://www.pretec.com/`
- **Pocket Co-Pilot GPS**—`http://www.pocketcopilot.com/`
- **Destinator GPS**—`http://www.destinator1.com/`
- **Pharos GPS**—`http://www.pharosgps.com/`
- **Teletype GPS**—`http://www.teletype.com/`

MULTIMEDIA AND I/O

Multimedia accessories are in many ways the flashiest of Pocket PC add-ons because they provide sizzle with sounds and imagery. These accessories are composed of surprising pieces of hardware, such as Pocket PC keyboards, VGA presentation cards, digital camera CF cards, audio amplifiers, and bar-code scanners.

KEYBOARDS

Text entry is a major limitation of any handheld device, including Pocket PCs. As efficient as you might get at using the stylus to write or pecking keys on the soft keyboard, you're unlikely to be able to match the speed and convenience of a traditional computer keyboard. That's why you might want to consider a portable keyboard for your Pocket PC at some point if you plan on entering a lot of data. Following are some of the major portable keyboards available as of this writing:

- **Compaq Micro Keyboard**—`http://www.compaq.com/products/handhelds/pocketpc/options/keyboards.html`
- **Compaq Foldable Keyboard**—`http://www.compaq.com/products/handhelds/pocketpc/options/keyboards.html`
- **HP Jornada Pocket Keyboard**—`http://www.hp.com/jornada/`
- **Targus Stowaway Keyboard**—`http://www.targus.com/`

PRESENTATION CARDS

Presentation cards enable you to connect a Pocket PC to a VGA monitor or LCD projector to share presentations with others. This is an incredibly useful accessory when you consider busy professionals who must travel and make presentations. Notebook computers are currently used quite often for these types of presentations, but there is no reason Pocket PCs can't be used. If you're interested in making presentations with your Pocket, take a look at the following presentation cards, both of which output VGA signals capable of being used with monitors or LCD projectors:

- **Presenter-to-Go**—http://www.presenter-to-go.com/
- **Voyager VGA**—http://www.colorgraphic.net/

DIGITAL CAMERA CARDS

In terms of pure gadget appeal, my favorite Pocket PC accessory is a digital camera card, which enables you to take digital photos using a Pocket PC. Digital camera cards are currently manufactured by Casio and HP and are available in the CF card format, which makes them usable in virtually all Pocket PCs. Both cameras extend above the CF slot on most devices, which is where the camera lens is located. Pictures taken with the cameras are automatically stored as JPEG images. Keep in mind that digital camera cards require a fair amount of power as compared to most other CF card add-ons, so expect your device to have a considerably shorter battery life when using a digital camera card. Following are the two digital camera cards currently available for Pocket PCs:

- **Casio Digital Camera Card**—http://www.casio.com/accessories/
- **HP Pocket Camera**—http://www.hp.com/jornada/

Unfortunately, both of these digital camera cards are designed to work solely with devices made by their respective manufacturers and therefore aren't capable of being used with other Pocket PCs.

AUDIO AMPLIFIERS

Even though Pocket PCs include the capability of playing music via MP3 and WMA music files, some devices are weak in terms of how much power they devote to audio playback. More specifically, hearing music on some Pocket PCs can be difficult when there is background noise, such as when listening in a car, even with the volume cranked up high. For these devices, you might want to consider using an audio amplifier, which boosts the audio signal coming out of the headphone jack of the Pocket PC to give you a better (or at least louder) listening experience.

The Boostaroo is an audio amplifier designed to boost the signal of audio and is perfectly suited for Pocket PC listeners. It is a small device powered by two AA batteries, and it plugs into the headphone jack of a Pocket PC. In addition to boosting the audio of a Pocket PC, the Boostaroo also provides three extra headphone jacks, which enable a total of four people to listen in at once. Now, when you're traveling by plane, everyone on your aisle can listen in together as you spin MP3 tunes. The Boostaroo doesn't have a volume control of its own; instead, it boosts the signal it receives. So, you still control the volume of the Pocket PC using the standard volume control. The big difference is that half volume with the Boostaroo is louder than full volume without it. For more information on the Boostaroo, visit the Boostaroo Web site at http://www.boostaroo.com/.

Another option for boosting the audio signal on Pocket PCs is the Koss EQ-50 audio amplifier. It performs a function similar to the Boostaroo, but it doesn't provide the extra headphone jacks. On the upside, the Koss amplifier includes a three-band equalizer that enables you to fine-tune the audio signal to some degree. This amplifier does include its own volume control, which might be seen as a benefit or a drawback depending on your own personal preference. The benefit would be that you can clip the amplifier to your belt and have an easily accessible volume control; the drawback would be the complexity of having two volume controls with which to contend. For more information on the Koss EQ-50 audio amplifier, visit the Koss Web site at http://www.koss.com/.

BAR-CODE SCANNERS

One application of Pocket PCs that hasn't been fully realized yet is that of mobile management and tracking of products and services. Many of these products and services are coded with bar codes that can be scanned and processed by a Pocket PC. Bar-code scanners enable you to scan bar codes with a Pocket PC. Specific applications of bar-code scanners range from catalog shopping by scanning item numbers to patient management by scanning medications and procedures in a medical environment. Following are several bar-code scanners available for use with Pocket PCs:

- **Socket Bar Code Laser Scanner CF Card**—http://www.socketcom.com/
- **Socket In-Hand Scan Card**—http://www.socketcom.com/
- **Socket Bar Code Wand System**—http://www.socketcom.com/
- **Symbol SPS 3000 iPAQ Bar Code Expansion Pack**—http://www.symbol.com/

GAME PADS

As surprising as it might seem, a couple of companies have created game pads for Pocket PCs that are designed to help improve the Pocket PC gaming experience. Granted, most Pocket PC 2002 devices include highly usable multidirectional pads and several push buttons, but Pocket PCs still don't quite compare to pure game devices such as Nintendo's GameBoy Advance. Besides, you might not be comfortable bashing the keys on your Pocket PC in a heated shoot-em-up game. For this reason and more, you have the option of buying a portable game pad that connects to your Pocket PC and provides a gaming interface similar to those found on popular game systems. The Zeta Joypad is a separate game controller that plugs into your device, whereas the Tigerex Q-Pad for iPAQ is a snap-on game pad designed to fit Compaq iPAQ Pocket PCs. To learn more about these game pads, check out the following links:

- **Zeta Joypad for Pocket PC**—http://www.beinteractive.co.kr/eng/
- **Tigerex Q-Pad for iPAQ**—http://www.tigerex.com.tw/

POINTING TOOLS

One accessory that you will inevitably find yourself needing is a new stylus. Whether you misplace it, it wears out, or you want to upgrade to a fancier one, the stylus is an accessory that practically every Pocket PC user will replace. Several styli are on the market, including straight replacements from Pocket PC manufacturers to fancy upgrades that include ball-point pens. There is even a small Pocket PC stylus that clips on to your finger, effectively making you the stylus. Following are some of the more popular styli you might want to con-sider when the time comes to replace or upgrade your stylus:

- Casio Combination PDA Stylus and Ballpoint Pen
- Fellowes FingerTip Stylus
- Fellowes PenCap Stylus
- Pilot Pentopia 2+1 Stylus
- Pilot Pentopia Dr. Grip 1+1 Stylus/Pen
- Pilot Chameleon Stylus/Pen
- Platinum Pen Mini Three Action PDA Stylus
- Platinum Pen Zepher Mini Three Action PDA Stylus
- Platinum Pen Dual Action PDA Stylus
- Platinum Pen Executive Three Action PDA Stylus

Most of these styli are available for purchase at retailers that carry Pocket PCs and acces-sories. Also keep in mind that each Pocket PC manufacturer offers replacement and often upgrade styli that are specifically designed for its devices.

→ For information about retailers that sell Pocket PCs and accessories, **see** "Retailers," **p. 495**.

CARRYING CASES

A relatively inexpensive accessory you might consider picking up for your Pocket PC is a carrying case. Most Pocket PCs come with a carrying case of some sort, but you can upgrade to a significantly nicer and more protective case if you so desire. If you carry your Pocket PC in situations in which it might be at risk of physical abuse, a rigid case might be a worthy investment. You also might consider a carrying case that folds open to provide space for other personal items, such as credit cards.

RhinoSkin makes several carrying cases that are designed specifically to hold Pocket PCs. From the sleek Executive Leather Case to the sporty RhinoPak 2000, cases are available to meet the needs of most Pocket PC users. The RhinoPak 2000 is a particularly interesting carrying case because it is designed for the rugged Pocket PC user. It resembles a mountain bike gear bag and includes elastic straps inside to secure your Pocket PC in place. Several pockets are included for storage of extra batteries and accessories. If you need extra space for other gadgets, you can move up to the RhinoPak 3000, which is similar to the RhinoPak 2000 but with extra room. At the other end of the spectrum is the RhinoPak 1100, which is a relatively slim-lined case with extra pockets for storing business cards, credit cards, and so on.

If you're looking for sleekness and style in a carrying case, check out Incase Designs's PDA Case for Pocket PCs. The oval shape of the case looks unique when compared to traditional rectangular cases. Even more unique is the graphite-colored neoprene material used for the exterior of the case. This case is definitely a winner if you want to get maximum style out of your Pocket PC.

If you think your Pocket PC might run the risk of being trampled by an angry mob, run over by a dump truck, or tied to a concrete block and tossed in a lake, the Otterbox is your dream come true. The Otterbox is not really sleek or stylish, but it will protect your Pocket PC like no other carrying case. Otterbox cases are designed to be crushproof and water resistant to 100-foot depths. They also float, which hopefully means you won't have to rely on the water-resistant feature. Not surprisingly, they have a lifetime guarantee. The Otterbox is available in a variety of sizes and colors and includes a handy cord for keeping it attached to your person.

APP

A

Following are links to the three case manufacturers you just learned about:

- **RhinoSkin**—http://www.rhinoskin.com/
- **Incase Designs**—http://stores.yahoo.com/goincase/
- **Otterbox**—http://www.otterbox.com/

Keep in mind that many other Pocket PC cases are on the market, and rather than list them all, I just wanted to point out some of the more interesting ones. Before you make a decision on a new case, you should check to see whether the manufacturer of your device offers a case specifically designed for your device. These cases can often be good choices because they are designed to fit the exact physical dimensions of a specific device.

While we're on the subject of carrying cases, I feel obligated to mention a product that you might think is a little outlandish at first. I'm referring to the Scott eVest, which is a futuristic vest designed to accommodate a plethora of electronics equipment. If you're a gadget lover on a serious level, the Scott eVest is probably right up your alley! It is designed to accommodate even the most sophisticated personal area network with an interconnected Pocket PC, mobile phone, pager, MP3 player, digital camera, portable keyboard, and headphones—not to mention room for a water bottle, wallet, and keys. To learn more about becoming a human carrying case for your Pocket PC and related gadgets, visit the Scott eVest Web site at http://www.scottevest.com/.

WHERE TO GO FOR MORE ABOUT POCKET PCS

In this appendix

ASSESSING POCKET PC RESOURCES

I could be arrogant and assume that I've included everything in this book that you could ever want to know about Pocket PCs. In addition to being arrogant, I would also be woefully wrong. It would truly be impossible for any one book to touch on every possible Pocket PC-related technology. Besides, Pocket PCs are changing rapidly, with new devices, accessories, and software appearing on a regular basis. For this reason, it's important for you to have some outlets for learning more about Pocket PCs.

This appendix directs you to resources that will likely prove invaluable as you continue your quest for Pocket PC knowledge. The Pocket PC resources you learn about in this appendix can be broken down into three major types:

- Web sites
- Publications
- Retailers

WEB SITES

Because the Web makes it possible to publish information virtually instantaneously, you'll likely find the Web the best place to go to learn more about Pocket PCs or to diagnose a particular problem. Although I am a big advocate of tinkering with computers and electronics to learn how they work, you can get a significant jump on learning tips and tricks by visiting a few informative Web sites. This book has touched on most of the more powerful Pocket PC tips and tricks, but I'm sure more are out there if you spend the time visiting some of the sites mentioned in the following sections. You'll also find these sites indispensable for product reviews, be it new Pocket PC accessories or a comparison of Pocket PC devices.

MICROSOFT'S POCKET PC WEB SITE

Not surprisingly, Microsoft lays claim to the official Pocket PC Web site, located at http://www.pocketpc.com/. This site actually covers all Microsoft's handheld initiatives, including Handheld PCs and mobile smart phones. Even so, the Pocket PC area of the site includes a lot of interesting articles, reviews, and how-to tips. I regularly visit this site to read new articles and learn about Microsoft's official take on certain Pocket PC issues.

POCKETNOW

PocketNow is a solid Web site devoted specifically to Pocket PCs. In it you will find articles, news, reviews, device comparisons, discussion forums, classified ads, and a concise but informative FAQ. The news section of the site is probably my favorite because it reports on the entire handheld computing world. The clean, professional layout of this site rivals Microsoft's site in terms of usability. You can visit PocketNow by pointing your browser to http://www.pocketnow.com/.

STEVE BUSH'S BRIGHTHAND WEB SITE

Many of the most interesting Pocket PC Web sites are hosted by individuals who feel strongly about the usefulness of handheld devices. One such individual is Steve Bush, who runs a handheld computing Web site called Brighthand that includes coverage of both Pocket PCs and Palm devices. Brighthand, which is located at `http://www.brighthand.com/`, began as a handful of articles and a discussion board but quickly grew to become a broad information repository for handheld device users. The discussion boards are probably the most valuable part of the Brighthand site because they see a fair amount of posts. In addition to managing and overseeing the Brighthand site, Mr. Bush is also a regular contributor to *Pen Computing* magazine, which you learn about a little later in this appendix.

DALE COFFING'S POCKET PC PASSION WEB SITE

If it was possible to single out one person as the biggest Pocket PC fan and expert, I'd have to lead you to Dale Coffing, who runs a Web site called Pocket PC Passion. The Pocket PC Passion Web site is located at `http://www.pocketpcpassion.com/` and is a great source of Pocket PC information that you are unlikely to find anywhere else. Mr. Coffing is the consummate Pocket PC tinkerer and has loads of great insider tips and tricks on his site. To give you an idea regarding the type of information on this site, Mr. Coffing includes instructions on how to build your own Pocket PC battery extender, as well as how to make a mobile phone cable and a car adapter to power your Pocket PC on the go. You might not have the desire to go to such lengths to enhance your Pocket PC experience, but it's still interesting to learn the possibilities. Beyond the hardware projects, Dale Coffing's Pocket PC page also includes a lot of great Pocket PC news links, rumors of upcoming devices and accessories, and numerous suggestions for improving the Pocket PC experience.

CHRIS DE HERRERA'S WINDOWS CE WEB SITE

Another individual who shows an incredibly high level of interest in Pocket PCs is Chris De Herrera, who runs a Web site called Windows CE that is somewhat similar to Dale Coffing's site. Mr. De Herrera's site, however, bills itself as "the most complete set of FAQs on Windows CE anywhere." This tells you that his site is set up more as a question-and-answer site, and also that it covers all versions of Windows CE, including Pocket PCs. Chris De Herrera's Windows CE Web site is located at `http://www.cewindows.net/` and has a section devoted to Windows CE 3.0, which corresponds to Pocket PCs. The Pocket PC section of the site includes a feature comparison of Pocket PC devices, useful tips and tricks, and an archive of Pocket PC news articles. The site is also a great place to learn about the origins of Pocket PC by exploring previous versions of Windows CE.

APP
B

THE GADGETEER

The Gadgeteer is a Web site devoted to handheld devices in general, including Pocket PCs, Palm devices, and other handhelds. The primary focus of the Gadgeteer Web site is reviewing devices, accessories, and other hardware gadgets related to the mobile computing. The compilation of device comparisons, reviews, and FAQs is nice to have at your fingertips. The Gadgeteer Web site is located at `http://www.the-gadgeteer.com`.

RICHARD KETTNER'S WIRED GUY WEB SITE

If you're interested in comparing devices and accessories or otherwise reading reviews of new Pocket PC technologies, you should visit Richard Kettner's Wired Guy Web site. Wired Guy is a well-organized Web site devoted to both Pocket PCs and Palm devices and is located at `http://www.wiredguy.com/`. Wired Guy is primarily a review site that provides thorough reviews of Pocket PC hardware, software, and accessories.

POCKET PC HELP

A Pocket PC Web site doesn't necessarily have to include original content to be useful. A good example of this is Pocket PC Help, which is a site that primarily serves as a repository of links to other Pocket PC Web sites. Pocket PC Help is located at `http://www.pocketpchelp.com/` and is broken down into several categories, including articles, news, hardware, software, and so on. One particularly interesting section of the site is Craig's Corner, where the host of the site, Craig Peacock, provides his own commentary and review of Pocket PC devices. Pocket PC Help is also one of the few user-oriented Pocket PC Web sites to include a programming section.

MYMOBILESTUFF SEARCH ENGINE

Believe it or not, there is now a search engine designed specifically for wireless handheld devices. MyMobileStuff is located at `http://www.mymobilestuff.com/` and serves as the first search engine to specifically target mobile content. What this means is that you can perform live searches from your Pocket PC and know that the resulting matches are designed for viewing by mobile devices. You won't have to worry about whether a Web site will scale down to fit on a Pocket PC screen because the search engine does the job of exposing only mobile-friendly sites.

PUBLICATIONS

Although it's hard to argue that Web sites can't be beaten for up-to-the-minute information on just about anything, including Pocket PCs, traditional printed publications also have their place. Even Pocket PCs with their ClearType technology won't completely replace printed material in the very near future, which is why I still find myself reading print magazines and newspapers on a regular basis. Add to this the fact that most magazines and newspapers have an online presence, and you simply can't ignore the value of a print publication. Following are a couple of magazines I recommend as valuable sources of Pocket PC insight:

- *Pocket PC Magazine*
- *Pen Computing*

Because Web sites typically try to keep things very bite-sized, you'll find that these magazines often spend more time delving into Pocket PC topics. Print articles are also often more accurate and better written, perhaps due to the fact that correcting mistakes in print is much tougher, whereas a Web page can always be updated.

Pocket PC Magazine

Although the magazine was around before Microsoft officially blessed the Pocket PC name, *Pocket PC Magazine* is a great resource for users of all Windows-powered handheld devices, especially Pocket PCs. The magazine is packed with tips, reviews, a download of the week, and a buyer's guide that is sure to grow as new Pocket PC devices and accessories continue to flood the market. The magazine is available at most bookstores and computer stores and online at `http://www.pocketpcmag.com/`.

Pen Computing

If you're looking for a publication that branches out beyond Pocket PCs to encompass all mobile computing devices, you should take a look at *Pen Computing*. *Pen Computing* covers a wide range of handheld devices, including both Pocket PCs and Palm devices. Although it doesn't focus solely on Pocket PCs, the magazine does help to provide perspective when it comes to the future of Pocket PCs and how they fit into the larger handheld computing market. *Pen Computing* is located on the Web at `http://www.pencomputing.com/` and is also available from most bookstores and computer stores.

Retailers

Now that you know where to go to learn more about Pocket PC hardware, software, and accessories, it doesn't hurt to know where you can buy them. Pocket PCs are available through most traditional office, electronics, and computer stores such as Office Depot, Staples, Best Buy, and CompUSA. In addition to these large brick and mortar retailers, many online retailers carry Pocket PC products. Some of the larger online retailers include Amazon.com, Beyond.com, and Buy.com.

Note

For a complete list of Pocket PC retailers, please refer to Microsoft's online list of retailers at `http://www.microsoft.com/mobile/pocketpc/hardware/wheretobuy.asp`.

App

B

Although a large online retailer can often offer rock-bottom prices, you might prefer dealing with an online retailer that specializes in handheld devices. Following are some online retailers that cater specifically to the handheld market:

- **Handango**—`http://www.handango.com/`
- **MobilePlanet**—`http://www.mobileplanet.com/`
- **PocketGear**—`http://www.pocketgear.com/`
- **Pocket PC Fanatic**—`http://www.pocketpcfanatic.com/`
- **CEShopper**—`http://www.ceshopper.com/`
- **smaller.com**—`http://www.smaller.com/`

- **Handheld Planet**—http://www.handheldplanet.net/
- **Data Anywhere**—http://www.datanywhere.net/

RESETTING YOUR POCKET PC

In this appendix

WHY RESET?

Unlike desktop and most notebook computers, Pocket PCs never truly shut down when you turn them off. When you power down a Pocket PC, the screen turns off and the device certainly looks like it's doing nothing, but everything in memory is actually preserved. That's why when you turn on a Pocket PC, you are instantly returned to the last thing you were doing, such as editing an e-mail document, reading an eBook, or playing a fierce game of Pac-Man. This functionality is sometimes referred to as *instant-on* and is an incredibly powerful feature.

The occasional downside of the Pocket PC instant-on functionality is revealed when applications don't perform properly. You no doubt are familiar with applications crashing on a desktop computer, resulting in you having to reboot to clean everything up. Rebooting is a part of my standard desktop computing ritual—if applications start acting strange or my machine starts noticeably running slower, a reboot is definitely in my future. Unfortunately, Pocket PC applications are also capable of crashing and causing problems with memory, in which case you need to be able to restart the device with a clean slate.

At this point, it's worth clarifying that two different logical areas of memory exist in a Pocket PC: active RAM and storage RAM. These memory designations help to distinguish between RAM that acts as a memory hard drive to store installed applications and application data (*storage RAM*) and RAM that is used by the Pocket PC operating system and applications to perform various processing tasks (*active RAM*). Storage RAM is a concept that doesn't currently exist on desktop and notebook computers. This is because all the RAM in a desktop or notebook PC is active RAM; desktop and notebook PCs use hard drives for application and data storage.

Note

> Pocket PCs also have ROM, which is used to hold the Pocket PC operating system and standard applications. Many Pocket PCs also have a special area of Flash ROM that serves as a safe storage area for data that might be modified but that isn't lost if you somehow lose battery power.

Restarting a Pocket PC with a crashed application is necessary when the active RAM has been corrupted by the application. In the vast majority of situations, this problem is associated with an application that doesn't behave properly, as opposed to the Pocket PC device itself. The only sure-fire way to deal with the problem is to reset the device, which is equivalent to rebooting a desktop PC. This type of reset is known as a *soft reset* because it clears only the active RAM. Another type of reset called a full reset, or *hard reset*, completely resets a Pocket PC to its factory settings. This second type of reset clears any data you have stored on a device, as well as any applications you have installed, and returns your device to the same state it was in when you first took it out of its box.

A hard reset essentially clears all the RAM in a device (both active and storage). The only reason to perform a hard reset is if you're having major problems and you need to completely clear your device and start over with a clean slate. A hard reset is somewhat akin to formatting the hard drive on a desktop PC, with the primary difference being that the Pocket PC operating system and standard applications are still present in ROM on the Pocket PC, whereas you have to manually reinstall all software on a desktop PC. As harsh as a hard reset sounds, it's still a handy feature if you want to start over with the device in the same state it was in when you bought it. For the record, a hard reset occurs naturally if you allow all the batteries in your device to completely run down.

PERFORMING A SOFT RESET

You'll typically want to perform a soft reset when an application has failed, leaving the device in a questionable state. An example of such a state is the device not responding when you tap the screen or press a button or when the animated wait icon stays up indefinitely. You might also opt to perform a soft reset if your device is acting sluggish, which indicates that you're running low on system resources. This can happen if an application doesn't do a good job of freeing memory after using it. Such occurrences are known as *memory leaks*, and it's the job of Pocket PC developers to do everything in their power to track down memory leaks before releasing an application.

A soft reset is very easy to perform and is identical across all Pocket PC devices. Every Pocket PC is required to have a reset button that is intentionally inset so it can't be pressed without using a pointed object such as a stylus. The reset button is usually quite small and inset within a hole in the case of your Pocket PC; please refer to the documentation on your specific device to locate the reset button. After you've located the reset button, performing a soft reset is a breeze. Just grab your stylus and follow these steps:

1. Turn the power on.
2. Press the reset button with the stylus and hold it for a couple of seconds.

Caution

If you are working in any applications, be sure to save or close anything you're working on because a soft reset closes any running applications without saving data. If your system is stable then you might also consider performing a backup just to be safe.

APP

C

After holding down the reset button for a second or two, the screen goes blank and then displays a startup screen that usually identifies the device manufacturer. You also might hear an audible chime to indicate that the device was reset. After a few more seconds, the Today screen appears, in which case the device has been successfully reset. Keep in mind that a soft reset deletes any data on your device that is in the process of being input or edited; in other words, anything that isn't yet saved is lost. Device settings and anything you've already saved are retained after a soft reset.

Part of the soft reset procedure is the device performing a memory check to ensure that there is no problem with the memory. If a memory problem is detected during a soft reset, the device displays an error message instead of the Today screen. You are then prompted to press the Action button to continue with the reset, in which case the device attempts to repair the memory problem. If memory cannot be repaired, another error message appears indicating that the memory error is fatal, in which case a hard reset is necessary. Pressing the Action button enables you to perform a hard reset, which erases all the RAM in the system, including saved data and installed applications.

Caution

Avoid using the backup feature in ActiveSync if you suspect a memory error because the corrupted memory will be part of the backup and will reveal itself when you attempt to restore the data. To avoid this situation, try to make a habit out of performing regular backups when there aren't problems.

PERFORMING A HARD RESET

Just as it is sometimesbeneficial to clean off the hard drive of a desktop computer and start anew, it is also sometimes necessary to perform a hard reset on your Pocket PC. You will have to perform a hard reset if memory gets corrupted and cannot be repaired. You also might have to perform a hard reset if you forget your password. If you like to tinker like I do, you accidentally might tinker too much and get your device into a state from which it can't recover, in which case a hard reset is probably in order. Even so, a hard reset is definitely a last resort and shouldn't be taken too lightly.

Unlike a soft reset, which is uniform across all Pocket PCs, the steps required to perform a hard reset are not the same across all devices. The next few sections explain how to perform a hard reset on each of the major types of Pocket PC devices available as of this writing. If information about your device isn't provided here, please refer to its documentation, which should contain directions on how to perform a hard reset.

Note

Most Pocket PC 2002 devices include a special area of memory that consists of Flash ROM, which isn't automatically cleared when you perform a hard reset. You must manually clear this area of memory after performing a hard reset if you'd like it to be empty.

COMPAQ iPAQ H3700/3800 SERIES

The reset button on Compaq iPAQ H3700 and H3800 devices is located on the bottom of the device, just to the right of the cradle connector. Following are the steps required to perform a hard reset on either of these lines of Pocket PCs:

1. Turn the power off.
2. Remove the device from the cradle, or unplug it from the USB cable.

3. Remove any memory storage cards that are installed.

4. Hold down any two application buttons on the bottom while depressing the reset button with the stylus.

5. Hold all three buttons for about 5 seconds until the screen starts to fade.

6. The screen will fade, and the device will power off. Turn it back on, and you're ready to go.

CASIO CASSIOPEIA E-200 AND HP JORNADA 560 SERIES

The Cassiopeia E-200 and HP Jornada 560 series Pocket PCs have a similar procedure for performing a hard reset. The reset button on the Cassiopeia E-200 is located on the left side of the device, just below the power button. The reset button on the HP Jornada 560 series of devices is located on the back of the device near the top, just to the left of the CF card slot. Following are the steps required to perform a hard reset on the Cassiopeia E-200 and HP Jornada 560 series devices:

1. Turn the power off.

2. Remove the device from the cradle, or unplug it from the USB cable.

3. Remove any memory storage cards that are installed.

4. Press and hold down the power button.

5. While holding down the power button, press the reset button with the stylus and hold it for a couple of seconds.

6. Press the Action button to confirm that you want to proceed with a hard reset.

7. Press the Action button again to confirm that you want to continue with the hard reset.

TOSHIBA E570

The Toshiba e570 has its reset button located on the left side of the device, about midway down. To perform a hard reset on the Toshiba e570, just follow these steps:

1. Turn the power off.

2. Remove the device from the cradle, or unplug it from the USB cable.

3. Remove any memory storage cards that are installed.

4. Press and hold down the power button.

5. While holding down the power button, press the reset button and then release the power button.

6. A welcome screen will appear, and you can then release the reset button.

APP

C

After resetting your device, it will be in the state it was in when you first purchased it. In other words, a hard reset leaves you with a fresh system that is devoid of any installed applications and data that you've stored on the device. Of course, the standard built-in applications will still be on the device because they are stored in ROM.

INDEX

Symbols

@ (at) symbols, entering, 44

` (accent mark), 90

' (quotation mark), 90

= (equal sign), 312

Numbers

40-bit encryptions, SSL (Secure Sockets Layer), 391

56Kbps modem cards, (56 kilobits per second modem cards), 482

128-bit encryptions, SSL (Secure Sockets Layer), 391

802.11b (Wi-Fi). *See* **Wi-Fi**

1942, Capcom game, 471

A

ABC tabs, contacts (navigating), 238

About icon, 44

accent marks (`), 90

accented characters (Letter Recognizer), 90

access
  encrypted terminal server access, SmartPass CE, 383
  Internet, set-top Internet devices, 10
  remote access, 140-141, 156
  wireless Internet access, mobile phones, 120-123

accessibility, wireless ISPs, 118

accessing
  applications (Pocket Controller), 157
  audible books, 430
  corporate address directories, 233
  eBooks, 412
  file attachments (e-mail), 228
  files, networks (File Explorer), 207-208
  Flash Format, 364
  Internet radio, 445
  keys, stylus (soft keyboards), 86
  Letter Recognizer settings, 89
  memory storage cards, 359
  micro hard drives, 360
  news headlines, AOL Instant Messenger (AIM), 170
  Pocket Excel toolbar, 305-307
  resources, 492-496
  stock quotes, AOL Instant Messenger (AIM), 170
  streaming content (networks), 440
  streaming multimedia (Pocket Internet Explorer), 444-446
  text notes, 424
  Today screen, 75-76
  virtual hard drives, 361, 368-369

  Web-based e-mail (Web surfing), 193-195
  wireless LAN cards, 484

accessories, CF (CompactFlash) cards, 480. *See also* hardware accessories

Account Manager, finances (Money for Pocket PC), 326-327

Account Register, transactions (Money for Pocket PC), 327-329

account registers, 323

accounts
  creating (Money for Pocket PC), 327
  information (Money for Pocket PC), 327
  MSN Messenger, 161-163
  My Docs Online, virtual hard drives, 366
  .NET Passport, MSN Messenger, 162
  security, 162
  synchronized accounts, specifying (Money for Pocket PC), 323

Accounts tab, 163

Acer, fingerprint-scanning hardware (security), 388

Action
  button, 36, 262
  hardware button, 243, 250, 293, 315

Activate My Pocket PC button, 413

Freeze Panes, 312
Full Screen, 307
Properties, 392
Recording, 290
Remove Split, 312
Sheet, 315
Split, 311
Status Bar, 303
Text Size, 192
Toolbar, 283, 305
Unfreeze Panes, 312
Writing, 286
Zoom, 306
Zoom, Custom, 307

comments, lost attribute (converted Pocket Word document), 281

CommonTime, Cadenza, 154

Communication Intelligence Corporations, Sign-On for Pocket PC, 389

communications
56Kbps modem cards, 482
Bluetooth networking, 484
digital phone cards, 483
GPS receivers, 485
infrared modems, 483
secure communications, security, 379
Transcriber, Gestures, 96-98
wired LAN cards, 484
wired modem cards, 482
wireless communications, 18-20
wireless LAN cards, 484
wireless modem cards, 482-483

CompactFlash memory cards. See **CF (CompactFlash) cards**

Compaq
Bluetooth networking, 484
fingerprint-scanning hardware (security), 388
Web site, 484
wired modem card, 482

Compaq Foldable Keyboard (portable keyboard), 485

Compaq iPAQ H3700/3800 Series, hard resets, 500

Compaq iPAQ H3800 Series, Pocket PC model, 25

comparing
active RAM and storage RAM, 498
devices, 37-38
expansion cards, 30
modem cards, 482
Palm and Pocket PCs, 15-18

compatibility
CF memory cards (digital cameras), 481
instant messaging, 169
wireless ISPs, 119-120

Complete Tasks check box, 261

components
hardware, 24
themes, 67

compressed files, opening (HandyZip), 372

compression
JPEG images, 371
Windows Media Audio, 435
Zip files, memory storage cards, 370-372

computers, handheld computers, 14

configuring Inbox (managing e-mail), 218

Confirm box, 64

Conflict Resolution drop-down list, 148

Connect
button, 224
command, 156, 224

connecting cradles, 46

Connection Manager, 126
connections, 139
creating, 127-138
dialing locations (creating), 138

corporate LAN connections, creating, 136-137
dial-up ISP connections, creating, 131-134
dial-up RAS connections, creating, 134-135
mobile phone connections, creating, 137-138
new connections, creating, 139
pass-through connections, creating, 129-131
public LAN connections, creating, 135-136
starting, 127
wireless modem connections, creating, 137-138

connections
Connection Manager, 138-139
corporate LAN connections, creating (Connection Manager), 136-137
creating (Connection Manager), 127-138
desktop PCs (GUI), 45-50
dial-up connections
ISP connections, creating (Connection Manager), 131-134
modem connections, wired modem cards, 482
properties, 128
RAS connections, creating (Connection Manager), 134-135
Ethernet, ActiveSync option, 146
infrared
ActiveSync option, 146
cradle networking, 113
Internet connections, 113, 180-183, 368
mobile phone connections, creating (Connection Manager), 137-138
network connections, 126, 217

cradles
ActiveSync installations, 47
connecting, 46
networking, 113

crashes, 498

Create In button, 183

Create Mobile Favorite button, 183

creating
accounts (Money for Pocket PC), 327
appointments, 77, 249-250
bookmarks, annotations (Reader), 422
bulleted lists (Pocket Word), 286
connections, Connection Manager
corporate LAN connections, 136-137
dial-up connections, 131-135
mobile phone connections, 137-138
pass-through connections, 129-131
public LAN connections, 135-136
wireless modem connections, 137-138
contacts (Pocket Outlook), 242-243
containers (Sentry 2020), 383
custom formulas (Pocket Excel), 304
dialing locations (Connection Manager), 138
documents, 77-79, 282-290
e-mail, 225
eBooks, 426-428
file attachments (e-mail), 229
files, templates (Pocket Word), 294
folders, mobile favorites, 182
formulas (worksheets), 312
maps (Pocket Streets), 338, 342, 345

mobile favorites, 183-184
My Documents folder (storage cards), 206
new connections (Connection Manager), 139
notes, 265-267
pushpins (maps), 346
tasks, 258-259
temporary files (Money for Pocket PC), 325-326
themes, 67, 73
background images (selecting), 71-72
dissected themes, 69
Start images, 68
Today images, 68
workbooks (Pocket Excel), 303-314

Credit Card, account registers (Money for Pocket PC), 323

crossing letters (Letter Recognizer), 90

CrossWord, Jimmy Software game, 469

Crypto API (Application Programming Interface), encryption tools, 379

Cryptographer for Windows CE, data encryption, 382

CSS (Cascading Style Sheets), Pocket Internet Explorer technology, 178

Cubicle Chaos, 457-458, 463

Currency button (Pocket Excel toolbar), 306

custom formulas, creating (Pocket Excel), 304

Customize tab, 184

customizing
ActiveSync, 148-150
appearances, contacts (Pocket Outlook), 240
Calendar, 250-255
Contacts, 244

handwriting recognition (Transcriber customizations), 101-102
information, Today screen, 76
inks (Transcriber Options page), 101
Letter Recognizer, 88-91
mobile favorites, 186-188
Money for Pocket PC, 333-334
My Info page (images), 75
New menu, documents (creating), 77-79
Notes, 271-273
Pocket Excel, 315
Pocket Word, 293-294
Reader, 425
scoreboard, Yahoo! Messenger, 172
soft keyboards, 86-87
Start menu, applications, 77
strokes (letters and symbols), 103
Tasks, 263-264
Transcriber, 100-104
Windows Media Player, 447-450
word-completion feature, 105

Cut command (Transcriber command), 96

D

data
deleting (Money for Pocket PC), 324
graphing, Pocket Excel (troubleshooting), 318
saving (soft reset), 499
synchronized data, 46, 113, 324

Data Anywhere Web site, 496

data encryptions
Cryptographer for Windows CE, 382
FileCrypto for Pocket PC, 382

expansion sleeves
  memory, selecting, 30
  wireless LANs, 115
  wireless modems, 116

expansion slots
  comparing, Palm and
    Pocket PCs, 17
  memory limitations, 28
  memory storage cards, 358
  MMCs (multimedia) cards,
    29

Explore button, 66, 147, 417

Explorer. *See also* **File
Explorer**
  button, 437
  digital multimedia files
    (copying), 437
  window, 147

**Export Map for Pocket
Streets command (Tools
menu), 343**

**Expresso Run, ZIOSoft
game, 466**

**Extended Systems Web site,
114**

**Extensible Markup
Language (XML), Pocket
Internet Explorer, 178**

**Extensible Stylesheet
Language (XSL), Pocket
Internet Explorer, 178**

extensions
  eBooks, .lit, 416
  file extensions, trou-
    bleshooting (File
    Explorer), 213
  Money, .mny, 323
  Pocket Excel, 300
  Pocket Street maps, 341
  Pocket Word, 278
  themes, 66

**external devices, wired
modems, 115**

**external power, brightness
level, 80**

**External Power tab
(Backlight Settings page),
80**

**F-Secure Corporation, 382,
403**

**faces, biometric authentica-
tion, 388**

**Favorite Synchronization
Options window, 184**

Favorites
  menu commands, Organize
    Favorites, 186
  mobile favorites, 182-188
  Pocket Internet Explorer,
    181
  updating, 183-186

features
  Find feature, contacts (navi-
    gating), 239
  flexibility, 12
  instant-on, 498
  mobility, 12
  user needs, 12
  word-completion (Word
    Completion tab), 105

**Fellowes FingerTip Stylus,
488**

Fellowes PenCap Stylus, 488

fields
  Category (Money for
    Pocket PC), 329
  Incoming Mail, 221
  Outcoming Mail, 221
  Subcategory (Money for
    Pocket PC), 329
  transactions (Money for
    Pocket PC), 329

**File As property, contact
appearances (customizing),
240**

**file attachments, e-mail,
227-230**

File Explorer
  background images, select-
    ing (Today screen), 74
  e-mail file attachments, cre-
    ating, 229
  files, 201-207
  folders, displaying, 200

  icon, 200
  networks, files (acessing),
    207-208
  software, 208-211
  starting, 200
  storage areas, 201
  troubleshooting, 212-213

file extensions
  eBooks, .lit, 416
  Money, .mny, 323
  Pocket Excel, 300
  Pocket Word, 278
  themes, 66
  troubleshooting (File
    Explorer), 213

File menu commands
  Build eBook, 427
  Connect, 156
  Disconnect, 157
  Guest, 104
  Master, 104
  New, 383, 386

**File Synchronization
Settings window, 295, 317**

**File Transport Protocol
(FTP), virtual hard drives,
361**

**FileCrypto for Pocket PC,
data encryption, 382**

files
  accessing, networks (File
    Explorer), 207-208
  adding, Synchronized Files
    list, 295
  application files, installing
    software (File Explorer),
    210
  CAB files, 209
  compressed files, opening
    (HandyZip), 372
  copying (File Explorer), 203
  creating, 77-79, 282-290,
    294
  deleting, 204, 292
  digital multimedia files, 436
    copying, 437-440
    *playing (Windows Media
      Player), 440-444*

formats
converted Pocket Excel document, 301
digital video, playing, 451
multimedia formats, Windows Media Player, 434-436
SKY formats, video (playing), 451

formatted documents, Word, 278

formatting
cells, worksheets (Pocket Excel), 308-311
memory storage cards, 362-365
text, 283-288
Web pages (Fit to Screen option), 192

Formula box (Pocket Excel), 312

formulas
altered attribute, converted Pocket Excel document, 301
cells, referencing (worksheets), 312
creating (worksheets), 312
custom formulas, creating (Pocket Excel), 304
spreadsheets, Pocket Excel, 302
worksheets, 312-314

Forward command (Inbox menu), 230

frames
lost attribute, converted Pocket Word document, 281
My Docs Online, 369

Freecell, Entertainment PocketPak game, 461

FreeDrive, virtual hard drive, 362

freezing panes, 312

From command (Inbox drop-down list), 231

FTP (File Transport Protcol), accessing virtual hard drives, 361

full backups, ActiveSync, 151

Full Copy command (Edit menu), 223

full reset (hard reset), 45, 500-501

Full screen command, 100, 307

Full Street Detail option (map background color), 350

FullHand Casino, Hexacto game, 467

functions, 312-314, 450

G

Gadgeteer (The) Web site, 493

Game Boy (Nintendo), mobile gaming, 456

games
Arcade PocketPak, 464
Capcom, 471
Entertainment PocketPak, 461-463
FLUX, 470
free games, Pocket gaming, 457-461
game pads, multimedia accessory, 487-488
Games PocketPak, 463
Hexacto, 467
installing (Pocket gaming), 458
Jimmy Software, 468-469
Virtual Game Gear, 460
ZIOSoft, 466

Games PocketPak, Microsoft Pocket gaming, 463-464

gaming, mobile gaming, 456. *See also* **Pocket gaming**

General Packet Radio Service (GPRS), wireless WANs, 117

gestures
check box, 87
communications, Transcriber, 96-98
Correction, 98-100
Quick Correct, 98
soft keyboards, 86
strokes, 97
Transcriber, 94

Get Full Copy command (Services menu), 223

Ghosts 'N Goblins, Capcom game, 471

GIF images, animated (Pocket Internet Explorer technology), 178

Global Positioning System (GPS), 351, 485

Global System for Mobile Communications (GSM)
expansion cards, mobile phones, 14
WANs (wide area networks), 116

Go To command, 310, 420

Go to Corrector command (Alternates menu), 99

GPRS (General Packet Radio Service), 117

GPS (Global Positioning System), 351, 485

Graffiti input method (Block Recognizer), 85, 91-92

graphical user interfaces. *See* **GUIs**

graphing data, Pocket Excel (troubleshooting), 318

Group button (Pocket Word toolbar), 289

grouping
files (File Explorer), 203
strokes, objects (Drawing mode), 289

Hotmail, 193-195

HP Jornada 25, 60, 501

hyperlinks
lost attribute, converted Pocket Excel document, 302
mobile favorites, 185

Hypertext Markup Language (HTML), Pocket Internet Explorer technology 177

I

I/O (input/output), 24, 33-34

IBM Microdrive cards (micro hard drive), 360

iconbars, Transcriber, 102-104

icons
About, 44
attachment, 228
AudiblePlayer, 431
Backlight, 79
bookmark, 422
Buttons, 262, 450
Command bar, 54
Connections, 127
drawing, 424
envelope, 228
File Explorer, 200
Flash Format, 364
Internet Explorer, 180
Memory, 57
Menus, 77-78
Microsoft Money, 326
Microsoft Reader, 418
Microsoft Streets & Trips, 343
Mobile Device, 147
Month view, 248
MSN Messenger, 168
My Device, 202
My Pocket PC, 147
Network Share, 207
Password, 63-64, 380
Pocket Excel, 303
Pocket Streets, 345
Pocket Word, 282

Power, 80
Pushpin icons, Tools menu (Pocket Streets), 346
Remove Programs, 57, 211
Sign-On, 389
Sounds & Notification, 252
speaker, 290
Start menu, 52
Terminal Services Client, 142
text note, 424
Today, 66
voice recording, 290
Yahoo! Messenger, 172

identification letters, contact appearances (customzing), 240

identifying Pocket PCs, troubleshooting, 58

IDs, user IDs (e-mail), 218

images
animated GIF images, Pocket Internet Explorer technology, 178
background, 69-73
component, themes, 67
creating, 68
JPEG, compression, 371
modified attribute, converted Pocket Word documents, 279
modifying, 68-69
My Info page, 75, 81
shared memory storage cards, troubleshooting, 373
storing (Today screen), 73
Theme Generator, 68
themes, 65
transparency (themes), 71

IMAP4 (Internet Message Access Protocol Version 4), 216

improving performance, Transcriber, 102

Inbox, 216
application, 226-227
command (Start menu), 225

configuring (managing e-mail), 218
drop-down list commands
From, 231
Received Date, 231
Subject, 231
e-mail, 217, 230-233
menu commands
Delete, 230
Edit, Check Names, 234
Forward, 230
Mark As Unread, 230
Mark for Download, 230
Move to, 230
My Text, 225
Reply, 230
Reply All, 230
synchronizing (IMAP4), 217

Inbox Options screen, 231

Inbox Tools menu commands, Emtpy Deleted Items, 231

Incase Designs, PDA Case (hardware accessory), 489

Include File Attachment option, 49

Incoming Mail field, 221

incremental backups, ActiveSync, 151

indentation, modified attribute (converted Pocket Word documents), 279

index formatting, modified attribute (converted Pocket Word documents), 280

Info tab (Flash Format), 364

information
accounts (Money for Pocket PC), 327
appointments, Calendar, 250
contacts, viewing, 243
encrypting, 62, 386-387
entering, Typing input mode, 283
notes, 265
owner information, 43, 62

ISPs (Internet service providers)
dial-up ISP connections, creating, 131-134
wireless ISPs, 117-120

italic, retained attribute (converted Word Pocket document), 279

Italic button (Pocket Word toolbar), 287

items, list items (Action button), 36

Items tab, 76, 264

J

Java applets, Pocket Internet Explorer technology, 176

Jerusalem virus, 396

Jimmy Software, Pocket, 26, 468-470

JimmyARK, Jimmy Software game, 469

jog dials, 36, 39

JPEG images, compression, 371

JS Overclock software, 26

K

Kensington PDA Saver, 377

keyboards. *See also* **soft keyboards**
information, entering (Typing mode), 283
limitations, 12
multimedia accessory, 485
portable keyboards, 485
text information, handheld input, 84
Transcriber, 98, 103

keys
accessing, stylus (soft keyboards), 86
Shift, Gestures, 87
Space, Gestures, 87

Killer Commut, Games PocketPak game, 463

Killer List of Videogames (KLOV) Web site, 464

Kingston micro hard drive, 360

KLOV (Killer List of Videogames) Web site, 464

Koss (audio amplifier), 487

L

LANs (local area networks)
cards, 484
corporate LAN connections, creating (Connections Manager), 136-137
networking, 114-115
public LAN connections, creating (Connections Manager), 135-136
wired, 114
wireless, 114

LapLink, PDAsync, 153

Large Keys radio button, 87

launch buttons, hardware, 35

launching
applications, 35, 53
Inbox application, 226
Pocket Controller, 155
Pocket Streets, 345

LCD displays, TFT (thin film transistors), 32

LDAP (Lightweight Directory Access Protocol), 233

Legendary Wings, Capcom game, 471

Lemonade Inc., Hexacto game, 467

Less Street Detail option (map background color), 350

Letter Recognizer
command (Input Panel menu), 88

customizing, 88-91
demonstrations, 91
input method, 85-91
settings, accessing, 89
symbols, entering, 88
text, entering, 88
toolbar, 91

Letter region, Input Panel (Block Recognizer), 92

Letter Shape Selector setting (Transcriber iconbar), 103

letters, 90, 240

levels, brightness levels (backlight), 80

Liberty trojan, 397

libraries
Digital Library, Amazon.com, 416
eBooks library, 412-419

Library
command (Reader), 420
screen (Reader), 418

Light Background option (map background color), 350

Lightweight Directory Access Protocol (LDAP), 233

LimeWire, MP3 application, 435

Limit Attachment Size To check box, 227

limitations
ActiveSync, 152
displays, 13
infrared ports, mobile phone connections, 122
keyboards, 12
memory, 27
mobile phones (networking), 116
Pocket Internet Explorer (Web surfing), 176-178
Psion Infrared Travel Modem, 483
RAM (random access memory), 27

How can we make this index more useful? Email us at indexes@quepublishing.com

Investments (Money for
Pocket PC), 330
Library (Reader), 418
New Container, 383
New Passkey, 386
Organize Playlists, 442
orientations, rotating, 103
PassKey Options screen,
387
Password Settings, 380
Payees (Money for Pocket
PC), 332
Pocket Internet Explorer,
178
setting, 66, 426
Today, 42-43, 73-76

scrolling
displays (Action button), 36
file lists, 293
workbook lists, 315

**SD (Secure Digital), memory
cards, 29, 358, 481**

**SDMI (Secure Digital Music
Initiative), Windows Media
Audio, 435**

**searching text, eBooks,
421-422**

**Section Z, Capcom game,
471**

**secure communications,
securtiy, 379**

**Secure Digital Music
Initiative (SDMI),
Windows Media Audio,
435**

**Secure Digital (SD) memory
cards, 29, 358, 481**

Secure Sockets Layer (SSL)
Pocket Internet Explorer,
391
secure communications, 379
security, 179

**securing workbooks, Pocket
Excel (troubleshooting),
318**

security
antitheft devices, 377
backups, 377

biometric authentication,
388-391
checking (Pocket Internet
Explorer), 392
data encryption, 378
encryptions, 383-387
files, encrypting, 383-386
folders, encrypting, 383-386
hackers, 376
Money for Pocket PC, 326
.NET Passport accounts,
MSN Messenger, 162
pass-through connections,
131
passwords, 63
Pocket Internet Explorer,
179, 391
power-on passwords,
380-383
SD (Security Digital) cards,
481
secure communications, 379
theft, 376
troubleshooting, 392
user authentication, 378
VPNs (virtual private networks), 139

**Sega 4-in-1, Virtual Game
Gear, 460**

**Sega Virtual Game Gear,
457-461**

**Select All command (Edit
menu), 273, 289**

**Select Synchronization
Settings window, 48**

selecting
background images (Today
screen), 73
categories, contacts, 240
cells, worksheets, 304
e-mail services, 220
files (File Explorer), 203
functions (worksheets), 313
list items (Action button),
36
memory (hardware), 30
passwords, 380
skins, Skin Chooser
(Windows Media Player),
448

strokes, objects (Drawing
mode), 289
workbooks (Pocket Excel),
314
worksheets, 304

**selection strokes, selecting
text (Transcriber), 96**

Send button, 225

**Send Meeting Request via
setting (customizing
Calendar), 251**

**Send Theme to Device
When Finished check box,
71**

sending
e-mail, 216-227
files (File Explorer), 204
messages, MSN Messenger,
164

Sentry 2020, 381-386

**Separate Letters Mode set-
ting (Recognizer tab), 101**

serial connections
cradle networking, 113
physical connection (desktop PC), 45-46

**serial infrared (SIR) ports,
33**

**serial ports, I/O port (hard-
ware), 33**

**server applications, remote
access (Terminal Services),
141**

servers
e-mail servers, network
connections, 217
mail servers, 216
proxy servers, corporate
LANs, 136

services
e-mail services, 220, 224
multiple e-mail services,
232
online services, antitheft
devices (security), 377

How can we make this index more useful? Email us at indexes@quepublishing.com

My Docs Online, 366
My Files folders, 368
storage, 361-362
virtual keyboards. *See* **soft keyboards**
Virtual PC, Macintosh (ActiveSync), 46
virtual private networks. *See* **VPNs**
viruses, 396-397
antivirus software, 401-403
detecting (antivirus software), 401
handheld devices, 397
Jerusalem, 396
Phage, 397
risks, 397-399
smart phones, 397
spreading, 399-401
Timofonica, 397
trojans, 396
troubleshooting, 404
worms, 397
VirusScan for Pocket PC (McAfee), antivirus software, 402
Visiting setting (time zones), 42
voice, biometric authentication, 388
Voice Bar, 229, 269-271, 290
voice recordings
e-mail, 229
managing (Recording mode), 290
icon, 290
Notes, 265-267
volume
notes, 269
speaker volume, Navigation bar, 52
VPNs (virutal private networks), 139
benefits, 140
connections, 139-141
secure communications, security, 379

W

WAN (wide area network)
mobile phones, 116
networking, wireless communications, 19
versus WLAN (wireless local area network), 19
wireless WANS, 117
WAP (Wireless Application Protocol), Pocket Internet Explorer, 179
WAV, multimedia format (Windows Media Player), 435
WDA (wireless digital assistant), 15
Web addresses. *See* **URLs (uniform resource locators)**
Web browsers
comparing, Palm and Pocket PCs, 17
Web-based e-mail, accessing, 193
Web Favorites, adding (Windows Media Player), 446
Web pages, 192
Web sites
Amazon.com, 411
AOL Instant Messenger (AIM), 169
Application Development Studio, 382
Applied Biometrics, 389
Arkon, 441
Atom Films, 451
Audible.com, 429
Barnes and Noble, 411
Boostaroo, 37, 487
Brighthand, 493
Capcom, 471
Cash Organizer, 335
CEShopper, 495
CNetX, 364, 371
CommonTime, 154
Communication Intelligence Corporations, 389
Compaq, 484

Crytpographer for Windows CE, 382
Data Anywhere, 496
Destinator GPS, 15
Enfora, 483
Extended Systems, 114
FLUX, 470
FreeDrive, 362
F-Secure, 382, 403
Gadgeteer (The), 493
Handango, 495
Handheld Planet, 496
Hotmail, 194
Intellisync, 153
Jimmy Software, 26, 470
Kensington, 377
Killer List of Videogames (KLOV), 464
Koss, 487
McAfee, 402
Michael Morrison, 176
Microsoft, 67, 492, 495
Microsoft Pocket PC Themes, 65
Microsoft Reader, 415-417
Minds@work, 361
MobilePlanet, 495
Monkeystone Games, 471
MSN Messenger, 161
My Docs Online, 362, 366
MyMobileStuff, 494
ParaGraph, 93
PDA Resources, 364
PDAsync, 153
Pen Computing, 495
Pharos GPS, 15
Pocket Co-Pilot GPS, 15
Pocket Gamer, 457
Pocket PC Fanatic, 495
Pocket PC Help, 494
Pocket PC Magazine, 495
Pocket PC Passion, 493
Pocket PC Themes, 65
Pocket Street, 340
Pocket Themes, 65
PocketGear, 495
PocketLock, 381
PocketMoney, 335
PocketNow, 492
PoQuick Money, 335
Portable Computer Enhancements, 28
Pretec CompactGPS, 351
Psion, 483

Read *10 Minute Guide to Pocket PC 2002* on Your Pocket PC!

Purchasers of *Special Edition Using Pocket PC 2002* have the opportunity to download the contents of the book *10 Minute Guide to Pocket PC 2002* in Microsoft Reader format, FREE!

To read this eBook from your Pocket PC, you must first have Microsoft Reader 2.0 installed. Microsoft Reader 2.0 is a free software application that allows you the pleasure and convenience of onscreen reading. Most Windows-powered Pocket PC 2002 devices already have it preinstalled; however, if you need to download the software application, simply go to http://www.microsoft.com/reader/downloads/pc.asp.

DOWNLOADING THE EBOOK FILES

Downloading the files is quite easy. Simply follow these instructions to start enjoying your onscreen reading:

1. Go to http://www.quepublishing.com.

2. Enter the ISBN of this title located on the back of the book (0789727498) into the box to pull up the Book Information Page.

3. Click the Downloads link to begin downloading *10 Minute Guide to Pocket PC 2002*. Click Save to save it to your computer.

4. From where you saved the downloaded file in step 3, double-click SEU10MG.exe to begin installing the electronic version of the book in Microsoft Reader format.

5. To install SEU10MG.exe, the installation program will prompt for a password from *Special Edition Using Pocket PC 2002* to verify you own the book. Keep the book handy during installation to reference this password.

6. After the file is installed, make sure your Pocket PC is connected and ActiveSync is running, and then transfer the chapter files to your Pocket PC.

7. See Chapter 22, "Reading eBooks with Reader," in *Special Edition Using Pocket PC 2002* for further instructions on using Microsoft Reader.